REPORT ON THE ADMINISTRATION OF
THE MADRAS PRESIDENCY DURING THE YEAR 1865 – 66

Volume - I

M

MAVEN BOOKS

REPORT ON THE ADMINISTRATION OF
THE MADRAS PRESIDENCY DURING THE YEAR 1865 – 66

Volume - I

MAVEN BOOKS

Chennai   Trichy   New Delhi

M

MAVEN BOOKS

This edition has been published in india by arrangement with Carson Books, UK

ISBN 978-93-5527-048-1 Maven Books

All rights reserved No. 44, Nallathambi Street,
Printed and bound in India Triplicane, Chennai 600 005

MJP 1245 © Publishers, 2023

Publisher : C. Janarthanan

Publisher's Note

The legacy of a country is in its varied cultural heritage, historical literature, developments in the field of economy and science. The top nations in the world are competing in the field of science, economy and literature. This vast legacy has to be conserved and documented so that it can be bestowed to the future generation. The knowledge of this legacy is slowly getting perished in the present generation due to lack of documentation.

Keeping this in mind, the concern with retrospective acquiring of rare books has been accented recently by the burgeoning reprint industry. Maven Books is gratified to retrieve the rare collections with a view to bring back those books that were landmarks in their time.

In this effort, a series of rare books would be republished under the banner, "Maven Books". The books in the reprint series have been carefully selected for their contemporary usefulness as well as their historical importance within the intellectual. We reconstruct the book with slight enhancements made for better presentation, without affecting the contents of the original edition.

Most of the works selected for republishing covers a huge range of subjects, from history to anthropology. We believe this reprint edition will be a service to the numerous researchers and practitioners active in this fascinating field. We allow readers to experience the wonder of peering into a scholarly work of the highest order and seminal significance.

Maven Books

CONTENTS.

SECTION IV.—REVENUE.

Section V—PUBLIC WORKS.

Section IX.—MILITARY.

SECTION X.—EDUCATIONAL.

APPENDICES.

APPENDIX—I.

LEGISLATIVE.

APPENDIX—II.

JUDICIAL.

APPENDIX—V.

MARINE.

APPENDIX—VI.

FINANCIAL.

APPENDIX—VII.

POLITICAL.

APPENDIX—VII.

EDUCATIONAL.

ANNUAL REPORT

ON THE

ADMINISTRATION OF THE MADRAS PRESIDENCY
DURING THE YEAR 1865-66.

SECTION I.—EXECUTIVE GOVERNMENT.

TOWARDS the close of the year under review, His Excellency Sir William Thomas Denison, K.C.B., whose tenure of office had expired, was succeeded as Governor by the Right Honorable Lord Napier, K.T., who arrived on the 27th March 1866.

2. On the 25th May 1865, His Excellency Sir John Gaspard LeMarchant, K.C.B., G.C.M.G., arrived, and assumed the command of the Madras Army in succession to Sir Hope Grant, G.C.B., who embarked for England on the 3rd June following.

SECTION II.—LEGISLATIVE.

3. The only changes in the constitution of the Council for mak- Additional ing Laws and Regulations were those caused by the appointment of Members. Mr. Alexander Forrester Brown, and Mr. John Dawson Mayne, who took their seats, as additional Members, on the 2nd December 1865, and 10th March 1866, respectively. The Honorable Messrs. Charles Pelly, Robert Orr Campbell, Gajala Lutchmenarasu Chetti, Garu, C.S.I., and Sir Sharaf-úl-omrah, Bahadur, K.C.S.I., were re-appointed as additional Members.

4. I. Act No. VI of 1865, or an Act " to enable the Governor Acts passed by "in Council to direct and prescribe what official seals Collectors, the Council. "Magistrates, and other Public Officers shall have and use," received the assent of the Governor General, and came into operation on the 19th of August 1865. This Act repeals Section X, Regulation II of 1803, and enables the Government to deal with the matter of official seals, as they may, from time to time, deem necessary.

1

II. Act No. VII of 1865, being an Act "to enable the Government "to levy a separate cess for the use of water supplied for irrigation "purposes in certain cases," received the assent of the Governor General, and came into operation on the 7th September 1865. This Act empowers the Government to levy a cess, in addition to, and distinct from, the land assessment, on account of water supplied from sources of irrigation constructed or kept up at the charge of the State.

III. Act No. VIII of 1865, or an Act "to consolidate and "improve the Laws which define the process to be taken for the recovery "of rent," received the assent of the Governor General on the 19th September 1865, and came into operation on the 1st of January 1866.

This is a very important Act, and occupied the consideration of the Legislature for more than two years. It empowers land-holders to collect arrears due to them, whether those arrears consist of the land tax which Zemindars and Inamdars collect, as authorized representatives of the Government, or of rent which proprietors have a right to levy from the tenants to whom they let their lands.

The necessity for legislation on this important subject had been long experienced in the Madras Presidency, owing to the doubts existing as to the construction to be placed on Regulations XXVII and XXVIII of 1802, II of 1806, and IV and V of 1822: and this need was latterly felt more strongly owing to a decision of the High Court, which reversed a previous decision of the Sudder Court, and unsettled the vexed question of the mutual rights of landlord and tenant. Besides codifying the old law, this Act simplifies the procedure to be followed in recovering arrears of rent, and gives the use of summary process, under certain restrictions, to all landlords, thus abolishing a somewhat anomalous provision of the old law, which restricted this privilege to those who paid revenue direct to Government.

IV. Act No. IX of 1865, or an Act "to amend the law relating "to the appointment of Municipal Commissioners for the Town of "Madras, and the management of its Municipal affairs, and to make "better provision for the Police, conservancy, and improvement of "the said town, and to enable the said Commissioners to levy taxes, "tolls, and rates therein," received the assent of the Governor General on the 3rd October 1865, and came into operation on the 1st November 1865.

V. Act No. X of 1865, or an Act "to provide for the appoint-"ment of Municipal Commissioners in towns in the Presidency of

"Fort St. George, and for the Police, conservancy, and improvement "thereof, and for the levying of rates, tolls, and taxes therein," received the assent of the Governor General on the 14th October 1865. Measures are being adopted to bring this Act into early operation in the larger towns. ACTS
PASSED.

VI. Act No. I of 1866, or an Act " to repeal Madras Act No. IV "of 1865, and to make provision for the administration of Military "Cantonments in the Presidency of Fort St. George," received the assent of the Governor General on the 31st January 1866. This Act comes into operation only in such Military Cantonments, and from such dates as the Governor in Council may direct. It has been extended to Bellary, Cannanore, Trichinopoly, Saint Thomas' Mount, and Wellington.

VII. Act No. II of 1866, or an Act " for the prevention of the "spread of disease among cattle in the Madras Presidency," received the assent of the Governor General on the 17th April 1866.

This Act was passed on the urgent representation of the Revenue authorities, and of Veterinary Surgeon Thacker, who was deputed by Government to investigate the causes of the murrain prevalent among cattle, and to suggest the appropriate remedies. The heavy losses inflicted upon the country, and the extraordinary apathy and carelessness of the agricultural community in the matter of contagion, necessitated legislative action.

VIII. Act No. III of 1866, being an Act " for the levy of a " District Road Cess," received the assent of the Governor General on the 17th April 1866.

The object of this enactment is to enable Government to raise funds for the construction and repair of minor roads, by local taxes imposed upon the owners and occupants of lands in the vicinity. This measure was considered necessary, since the increasing demands on the general revenues, render it improbable that the Government will ever be in a position to do more than complete and maintain the chief lines of communications.

5. A Bill, the object of which is to amend the law relating to the custody of prisoners within the local limits of the original jurisdiction of Her Majesty's High Court of Judicature at Madras, has passed the Council, and now awaits the assent of the Governor General. Bill passed,
but not yet as-
sented to.

GENERAL.

SECTION III.—JUDICIAL.

GENERAL.

Whipping Act.   6. The power of awarding corporal punishment for certain offences was restored to the Criminal Courts by Act VI of 1864. During the year under review the Act has worked satisfactorily. The power given by it has been more freely exercised than in the year immediately following its enactment. The Subordinate Magistrates of the second class, in particular, have been more ready to recommend whipping, where it appeared a suitable punishment. The Act does not permit them to sentence to whipping, unless specially empowered by Government, and it is probable that for some time many of them were not aware that it was competent to them to refer their proceedings to their superiors, with a view to a sentence of whipping being passed.

Jury system.   7. The Jury system has been introduced into seven Districts only, viz., Chittoor, Cuddapah, Rajahmundry, Tanjore, Tranquebar, Cuddalore, and the Vizagapatam Agency. On the whole, it appears to have worked favorably, but the measure of success attained is chiefly attributable to the careful selection made of offences to which it should be applicable. These are, theft (Penal Code, Sections 379, 380, and 382), robbery (Sections 392—5, 397—402), house-breaking (Sections 451—9), receiving or concealing stolen property (Sections 411, 412, 414, 461). The Jury system has now been in operation for four years, but it is not proposed to extend it to other Districts at present.

Under Section 329 of the Code of Criminal Procedure, Jurors and Assessors are to be selected from among persons residing within ten miles of the Court, but power is reserved to Government to extend the distance, if they think fit. In the Chittoor Zillah it has been increased to fifteen miles, in Tranquebar to twenty-five miles, owing in both cases to the small number of qualified persons to be found within the original distance.

Small Cause Courts established in certain Military Cantonments.   8. Under Madras Act I of 1866, Courts of Small Causes have been established in the Military Cantonments of Bellary, Cannanore, Trichinopoly, Saint Thomas' Mount, and Wellington, for the trial of suits for sums not exceeding Rupees 200.

4

9. In 1864 a temporary Principal Sudder Ameen was appointed GENERAL. to Coimbatore to assist the Civil Judge in clearing off the heavy arrears Temporary appointment of a with which his file was burdened. In September 1865 this work was Principal Sudder completed, and the Principal Sudder Ameen was then moved to Chittoor, batore. where the arrears of the Civil Court will give him full occupation till April or May 1866. To relieve the Civil Judge of Cuddalore, the Judge of the Court of Small Causes at that station has been invested with the powers of a Principal Sudder Ameen.

10. The Judge of the Court of Small Causes at Masulipatam has Alterations in Jurisdictions, exercised the powers of a Magistrate within the town of Masulipatam, since the Court was first established in 1863. In the year under review his Magisterial jurisdiction was extended over the revenue Taluk of Masulipatam and two adjacent Taluks.

On the passing of (Madras) Act IV of 1863, the Principal Sudder Ameen of Salem was invested with special jurisdiction throughout the Salem Zillah. This, in effect, gave him exclusive jurisdiction over all suits of the nature of Small Causes, for sums between fifty and 500 Rupees. To remedy the inconvenience which this entailed on the inhabitants of distant parts of the Zillah, the special jurisdiction has been limited to the town and revenue Taluk of Salem.

On the passing of the same Act (IV of 1863) the Judge of the Small Cause Court of Negapatam was vested with exclusive special jurisdiction. He had also been vested with the powers of a Principal Sudder Ameen. The work thus devolving upon him was found to be more than he could properly perform, and as there appeared to be no reason why the District Moonsiff of Negapatam should not have the jurisdiction possessed by all other District Moonsiffs over Small Causes of a value not exceeding fifty Rupees, the Judge of the Small Cause Court has been divested of his exclusive jurisdiction.

11. Three District Moonsiffs' Courts were abolished during the Abolition of certain District year; two in the Tanjore, the third in the Madura Zillah. They were Moonsiffs' all Courts which had been temporarily established to assist in clearing Courts. the files of the regular District Moonsiffs' Courts, and had accomplished the purpose for which they were opened.

12. The following is a detailed account of the working of the Registration system of Registration of Deeds, &c., introduced at the close of the preceding year.

5

REGISTRA- 　　　13. The total number of registrations during the year was
TION OF AS- 1,39,792. Of these, 39,708 were deeds of gift, of sale, and of parti-
SURANCES.
Total number tion, and other absolute transfers of immovable property; 69,214
of registrations. were leases, mortgages, and other temporary or conditional transfers
of immovable property ; 10,959 were memoranda of decrees, and
orders of Court, and awards of arbitration; and 19,911 were bonds,
contracts, and miscellaneous instruments affecting movable property.

Number of 　　　14. The above number gives an average per mensem of 11,649;
registrations in
each. the average number of registrations per mensem during that portion
of the previous official year, in which the Registration Act was in force,
was only 3,268. The number of registrations gradually increased from
the commencement of the year under review until August ; there was
a marked increase in the number of instruments registered during the
months of November and December, in consequence of the expiration,
on the 1st January, of the time allowed for registration of such documents.

Number of 　　　15. The amount of registration varies greatly in the different
registrations in
each District. Circles of Registration. There are four Circles in which the registrations
range from 10,000 to 15,000. In nine Districts the registrations range
from 5,000 to 10,000 ; in the nine other Districts registration falls
below 5,000.

Offices in 　　　16. There are many offices in which the number of registrations
which little or
no registration has been very insignificant, and four in which not a single registration
has taken place. has taken place. Fourteen of these offices have been abolished, and it
is proposed to abolish twenty-two more.

Rates of op- 　　　17. The number of instruments voluntarily registered continues
tional and com-
pulsory registra- to bear a satisfactory ratio to the number of those of which the
tion. registration is compulsory. Out of a total number amounting, exclusive of memoranda of decrees, orders of Court, and awards of arbitration,
to 1,28,833, the number of instruments the registration was compulsory
was 73,530 ; of those the registration of which was optional 55,303.

Special regis- 　　　18. The total number of instruments specially registered under
tration. the provisions of Sections 51 and 52 was 12,715. The proportion of
instruments specially registered was extraordinarily large in the
Godavery and Kistna Districts, and extraordinarily small in Tellicherry
and Calicut.

G

19. The total number of instruments registered under Section 17 REGISTRA-
of the Registration Act during the official year was 17,892, nearly TION OF AS-
SURANCES.
half of which were presented in Tanjore, Tranquebar, and Salem.   Registration
of instruments
20. In twenty-eight cases registration of instruments, refused under Sec. 17.
in the first instance by the registering officers, was allowed by order of under orders in-
Court, on regular Suit brought to enforce the same. The reason of sued by Courts.
refusal was, in almost every case, the non appearance of the party
executing the instrument.

21. The number of appeals preferred to the District Registrars,   Registration
ordered by Dis-
under Section 62, was twenty-three. Nine instruments, which Sub- trict Registrars
on appeal.
Registrars had refused to register, were registered under the orders of
District Registrars.

22. Ninety-six sealed covers purporting to contain wills, codicils,   Deposit of
sealed covers.
and authorities to adopt were deposited during the year. One cover
was withdrawn, and fifteen were opened on the death of the depositors.

23. The total number of general Powers of Attorney attested   Powers of Attorney attested.
under the amended table of fees, since August, is 473—the number of
Special Powers attested 1,985.

24. One thousand three hundred and eighty-six applications for Attendances at
private resi-
the attendance of Registering Officers at private residences, and for dences.
issue of commissions to examine persons unable to appear, have been
complied with since August; previous to which time no fee was ex-
acted for such processes: under the amended table, a fee of Rupees ten
is charged on every such attendance.

25. No case has occurred of a registered instrument being declared, Invalid instruments.
by the Civil Courts, invalid or forged.

26. The table of fees originally sanctioned having been found   Fees.
inadequate to provide a reasonable amount of remuneration for the
Registering Officers, or to meet the expenses incurred by Government,
an amended table was sanctioned, and came into force on the 1st
August. Some of the new charges for which provision was made in
this amended table have been already noticed. The only other
changes of importance were doubling the fee for registering instruments
not exceeding Rupees 100, 500, and 1,000 in value, which, under the
old table, was four Annas, eight Annas, and one Rupee respectively, and

REGISTRA- increasing the fee for instruments between Rupees 1,000 and Rupees
TION OF AS- 2,500 in value, from two to three Rupees. These changes have
SURANCES. been attended with some success. As, however, the collections were still
insufficient to render the department self-supporting, certain modifications in the rules were under consideration, but further changes were
rendered necessary by the passing of the Indian Registration Act, and
the amended table of the 15th August remained in force until the end
of the official year.

Commission 27. The commission realized by the Registrars of Districts in the
drawn by Regis-
tering Officers. Provinces has averaged Rupees 133-10-0 per mensem, ranging between
Rupees 30-9-9 the lowest, and Rupees 309-12-10 the highest, monthly
average. This commission was drawn up to the 1st April 1866 at the
rate of twenty-five per cent. on the amount collected in each District.
In March, Government decided that Registrars, when holding the office
in conjunction with another appointment, should receive twenty-five
per cent. on the fees up to Rupees 600, and ten per cent. on any sum
above that amount.

The average amount of commission drawn by the 331 Deputy
Registrars has been Rupees 16-14-4 per mensem.

Financial 28. The total collections amounted to Rupees 1,54,232-10-0, the
results. expenditure was Rupees 1,76,367-3-9 ; the loss entailed upon Government during this year by the Registration Department is thus
Rupees 33,805-7-11.

CIVIL JUSTICE.

Number of Suits. 29. At the close of the year 1864, 61,641 original suits remained
undecided. The number instituted in 1865 was

(a) 1864... ... 249,537
    1865... ... 231,718

168,129, and 1,948 were remanded or re-admit-

Decrease ... 17,819

ted, making a total of 231,718. This is 17,819*(a)*
less than the number before the Courts in the

(b) 1865... ... 170,077
    1864... ... 159,401

previous year, although in the number of suits

Increase ... 20,676

instituted and re-admitted, there was an increase
of 20,676*(b)* as compared with 1864. The

falling off in the total number of suits is due to the small number
of suits in arrears pending at the commencement of the year as
compared with 1864.

These 231,718 suits came before the different Courts in the proportion shewn in the following Statement·

3

Panchayets	653	CIVIL JUSTICE.
Village Moonsiffs	52,107	
District Moonsiffs in their ordinary jurisdiction ...	89,933	
Do. under Madras Act IV of 1863 ...	70,470	
Cantonment Small Cause Courts	331	
Principal Sudder Ameens in their ordinary jurisdiction	2,053	
Do. do. under Madras Act IV of 1863...	3,366	
Assistant Agents	17	
Civil Judges and Agents in their ordinary jurisdiction	1,180	
Do. do. under Madras Act IV of 1863.	379	
Judges of Small Cause Courts	10,876	
Do. do. in the exercise of the powers of a Principal Sudder Ameen	353	

231,718

Of the total number 169,397, or 73 per cent., were disposed of, leaving 62,321 undecided at the close of the year. The number determined is less by 18,499(*a*) than the number disposed of in 1864, but it must be remembered that eight District Moonsiffs' Courts were abolished in the course of the years 1864 and 1865. The number remaining undisposed of is slightly in excess of the number at the end of the preceding year, but far less than the number pending at the close of 1863(*b*).

Disposed of.
(*a*) 1864 187,896
1865 169,397

Decrease ... 18,499

Pending at the close of the year.
(*b*) 1865 ...62,321 1863 .. 90,136
1864 ...61,641 1865... 62,321

Increase.... 680 Decrease. 27,815

The Judicatories by which the above 169,397 suits were disposed of are shewn in the following table :—

	Ordinary Suits.	Small. Causes.	Total.
Panchayets	552	...	552
Village Moonsiffs	40,166	...	40,166
District Moonsiffs	47,694	65,510	113,204
Cantonment Small Cause Courts	...	234	234
Principal Sudder Ameens ...	884	3,108	3,992
Assistant Agents	7	...	7
Civil Judges and Agents ...	503	339	842
Judges of the Small Cause Courts	...	10,193	10,193
Do. do. in the exercise of the powers of a Principal Sudder Ameen	207	...	207
	90,013	79,384	169,397

B

CIVIL
JUSTICE.
Mode of disposal of Suits.

30. Of the ordinary suits disposed of by the several Courts 39,216, or forty-three per cent., were decided on the merits in favor of plaintiffs, and 11,516, or thirteen per cent., in favor of defendants ; 10,417 were dismissed for default; 26,203 were adjusted or withdrawn; and 2,661 were disposed of in other ways. Of the Small Causes disposed of by District Moonsiffs, &c., under Act IV of 1863 (Madras), 36,757, or fifty-three per cent., were decreed on the merits for plaintiffs, and 8,851, or thirteen per cent., for defendants ; 3,463 were dismissed for default; 18,523 were adjusted or withdrawn; and 1,363 were otherwise disposed of. Of those disposed of by Courts of Small Causes, under Act XLII of 1860, 6,158, or sixty per cent., were decreed on the merits for plaintiffs, and 937, or nine per cent., for defendants; 512 were dismissed for default; and 2,586 were adjusted or withdrawn. And of those disposed of by the Cantonment Small Cause Courts 173, or fifty-one per cent., were decreed on the merits for plaintiffs, and ten, or three per cent., for defendants ; fourteen were dismissed for default; thirty-six were adjusted or withdrawn ; and one was disposed of in some other way.

Duration of Suits.

31. The average duration on the files of the suits disposed of by the Lower Courts was as follows :—

	Ordinary Suits.			Small Causes.		
	Y.	M.	D.	Y.	M.	D.
District Moonsiffs　...　...　...	0	9	0	0	0	29
Cantonment Small Cause Courts　...	...	...	...	0	0	12¼
Principal Sudder Ameens　...　...	1	3	16	0	0	21
Assistant Agents　...　...　...	0	9	18	...	...	...
Civil Judges ...　...　...　...	1	1	17	0	1	10
Judges of the Small Cause Courts　...	...	...	...	0	0	22
Do.　do.　in the exercise of the powers of a Principal Sudder Ameen.	0	9	10	...	...	...

Classification of Suits.

32. The suits newly instituted during the year may be classified as follows :—

For rent and revenue derivable from land　...　...	5,646
Lands　...　...　...　...　...　...	13,395
Real property, such as houses, &c.　...　...　...	5,192
Debts, wages　...　...　...　...　...	1,41,156
Caste, religion, &c.　...　...　...　...	458
Indigo, Sugar, &c.　...　...　...　...	2,282

10

33. The aggregate value of the property at stake in the original suits pending at the close of the year amounted to 1,50,22,438 Rupees. CIVIL JUSTICE. Value.

34. In the course of the year 15,274 appeals came before the Courts subordinate to the High Court, inclusive of those pending at the close of 1864. Of these 8,711 were disposed of as shewn below, leaving 6,568, of the value of Rupees 15,08,287, undetermined at the close of the year. 1,766, or twenty per cent., were decreed on the merits in favor of appellants, and 2,974, or thirty-four per cent., for respondents; 181 were remanded to the Lower Courts; 282 dismissed for default; 219 adjusted or withdrawn; and 3,289 were disposed of in other ways. The average duration of appeals was eleven months and seven days before the Civil Judges, ten months and two days before the Principal Sudder Ameens. And eleven months and twenty-nine days before the Judges of Small Cause Courts vested with the powers of a Principal Sudder Ameen. In addition to the Original and Appeal Suits shewn above, 93,318 applications for execution of decrees, and 155,568 petitions of a miscellaneous character, were disposed of by the Lower Courts, leaving a balance of 13,644 of the former, and 3,526 of the latter. Appeals, &c., in Lower Courts.

35. On the Original Side of the High Court, besides ninety-eight suits that were pending on the 31st December 1864, 358 were instituted. Of these 162 were disposed of on merits at the settlement of issues, and eighty-four on final disposal; twenty-eight were dismissed for default; nine were withdrawn with leave to bring fresh suits, and seventy-three absolutely. Twenty-two petitions for leave to sue "in formâ pauperis" were also disposed of, and in addition, fourteen suits and plea side actions, remaining from the late Supreme Court, were heard and determined. Thus on the 31st December 1865 there were 100 suits pending under the Procedure Code, besides Ecclesiastical suits and Interlocutory orders. Suits in High Court, Original side.

36. Before the High Court, in its Appellate Jurisdiction, there were pending, at the close of 1864, forty-eight Regular and 156 Special appeals, to which eighty-seven Regular and 661 Special appeals were added in 1865, making a total of 135 Regular and 817 Special appeals pending and instituted. In the number newly filed as compared with the previous year, there was an increase of four Regular and 174 Special appeals (a). Eighty-seven Regular and 544 Special appeals Appellate side.

(a)	Regular.	Special.
1865.......	87	661
1864.......	83	487
Increase,	4	174

CIVIL
JUSTICE.

were disposed of, and at the close of the year there remained on the file forty-eight Regular and 273 Special appeals. Of these only seven Regular and five Special appeals were filed previous to 1865.

Mode of disposal, and duration.

37. The manner in which the decided appeals were disposed of is shewn below :—

	Regular.	Special.
Decrees confirmed	52	456
Do. amended	5	18
Do. reversed	19	28
Suits remanded	8	13
Appeals dismissed for default		22
Do. adjusted or withdrawn		3
Do. otherwise disposed of	3	4

The average duration of the appeals disposed of was four months. The total value of those depending at the close of the year amounted to Rupees 14,01,125.

Of 321 Civil Petitions brought before the Court, 262 were disposed of, viz. :—

Orders confirmed	204
Do. reversed	40
Dismissed for default	9
Otherwise disposed of	7

Referred cases.

38. Thirty-two cases were referred for the Judgment of the High Court, under Section 13' Act XLII of 1860, and Section 28, Act XXIII of 1861. Of these thirty were disposed of within the year.

Criminal petitions.

39. The High Court also disposed of 185 of the 203 Criminal Petitions brought before them, viz. :—

Dismissed after hearing without perusal of record ...	157
Orders or sentences of Lower Courts confirmed after perusal of record (of which two were under Section 404 of the Code of Criminal Procedure)	16
Do. amended do. do.	3
Do. released without perusal of record ...	2
Do. do. after perusal do. ...	5
Otherwise disposed of without perusing record... ...	1
Do. after perusing the record	1

Sentences of death referred for confirmation.

40. Eighty-five trials, in which sentence of death was recorded by the Session Court, were referred for the confirmation of the High Court

12

of the eighty-five, all but two were disposed of within the year, as

follows :—

Sentences confirmed	76
Modified or amended	2
Released	4
Remanded to Session Court	1

41. Sixty-eight references were made to the High Court under Section 434 of the Code of Criminal Procedure. The sentence or order of the Lower Courts was reversed in forty, and modified or amended in seven. In the remaining twenty-one there was no error on a point of law to justify the High Court's interference.

References under Sec. 434, Code of Crimi-nal Procedure,

POLICE.

42. The strength of the Provincial Force of the Madras Presidency, exclusive of the Town of Madras, was, on the 30th April 1866, as follows :—

Force.

Inspector General and supervising Staff	6
District Superintendents	21
Assistant Superintendents	22
Inspectors...	453
Constabulary of all ranks	23,249
	————
	23,751

43. The full permanent establishment is 24,467 men. The Force was, therefore, 2·8 per cent. under strength.

Distribution.

The services were distributed as follows :—

On purely State services—

Revenue—Salt Preventive Establishment.	1,528	
Do, Inland Frontier Preventive do	184	
		1,662
Convict Jail Guards		1,276
		2,938
On General Police duties—		
Effective strength in rural parts	19,124	
In Towns	1,689	
		20,813

44. Excluding Revenue Preventive Establishments, the proportion of rural Police to rural populations (23,201,200) is one to 1,212; of Town Police to Town populations (1,005,309) one to 536; on the whole population of the Presidency the proportion of Policemen is one to 1,019 inhabitants. In England and Wales the proportion is one Policeman to 906 (1864). In Ireland the average proportion of Police to population is one to every 417.

Proportion to population.

45. The local Village Establishment of South Arcot (2,570 *Talari*) are paid from the Police Budget, Rupees 21,861; and there are 472 (at a cost of Rupees ·12,204) local watchers maintained in unhealthy ghauts, &c., chiefly in the Northern range.

Village Esta-blishment debit-ed to Police,

POLICE.
Cost.

46. The entire cost of the Police was borne by the State during the year, viz., Rupees 35,77,653, as follows :—

In Wages and Allowances ... ... Rs.	31,08,964
In Clothing, Accoutrements, &c ... .'	3,29,386
In Office Charges, Rent, Stationery, and Miscellaneous charges...	1,05,238
Constabulary Total...	35,43,588
Add Village Watchers of South Arcot, &c.	34,065
Grand Total...	35,77,653

Of the above gross charge the following sums are debitable to purely State services :—

Police over Convict Establishments ... ... Rs.	1,29,200
Salt Preventive, do.	1,30,020
Inland Frontier, do.	14,360
Total...	2,73,580

The actual cost of the Police for the Presidency, exclusive of the Madras Town Police, was Rupees 33,04,073.

The average cost of each Policeman for the year was Rupees 150, or £15. In England and Wales the cost (1864) was £74-10-0 per man, and in Ireland (1864) £55-15-4.

The annual cost of Police per head of the population of the Madras Presidency, excluding State services, was 2¼ Annas, or about 3¼d. per inhabitant. In England and Wales, and in Ireland these charges are respectively 1s. 7¾d. and 2s. 8¼d.

The total expenditure upon Police, from Imperial Funds, was 35,04,640 Rupees.

Madras Town
Police.

47. The total strength of the Madras Town Police during the year 1865 was, inclusive of the Marine and Mounted Police, 983 ; the proportion, exclusive of the Marine and part of the Preventive Force employed on special duty, is one to 600 inhabitants. The total cost (exclusive of the Marine Force which it will be seen is a self-supporting body) was 1,98,567.

Marine Police.

48. The Marine Police has worked satisfactorily, fully answering the purpose of which it was raised, imports and exports are now effected almost without loss. The amount realized from the proceeds of the fee charged amounted to 31,662 Rupees, while the total cost was only 29,162 Rupees.

European Va-
grancy.

49. The subject of European vagrancy forces itself prominently forward ; the Commissioner of Police remarks that it " is an evil, which although not so fully developed here as in Calcutta and Bombay, still exhibits a tendency to increase. Europeans are largely employed on Plantations, Railway, and Irrigation or other works. They are dis-

POLICE.

charged for drunkenness or other causes, and forthwith become mere loafers, without any possible means of livelihood. The ranks are swelled by discharged or run-away seamen of indifferent character, and importations from Australia, who come over with horses and remain here to "better themselves," which they seldom succeed in doing. There is no mere manual labor to be found for Europeans in India. Without money or employment, they are driven to beg, and this begging too frequently assumes the form of threat when they visit houses which they find to be tenanted by ladies only. The conduct and appearance of these disreputable tramps cast discredit on the ruling race. Sooner or later the matter will call for Legislative action."

50. Towards the close of the year outbreaks occurred in the Hill Tracts of Vizagapatam and Ganjam. In the first district the Sowrahs, a savage and truculent race, inhabiting the Hill tracts and the north of Jeypore, attacked a party of Police headed by the District Superintendent, who had gone into the Hill Tracts to establish a Police Station, and forced it to retire. A stronger force was shortly afterwards moved up, and a Station established in a central spot. In Ganjam the rising, which originated in the Kuttaya country, an outlying tract to the west of the Chinna Kimedy Malayahs, was more serious, and assumed the form of an extended insurrection, which beginning on the 13th November 1865, and involving no less than 380 villages, was not fully quelled until the 5th of the following January, and that not without considerable loss of life. A subsequent rising, which occurred at the end of January, in another part of the Ganjam Hills, was promptly and effectually suppressed by the Police under the personal direction of the Agent, Mr. Gordon Forbes. With the view of preventing a recurrence of these murderous outbreaks in the Ganjam Hills, and in order that they may be dealt with promptly when they do occur, it has been arranged that the Assistant Agent and Assistant Superintendent of Police shall reside in the Hill tracts during a considerable part of every year. The Police force has also been considerably strengthened. In the Jeypore and Golcondah Hill country, fifteen new stations have been taken up, and the country is now fairly occupied. No extension has taken place in other parts. The constitution of the Force has remained unaltered; and the principles laid down are being persistently worked out with success. There has been, on the whole, a steady improvement in every respect throughout all the grades of the Force.

Outbreaks in the Hill Tracts of Vizagapatam and Ganjam, and strengthening of the force in those Tracts.

State of the Force.

15

POLICE.

General remarks.

51. District Officers worked well and with success during the year ; and, save in the Northern Range, suffered less in health than in previous years. All subordinate grades are improving in the knowledge and efficient performance of their duties. In respect to internal

Internal economy.

economy the stability of the Force has improved, the annual casualties having fallen from twenty-one per cent. in 1863 to sixteen per cent. in 1865. No increase took place in the number of Policemen who were tried for offences, and the number of punishments and dismissals declined considerably. The proportion of men in the Force who are able to read and write has risen from thirty-six per cent. in 1863, to 58·9 per cent. ; and the number who pass the tests of their rank is steadily increasing. Miscellaneous duties are, on the whole, fairly performed. An accurate knowledge of the criminal classes is being acquired by the Police. As respects *crime*, it appears that during a year of great pressure, crime was repressed, and detection improved. A further increase of the numbers of offenders incarcerated in Jails, evinces greater success in bringing offenders to justice. A considerable decrease of crime, under all important heads, occurred during the year under review as compared with the preceding year. Under offences against the persons, this decrease was nineteen per cent. ; under robbery twenty-two per cent. ; under dacoity thirty per cent. A further decrease of thirty-five per cent. occurred in torch-light gang-robbery and in house-breaking of 5·6 per cent. On the other hand, the per-centage of detection improved. In fifty per cent. of all important offences, detection was successful, and offenders punished ; against 41·6 per cent. in 1864. And 70·1 per cent. of all persons arrested and proceeded against, were convicted. In 47·1 per cent. of all murders, offenders were brought to justice. In twenty per cent. of all robberies, 25·8 per cent. of all dacoities (44·9 per cent. of all torch-light dacoities), and 16·3 per cent. of all burglaries, offenders were convicted. These results, while they are not all that must be aimed at, evince a steady improvement, and, in some respects, bear comparison with the statistics of crime, and the result of the Police work in England.

Distribution of Savings.

52. The service becomes gradually more stable and popular. The distribution of savings on the Budget grant as batta, gave a small increase of pay to the lower grades which was much needed ; and the prospect of pension is telling. Recruits are more easily obtained ; dismissal from the service

Force.	Discharged and dismissed.	Resigned and deserted.	Died.	Total.	Per cent.	Enlistments.
23,660	1,902	1,431	408	3,741	15·8	4,029

becomes a real punishment, and men resign and desert less readily. The casualties of the year involved 3,741 men, or 15·8 per cent. of the Force, against eighteen per cent. in 1864-65, and twenty-one per cent. in 1862-63. Dismissals averaged 6·8 per cent. during the year under review, against 8·2 per cent. in 1864, and a still higher proportion in previous years. Six per cent. of the casualties of the year occurred through resignation and desertion; against 7·4 per cent. in 1864-65, and 8·7 per cent. in 1863-64. The number of deaths which occurred during the year was 408, or 1·3 per cent. of the strength, against 363 in 1864-65, and 375 in 1863-64, respectively. Police work is trying to the health of all ranks. Ten European Officers, or one in five, proceeded to Europe on sick furlough during the year; four were from the Districts of Ganjam and Vizagapatam, where the disturbances in the hills taxed the Force to the utmost. Of the whole Force, 8,553 men, or 36·1 per cent., were treated in Hospital.

POLICE. Casualties.

Health.

53. Four hundred and thirty-three Policemen, or 1·8 per cent. of the Force, were convicted, as shown in the margin, of offences under Criminal and Departmental Laws. The number of delinquents and proportion of the Force implicated, were exactly the same in 1864. These convictions are now almost entirely confined to the lowest grades of the Constabulary; and the circumstances attending the offences are such that nearly all the charges—407 out of 433—are summarily disposed of by the Magistracy.

Offences for which Policemen were tried and convicted.

	No. of Force.	Murder.	Culpable homicide.	Hurt, Assault and Criminal Force.	Dacoity.	House-breaking.	Theft, Breach of trust, &c.	Bribery and Extortion.	False evidence and Forgery.	Negligent escape.	Miscellaneous.	Total.	Per-centage.
By Magistrates ...	23,660	..	...	46	.	1	60	65		4	80	151	407	1 7
By Courts	..	1	2	3	2	1	3	1	6	.	7	26	...
Total ...	23,66(	1	2	49	2	2	63	66	10	80	158	433	1·8

54. The condition of the Force in respect to education is, on the whole, rising steadily. Fifty-nine per cent. of all ranks as they stood on the 31st December 1865, were able to read and write. In 1864 the proportion was fifty per cent.; in the preceding year, it was as low as thirty-six per cent. The hopelessly ignorant decrease in numbers, and the officers of several Districts are now able to refuse recruits who are wholly illiterate, while hundreds

Education and Instruction.

State of Education in the Force.

Force.	Number who neither read nor write.	Number who read and write.	Per-centage of the latter in the Force.
23,660	9,405	14,122	59·6

POLICE. of men have taken advantage of the facilities afforded at district head quarters, and learnt to read and write after joining the Force.

District Schools and Instruction.

55.　3,804 men, or 16·0 per cent. of the whole Force, were under

Force.	Instructed in Head Quarter School.		Passed Test prescribed for Rank.		Passed Special Test.
	No.	Per-cent-age of Force.	No.	Per-cent-age of Force.	
23,660	3,804	16·0	1·520	6·4	70

instruction in the head quarter schools of all Districts during some part of the year under review ; and 1,590 passed the test of their rank, or the special test, against 2,835 who were under instruction, and 1,573 who passed the test of this rank in 1864. Seventy Police Officers chiefly Inspectors, passed the Special Test Examination during the year, against forty-one in 1864 and six in 1863 respectively. The children of Constables at head quarters are instructed in classes maintained for that purpose.

Castes and Races,

	Force.	Europeans.	East indi-ans, &c.	Brahmins.	Sudras.	Other Hin-dus, &c.	Mahome-dans.
Inspectors.	427	54	78	91	162	12	30
Constables.	23,250	41	452	596	12,346	2,843	7,472
Total.	23,677	95	530	687	12,508	2,856	7,502

56.　The general relative proportion of Castes and Races constituting the Force, scarcely varies from year to year. Sixty-five per cent. are Hindus of all races : thirty-one per cent. are Mahomedans.

Buildings and Huts.

57.　The grant for the year for Police buildings was 70,000

Huts.		Station Houses.	
No. con-structed.	Cost.	No. con-structed.	Cost.
517	30175	44	15,553

N. B.—Two Hospitals were con-structed or adapted at a cost of Rupees 556.

Rupees, of which 11,774 lapsed as unex-pended on the 30th April 1865. The sum spent was Rupees 58,226. Of this sum a considerable portion went to complete works commenced during the preceding year. In 1865, 517 huts were constructed at a cost of Rupees 30,175, and forty-four station-houses at a cost of Rupees 15,553. Much still remains to be done towards providing healthy shelter for the Police in outlying stations. Bad accommodation is one of the chief causes of sickness. In the hill tracts no shelter can be procured except what is constructed at public expense ; and in other parts of the country the Police is practically quartered on the villages wherever huts are not provided.

58. Receipts on account of the Superannuation Service Fund, **POLICE.** during the year amounted to Rs. 1,27,144. The credits from the same Superannuation Service Fund. sources in 1864-65 being Rs. 1,07,093. The balance at the credit of the service at the close of the year was Rupees 5,08,610. No pensions have been granted as yet.

59. The Police executed 34,934 warrants, and arrested 38,886 per- Miscellaneous duties. sons, and served Processes exe- 286,305 summonses cuted. on 291,621 per- sons ; in all 321,239 processes issued to compel appearance of 330,507 persons. The steady decrease in the number of persons compelled

	WARRANTS.		SUMMONS.		TOTAL.		Proportion to Population.
	Process- es.	Persons.	Process- es.	Persons.	Process- es.	Persons.	one in
Grave cases.	14,241	15,580	60,874	61,173	75,115	76,753	315
Minor cases.	20,693	23,306	225,431	230,448	246,124	253,754	95
Total...	34,934	38,886	286,305	291,621	321,239	330,507	...

Search Warrants.
Number of Warrants... 2,705
Number of houses searched 3,642

to attend Courts by criminal processes continues. In 1863, 465,075 persons, and in 1864, 417,459 persons respectively were arrested or summoned. The decrease has been 28·9 per cent. in three years. In grave cases, one in 315 of the population appeared before a Court in 1865 ; whereas one in 276 was compelled to attend in 1864. The most marked change, however, appears under the head of minor cases. In 1863, the Returns shewed 381,845 persons brought up by warrant and summons in minor cases; in 1864, 330,023; during the year under review, 253,754 persons only were compelled to attend the Courts, showing a decrease of about one-third within three years. In 1863, one in every sixty-one of the population was compelled to appear ; in 1864, one in seventy-three ; in 1865, one in ninety-five.

60. The average daily number of convicts Jails. guarded by Police in all Jails during 1865-66 was 8,141. Twelve hundred and two Constables of all grades were employed at a cost of Rupees 1,36,848. The same steadily progressive increase in the number of prisoners in Jails which has obtained for some years, was maintained, giving an increase of 25 per cent. in six years.

No. of convicts.	Consta- bles.	Cost.
8,141	1,202	1,36,848

Number of Convicts in Jails.
Prior to 1860 about	6,045
1860-61 ,,	6,424
1861-62 ,,	7,953
1862-63 ,,	7,422
1863-64 ,,	7,731
1864-65 ,,	7,879
1865-66 ,,	8,141

61. The Police guarded in Magistrates' lock-ups 15,212 persons Subsidiary Prisons. convicted and sentenced by Magistrates to imprisonment for a term

19

POLICE. of less than one month, the average duration of such sentences being about nine and a half days each. In 1864 and 1863 the number of convicted persons confined in casual wards was 15,931 and 15,330 respectively. The average duration of confinement being in both years, eight days.

Prisoners escaped and re-captured.

62. Four hundred and sixty-seven persons escaped from custody during the year, of whom 308 were re-captured. Forty-five escaped from Convict Jails, of whom twenty-five were re-captured. Seventy-five escaped from the casual wards or subsidiary Jails attached to Magistrates' offices—very few of which are in any respect fit places for custody ; sixty were re-captured. 342 escaped from Police lock-ups or from Police custody while in transit, of whom 219 were re-captured. The number of escapes from Police lock-ups is caused in many cases by the insecurity of these places of temporary confinement. Eighty Police Officers were convicted of culpable negligence in regard to a portion of these escapes.

From Jails.		From Subsidiary Jails.		From Police custody.		Total.	
Escaped.	Re-captured.	Escaped.	Re-captured.	Escaped.	Re-captured.	Escaped.	Re-captured.
45	25	75	60	342	219	467	308

Revenue duties.

Statement of Salt Thefts during the year 1865.

63. All preventive duty relating to the Salt monopoly devolves on the Police, as well as guarding Stores, &c. The value of salt guarded in Store was 120 lakhs of Rupees, and 87 lakhs worth of Salt was watched in process of manufacture in the open swamps. 386 cases of theft, &c., of Salt, were reported, the value of the property stolen being Rupees 1,172 ; 653 persons were arrested by the Police, of whom 437, or sixty-seven per cent., were convicted. Experience has shown that the establishment must be strengthened in some Districts.

Districts.	Value Store on average of the year.	Value manufactured.	Number of cases of Thefts.	Value of Salt Stolen.	Number of Arrests.	Number of Convictions.
	1	2	3	4	5	6
	RS.	RS.		RS.		
Ganjam	8,78,896	10,27,395	107	337	296	177
Vizagapatam. ...	3,37,093	37,454	20	35	45	38
Godavery	3,46,694	64,963	...	...	...	...
Krishna	12,16,311	6,24,903	7	14	6	4
Nellore	17,93,068	12,03,195	83	29	39	32
Madras	27,53,009	30,52,528	77	348	66	42
South Arcot ..	12,43,053	2,53,417	94	264	124	89
Tanjore	6,70,969	16,55,938	10	44	15	12
Madura	6,90,489	6,22,228	12	23	27	15
Tinnevelly	17,67,106	7,39,704	14	71	21	8
South Canara.. ..	3,42,687	55,276	12	7	20	20
Total ..	1,20,39,375	87,37,001	386	1,172	653	437

64. The first step towards effective prevention and detection of crime by the Police, is a thorough knowledge of the criminal classes whom they have to observe, and of their places of resort. To this important object the attention of the Police has been earnestly directed throughout the Presidency, and

Range.	Known thieves and depredators.		Receivers of stolen property.		Total.	Houses of bad repute		
	Males.	Females.	Males.	Females.		Drink shops frequented by thieves.	Of receivers of stolen property.	Notorious gambling houses.
Northern	2,477	93	479	73	3,122	841	332	400
Central	4,483	110	596	70	5,259	471	284	349
Southern	2,905	30	361	57	3,353	529	314	123
Western	1,107	25	160	21	1,313	72	29	143
Total	10,972	258	1,596	221	13,047	1,913	959	1,015
Add Suspected persons.	16,000	550	...	...	16,550	...	...	...
Vagrant and wandering gangs.	5,333	2,326	...	...	7,659	...	...	...
Total	32,305	3,134	...	...	37,256	...	...	...

information has been in course of collection for some years. Fair accuracy is now attained in most Districts. The returns comprise only thieves and depredators who are known to be actually practising on the public, but not persons who, although they may have been convicted as offenders, are not suspected of continuing dishonest practices. 10,972 known thieves and depredators, male and female, are returned by the Police; or including known receivers, in all 13,047 persons. To these must be added 24,209 suspected persons, 16,550 wandering gangs, and 7,659 believed to be engaged in crime. In all 37,256 persons are noted by the Police who, from their habits, must be set down as belonging to the criminal classes. The proportion of the criminal classes at large, thus returned by the Police to the population is one to 655. In England the proportion of criminal classes (deducting prostitutes) to population is one to 226 (1864), and in Ireland (making the same deduction) one in 327 (1863). Comparing the number of criminals already convicted and confined in prison, with those still at large and known to the Police, the proportion in England is 24·4 to 100 at large (1864), in Ireland 23·7: in the Madras Presidency the proportion of sentenced convicts to depredators at large is about 21 to 100. The prostitutes of India are not returned as belonging to criminal classes, as are all low prostitutes in England. These women are, however, observed, and their numbers registered in Cantonments where there are European Soldiers. There were 762 such prostitutes in Cantonments at the end of 1865. One thousand and fifteen notorious and open gambling houses are returned. The unchecked gambling which prevails in almost every town of the Presidency is a most serious evil.

21

POLICE.
Season.

65. The year 1865 was another year of the series of bad seasons, during which the pressure of dire want has been increasingly felt by the poor. The commonest necessaries of life commanded extravagant prices throughout the year. Yet crime was successfully repressed, and a marked decrease occurred under every important head of offence. The per-centage of cases in which offenders were brought to justice ran up considerably; and the proportion of convictions to arrests, and of convictions to offences committed, improved.

Crime.

Accidental
Deaths.

66. A further increase in the number of accidental deaths reported is indicative of improved intelligence and observation. 7,086 lost their lives accidentally, viz., 4,056 males, and 3,030 females, against 6,321 in 1864. 4,967 were drowned, 2,119 lost their lives by other accidents.

Drowned.		By other causes.		Total.
Males	Females.	Males.	Females.	
2,459	2,508	1,597	522	7,086

In India the loss of human life from accidental causes is not excessive, as compared with England and Wales. In Madras, on the average, one in every 3,635 of the inhabitants is killed by accident every year; in England the proportion, on an average of six years (9,485), is one in every 2,115.

Suicide.

67. One thousand two hundred and forty-two persons (482 males and 760 females) committed suicide. Men resort to drowning and hanging in equal numbers. Six out of seven women who destroy themselves prefer the water. The average number of suicides for five years (1,145) was exceeded in 1865—the increase may be attributed in part perhaps, to better observation, but chiefly to increased destitution.

Males.	Females.	Total.
482	760	1,242

Several women are reported to have jumped into wells, taking with them one or more of their children. The yearly average proportion to the population of persons who commit suicide is nearly one in every 20,000. In England and Wales the proportion of suicides to population, on an average of six years (1,319), is one in 15,200. Some suicides no doubt pass unchallenged in India, and there really exists a near analogy in respect to self-murder between the two populations, except that twice as many males destroy themselves as females in England, while the reverse is the condition of India. 581 attempts were made to commit suicide in England and Wales in 1862—in Madras 202 attempts were reported in 1865. In respect to murder too the same analogy holds good. In Madras,

on an average of five years, it is found that one in 97,680 of the population   POLICE.
falls by the hand of an assassin ; in England and Wales, one in 91,210.

68. The destruction of human life and dwellings by fires during   Fires.

Fires reported.	Houses burnt.	Value of property destroyed.	Lives lost.
7,150	33,276	6,63,361	116

the year largely exceeded that of the previous years—7,150 fires occurred, 116 persons were burnt to death, and 33,276 dwellings of all kinds were consumed, involving a loss of above six and a half lakhs of Rupees worth of property. In 1864, 6,401 fires occurred, and caused the loss of ninety-six lives; 27,410 dwellings, and property to the value of eight and a half lakhs. By far the greater number of fires are accidental, but mystery hangs over the origin of many, which, though not proved to be, are no doubt the work of incendiaries.

JAILS.

69. The daily average number of prisoners in confinement during   Number in Jails.
the year, was 8,150, and the number in Jail on the 31st December 1865 was 9,437.

70. There were 1,055 deaths, being at the rate of 12·944 per cent.   Deaths.

71. The greatest mortality has been in the undermentioned Jails,   Mortality in Jails.
viz., Calicut, Rajahmundry, Cochin, Nellore, Tellicherry, Madura, Guntoor, Vizagapatam, Mangalore, Berhampore, Palghat, Tinnevelly, and Salem.

72. The Jail at Calicut has always been unhealthy, and was much   Calicut.
crowded during the past year. In the month of March last, it was relieved by the transfer of 128 prisoners, which reduced the number of inmates to about 200, being sixty less than the Jail can accommodate at the regulated allowance of cubical space to each individual. The effects of this measure have been beneficial, as against nineteen deaths in February and thirteen in March, there were only two in April, two in May, and two in June ; but the building is unsuitable for its present purpose, and has been condemned. Out of the large number of casualties, viz., 195, forty-eight died of cholera, which broke out in the middle of June, and terminated on the 8th July ; eighty-three in all were attacked, of whom thirty-five recovered, being a somewhat larger proportion than usual. Thirty-eight died of dysentery and diarrhœa,

JAILS. twenty-five of atrophy, twenty-four of anasarca, seventeen of rheuma-
tism, and thirteen of fever.

Rajahmundry. 73. The mortality in the District Jail at Rajahmundry is also to
be attributed to overcrowding, and partially, in the opinion of the
Medical Officer, to taint in the building. In the month of April last,
sixty prisoners were removed to the Central Jail, and the walls were
scraped and cleaned. These measures were also followed by good
results, as there were no casualties in May or June.

Cochin. 74. In the Jail at Cochin, out of sixteen deaths, fourteen were
from cholera, which was prevalent all through the State in the months
of June and July. The prisoners were otherwise healthy.

Nellore. 75. At Nellore, out of 115 deaths, ninety-eight were from cholera,
which broke out virulently in March and April, on which occasion
ninety-four* persons died. The disease, which seemed to have been
absent from the town between March and October, again appeared in
Jail in the month of August, but in a much milder form, only four
casualties having occurred. On both of these occasions the prisoners
were encamped. With the exception of this epidemic, the Jail was
generally healthy.

Tellicherry. 76. At Tellicherry, where there were forty-four deaths, the principal mortality was from cholera, of which twenty-four persons died.
In the month of June last, Dr. Thompson, the Superintendent of the
Jail, reported the very damp state of one range of wards, which he
attributed to the fact of their resting against a mass of earth filling
the space between them and the fort wall. This earth is now being
removed by convict labor, and certain alterations to the building are
being carried out. The Superintendent confidently expects that
these measures will have a very beneficial effect.

Madura. 77. There were forty-five deaths at Madura, of which sixteen
were from cholera, and fifteen from diarrhœa. The Jail being in the
heart of the town, which is visited yearly by cholera, the disease generally appears in the Jail at the same time. This building also has been

---

* This is the outbreak referred to in paragraph ninety-two of the Administration Report
for 1864-65.

The statements annexed to the report on Jails except those which relate to money
payments and receipts, refer to the Calendar year, and consequently include the first four
months of the official year 1864-65.

condemned, and orders have been issued for the erection of a new Jail JAILS, outside the town.

78. The deaths at Guntoor were sixty-two, of which twenty-three Guntoor. were from anasarca, which shewed itself in July, and which, in the opinion of the Medical Officer, was induced in a great measure by the over-crowded state of the Jail. In September, 154 convicts were transferred to Rajahmundry and Masulipatam. From that time there has been a marked improvement in the general health of the prisoners, and no serious sickness has since prevailed.

79. At Vizagapatam, out of sixty deaths, twenty-seven were from Vizagapatam. cholera and nineteen from anasarca. Cholera appeared in an epidemic form in May, June, and July, and in a sporadic form in December. The mortality was augmented by the presence of prisoners from the Hill Tracts, twenty-four of whom died. A small Jail, for the reception of this class of convicts, is now being built at Parvuttipur, a town in the immediate vicinity of the hills. The health of the prisoners from the low country, when not visited by epidemic disease, is generally good.

80. Of the forty-five deaths at Mangalore, twenty-three were from Mangalore. diarrhœa and sixteen from atrophy. The Medical Officer is of opinion, that the mortality is to be mainly attributed to the effects of incarceration under the system of diet then in use, and he anticipates much benefit from the introduction of the present more liberal scale, and also from that of intramural labor, which is now being carried out to some extent.

81. Of forty deaths at Berhampore, eighteen were from anasarca, Berhampore. twelve from diarrhœa and dysentery, and six from cholera. This Jail has been much crowded, and has been relieved, from time to time, by drafts to other Jails ; but as these measures proved insufficient, huts are now in course of erection. The great increase of prisoners in this Jail is no doubt to be attributed to the distress in the District.

82. There were thirteen deaths at Palghat on an average daily Palghat, strength of eighty-eight convicts, and the per-centage is, therefore high ; but these casualties were principally amongst prisoners transferred from other Jails, particularly those received from the Hills. The health of the prisoners who had been any time in the Jail was good.

83. At Tinnevelly there were thirty-four deaths, of which twenty- Tinnevelly, seven were from diarrhœa and dysentery. This building is not suited

D

JAILS.   for a Jail, and as it cannot be easily altered or added to, it is intended to build a new one. The death-rate for the past year has been heavy, but still not so much so as in the two years immediately preceding.

In 1863 it was 15·58 on the average strength.

In 1864 „   19·5   do.

In 1865 „   11·9   do.

The Medical Officer attributes the improvement to a change in the diet, and to the fact that, during the year under review, the Jail was not so much crowded as it was in the two preceding years.

Salem.   84. At Salem there were fifty-five deaths, of which twenty-nine were from diarrhœa and dysentery, nine from atrophy, and seven from anasarca. The mortality in this Jail is somewhat increased by transfers of sick from the Hills.

Lawrence Asylum Works.   85. The health of the convicts at the Lawrence Asylum Works was good during the whole year, the total number of deaths having been nineteen on an average daily strength of 334. The officer in charge reports that men who are cheerful, and who make up their minds to the change of climate, and to the distance from their native country, improve considerably in strength, and enjoy very good health. He also points out a remarkable difference between the rate of mortality amongst the Tamil-speaking men, and those who speak Telugu. The subjoined table shews the difference in the health of those two classes during the year 1865.

Language.	Admission to strength.	Deaths to strength.	Deaths to admission.
Telugu men	97·2	11·2	11·4
Tamil men	85·6	4·0	4·8

This fact has been borne in mind in the recent selections of men for labor on the hills.

Cost.   86. The expenses, exclusive of Police Guards and buildings, amounted to Rupees 4,86,947, of which Rupees 3,24,343 were on account of food. The cost per prisoner was Rupees 56-1-7 per head, that for last year having been Rupees 56-11-3.

Estimated value of convict labor.   87. The estimated value of convict labor during the year was Rupees 75,796.

Jail manufactures.   88. The only Jails in which manufactures were carried on are those at Chingleput, Cuddalore, Chittoor, Berhampore, Mangalore, and Salem. They have now been commenced at the Central Jail, Rajah-

26

mundry, and will be soon introduced in that at Coimbatore. The trades have been principally weaving, paper-making, rattan work, and mat and rope-making.

JAILS.

89. In the last Administration Report reference was made to the measures which were being taken, or which were in contemplation, for increasing the amount of Jail accommodation. It was stated that a new District Jail was in progress at Vizagapatam, and that Central Jails at Coimbatore and Rajahmundry were approaching completion. The Vizagapatam Jail is nearly finished, but the two Central Jails have not progressed as rapidly as was expected. Both these Jails, however, have been occupied since January, and now afford accommodation to about 1,000 prisoners. It is hoped that the two Jails will be completed by the end of the present year.

New Central Jails.

Of the three other Central Jails which are required for this Presidency, it has been determined to build one at Vellore instead of at Bellary, as was originally intended, difficulty having been experienced in finding a suitable site with a sufficient supply of water at the latter station, while the expense of building there would be much greater than at Vellore. Central Jails are also to be built at Cannanore and Trichinopoly. At Cannanore the site has been fixed on, and buildings have been erected for a gang of convicts who are to be employed upon the works. At Trichinopoly, owing to a difficulty in finding good water, the question of site has not yet been determined, but this difficulty has now been overcome, and it is hoped that at both stations considerable progress will have been made in the erection of the Jail buildings during the ensuing year.

90. The new District Jail at Madura, one of those adverted to in the last Administration Report, has been commenced, and at Calicut, a site has been selected, and a plan and estimate sanctioned for a new Jail. Orders have also been issued for various alterations and improvements which are required in the existing District Jails at the stations specified in the margin; and at Parvuttipur, in the District of Vizagapatam, a Jail is now in course of construction for the reception of prisoners belonging to the hill tribes, to whom removal to the coast is in most cases fatal. The question of improving the Jail accommodation in this Presidency is one which, for some time past, has engaged the

District Jails.

Rajahmundry.
Guntoor.
Nellore.
Bellary.
Kurnool.
Chittoor.
Vellore.
Tranquebar.
Tanjore.
Trichinopoly.
Tellicherry.
Ootacamund.

27

JAILS.
serious attention of the local Government. Want of funds is the main reason why so little progress has yet been made in carrying out this important object. In December last, an urgent application was made to the Government of India for a special grant of two lakhs, in addition to the sums entered in the Public Works Budget for the current year, for building additional Jails. More recently the subject has been again brought under notice in a Minute by His Excellency the Governor, in which His Lordship has reviewed at length the requirements of this Presidency in the matter of Jail accommodation, as well as the necessity of providing better accommodation for lunatics, and which has resulted in an additional grant of Rupees 1,20,000 being sanctioned by the Supreme Government. Copies of the correspondence will be found in the Appendix.

European prison, Ootacamund.
91. The European Prison at Ootacamund is in good order. The average daily number of prisoners, during the year, was fourteen. They were employed in sawing wood, making rope and mats, tailoring, and rattan work. There were no deaths, and the health of the prisoners generally was very good.

Charge of District Jails.
92. In September last, all the District Jails in the Presidency with the exception of those at Bellary, Trichinopoly, Cuddapah, and Ootacamund, were placed under charge of the Zillah Surgeons. At Trichinopoly and Bellary the Cantonment Magistrates, and at Ootacamund the Joint Magistrate, have charge of the District Jails, and at Cuddapah the Jail is under one of the Assistant Magistrates, acting under the general supervision of the Magistrate of the District. In the Central Jails at Rajahmundry, Coimbatore, and Salem, the superintendence of the Jail has been made a distinct charge.

Penitentiary.
93. The total cost of maintenance for a daily average of 377 prisoners in the Madras Penitentiary was Rupees 28,282-15-5, against Rupees 31,209-14-11 for a daily average of 379 prisoners in 1864-65. The difference of expenditure is due chiefly to the larger disbursement in the former year for additions, alterations, and repairs. The daily average of European prisoners in 1865-66 was 38, and the gross cost of each Rupees 185-12-11. The daily average of Native prisoners was 339, and the gross cost of each Rupees 62-9-7. 5,139 prisoners were lodged in the Penitentiary, the daily average being 380. There were only 267 admissions into Hospital during the year, and fifteen deaths, or four per cent on the daily average, Seven of these

deaths were from cholera, and excluding this disease the death ratio
would fall to two per cent. Cholera made its appearance in the
month of August, but although the Jail was then somewhat crowded
with prisoners awaiting transportation, and the disease was raging in
Chintadripett, just on the opposite bank of the Cooum, yet the epidemic gained no hold over the Penitentiary, the seven deaths being
spread over an interval of about three weeks, after which the disease
disappeared. This result is probably due to the vigilant care exercised
by the Superintendent, Mr. Owen, in keeping the Jail precincts clean
and wholesome. 694 prisoners for transportation passed through the
Jail. Of those condemned to imprisonment only eight were for periods
between two and five years, and forty-five for periods between one and
two years. The great majority are short sentenced prisoners, for
periods of six months and under. This makes it difficult to organize
a remunerative system of skilled labor in the Penitentiary. At present,
rope making is the only branch of intramural work provided for hard
labor prisoners. The sum realize d by the sale of ropes was only Rupees
375-1-0, and after deducting the cost of materials the nett profit was
only Rupees 249-12-0. The value of labor supplied to Public Works
is estimated at Rupees 2,859-2-0, at 1½ Anna per man; the ordinary
wages of a cooly being three Annas. It may be possible to utilize the
labor at the Penitentiary somewhat more than at present, so as to
bring in a larger return towards defraying the expenses of the Institution.

SECTION IV.—REVENUE.

Gross Revenue.　94. The Revenue of the year 1865-66 amounted to Rupees 6,33,17,129, exceeding that of the year 1864-65 by Rupees 7,15,652.

Charges.　95. The charges aggregated Rupees 66,50,318, or little more than ten per cent. on the Revenue, and were Rupees 3,26,448 more than in the preceding year. The increase was owing chiefly to the revision of the Revenue Establishment, and to the purchase of a large quantity of Arrack for the Abkarry shops of Madras.

Net Revenue.　96. The *net* Revenue of the year was Rupees 566,66,811, or Rupees 3,89,204, more than in the previous year, notwithstanding a clear loss of Rupees 7,80,000 by the abolition of the Income Tax.

The subjoined statements shew the Receipts and Charges of the last five years :—

Receipts.

	1861-62.	1862-63.	1863-64.	1864-65.	1865-66.
	Rupees.	Rupees.	Rupees.	Rupees.	Rupees.
Land Revenue ... } Forest Revenue ... }	411,25,379	420,64,980	429,65,352	{418,11,620 2,92,527	429,17,664 3,21,581
Abkarry	33,29,961	35,03,651	40,51,918	39,60,490	41,42,805
Income Tax	25,48,110	23,18,250	16,45,522	14,65,652	6,70,543
Mohturpha, or Tax on Professions, &c.	3,11,644	4,780	2,456	2,518	...
Sea Customs	20,94,896	17,66,809	20,37,373	18,10,046	19,51,019
Land Customs	2,71,484	1,94,084	2,61,146	2,28,733	1,34,468
Salt	86,00,532	91,26,362	89,79,243	103,45,973	101,12,489
Stamps	30,14,598	20,98,040	23,81,746	26,83,918	30,66,558
Miscellaneous Items... ...	75,295	...	...	...	...
Total...	613,72,399	610,76,956	623,24,756	626,01,477	633,17,189
£ Sterling...	61,37,239	61,07,695	62,32,475	62,60,147	63,31,712

Charges.

	1861-62.	1862-63.	1863-64.	1864-65.	1865-66.
	Rupees.	Rupees.	Rupees.	Rupees.	Rupees.
Land Revenue including Board of Revenue, Settlement Officers, and Revenue Survey ... ... }	45,69,178	42,72,371	39,24,787	{ 38,12,095	39,54,934
Forest Revenue				1,58,616	2,60,044
Abkarry	1,35,438	1,51,181	1,39,817	1,56,831	2,70,417
Income Tax	1,15,900	72,923	37,900	32,506	17,483
Mohturpha, or Tax on Professions, &c.	5,783	1,187	...	...	...
Sea Customs	1,57,635	1,49,620	1,48,901	1,58,630	1,57,195
Land Customs	22,944	15,677	14,292	10,408	8,489
Salt	11,02,451	11,66,797	9,15,864	14,25,062	14,98,792
Stamps					
Allowances to District and Village Officers	1,14,673	1,32,765	1,43,305	1,49,131	1,24,113
			3,30,472	3,60,015	3,58,901
Miscellaneous Payments	...	83,460	1,39,122	66,311	...
Payments made for the relief of the sufferers by the late inundation at Masulipatam and Cuddalore... ...	...	...	...	...	...
Total...	62,24,002	60,45,981	57,94,460	63,29,605	66,50,318
£ Sterling...	6,28,400	6,04,598	5,79,446	6,32,960	6,65,031

97. The Revenue was realized with facility. The sum collected Realization of Revenue. by resort to coercive processes was Rupees 50,000. This amount, though double that collected in the same manner in 1864-65, bears an insignificant ratio to the total Revenue.

98. The season was even more unfavorable than in the pre- Season. ceding year. In Ganjam the excessive drought necessitated extraordinary measures for the relief of the people. The Eastern and Inland Districts all suffered more or less from want of water, and on the Western Coast there was unusual drought during the last five months of the year. The fact that the revenue not only remained undiminished, but even increased during such a season, is a remarkable proof of the prosperity of the Presidency, and the stability of its resources.

99. The public health was, in most parts of the Presidency, Public Health. equal to the average. In Ganjam and the Godavery Districts however, cholera and small-pox were very prevalent; and in Malabar and North Arcot the former disease appeared during some months of the year. Cattle suffered from want of water and pasture, but murrain was not prevalent except in Coimbatore.

100. Prices steadily advanced. The statement given in the margin Prices. shews that the chief articles of food cost more by from forty to fifty percent. than they did five years ago. Unfortunately the nature of the season restricted the demand for labor, and there

Items.	1860-61.	1861-62.	1862-63.	1863-64.	1864-65.	1865-66.	Per-centage of increase during the last 5 years.
	RS.	RS.	RS.	RS.	RS.	RS.	RS.
Rice, 2nd sort, per garce.	307	333	346	352	411	431	40
Paddy, do. do. ...	138	151	152	158	189	198	43
Cholum, do. ...	164	186	201	214	227	260	59
Cumboo, do. ...	158	167	173	186	209	237	50
Raggy, do. ...	160	172	175	185	210	231	44
Veragoo, do. ...	110	133	139	132	161	164	49
Wheat, do. ...	425	443	445	553	668	700	65
Cotton per candy ...	59	93	159	270	227	151	156

was, doubtless, much distress among the laboring classes, as well as those possessing only fixed incomes of small amount.

101. Notwithstanding the character of the season, the area under Cultivated area. cultivation increased by 1,87,012 acres. The marginal abstract shews

Year.	Acres under cultivation.	Assessment.
	Acres.	Rs.
1861-62 ...	144,50,718	319,06,152
1862-63 ...	151,43,279	327,19,710
1863-64 ...	158,34,170	338,11,122
1864-65 ...	158,49,668	323,61,309
1865-66 ...	160,56,675	323,24,934

the area of cultivation and its assessment for the last five years. The decrease in the assessment for the last year, was caused by a reduction of the tax on land irrigated from private wells.

Forest Revenue.

102. The Forest accounts are, in accordance with orders from the Government of India, exhibited separately from those of the Land Revenue. The receipts amounted to Rupees 3,21,581, the charges of conservancy to Rupees 2,60,044, and the net revenue to Rupees 61,536. The deficiency in the receipts resulted principally from the relinquishment in July of the tax on bamboos. This tax has since been re-imposed in many parts of the Presidency. The increase in charges is due partly to the fact that the extensive Golcondah forests in Vizagapatam, the Chenat Nair and Bolumputty belt in Coimbatore, and the Alwarkurchi forest in Tinnevelly, were taken under management, for the first time, during the year.

In spite of extensive fires, the value of timber in store was increased by Rupees 1,06,645. The Javady and Yellagiri Hills, between the Salem and South Arcot Districts, were explored, and large quantities of Satinwood and Sandalwood discovered. Good progress was made with the Teak nurseries at Muddumally and Nellambur, and with the planting of Acacias and Eucalypti on the Neilgherries and other hill tracts. Many valuable forest trees have been introduced from Australia, and are thriving beyond expectation.

Abkarry.

103. The Abkarry revenue increased by Rupees 1,82,315, but most of this arose from realization of arrears.

Salt.

104. The Salt revenue shewed a decrease of Rupees 2,33,484, which was entirely owing to the fact that, in 1863-64, a large amount was credited in the Madras District in adjustment of long outstanding balances.

The quantity of salt sold for home and inland consumption decreased by three lacs of maunds, as will be seen from the annexed statement. This was owing to the large stocks purchased by salt dealers in the previous year. The price of salt, during the latter part of the year, was raised from Rupees 1-8-0 to Rupees 1-11-0 per Indian Maund of 82¾ lbs.

Items.	1861-62.	1862-63.	1863-64.	1864-65.	1865-66.
	In. Mds.	In. Mds.	In. Mds.	In Mds.	In. Mds.
Home consumption.	27,30,757	28,49,502	29,74,214	32,36,772	33,30,837
Inland do.	30,91,008	32,72,713	31,25,278	37,09,269	33,50,364
Total...	58,21,765	61,22,215	60,99,492	69,46,041	66,81,201
Exportation	6'1,116	4,16,286	3,03,127	5,32,018	12,86,965
Grand Total...	64,32,881	65,38,501	64,02,619	74,78,059	79,68,166
	RS. A. P.	RS. A. P.	RS. A. P.	RS. A. P.	RS. A. P.
Government price for Salt per Indian Maund.	1 6 0 1 8 0	} 1 8 0	1 8 0	1 8 0	{ 1 8 0 1 11 0

105. The revenue from Stamps increased by Rupees 3,82,640. The **Stamps.** operation of the new Registration and Abkarry Acts, the establishment of Courts of Small Causes, and the increased facilities for obtaining stamps offered by the discount system of sale, which has been introduced into many Districts, account for this result.

106. The Income Tax Act was in force for only three months of the **Income Tax.** year, and the receipts consequently diminished by Rupees 7,95,104.

107. The Sea Customs revenue partially recovered the effects of **Sea Customs.** the depressed state of trade in 1864-65, when the revenue fell by Rupees 2,27,327. It has this year risen by Rupees 1,40,973; but is still considerably below the revenue of 1863-64. The increase is due to large imports of spirits at Madras ; and to increased exports of grain and oil seeds from Tanjore, South Canara, and the Godavery.

The increased duties imposed on exports, towards the close of 1864-65, were removed early in the year under report, and the amount of additional duty which had intermediately been collected was refunded, to the amount of Rupees 1,04,233.*

108. There was a falling off of Rupees 94,268 in the Custom's duties **Land Customs.**

RS.
1864-65 2,28,733
1865-66 1,34,465

collected on the frontiers of foreign territories, owing to the arrangements effected last year with the Travancore and Cochin States, with the view of freeing interportal trade from taxation and assimilating the Tariffs and duties of these States with those of British India.

* Sea Customs .... Rs .1,00,161
Land Customs....... .. .. „ 4,071
                                           1,04,233

E   33

Foreign Trade.　109.　A comparative statement is given in the Appendix, shewing the declared value of the Exports and Imports of the Madras territories during the last ten years. 'In the present year, the exports and imports have exceeded those of any previous year, the value of the merchandize exported having been upwards of nine millions sterling, and that of the imports not very far short of five millions. It may be inferred from the same table, that the pressure exercised upon trade by the present rates of import and export duties, is moderate ; for in 1860-61, when the value of the exports was just one-half what it is at present, the export duty collected exceeded that of the year under report by twenty per cent. ; while on merchandize, valued at only a little over three millions sterling, an import duty of seventeen lacs of Rupees was collected, against a present import duty of twelve lacs, on merchandize valued at nearly five millions.

110.　In the Appendix will also be found a comparative analysis of the principal articles of export and import trade in 1865-66. There has been an increase in the value of the Import trade in Spirits, Wines, Tea, plain and printed Piece Goods, Silk Piece Goods, Paddy, Timber, and Planks, and in Railway and Naval Stores. In raw Silk and Woollens, Malt liquors, Metals, and Rice there was a decrease.

In exports, the increase was marked in Coffee, Cotton, Wool, Drugs, Indigo, Rice, Molasses, Coir, Provisions, and Spices. There was a decrease in Fruits and Nuts, Paddy, Grain, Oil-seeds, and Sugar.

The subjoined statement gives the export trade in staple articles, both in quantity and value, for the last three years. There has been a steady increase in the export of Coffee, Cotton wool, Cotton Piece Goods, Spices, and Molasses, while the export trade in Indigo, Oil, and Rum has fallen off.

Articles.		1863-64.		1864-65.		1865-66.	
		Quantity.	Value.	Quantity.	Value.	Quantity.	Value.
Coffee	lb.	27,333,127	Rs. 65,85,671	31,424,319	Rs. 76,84,938	34,527,695	Rs. 78,13,843
Cotton Wool	,,	72,490,686	447,18,112	73,101,578	401,18,937	120,034,216	4,84,15,248
Cotton Piece Goods	Pieces.	679,837	16,36,131	576,787	15,60,671	762,303	20,45,963
Indigo	lb.	2,093,784	40,37,259	1,530,508	33,35,915	1,600,925	34,57,079
Rice	Qr.	339,563	68,75,295	323,901	60,51,255	373,326	65,88,483
Hides and Skins	No.	4,469,832	20,62,978	4,278,270	19,39,439	4,443,327	19,81,107
Oils	Gals.	3,818,018	37,12,229	2,777,237	25,07,457	1,592,962	15,43,435
Coir and Coir Rope	Cwt.	210,672	11,95,399	178,587	9,90,206	217,907	12,27,660
Oil, &c., Seeds	Qr.	140,518	26,64,306	158,262	27,57,538	133,609	22,69,161
Spices	lb.	16,388,502	20,23,356	15,387,510	21,65,851	18,529,039	23,59,650
Rum	Gals.	27,908	44,533	1,046	1,606	344	518
Sugar	Cwt.	243,356	25,51,907	224,181	22,40,991	199,116	13,36,873
Molasses or Jaggery	,,	170,053	7,99,498	155,743	9,28,059	220,443	14,08,928

111. The area under Cotton cultivation has again diminished, but the quantity exported is still increasing. The subjoined table shews the Cotton wool exports in quantity and value, and the area under Cotton cultivation for the last ten years. *Area under Cotton cultivation.*

Years.	Quantity.	Value.	Area under Cotton.
	lbs.	Rs.	
1855-56··· ...	21,013,464	25,21,351	7,97,504
1856-57... ...	53,988,065	72,22,286	9,38,047
1857-58... ...	55,015,309	87,71,724	9,32,285
1858-59... ...	38,652,542	61,17,902	10,41,848
1859-60... ...	82,512,521	95,97,135	9,96,658
1860-61... ...	78,822,027	112,91,211	10,60,558
1861-62... ...	87,544,471	170,40,215	9,77,728
1862-63... ...	62,374,133	238,12,882	13,62,438
1863-64... ...	72,490,886	447,18,112	18,24,763
1864-65... ...	73,101,578	404,18,937	17,42,078
1865-66... ...	120,034,216	484,16,348	15,16,076

112. The following statement shews the course of the Cotton trade for the last three years. It will be remarked that out of 1,071,734 cwt. exported, no less than cwt. 1,016,254 went *direct* to England. *Cotton Trade.*

Ports.	1863-64.		1864-65.		1865-66.	
	Quantity.	Value.	Quantity.	Value.	Quantity.	Value.
	lbs.	RS.	lbs.	RS.	lbs.	RS.
United Kingdom	62,087.480	387,07,488	66,245,553	370,04,081	113,820,463	4,61,47,318
Ceylon	833,360	4,71,027	93,560	90,829	255,182	1,01,140
France	7,598,156	43,36,030	5,170,828	25,31,719	3,960,250	13,04,150
Maldive Islands ...	224	165	84	31	1,217	272
Bombay	1,209,300	6,93,537	900,543	4,00,929	1,263,038	5,93,274
Calcutta	600,100	4,08,650	406,838	2,28,739	484,217	1,80,556
Travancore ...	40,099	19,611	34,776	14,242	32,382	17,921
Indian Fr. Ports	121,550	81,163	220,172	1,42,870	205,556	69,459
Concan	617	441	8,682	3,269	2,652	828
Chittagong ...	...	...	14,542	2,198	9,259	1,430
Total...	72,490,886	447,18,112	78,101,578	404,18,937	120,034,216	484,16,348

113. The annexed statement shews the receipts and expenditure of the District Road Fund for the last six years. It continues to increase steadily, and is yearly exercising a most beneficial effect in developing the resources of the country. *District Road Fund.*

Receipts. Expenditure.
1860-61 ... 3,64,858 2,54,218
1861-62 ... 2,83,079 3,08,116
1862-63 ... 3,88,113 8,30,165
1863-64 ... 4,04,701 4,30,909
1864-65 ... 5,44,075 4,45,610
1865-66 ... 6,47,290 7,15,313

114. The out-door work of the Inam Commission was completed throughout the Presidency, and the services of the two Deputy Collectors who were retained at the commencement of the year were dispensed with. The number of cases settled by the Deputy Collectors was 7,083. In the central office titles were confirmed for all the cases pending, amounting in number to 22,324, and involving an extent of land measuring acres 7,35,438, and bearing an assessment of Rupees 12,64,102 ; a large number of appeals were heard and disposed of, and a considerable amount of work connected with the winding up of the Commission was gone through. The addition made to the annual revenue, in the shape of quit-rent imposed on Inams for enfranchisement, during the year, amounted to Rupees 1,14,013, while the cost of the Commission was Rupees 1,23,918. Inams bearing an assessment of Rupees 23,000 were fully assessed, chiefly on account of the non-appearance of the holders to claim the Inams within the time prescribed by the rules. These Inams are reported to consist, for the most part, of unprofitable lands, and to have been in consequence abandoned by the proprietors. The cost of the Commission from the commencement of its operations in 1859, has been Rupees 9,44,122. The subjoined statement shews the results which have been effected. The additional annual revenue gained by the operations of the Commission amounts to Rupees 15,06,017.

Description of Inam.	Number of Titles confirmed.	Extent in Acres.	Value or estimated Assessment.	Existing Jodi paid thereon.	Additional quit-rent stipulated to be paid for enfranchisement.	Additional quit-rent not agreed to be paid.	Number of cases decided by the Deputy Collectors.
Devadayam and Dhurmadayam, or religious and charitable grants of a permanent character	91,830	16,17,249	27,94,638	1,53,139	35,371	...	
Personal grants enfranchised at the option of the Inamdars, 1,61,503, compulsorily 85,866.	2,47,388	34,68,092	51,20,600	5,54,181	6,72,351	...	
Personal grants not enfranchised and confirmed on present tenures only.	6,831	1,49,705	2,03,701	32,746	...	35,175	Personal Inams 3,46,946
Miscellaneous Service Inams enfranchised compulsorily.	15,334	3,13,004	3,65,478	49,074	1,35,946	...	
	3,61,383	55,48,050	84,83,817	7,99,133	8,43,668	35,175	
Government Village Service Inams, enfranchised at five-eighths of their Assessment.	20,052	9,33,726	10,86,361	1,30,592	5,74,299	...	Service Inams 2,01,736
Total...	3,81,435	64,81,776	95,70,178	9,29,655	14,17,967	35,175	
Inams fully assessed...	...	82,597	1,03,648	15,598	88,050		
Net Assessment...	...	...	...	...			
Total...	...	...	...	...	15,06,017	...	

Number of Title Deeds issued 3,04,278.

	No.	RS.	A.	P.
Number of cases redeemed, ...	375	...		
Quit-rent redeemed........		656	11	1
Amount paid in redemption		13,133	13	4

115. In 1865-66, 384 villages, containing 1,615 square miles of Survey. country, were surveyed; 811 villages, containing 1,787 square miles, were mapped; and the maps of 746 villages, containing 1,250 square miles, were lithographed. The Survey Department was at work in 707 villages, containing 1,633 square miles, at the close of the year. The demarcation of two Districts was commenced. The correct areas of

	RS.	A.	P.
District Establishment	4,06,122	0	5
Central Office	39,784	3	2
Lithographic Establishment	9,299	2	2

1,742 villages, containing 3,854 square miles, were ready for settlement purposes. The total expenditure in the Survey Department amounted to Rs. 4,55,205-5-9. The average cost of completed work has been Rupees

	RS.	A.	P.
Krosur	71	2	9
Guntur	99	15	2

85-9-0 per mile; or Rupee 0-2-2 per acre, including surveying, mapping, lithography, and computation of areas.

116. Field operations were carried on during the year by the Settle- Settlement ment Department in the Districts of Kurnool, Cuddapah, Coimbatore, Tinnevelly, and Kistna. In the last named District, the work consisted chiefly of the re-classification of villages, the settlement accounts of which had been lost in the cyclone of 1864. The total area demarcated was 2,625 square miles, and the area classified (including that re-classified) 1,916 square miles. The demarcation of Tinnevelly was completed. The new settlement was successfully introduced in the central and eastern deltas, and in most of the upland talooks of the Godavery District; the total number of villages settled being 463. In Kurnool proper the settlement was introduced in 106 villages, for which survey areas had been received. In the Kistna District the whole of the Masulipatam division, with the exception of a few villages in two taluks, was brought under the new settlement. The settlement of the Trichinopoly District, nearly completed in 1863-64, was brought to a close in the year under report, and the settlement registers were printed. The total expenditure, during the year, was Rupees 3,59,290. This sum includes Rupees 25,452, paid out of the funds of the department to Settlement establishments working in the Districts of Vizagapatam, Nellore, Madras, and Tinnevelly, under the orders of the Collectors.

117. The operations of the District Printing Presses, during the last District Presses. two years, are shewn in the following statement. Work to the value of Rupees 1,32,444 was executed at a charge of Rupees 51,906 in 1864-65, and work worth nearly a lac and a half of rupees in 1865-66, at a cost of little more than one-third of that sum.

		Estimate of value of work done.		Expenditure.
1864-65	Rs.	1,32,444	Rs.	51,906
1865-66	„	1,48,595	„	52,388

Revision of Establishments.   118.   The revised establishments of the Revenue Department underwent some further modifications during the year under report. The salary of the office of Head Clerk on the Collector's establishment was raised ; the pay of the Taluk Serishtadars was equalized ; and some minor alterations were made in other offices.   The establishment of the Salt department was again revised, in consequence of alterations and improvements which have been made of late years at the Salt stations.

Examination of officials.   119.   The result of the Special Test Examination in the Revenue Department is given in the margin.

Deputy Collectors and Magistrates	41
Tahshildars, Deputy Tahshildars, Serishtadars, and Sub-Magistrates	122
Salt Superintendents	13
Superintendents of Sea Customs ...	11
Translators for lower grade	65

The number of persons who qualified themselves for the posts of Tahsildar, Sub-Magistrate, and Taluk Serishtadar was double that in 1864-65, but many of them were unfitted to occupy these important situations from want of experience.   The arrangements referred to in last year's Report, however, suffice to prevent the administration of the country from being placed in inexperienced hands, and the Modified Special Test Examinations resulted in the success of fifty-two officers, who were thus shewn to be fitted for the grades above referred to by special knowledge, as well as by tried ability and prolonged service.

Improvement of Agricultural system.   120.   The experimental farm at Sydapet, in the vicinity of Madras, was continued during the year with fair promise of ultimate success. The use of a superior description of agricultural implements is attracting the attention and interest of the agricultural classes.

In order to obtain complete information as to the system followed in native agriculture, exhaustive reports upon the subject were prepared in all the Districts of the Presidency, and a mass of valuable information, regarding soils, crops, modes of culture, &c., was collected, which will furnish important data for agricultural experiments, and for future adjustments of the Government demand upon the agricultural classes.

Sale of Waste land.   121.   As in 1864-65, only a very small quantity of land was sold under the rules for the sale of unassessed waste, and that only in the Districts of Ganjam and Coimbatore.   In the former District 207 acres were sold in freehold for Rupees 8,265, and in the latter 166 acres for Rupees 832. A small extent of land was also sold, under the special rules, on the Neilgherry and Shervaroy Hills, and in the Wynaad.

122. Notwithstanding the unfavorable character of the season, unprecedented progress was made in the Chinchona plantations. The average rate of propagation increased from 21,200 to 48,968, and the total number of plants was doubled during the year, and amounted to 11,56,070 on the 1st May 1866. These very satisfactory results are mainly due to the circumstance that the trees which were first planted out (in August 1862), and which are now from twelve to twenty feet high, and from eleven to twenty-two inches in diameter at the bole, have already produced millions of excellent seeds. The bark of the oldest plants has increased in thickness and improved in appearance, and the yield of crystallized sulphates has been ascertained by recent analysis to be no less than ten per cent. It has been proved that strips of bark may be removed from the trees without injuring them, if moss be immediately applied, and that by mossing the trees before the bark is stripped off, the latter may be immensely improved both in thickness and quality. Now that seeds are produced in abundance, the number of plants may be rapidly increased to any desired extent, and the cultivation may be readily extended to all favorable localities. *Chinchona cultivation.*

123. In the Tea plantations 1,700 plants were raised from Assam seed, in the course of the year, and the total number is now 13,500. Some of them have flowered, and a supply of fresh and good seed will soon be available for the public at a fair price. The price of plants is now one anna or three half pence each,—a good many are being distributed gratuitously to the inhabitants of the hill tracts, and a large number sold to planters. *Tea plantation.*

124. Continued attention was paid, through the year, to the raising of plantations to replace the forests which are gradually diminishing. The villagers in all districts have been stimulated to raise village topes, and in some parts of the country, very favorable results have attended the exertions of the district officers. Nurseries for young trees are in process of formation in all the districts, and endeavours have been made with fair success to plant the sandy tracts along the seashore with the Casuarina. In Nellore, an experimental plantation of firewood has been commenced, and tracts reserved elsewhere for like purposes. *Plantations.*

125. Agricultural exhibitions were held in the Districts of Nellore, Bellary, and Tinnevelly. As in previous years, the cattle shew at *Exhibitions.*

Cattle-disease. Addanki, and the Agricultural exhibition at Nellore, were decidedly successful. Elsewhere the attempt to arouse any general interest was a failure.

126.   The preservation of agricultural stock from disease received special attention during the year. Mr. Thacker, Veterinary Surgeon, was engaged in careful and protracted inquiries on the Neilgherry Hills and in other parts of the District of Coimbatore, where a new and virulent form of disease, akin to the well known " Rinderpest, had broken out. He has succeeded in discovering a course of treatment which he considers will, in a great measure, check the progress of the malady, and he is still prosecuting his investigations.

Municipal action. 127.   Municipal action has gradually become more general throughout the country, and in several districts considerable sums have been raised by private subscription for sanitary and other public purposes. The several voluntary Town Associations, which were referred to in the reports of previous years, and which worked satisfactorily in the Districts of Vizagapatam, Godavery, and Bellary, during the year, will shortly be merged in the Municipal Committees about to be formed under the Towns Improvement Act.

Rent recovery law. 128.   The law for the recovery of rent was brought into operation on the 1st January 1866, and promises to be most beneficial in its results.

SECTION V.—PUBLIC WORKS.

129. The Imperial Public Works grant, inclusive of private   ALLOT-
contributions, amounted to Rupees 64,46,658, which was distributed as   MENT.
follows :—

New Works	... Rs.	23,73,278
Repairs	... „	22,64,146
Tools and Plants	... „	1,67,908
Establishments	... „	16,41,326

130. The outlay during the year was Rupees 63,15,358, as shewn   Expenditure.
below :—

On New Works	... Rs.	22,11,009
„ Repairs	... „	22,95,207
„ Tools and Plants ...	... „	1,68,570
„ Establishments ...	... „	16,40,572

131. The expenditure on Works fell short of the allotment by   Expenditure contrasted with allotment and with the outlay in previous year. only Rupees 1,31,208, but it was less than the outlay in 1864-65 by Rupees 8,59,725, owing to the Imperial grant for that year having exceeded the assignment for 1865-66 by Rupees 8,51,495.

132. Except in the Ganjam, Vizagapatam, Madura, and Tinne-   Rates of Labor. velly Districts, and in parts of Cuddapah and Tanjore, where they were on the increase, rates of labor continued nearly the same as in 1864-65·

133. Statements shewing the outlay in each District from   Statement of expenditure, &c., given in Appendix. Imperial and Local Funds, and the expenditure on the more important works which were under execution, as compared with their estimates and allotments, will be found in the Appendix.

134. The following is a brief account of the progress made upon   Progress made upon important works. the principal works undertaken during the year.

135. Rupees 3,899 were laid out in completing a school-room   MILITARY. for the use of the Horse and Foot Artillery, and Quarters for an   Military Buildings at Bellary. Apothecary at Bellary. Good progress was made with the construction of the Artillery married Quarters at that station, and Rupees 9,878 were expended in] preparing and fixing wood work for the verandahs and for the main roof. The walls of nine Quarters for Non-Commissioned Officers of Artillery at Bellary were built up to the

MILITARY. full height at an outlay of Rupees 11,180, and Rupees 6,646 were expended in altering existing Quarters so as to secure better ventilation. One range of the barracks occupied by the Artillery at Bellary was re-roofed, and a second nearly so, at an outlay of Rupees 9,170; and Rupees 3,144 were spent in cutting channels for the purpose of supplying water to the Native Infantry Lines, and to the Fort ditch.

Kurnool Fort Ramparts. 136. The ramparts of the Fort at Kurnool, which completely shut out the air from a great part of the town, were levelled at a cost of Rupees 7,796.

Sea Face Batteries in the Fort. 137. In connection with the project for altering the Sea-face Batteries of Fort Saint George, two shot heating furnaces, and ten gun-platforms were constructed at an outlay of Rupees 2,771, and Married Quarters in do. Rupees 21,304 were spent in completing the married Quarters within Bakery at Madras. the Fort. The construction of a Soojee Mill and Bakery at Madras was put in hand, and Rupees 15,000 were laid out in raising the walls of the building to a height of eleven feet. It is expected that the work will be completed by the 30th September next.

Horse Artillery Lines and Reserve Powder Magazine at Saint Thomas' Mount. 138. The alterations to the Horse Artillery Lines at Saint Thomas' Mount, to fit them for the accommodation of the Batteries, were nearly finished, and Rupees 24,870 were expended upon that work, and upon the construction, at the same station, of a Reserve Powder Magazine, the walls of which, as well as a portion of the arched roof, were completed.

Rest houses in the Madras and Salem Districts. 139. Two Rest houses, one at Avady in the Madras District, and another at Jollarpett, in the Salem District, were built at a total cost of Rupees 5,894.

Race Course Barracks at Bangalore. 140. Notwithstanding some delay in fixing the sites of the several buildings, and in preparing detached plans, considerable progress was made with the new Race Course Barracks at Bangalore, on which the outlay amounted to Rupees 92,558. Two ranges of Barracks, Quarter Master Serjeants' Quarters, Provost cells, and Skittle alley were completed. The Orderly room, School Master's and Mistress' quarters, Trumpet Major's and Band Serjeant's quarters, and Powder Magazine were nearly finished, and the foundations and basement of the subsidiary buildings of the Hospital were in a forward state.

141. The additional buildings required at the present Cavalry **MILITARY.** Barracks at Bangalore, to fit them for the occupation of an Infantry Cavalry Barracks at Bangalore. Regiment, were commenced. Nearly the whole of the brickwork and part of the terracing of the first main block were completed ; two other blocks were in progress, and the foundations of the Powder Magazine were in a forward state. The outlay was Rupees 47,027.

142. Rupees 18,822 were expended on the foundations and Bakery and Water supply at Bangalore. basement of the new Commissariat Bakery at Bangalore.

In connection with the Ulsoor water project at that station, on which the outlay amounted to Rupees 18,083, the pumping machinery was put up, and the walls of the engine house were raised to a height of nine feet. The filter was partly completed, and the walls of the sides of the pure water basin were raised to the full height.

143. The Racket and Fives Court at Trichinopoly, which was Military Buildings at Trichinopoly. commenced in April 1864, was completed with a further outlay of Rupees 3,638, and Rupees 12,279 were expended in finishing the family Quarters for the Artillery at that station, and in adding court-yards and out-offices to those buildings. The Parcherry in the vicinity of the European Infantry Barracks at Trichinopoly was removed, the ground levelled, and nearly all the claims to compensation disposed of. The total outlay on these improvements was Rupees 25,819, of which Rupees 2,817 appertains to 1865-66.

144. Rupees 1,15,541 were expended in connection with the Law- Lawrence Asylum at Ootacamund. rence Asylum Works at Ootacamund, in the Coimbatore District. The sites of the buildings for the Male and Female Asylums and for the Hospital were excavated, and the tramway from the brickfield to the former of these sites was completed, as also the road of approach, the workshop, water channels, and servants' Quarters.

145. With the exception of one block at Cannanore, the whole Cannanore and Calicut. of the married Quarters at that station, at Calicut, and at Malliapooram, Married Quarters in the Malabar District. in the Malabar District, were completed at a cost of Rupees 1,08,192, of which Rupees 49,065 were laid out during the past official year.

146. Four of the six radial blocks of the District Jail at Vizaga- **CIVIL.** patam were finished, and the other two, as well as the central Guard District Jail at Vizagapatam. house were partially roofed in. Good progress was made with the foundations of the Jail wall and Jailer's quarters, and a well was sunk to a depth of eighty-five feet. The outlay, during the year, amounted to Rupees 7,479.

CIVIL.

Central-Jail at Rajahmundry.

147. In connection with the new central Jail at Rajahmundry, in the Godavery District, Rupees 36,441 were expended on the completion of four radial blocks, four workshops, central warder, six sides of the enclosure wall, three partition walls, four towers and inner palisade, and considerable progress was made with the other parts of the building, and with the construction of the Jailer's Quarters. A well, twenty-two feet in diameter, was sunk to the depth of seventy-two feet.

Salem Jail.

148. An outlay of Rupees 418 was incurred in finishing the upper story of the Salem Jail.

Central Jail at Coimbatore,

149. In connection with the new Central Jail at Coimbatore, Rupees 1,46,888 were laid out in completing the outer and inner walls of twelve sides, as well as two barracks of four rooms, the foundations of two others of eight rooms, seven workshops, three cook-rooms, central warder, and Jailer's quarters. Good progress was made with the solitary cells, guard-room, and the hospital enclosure wall, and several hundred prisoners are now in actual occupation of the finished parts of the building.

Taluk Cutcherries in the Nellore and Madras Districts.

150. A strike amongst the workmen retarded the progress of the Taluk Cutcherry at Ongole, in the Nellore District. The walls of the building were raised to their full height, and the doors and windows were completed, at an expenditure of Rupees 4,884. An outlay of Rupees 2,742 was incurred in completing the Taluk Cutcherry at Madrantacum, in the Madras District.

Post Office at Cuddapah, and Taluk and other Cutcherries in the Cuddapah, Kurnool, and Bellary Districts.

151. A new Post Office at Cuddapah, a Cutcherry for the Head Assistant Collector at Hospett, in the Bellary District, and the enlargement of the Taluk Cutcherries at Nandikatkoor and Ravalcotta, in the Kurnool District, were completed at a total cost of Rupees 8,213, of which Rupees 5,540 were laid out in 1865-66. Rapid progress was made with the re-roofing of the Hospett Taluk Cutcherry, and Rupees 3,754 were expended upon that work and upon the construction of a similar building at Pullumpett, in the Cuddapah District, the progress of which was greatly retarded owing to the difficulty which was experienced in procuring the wood work for the roof.

Paper Currency Office and Lunatic Asylum at Trichinopoly.

152. Rupees 6,162 were expended in providing accommodation for the Paper Currency Department at Trichinopoly, and in completing the alterations to the old abandoned Jail at that station, to adapt it for a Lunatic Asylum.

153. Two wings were added to the building occupied by the Government Office in Fort Saint George at an expense of Rupees 11,620; and Rupees 36,811 were laid out in finishing the new wing and upper story of the General Hospital at Madras. The Public Works Store and Workshop buildings at the Presidency, which were left unfinished on the 30th April 1865, were completed during the year at a further outlay of Rupees 28,680. A Foundry, in connection with the Government Workshop, was commenced, and Rupees 6,000 were spent in laying the foundations and raising the basement. An upper story to the East face of the Revenue Board Office, at Chepauk, was under construction, and four-fifths of the work were completed with an outlay of Rupees 8,734.

CIVIL. Government Office, General Hospital, Public Works Workshop, and Foundry, and Revenue Board Office.

154. The Court-house at Cuddalore, in the South Arcot District, upon which Rupees 12,698 were laid out during the year, was completed at a total cost of Rupees 48,979.

Court House at Cuddalore.

155. Rupees 7,492 were expended at the Madras Salt Cotaurs in completing the western platform, turfing the slopes, and constructing stone steps from the platform to the canal. A new platform was built at Home's Gardens, in the Madras District, at a cost of Rupees 1,771. In the Tanjore District good progress was made with the excavation of a trench, and in carrying out other improvements to the salt platform at Tranquebar. The outlay on these works and on the salt platform, with surrounding wall, watch house, and Superintendent's Cutcherry at Negapatam, which was completed and made over to the Revenue Department, amounted to Rupees 10,201.

Salt Works at the Presidency, and in the Madras and Tanjore Districts.

156. The project for the supply of water to the Government house at Guindy was completed with an expenditure of Rupees 10,151.

Guindy Government House Water Supply Project.

157. Rupees 11,517 were appropriated to the raising of the crest of the Godavery anicut and to the addition of a rough stone apron. An outlay of Rupees 16,593 was incurred in completing the construction of a step in rear of the body of the Palar anicut, and in lengthening the head sluice, and extending an aqueduct and three bridges in connection with the Cheyaur anicut in the North Arcot District. An anicut was built across the Cheyaur river, in the South Arcot District, at an outlay of Rupees 3,280.

Agricultural. Godavery, Palar, and Cheyaur anicuts.

AGRICUL-
TURAL.
Nizampatam
canal.

158. The tidal lock on the canal from Seetanagaram, on the Kistna river, to Nizampatam, was opened in November last, and there is now through communication, on the Guntoor side of the delta, from Bezwara to the sea. The Nallawada calingulah was completed, the tidal lock calingulah was commenced, and the channel was deepened in various parts at an outlay, during the year, of Rupees 13,903.

Channel from
Valabapuram to
tide-water.

159. Rupees 15,701 were expended on the widening of the channel from Valabapuram to tide-water in the Kistna District. The large calingulahs at Penumudy and Brattiprole are ready for use, and that at Kollur is approaching completion.

Head of main
canal from Seeta-
nagaram to Doog-
geralla.

Pollairoo chan-
nel.

160. About one-half of the total excavation which is required for the enlargement of the head of the main canal from Seetanagaram to Dooggeralla, was completed. The widening of the lower portion of the Pollairoo channel was retarded by sickness amongst the workmen and scarcity of labor, but the excavation of the Bantumilly channel was nearly completed, while good progress was made with the widening of the old Polraz-Codu. The expenditure on these two projects, in the Kistna District, amounted in the aggregate to Rupees 15,430, against an assignment of Rupees 15,500. The Commamoor channel, in the same District, upon which Rupees 18,254 were expended, will be navigable this year from Dooggeralla to the Alluru, but through communication, with the Masulipatam side of the delta cannot be established until the lock at Dooggeralla has been completed. The drainage of the Romperu swamp was commenced, and sufficient will be accomplished by the end of August to aid materially in the restoration of this fertile tract of country.

Commamoor
Channel.

Channel from
Aukamarru lock
to Sultanagram
bridge.

161. A channel was excavated from the Aukamarru lock to the Sultanagram bridge, in the Kistna District, at a cost of Rupees 12,669, of which Rupees 4,227 were laid out in 1865-66. Rupees 9,997 and 4,495, respectively, were expended in completing the re-construction of a tunnel under the Masulipatam canal, near Sultanagram, in the same District, and in strengthening the embankments of the Idur and Labur branches of Jaffer Sahib's channel in Nellore. These latter works are on the verge of completion, and are ready to receive a full supply of water during the next season.

Tunnel under
Masulipatam
Canal.

Branches of Jaffer
Sahib's channel.

Improving head
of Vadavaur.

162. The existence of cultivation on the land through which the channel is to pass precluded the commencement of operations fo

the improvement of the head of the Vadavaur, in the Tanjore District, till
the middle of March. Rupees 1,900 were, however, expended in carrying
out the masonry works, which are in an advanced state, and in executing a portion of the earthwork. An outlay of Rupees 28,530 was
incurred in the restoration of seventy-seven out of 172 running
feet of the lower Coleroon anicut in Tanjore, and in extending the aprons
of some of the sluices. The construction of six surplus sluices on the
north, and ten on the south bank of the Coleroon, in the Trichinopoly
District, was on hand, Rupees 7,095 having been laid out upon an
estimate of Rupees 20,300.

*AGRICUL-
TURAL.*
Re-building por-
tion of Coleroon
anicut. &c.
Constructing
sluices on bank
of Coleroon.

163. In the Ganjam District, an expenditure of Rupees 13,552 was
incurred in completing 130 bridges and tunnels, and in laying down the
earthwork of nearly twenty-two miles of the roads from Aska to
Russelcondah, and from Bullepudra to Kurchooly. Good progress was
made with the construction of the road from Mojagudda to Sunkera-
kole, on which twenty-five bridges, seven road dams, and twenty-three
miles of earthwork were finished at an outlay, during the year, of
Rupees 2,222. A sum of Rupees 28,090 was spent in the completion of
the road from Aska to Ganjam, and in the partial construction of a pile
bridge. In the Vizagapatam District, nearly all the masonry works on
the road from Vizianagram to Cassipur, up to the twenty-eighth mile
stone, were completed, and it is expected that, for this distance, the
line will shortly be available for cart traffic. The earthwork of
eighteen miles, and the graveling and metaling of sixteen others, on
the road from Vizianagram to Bowdara, as also a large number of
masonry works, were finished, and a bridge of five arches, of thirty feet
span, was partially built. The outlay on these two roads amounted to
Rupees 23,571.

Communications.
Roads in Gan-
jam and Vizaga-
patam.

164. Rupees 16,123 were spent in carrying out the works connected with the project for the cross drainage of the Ellore high level
canal in the Godavery District. Some alterations were made to the
Ellore aqueduct, and a sub-passage of five vents, as well as a large
inlet and outlet for the East branch of the Tumiler, were nearly finished.
The masonry of the iron girder bridge at Cocanada, in the same
District, was completed with a further outlay of Rupees 15,000, and
the girders, piles, and screws were prepared, and are now ready for use.

Do. in Go-
davery.

165. Rupees 8,862 were spent in the construction of two bridges,
one at Sultanagram on the Masulipatam and Hyderabad road, and

Do. in Kistna.

ROADS.　another across the Commamoor channel at Chabrole, in the Kistna District. The bridges were completed with the exception of the parapets and approaches.

Roads in Nellore.　166. The road embankment across the Musanur valley in the Nellore District is in an advanced state; the Musanur bridge was all but completed, and another bridge at Pillavagu was in progress. Two bridges were constructed on Trunk Road No. 6, and the foundations of a third were laid. On the Ongole and Kotapatam road, a bridge of nine arches, two barrel drains, and a road dam, besides a large quantity of metaling were completed, and it is expected that the entire work will be finished in 1866-67. The aggregate outlay during the year, on these three projects, was Rupees 22,743 from Imperial, and Rupees 2,796 from Income Tax Funds, from which latter source Rupees 1,497 were spent in completing eighteen miles of the Nellore and Dorenal road with the necessary masonry works.

Do. in 'Cuddapah.　167. In the Cuddapah District, Rupees 5,951 were laid out in completing the Feeders to the Rajampett and Ontimitta Railway stations, and in forming the road between the town of Nundalur and the Nundalur Railway station.

Two bridges and two ramps were constructed over the Mahal and Piler rivers on Trunk Road No. XI, at a cost of Rupees 8,427.

Do. in Cuddapah and Bellary.　168. Several masonry works and one mile of the road from Cuddapah to Bellary were constructed, seven and a half miles were metalled, and three gravelled, at an outlay of Rupees 16,101, of which Rupees 7,124 were from Income Tax Funds.

Dr. in Cuddapah and Kurnool.　169. Owing to changes amongst the Executive Officers, the construction of the road from Cuddapah to Nundial was delayed; but Rupees 15,994 were nevertheless spent upon the line, with much advantage. A large number of masonry works was built, and a good quantity of material was collected.

Do. in Kurnool.　170. The east wall of the viaduct across the ravine near Rájunánugunta on the Nandy Kanama Ghaut, in the Kurnool District, which was left unfinished in April 1865, was completed at a further outlay of Rupees 154, the aggregate expenditure on the work being Rupees 54,538, upon an estimate of Rupees 54,540.

Do. in Madras and North Arcot Districts.　171. A sum of Rupees 6,026 was appropriated from Income Tax Funds to the construction of roads from Satiaved to Cowrapet, from

Trivellur to Nagalapuram, and from Utucottah to Satiaved, in the ROADS.
Madras District ; and Rupees 2,082 were expended from the same source
to complete the road from Arcot to Arni, in the North Arcot District.

172. The rebuilding and widening of the ten arches of the Roads in South Arcot.
Guddilam bridge, in the South Arcot District, were successfully carried
out at a total cost of Rupees 15,296, of which Rupees 7,056 were
expended in 1865-66.

173. Owing to the scarcity of labor, it was found impossible to Do. in Salem.
spend more than Rupees 4,478, out of an allotment of Rupees 6,000,
on the road from Ussur to Mallur, in the Salem District. Most of
the tunnels and nearly all the earthwork were completed. Rupees
4,341 were laid out in forming two miles of the road from Taraman-
galam to the Suramangalam Railway station. The construction of
a bridge of nine arches, of thirty-six feet span, across the Vellar river, at
Talewassel, and the formation of a cart track between Palakod and the
Morapur Railway station, were in progress from Income Tax Funds.
The aggregate outlay on these works was Rupees 7,926. The bridge
was completed, and six miles of the road were formed.

174. Owing to the difficulty of obtaining gravel, the progress Do. and Canals in Tanjore.
of the two Railway feeders terminating at Negapatam and Kivalur, in
the Tanjore District, was much retarded, the expenditure during the
year having been limited to Rupees 1,956. The first of these roads
is six miles long, of which five and a half were metalled. The earth
and masonry works on the other line were completed. The canal from
Negapatam to Tritrapundi, in the same District, upon which an outlay
of Rupees 5,924 was incurred, was finished, with the exception of the
parapets of the Chundravadi bridge and the plastering of some of the
under-tunnels. The project for completing the navigation between
Negapatam and Vedarniem was on hand, and Rupees 3,797 were laid
out in the construction of three large under-tunnels.

175. Rupees 1,59,918 were expended on the Coonoor, Burghoor, Ghauts in Coimbatore and Malabar.
and Gudalur ghauts in the Coimbatore District, and on the Tamber-
cherry and Periah ghauts, and the Karkur ghaut and road in
the Malabar District. Of the entire length (sixteen miles) of the
Coonoor ghaut, the upper three and a quarter miles were fully completed,
and another mile and a quarter nearly so. Rapid progress was made
with the lower four miles, and all the earthwork of the intermediate por-

ROADS.

tions was finished. The bridle-path throughout the Burghoor ghaut was completed, and all labor is now concentrated in opening the Southern part to a width of twelve feet. The trace through the Gudalur ghaut was made and opened as a bridle-path, and several miles of the road were cut nine feet out of the solid. The road and bridge work between the foot of the Tambercherry ghaut and Pudupady were completed, and the lower seven miles of the ghaut itself were made practicable for carts. A most successful trace through the Periah ghaut was worked out, and opened as a bridle-path, which is now being made available for wheel traffic. Very little progress was made on the Karkur ghaut itself, but there is every probability that the whole line will be available as a dry-weather cart-road to carry the next season's coffee crop to the head of the navigation of the Beypore river at Ariacode.

Roads and bridges in Malabar and South Canara.

176. The Kulpatty bridge, near Palghat, in the Malabar District, was completed and opened for traffic at a cost of Rupees 30,494, of which Rupees 5,759 was the outlay during 1865-66. Rupees 45,271 were expended from Imperial and Income Tax Funds on the Terriot road, and on the road between Vythery and the Mysore frontier in the Wynaad. On the former, three bridges and a boat platform were completed, three other bridges were in course of construction, the road itself was made passable for carts throughout, and the widening of the new trace was in progress. On the road to the Mysore frontier, the embankment from the Challipoya river to the Challipoya bazaar, and the roadway from Sultan's Battery to within half a mile of the Kallur river were nearly completed, and good progress was made on two miles of the road beyond Pungulycotta. In connection with the road in the South Canara District, to connect Mangalore and Cannanore, fifty-one miles from Pani Mangalore to the head of the river navigation at Canyengode were opened from four to eight yards in width, and made fully passable for carts in dry weather. The expenditure amounted to Rupees 3,462.

Do. in Madura.

177. Four miles of the road from Tirumangalam to the Coimbatore boundary, in the Madura District, with twenty-two platform tunnels and eight road dams, were completed at a cost of Rupees 12,474, of which Rupees 1,566 were from Income Tax Funds. Rupees 8,545 were expended, in the same District, in the construction of a bridge of seven arches of forty feet span across the Shanmugannady river. Four

of the piers were built to a height of six and a half, and two to a height of ten and a half feet. The eastern and western abutments and wings were raised five and ten feet respectively, and two of the arches were turned.

178. The construction of a Light house at Cocanada, in the Godavery District, with a Flag staff, groynes, &c., was completed at a total cost of Rupees 73,011, of which Rupees 2,666 were laid out during 1865-66.

179. In the Kistna District, Rupees 8,403 were expended on the fresh water channel from the Sultanagram bridge to Robertson's Pettah, and very fair progress was made with the masonry of the conduit. The reconstruction of the Sea embankment from the Tidal calingulah to Gilkuldundy, on which Rupees 7,144 were spent, was approaching completion, and a large number of trees was planted for the purpose of consolidating and strengthening the banks.

Good Water
channel in Kist-
na District.
Sea embank-
ments in do., from
the tidal calingu-
lah to Gilkul-
dundy.

180. In connection with the project for cutting the inner angle of the reef channel at Paumbem, in the Madura District, Rupees 1,746 were expended in removing 17,529 cubic feet of stone, and 1,13,143 cubic feet of silt and gravel.

181. A list of the principal works which were undertaken from the District Road, Educational, and Port Funds by Officers of the Public Works Department is given in the Appendix.

182. Rupees 22,95,207 were spent in keeping in repair 682 Military buildings, 590 Civil buildings, 900 channels, 1,405 tanks, four calingulahs, eighty-six sluices, 465 dykes, eighty anicuts, nine locks, ninety-eight drainages, three irrigation dams, 8,078 miles of road or canal, and 167 bridges, tunnels, and road dams. The largest expenditure was incurred on the following works :—

Godavery.	Godavery anicut	... ...	Rs.	34,945
	Cocanada canal...	••• ••• •••	„	13,493
	Godavery river banks ···	... ...	„	32,638
	Cocanada river and bar	... ...	„	15,954
Kistna.	Masulipatam canal and minor branches		„	26,053
	Ellore	do.	do.		6,282
	Pullairoo	do.	do.	„	12,922
	Nizampatam	do.	do.	„	16,474
	Kistna anicut	do.	do.	„	11,969

MISCELLA-
NEOUS.

Bellary.
{ Tungabuddra channels   ...   ... Rs.   13,632
{ Karagal anicut   ...   ... „   5,160
{ Sirgoopah and Dassamur channels ...   „   6,033

Presidency.—Fortifications of Fort St. George   ...   „   8,400

Madras
District.
{ Canal north and south of Madras ...   „   11,345
{ Salt channels at Veyalur ...   ...   „   9,316

Dowlaishweram
Workshop.

183.   The amount which was charged for work turned out from
the Dowlaishweram Workshop, during the year, was Rupees 1,48,324, of
which Rupees 1,42,692 were for new works, and Rupees 5,632 for
repairs. The work performed for private parties was valued at Rupees
4,706.   The workshop was chiefly employed in making up lattice and
plate girders, timber truss bridges, roof trusses, iron barred doors, and
cast-iron shutter posts for the anicut, &c., and in altering the Paumbem steam-tug, and repairing steamers, dredges, and boats.

ACCOUNTS.

184.   Under instructions from the Government of India, a
revised system of account was brought into operation from the 1st May
1865, the principles upon which it was framed being that the accounts
shall be based upon actual disbursements of cash ; that every disburs-
ing officer shall obtain a monthly clearance for his expenditure ; that
a clear distinction shall be maintained between the accounts of cash
and stock ; and that all receipts and expenditure, whether from Imperial or Local Funds, shall be brought into the regular Public Works
accounts, so as to be finally passed through the books of the Controller.
Temporary establishments were sanctioned for finally closing the
accounts of the department up to 30th April 1865, and, during the year,
bills for Rupees 49,25,336 were received and disposed of in the
Office of the Controller of Public Works Accounts, in adjustment of
the expenditure of the years 1861-62 to 1864-65.   The amount thus
adjusted includes an outlay of Rupees 7,59,980 from Local Funds.   The
balance remaining to be accounted for on the 30th April 1866 was
Rupees 5,41,326, of which Rupees 1,25,921 represent the expenditure
from Local Funds.

RAIL-
ROADS.
South   West
line.
Mileage open
for traffic.

185.   The mileage open for traffic upon the South Western line
remains the same as at the close of the last official year. Including
the Bangalore branch, 492 miles have been worked throughout the
year now under review.

Increase   in
Receipts.

186.   As compared with the year 1864-65, the increase in receipts
for passenger traffic amounts to Rupees 1,54,934, for goods to 3,88,192 ;

a reference to the tabular statement in the Appendix shews that this increase is due as much to the enlargement of traffic as to the enhanced rates which have been enforced since November 1865.

RAIL-
ROADS.

187. The working expenses, during the half-year ending Decem- Financial state.
ber 1865, amounted to 43·93 per cent. upon the gross receipts, the total
expenditure was 5,74,83,103, and the net profits at a rate slightly
exceeding four per cent.

188. The only large work in progress on this line, during 1865-66, Kuddulhoon-
has been the construction of the bridge across the Kuddulhoondy dy Bridge.
river, upon the West Coast. It is intended to replace the present
wooden structure by an iron girder bridge supported upon iron piles ;
but the progress of the work has been considerably delayed by the
discovery that the firm stratum, which had been reached in the
trial borings, was only a few feet in thickness, and that a permanent
bearing for the piles could not, in some places, be obtained at a less
depth than seventy feet below the rail level.

189. At the close of the last official year the North West line North West
was open for traffic from the Arconum Junction as far as Reddipully, a line.
distance of seventy-nine miles. On the 1st September 1865, the line Mileage.
was further opened to Cuddapah, forty miles beyond Reddipully.
The average length of line open for traffic during 1865-66 has, therefore,
been 106 miles.

190. The increase in receipts for passenger traffic has been Increase in Traf,
Rupees 78,066 as compared with 1864-65, and in goods there is an fic Receipts.
advantage of Rupees 2,75,549 over the present year.

191. The working expenses for the half-year ending December Financial re-
1865 were 26·92 upon the gross earnings, a very low per-centage, sults.
which is attributable to the use of iron pot sleepers, and to the substitution of wood for coal. The total expenditure has been Rupees
1,23,50,577, and the net profits at the rate of four and a half per cent.

192. The progress made during the year 1865-66 upon the Progress.
portion of this line under construction has been satisfactory. The
opening of the portion between Reddipully and Cuddapah, upon the
1st September 1865, has been abovementioned. A further extension Extension.
of about thirty-five miles, between Cuddapah and Moodanoor, is expected to be opened for traffic during August 1866. Beyond Moodanoor the
works are making fair progress, but owing to the large bridges

RAIL-
ROADS.

Opening line
to Gooty.

required to carry the line over the Chittravutty and the Pennair rivers, there is no likelihood that the line will be opened for traffic to Gooty until 1868. Some parts of the line beyond Gooty have been given out on contract; but little has yet been done save completing the surveys, and collecting materials for the large bridge over the Toom-

Junction with
Great Indian
Peninsula Rail-
way at Raichoor.

budra river. The junction with the Great Indian Peninsula Railway at Raichoor will probably be effected in 1870.

Great Sou-
thern of India
Railway.

Mileage.

193. The length (seventy-nine miles) of line open for traffic has remained the same as in the past official year. It is expected, however, that a portion of the Errode extension, from Trichinopoly to Caroor, a distance of forty-seven and a half miles, will be opened for traffic in July 1866, and from Caroor to Errode, a distance of forty miles, about May 1867.

Increased Traf-
fic.

194. In the year under report, the receipts on passenger traffic shew an increase of Rupees 31,189, and the goods traffic shew an increase of 29,498 Rupees, as compared with the year 1864-65.

Financial re-
sult.

195. The working expenses were, during the year under review, 49·93 per cent. upon gross receipts, the aggregate expenditure up to 31st December 1865 were Rupees 85,76,975, and the per-centage of net profits was nearly 2¼.

Progress.

Extension.

196. The works on the Errode extension have progressed very satisfactorily, and, if the permanent way materials expected from England arrive in proper time, there is every prospect of the line being opened to Errode, the point of junction with the Madras South West Railway, during the next year.

The permanent way on all three lines is in good order, and the working and management of the Railways have been most satisfactory.

Indian Tram-
way Company.

Tramway be-
tween Arconum
and Conjeveram.

Mileage.

197. The tramway, or, more correctly, the light railway, constructed by this Company between the Arconum Junction, on the line of the Madras Railway, and the town of Conjeveram, was partially opened for traffic upon the 8th May 1865.

198. The remainder of the line, completing the whole distance of nineteen miles, was opened for traffic on the 1st August 1865.

No Traffic
Returns.

199. This line has been constructed without a guarantee, and no information regarding the amount of its traffic is as yet available,

200. The estimates sanctioned by Government, up to the close of **MADRAS** 1864-65, amounted to Rupees 68,42,586-8-0, and provided for the con- **IRRIGATION** struction of the main canal from the commencement to the end of the **AND CANAL COMPANY.** ninth section, in the 178th mile, with the anicut and head works at Estimates sanc.‑tioned up to Sunkasala, on the Tumbuddra, for the Somaiswaram anicut, where the close of previous Pennér enters the Nellore District, and for a few distribution works work provided and station buildings. for by them.

201. The estimates sanctioned during 1865-66 amounted to Estimates sanc‑tioned during Rupees 10,67,389-9-10, the particulars of which are given in the the year. Appendix.

202. The sanction of Rupees 8,02,811 for the main canal in the Estimates can‑celled during the ninth section, 143rd to 178th mile, was, at the request of the Company, year. cancelled; and the estimate of Rupees 11,884, for distribution works connected therewith, was also removed from the list of sanctions.

203. The subjoined statement shews the difference between the Comparison between origi‑ original estimates of the cost of works under construction by the Com- nal and revised estimates sanc‑ pany, and the estimates for those works as revised and sanctioned up tioned up to the close of 1865-66. to the end of the year under notice. These higher estimates have been exceeded, in some cases, to a considerable extent.

Description of Work.	Original Estimates.			Present Estimates			Increase.		
	RS.	A.	P.	RS.	A.	P.	RS.	A.	P.
Kurnool anicut	3,03,080	0	0	3,03,080	0	0	Abandoned		
1 mile of canal from anicut	65,000	0	0	65,000	0	0	Do.		
Sunkasala anicut and head works	1,25,000	0	0	4,10,292	0	0	2,85,292	0	0
1st Section, main canal, miles 18	4,60,000	0	0	8,56,777	0	0	3,96,777	0	0
Hindry aqueduct	1,15,000	0	0	2,46,029	8	0	1,91,029	8	0
2nd Section, main canal, miles 14 } 3rd do. do. do. 11 }	7,22,500	0	0	19,60,655	0	0	12,38,155	0	0
4th do. do. do. 17 } 5th do. do. do. 12 }	5,19,830	0	0	16,93,082	0	0	11,73,252	0	0
6th do. do. do. 19	3,02,525	0	0	3,80,529	0	0	78,004	0	0
7th do. do. do. 23	2,33,160	0	0	2,35,850	0	0	2,690	0	0
8th do. do. do. 28	4,37,410	0	0	7,36,830	0	0	2,99,420	0	0
9th do. do. do. 35	...			...			Cancelled.		
Distribution works *	25,520	0	0	25,738	0	0	218	0	0
Buildings	87,526	15	8	1,02,099	9	10	14,572	10	2
Somaiswaram anicut	1,33,000	0	0	1,62,470	0	0	29,470	0	0
Line of Telegraph	44,116	0	0	44,116	0	0	...	...	...
	36,03,667	15	8	72,22,548	1	10	36,18,880	2	2
Deduct retrenchment from main canal, 4th Section, Rs... 1,24,872 Do. Buildings, do. „ 2,395									
1,27,267	...	...	...	1,27,267	0	0	...	...	...
	36,03 667	15	8	70,95,281	1	10	34,91,613	2	2

* Exclusive of Rupees 11,884, for which the estimate was cancelled with the 9th section main canal estimate.

MADRAS
IRRIGATION
AND CANAL
COMPANY.
Retrenchments
from expendi-
ture.

204. When sanctioning supplemental estimates for works in the 4th Section, or Nagatore Division, the Government considered it necessary to decline to sanction the debit to guaranteed capital of a part of the expenditure incurred, as there was confessedly no work to shew for it. The amount retrenched is shewn at the foot of the above state-ment.

Expenditure.

205. The expenditure up to the close of the year on construc-tion, including special superintendence, was Rupees 58,04,785　4　10

The cost of the permanent establishment—

Controlling	...	...	Rs.	5,81,634	7	11		
Executive	...	...	„	11,78,539	7	5		
							Rs.	17,60,173 15 4
Miscellaneous	...	...	...	...	...	„		2,66,218 10 4
Store charges unadjusted ...		...	...	...	„			1,04,964 8 2
General plant in use on works	...	...	...	„				4,12,385 2 9
Revenue Account ...	...	...	....	...	„			6,781 8 5
Stores	...	...	...	...	...	„		4,99,450 11 7
						Total Rs....		88,54,759 13 5

Portion of the
line of main
canal between
the end of 9th
Section and
Somaiswaram.

206. This portion of the line includes the 10th, 11th, and 12th Sections. During the year the surveys and levels for the 12th Section were completed. It is not intended to bring forward the estimates for sanction at present.

Portion of line
of canal in Nel-
lore.

207. The investigations for the Company's project in the Nellore District have been continued, and the surveys and levels for a high level irrigation canal completed up to the watershed—sixty-six miles from the head. Enquiries are still being carried on in order to place the Board of Directors of the Company in possession of reliable informa-tion regarding the probable cost, and remunerativeness, of the whole length, from Somaiswaram to the sea, a distance, by the line of the canal, of from ninety-five to one hundred miles.

State of the
works.

208. The progress of the works, and the results of the trial of those which have been completed, so as to allow of entire or partial working, are as follows :—

Sunkasala Ani-
cut and head
works.

209. The Anicut received no injury of any moment from the freshes of the year, though these lasted for an unusually long period, and reached a fair average height. The water was shut off from the part previously breached, and the repairs, which were stopped by the early freshes, have since been completed. The rocky bed of the river

suffered from the overfall, but the prevention of further injury from
this cause is engaging attention. The Head Works stood well.

210. Water passed down the first section of the main canal
throughout the season, and the works generally were found to be in
an efficient state. About 650 acres of land were irrigated, and the
town of Kurnool was supplied with water.

211. This large Aqueduct, which has a clear waterway of ninety-
four feet, with a maximum depth of eight feet, has been completed,
with the exception of a small part of the superstructure. The
additional works undertaken to stop leakage through, and around, the
Aqueduct have been successful, and water was carried across it for
several months.

212. The Kadrabagh Aqueduct in the twenty-third mile, and
the heavy embankments connected with it, delayed the passing down
of water until late in the season, and it was found, when these works
had been secured, that a wall in the twenty-fourth mile required
strengthening, and that the high banks lower down needed to be very
gradually tried, in order that their settlement might be regular, and
that all risk of breaching might be avoided. The leakage through the
gravelly banks and stony sub-soil also was so great, that the supply
of water brought down by the first section proved insufficient,
without considerable delay, to fill up the numerous small valleys
between the spurs of the Jaggernath hills, which are crossed by the
single bank of the canal in this section; consequently, at the end of
December, after which water is not available for the canal from the
Tumbuddra, the supply had been carried only twenty-eight and a quarter
miles, instead of as was intended, and expected, to the fifty-third mile
in the fourth section. The walls, embankments, revetments, &c.,
received careful attention, and were strengthened wherever they were
found, or appeared to be, too weak, in readiness for the early freshes
of the coming year.

213. The more important works in the third section—those
necessary to the supply of as much of the maximum supply as was
likely to be required, have been in progress; while other works are
postponed, until the requisite funds become available.

214. In the upper half of this section the progress made has
been good; and below, the heavy embankments are in a much better

MADRAS IRRIGATION AND CANAL COMPANY.
state than at the commencement of the year, but the small amount of guaranteed capital remaining unexpended has led to the curtailment of operations, and, during the latter half of the year, the intention of pushing on the works from the fifty-third to the seventy-third miles was abandoned.

5th Section, Main Canal, 12 miles.
215. The work done in this section has been on a limited scale. The Teragopila aqueduct and its embankments made fair progress; otherwise, expenditure has been very much restricted, and towards the end of the year, almost ceased.

6th Section, Main Canal, 19 miles.
216. In the upper six miles, which will alone carry irrigation water, the works were pushed on satisfactorily up to the time when it was resolved to confine expenditure to the first four sections.

7th Section, Main Canal, 23 miles.
217. The anicut at the head of this section, across the Couli, received considerable damage from the year's freshes, and it is the intention of the Chief Engineer of the Company to modify the plans, but the requisite estimates have not yet been submitted. The general progress of the works of the section was slow, and the exact arrangements for passing the Byup-Gudoor tank in the 99th and 100th miles, and for crossing the supply channel of the Nundial tank in the 105th mile, have not been decided upon, or at least were not submitted for sanction. This is the last section on which any work was done.

8th Section, Main Canal, 28 miles.

Comparative Progress.
218. The subjoined statement will shew the comparative progress made during 1864-65, and in the year under review, and also the extent to which expenditure was restricted by the exhaustion of the original capital of one million, raised under guarantee.

	1864-65.			1865-66.														
				1st Quarter.			2nd Quarter.			3rd Quarter.			4th Quarter.			Total.		
	Rs.	A.	P.	Rs.	A.	P.	Rs.	A.	P.	Rs.	A.	P.	Rs.	A.	P.	Rs.	A.	P.
Anicut and head works at Kurnool.	425	1	2	...			...			...			...			...		
Do. do. at Soonkasala.	56,320	3	11	18,796	3	9	3,168	6	7	503	14	2	11,911	13	9	29,380	6	3
Do. do. at Somaiswaram	41,587	15	7	2,626	14	1	1,462	15	2	870	12	2	1,260	13		6,221	6	6
Aqueduct across the river Hindry	42,363	5	3	8,328	10	9	1,015	5	5	916	9	2	5,702	3	6	15,961	13	1
Canal for 1 mile	...			...			...			...			...			...		
South Main Canal, 1st Section	1,39,874	7	9	33,461	10	9	10,212	1	2	7,635	15	7	10,285	2	11	61,594	16	5
Do. 2nd & 3rd do.	8,30,991	15	6	1,95,922	5	9	1,38,887	12	4	72,680	13	5	34,369	10	9	4,41,860	10	3
Do 4th and 5th do	4,47,126	12	11	1,18,940	8	4	81,085	0	1	1,04,646	8	7	57,145	8	0	3,61,811	9	6
Do 6th do.	1,53,129	2	10	19,909	5	6	8,743	10	11	8,641	7	10	4,724	6	6	42,008	14	9
Do. 7th do.	94,372	0	3	19,247	2	0	23,093	9	9	12,127	6	1	1,985	7	2	56,453	3	0
Do. 8th do.	1,38,204	14	3	35,748	3	6	26,525	0	10	22,775	3	7	1,486	3	8	86,534	11	7
Total ..	19,33,208	13	5	4,47,981	0	5	2,94,193	14	6	2,30,781	4	7	1,28,871	5	4	11,01,827	8	10

219. These most important distribution works made little or no **MADRAS** progress. The amount sanctioned was Rupees 25,738, but the total **IRRIGATION AND CANAL** expenditure was only Rupees 7,889-14-1, and no fresh estimates were **COMPANY.** submitted for sanction during the year.

Distribution works.

220. The establishment employed in the Bellary Division has Bellary Division investiga- been engaged in completing the investigations, which were in progress tions. during the previous year, regarding the project for a canal from Vala-vapore on the Tumbuddra to Bellary. Bellary is so situated that it is impracticable to supply it with water without the construction of expensive and difficult works, but both the Station and the District are so distressed for want of water, that it seems probable that it will be considered advisable to undertake the canal, even at the outlay which will be necessary. It is not probable, however, that the Company will be in a position to take up this project, unless as an entirely distinct work from the Kurnool canal, and under special conditions.

221. The average labor employed on the Company's Canal Supply of labor. works during the first eight months of the year, and that of the preceding year, was as follows :—

							1864-65.	1865-66.
Coolies	...	...	...	...	...	...	16,707	8,119
Artificers	...	...	...	...	...		1,231	682
Carts	...	...	...	...	...	...	750	402
Cattle	...	...	...	...	...	...	1,966	909

The falling off was not due to failure of supply, but to the reduction of expenditure.

222. The Company have asked for an increase per acre of Water rates for irrigation. rupees two to the rate for ordinary irrigation for one crop, and for proportionate increases to other rates. No change has as yet been sanctioned.

223. The rate for this description of supplies was fixed by Act Rate for supplies of water for purposes other than that of irrigation. No. XXX of 1865, of the Government of India, at one Rupee for 400 cubic yards of water, as a maximum charge.

224. The draft of these Rules was sent to the Agent and Man- Rules for Irrigation revenue and Tolls revenue accounts. ager in December 1864, for the consideration of the Board of Directors, who have not yet furnished the Government with their views on the subject.

IRRIGATION AND CANAL COMPANY.
Amount drawn during the year and up to its close in India.

225. The amount drawn by the Company's Agent from the Government Treasury in India, during the year, was Rupees 11,43,298-6-7, and the total amount up to its close Rupees 86,57,511-4-7.

Expenditure in and up to the end of the year.

226. The amount expended, under all heads, during 1865-66 was Rupees 13,82,548-9-7, and the total up to the close of the year Rupees 88,54,759-13-5. The cash balance on the 30th April was Rupees 1,71,579-6-11.*

Expenditure by the Board of Directors in England.

227. Up to the close of the year the expenditure in England, incurred by the Board of Directors of the Company, amounts to Rupees 3,38,342-6-11. † The amount shewn in the Administration Report for 1864-65 was Rupees 6,49,170, but this sum, by mistake, included Rupees 3,58,179-13-9 for value of stores supplied by the Board of Directors, and brought into the Indian accounts, and which, therefore, should have been excluded from the Home expenditure.

Abstract Statement of expenditure received from the Agent.

228. The Abstract Statement of expenditure during the year is shewn in the Appendix.

State of Audit of expenditure.

229. The following is a summary of the state of audit of the expenditure incurred by the Company :—

	RS.	A.	P.
Amount drawn from Government up to the 30th April 1865 ...	75,14,212	14	0
Do. during 1865-66...	11,43,298	6	7
Value of Stores supplied by the Board of Directors up to 30th April 1865, and brought on the Indian accounts	3,58,179	13	9
Do. do from 1st May 1865 to 31st January 1866.	3,647	11	4
Amount under deposit on account of undischarged securities of the employés, &c., up to 31st January 1866	7,187	3	7
Agents's liabilty...	90,26,526	1	3

	RS.	A.	P.
* Actual balance ...	1,79,848	15	0
Deduct deposits of contractors and others ...	8,269	8	1
	1,71,579	6	11

† As per capital accounts for April 1866, received from Home Government	RS.	A.	P.
	7,00,170	0	0
Do. do. value of stores supplied by the Board of Directors as per form P. for April 1866	3,61,827	9	1
	8 38,342	6	11

Expenditure debited to permanent heads of charge in the accounts up to 30th April 1865	67,16,241	6	3
Do. do. in the accounts from May 1865 to January 1866 ...	11,71,060	3	3
Do. objected to, pending explanation	60	0	0
Do. Retrenched	1,27,372	0	0
Do. under floating heads in the accounts, but not yet debited to appropriate heads of charge ...	1,36,157	11	2
Amount remaining to be accounted for by the Agent	8,75,634	12	7
Total...	90,26,526	1	3

MADRAS IRRIGATION AND CANAL COMPANY.

230. The extent of land made over to the Company's Chief Engineer by the Revenue authorities during the year was—

Extent of land made over to the Company from April 1865 to April 1866.

Under Class A. ... ... Acres 2,342·52
   ,,   B. ... ...   ,,   72·23
   ,,   C. ... ...   ,,   4·44

The extent of land provided for road diversions, under class D, was acres 4·66.

The extent of land transferred up to the close of the year, and the amount of compensation paid are subjoined.

Class A. ... ... Acres 10,367·22
  ,,   B. ... ...   ,,   2,817·09
  ,,   C. ... ...   ,,   18·54
  ,,   D. ... ...   ,,   44·64

                                    13,247·49

Compensation ... ... Rupees 57,970   7   2
Deduct for trees, &c.... ... ...   ,,   2,956 11   5

Net amount paid... ... ...   ,,   55,013 11   9

231. The amount received up to the 30th April 1866 on account of the Irrigation Revenue of the Company was—

Amount received on account of Irrigation Revenue.

For first crop ... ... Rupees 2,416   2   0
  ,, second ,, ...   ,,   129 11 11
  ,, occasional irrigation ...   ,,   35 10   0

                             2,581   7 11

232. The cultivation supplied with water was situated in seven villages of the Ramulcotta Taluk of the Kurnool District. Water was supplied to the town of Kurnool, but no payments for the supply appear to have been made up to the close of the year

Water supply.

SECTION VI.—MARINE.

Violation of the Marine Law XXII of 1855,

233. The infractions of the Indian Passenger Act were trifling, and did not call for special notice ; no complaints were received of breaches of the Port Conservancy Act.

of Act XXI of 1858.

The Commander of the steamer " Punjab" was fined Rupees fifty, for sailing from the port of Cocanada without the certificate required by Act XXI of 1858.

Port Funds.

234. The Port Funds, with the exception of those at Ganjam and Vizagapatam, which shew an aggregate deficit of Rupees 727-4-0, have a balance at their credit : the total receipts for the year under report were Rupees 1,41,353, and the disbursements Rupees 1,20,109.

Wrecks.

235. There were only four wrecks on the Madras coasts, but three vessels ran ashore, and were afterwards floated off, the steamers " Madras" and " Arabia" near Cocanada, owing to inattention to the lead ; and a Dutch schooner, the " February," from Bankok to Bombay, grounded thirty miles north of Cochin.

Cyclone.

236. A cyclone occurred on the 25th and 26th of November last, when there were thirty-one vessels at anchor in the roads ; one, the " Polly," remained, and was burnt to the waters edge ; of the thirty which put to sea, the " Great Britain" has not since been heard of ; three were abandoned, five were dismasted, eleven were severely damaged, and ten were almost uninjured. Some anxiety was felt regarding the " Devonport," which, with the " Star of India," was known to be on the way from Rangoon to Madras with the 3rd Battalion 60th Rifles on board. She arrived on the 8th December, under jury masts, having been totally dismasted on the 26th November. Ten or twelve native followers had been washed overboard.

Port Conservancy. Bimlipatam.

237. In consequence of the failure of rain last season, the bar of the river at Bimlipatam has completely closed, and the back-water has become very shallow.

Vizagapatam.

238. The new building, comprising Sea Customs and Marine Offices, has been completed. An advance of Rupees 5,000 has been made by the Municipality of this place towards the construction of a ghaut and a commercial building.

239. The bank off Hope Island continues to extend, driving the ships further north for an anchorage. The buoys have consequently been taken up, repaired, and moored again in suitable positions. MARINE.
Cocanada and
Coringa.

The Hope Island lighthouse and Superintendent's quarters have been repaired, and substantial huts built for the native attendants.

240. The pier sustained some damage during the cyclone of the 25th and 26th November, when the sea was exceedingly heavy, but it would probably have escaped injury had it not been for the massive upright and horizontal fender beams, with which the T head was fitted, and which offered such resistance to the waves that the upper ends of the piles were forced from six to ten inches shorewards, and the braces bent and broken. No other damage was sustained except the washing away of some of these beams. The remainder have since been removed, and hanging spar fenders substituted. Tables will be found in the Appendix, shewing the number of boats and rafts that came to and left the pier during the twelve months, and the amount of tolls collected. During the past year, and, more particularly, during the cyclone before mentioned, the depths of water along the pier have much decreased, the sand having accumulated in some parts four to six feet, causing, in a heavy sea, a break, which occasionally endangers boats. The upper reservoir for the supply of water from the pier has been completed, but the flow is still so slow that very little advantage is gained by it, and ships have to be watered, as before, from the beach. Madras Pier.

241. The lighthouse is in good order. Madras Light-
house.

242. The jetty or sea-wall, built for confining the scour of the river, was much damaged during the last cyclone, and is undergoing repair. The bar continues very shallow, and at half tide, boats have much difficulty in going in or out. The flag staff has been repaired, and as the port fund can now bear the expense, it is proposed to obtain from England a better description of lantern. Negapatam.

243. The trade through these channels increased by 196 vessels in the last calendar year. Paumben.

244. A jetty has been built at this port, partly at the expense of the local community. Tuticorin.

245. The light column is in course of construction; the new jetty and a landing place have been completed; and a coal godown capable of storing 300 tons, has been built. Cochin.

SECTION VII.—FINANCIAL.

New system of Account and Audit.

246. The new system of Audit and Account, framed by the English Commissioners, came into operation in this Presidency on the 1st of July 1865. Among the principal changes, which it involved, may be noticed the amalgamation of the offices of Audit and Account, the abolition of the office of Civil Paymaster, and the creation of the office of Deputy Accountant General; the substitution of Post Audit for Pre-Audit, except for charges payable at the Presidency, which are now passed and paid by a separate Officer, subordinate to the Accountant General, styled the Examiner of Claims; the separation of the Accounts of the Civil Department from those of the Military and Public Works Departments, and of Cash from Store accounts; the abolition of inter-Presidential and inter-Provincial adjustments, save in a few exceptional cases; the discontinuance of the annual statement of receipts and disbursements, and the preparation, in lieu of it, of finally audited monthly accounts, and receipts, and charges, which are submitted to the Financial Department, Calcutta, within six weeks of the close of the period to which they relate. In consequence too of this amalgamation, a reduction of forty-six hands has been effected in the strength of the two establishments, with a net saving to Government of Rupees 3,816 per annum.

Comparison of the Actuals with the Estimate for 1865-66.

247. The total amount of Revenue realized from all sources, during the year 1865-66, was Rupees 6,88,10,000, being Rupees 8,37,880 above the receipts of the previous year. The expenditure amounted to Rupees 2,54,32,000, or 11,27,360 above that of 1864-65.

Revenues and Charges.

248. The following statements shew the entire revenues and charges of the Presidency during the last four years :—

64

Statement shewing the Territorial Revenues and Expenditure of the Madras Presidency, during the years 1862-63 to 1865-66.

		Actuals 1862-63.	Actuals 1863-64.	Actuals 1864-65.	Actuals 1865-66.
	REVENUES AND RECEIPTS.	RS.	RS.	RS.	RS.
I	Land Revenue	4,22,16,760	4,29,97,990	4,18,46,450	4,30,69,000
II	Tributes and Contributions from Native States...	34,46,430	34,46,430	34,46,430	34,46,400
III	Forest...	1,83,550	2,45,060	2,98,510	3,12,706
IV	Abkaree	37,27,570	40,51,650	39,60,540	41,47,000
V	Income Tax	23,19,430	16,49,580	12,81,600	6,11,000
VI	Customs.	19,64,980	22,98,320	20,38,780	20,85,000
VII	Salt	91,27,700	89,92,720	1,03,60,780	1,01,20,000
IX	Stamps.	21,25,580	23,84,420	26,91,090	30,65,000
X	Mint	6,99,340	11,06,960	9,47,340	6,84,000
XIII	Law and Justice	2,94,750	4,06,616	4,31,510	6,01,000
XIV	Police...	30,410	53,380	56,300	74,000
XV	Marine.	19,630	62,170	32,469	31,260
XVI	Education	42,550	47,380	45,850	49,500
XVII	Interest ..	29,350	71,620	96,920	1,08,000
XVIII	Miscellaneous.	6,88,740	5,69,960	4,37,660	4,96,900
	Total, Civil Department...	6,69,09,470	6,93,73,239	6,79,72,120	6,88,10,200
	Military Department	23,43,520	16,21,880	14,61,560	11,50,000
	Public Works do	4,05,750	4,89,120	4,03,440	2,54,000
	Postal do	4,63,960	5,18,740	5,42,290	5,15,000
	Telegraph do	1,49,860	1,82,070	7,97,020	2,86,000
	Total ..	7,03,72,564	7,11,85,140	7,05,76,450	7,13,45,000
	EXPENDITURE.				
*2	Interest on Service Funds and other Accounts...	8,17,660	5,65,570	7,69,380	9,04,800
3	Allowances, Refunds and Drawback...	10,81,850	2,52,620	1,20,180	3,01,300
4	Land Revenue.	40,90,770	37,11,620	38,42,090	39,34,700
5	Forest	1,93,420	2,69,240	2,18,520	2,55,500
6	Abkaree	1,51,150	1,39,920	1,56,830	2,79,400
7	Income Tax	65,590	87,900	32,410	17,400
8	Customs...	1,65,500	1,63,190	1,69,040	1,65,700
9	Salt ..	11,77,450	9,15,460	14,25,060	14,90,800
11	Stamps	1,90,550	97,210	1,08,160	1,24,100
12	Mint...	2,49,070	8,57,920	3,12,160	2,11,800
13	Allowances to District and Village Officers	11,80,870	12,69,340	12,54,040	12,78,700
16	Administration and Public Departments	36,38,43	33,89,320	36,74,850	38,89,000
17	Law and Justice	35,25,270	31,91,180	33,43,590	38,41,80
18	Police	2,08,260	84,160	93,590	2,80,060
19	Marine.	6,61,190	6,99,010	7,37,060	7,58,900
20	Ecclesiastical	3,62,800	3,80,120	4,06,810	3,97,100
21	Medical Services	3,10,890	4,54,690	4,73,050	4,93,700
22	Stationery and Binding	2,69,750	2,23,740	2,55,900	3,10,000
23	Political Agencies ...	1,89,470	96,030	66,710	90,800
24	Allowances and Assignments	31,63,590	36,33,430	29,98,710	29,71,900
25	Miscellaneous...	3,94,900	6,50,870	7,25,630	6,70,100
27	Superannuations, &c.	14,49,310	29,65,070	25,72,000	25,50,000
	Total, Civil Department...	2,35,59,810	2,41,57,780	2,43,64,640	2,51,32,000
	Military Department	3,22,83,790	2,96,53,020	2,19,92,790	2,15,46,000
	Public Works do	80,76,470	70,36,020	82,16,300	73,73,800
	Postal do	6,23,400	6,19,810	6,21,610	5,93,800
	Telegraph do	3,28,380	3,02,180	3,15,200	2,91,900
	Total ..	6,48,71,550	6,17,68,810	5,45,50,570	5,53,37,700

249. The actual cash balance on the 30th April 1866, amounted to Rupees 2,51,87,900, shewing an increase of Rupees

Cash Balance on 30th April 1866.

---

* The increase in this item is owing to the gradual increase of the Service Funds deposited with the Government.
† Increase owing to the purchases appearing under this consolidated head, instead of being charged in each Department as heretofore.
‡ Decrease due to diminished remittances of Specie.
§ Decrease attributable to the annually diminishing charges connected with the Civil Service Annuity Fund.
N.B.—The variations in the other items will be found explained in the Departmental Sections of this volume.

16,64,200 above that on the 30th April of the previous year. This increase is chiefly due to the fact of the remittances made during the year 1865-66, both by Bills and Specie, to Calcutta and Bombay having amounted only to Rupees 7,00,000,* whilst in the previous year it was Rupees 99,00,000, exclusive of remittances in transit at the commencement of that year.

Comparison of cash balances for the past five years.

250. The amounts of the actual cash balances in the several treasuries, at the beginning and termination of the last five official years, are as follow:—

Years.	Cash Balances at the beginning of the year.	Cash Balances at the termination of the year.	Increase..	Decrease.
1861-62	2,18,39,800	2,92,87,900	74,48,100	......
1862-63	2,92,87,900	3,77,81,700	84,93,800	......
1863-64	3,77,81,700	3,17,78,000	......	60,03,700
1864-65	3,17,78,000	2,35,23,700	......	82,54,300
1865-66	2,35,23,700	2,51,87,900	16,64,200	......
		Total...	1,76,06,100	1,42,58,000
		Deduct Decrease...	1,42,58,000	
		Net Increase...	33,48,100	

Demand for small coins in the Mofussil.

251. The demand for small coins in the Provinces is becom_ing less each year. The value of small silver sent in 1865-66 amounted to Rupees 90,000 only, and of copper Rupees 59,200, shewing a reduction of Rupees 3,13,000, or 77·6 per cent., in the former, and of Rupees 2,80,500, or 82·6 per cent., in the latter, compared with the preceding year. In addition to the above remittances, about Rupees 60,000 worth of copper coins were despatched to the Superintendent of Coorg in 1865-66, leaving a balance of about Rupees eight lacs worth available for remittance to other Presidencies, exclusive of a reserve of about Rupees 1,38,000, which it is expected will suffice to meet the demands of the local treasuries for 1866-67.

---

* This does not include Rupees 6,00,000, in transit on 30th April 1866.

252. The following table shews the imports and exports of coin and bullion by sea during the last five years:— Imports and Exports of Coin and Bullion.

Years.	Imports.			Exports.		
	By Go-vernment.	By In-dividuals.	Total.	By Go-vernment.	By In-dividuals.	Total.
1861-62	...	2,22,85,900	2,22,85,900	3,00,000	36,58,486	39,58,486
1862-63	51,02,833	2,52,84,057	3,03,86,890	35,40,000	26,50,551	61,90,551
1863-64	44,30,000	3 16,45,985	3,60,75,985	160,03,000	63,36,284	2,23,39,284
1864-65	...	3·03,13,958	3,03,13,958	89,52,000	91,98,942	1,81,50,942
1865-66	...	3,66,42,492	3,66,42,492	62,00,600	64,09,623	1,26,10,223

253. The receipt of silver into the Mint, and the value of the coin by weight delivered to the Bank of Madras during 1865-66, has been as follows:— MINT.
Silver receipt.

	RS.	A.	P.
Balance in the Mint on the 1st May 1865	4,77,785	9	2
Received from Merchants...	53,78,581	6	4
Uncurrent silver coin received from the Bank of Madras for re-coinage	77,131	9	8
	59,33,498	9	2

Weight of coin delivered to the   RS.   A.   P.
Bank of Madras   54,49,942   12   0
Balance in the Mint   4,90,350   13   3   59,40,293   9   3

Excess...   6,795   0   1

The excess above exhibited is exclusive of silver in the dross, and is at the rate of about 124 Rupees for each lac in value coined and remitted to the Bank of Madras. The particulars are as follow :—

	RS.	A.	P.
Pre-melting Room.—Recoveries from the refuse dross and sweepings	597	12	11¼
Melting Room.—Difference of the value of the metal with which the melter is debited and of the weight returned	5,296	10	7¼
Laminating Room.—Difference of weight delivered and returned	4,822	7	0½
	10,716	14	7¼
Deduct wastage in milling, cleaning, and stamping the coins	3,921	14	6¼
Net excess...	6,795	0	1

MINT.

Number and value of silver & copper pieces coined, with rates of coinage.

254. The following is a statement of the number and value of each denomination of silver and copper pieces coined and remitted, together with the rates at which the coin has been manufactured.

	Pieces.	Value.				Rs.	A.	P.
		RS.	A.	P.		RS.	A.	P.
Single Rupees ..	54,31.088	54,31,088	0	0	At 1 ₁⁴₄ per cent.	78,133	6	8
Quarter do ...	74,230	18,5 57	8	0	,, 3 ,, ,,	556	11	7
	55,05,318	54,49,645	8	0				
Half Annas ...	143,69,280	4,49,040	0	0	,, 177 Rs. per lac.	25,433	10	0
Quarter do ...	288,44,160	4,50,690	0	0	,, 100 ,, ,,	28,844	2	6
Single Pies ...	108,88,320	56,710	0	0	,, 50 ,, ,,	5,444	2	6
	541,01,760	9,56,440	0	0				
Grand Total...	596,07,078	64,06,085	8	0		1,38,412	1	3

Receipts of Merchants' bullion from May 1860.

255. The receipts of merchants' silver bullion, during each month for the past six years, are given below :—

	1860-61.	1861-62.	1862-63.	1863-64.	1864-65.	1865-66.
	Tolas.	Tolas.	Tolas.	Tolas.	Tolas.	Tolas.
May	4,29,404	3,84,604	2,59,498	61,463	6,44,696	2,20,520
June	8,19,407	1,61,830	2,21,975	2,45,589	13,82,769	40,415
July	5,75,206	3,01,685	2,81,604	3,55,680	5,41,942	58,415
August ...	1,86,245	2,66,005	3,38,456	2,19,595	4,97,943	17,219
September...	3,11,678	6,66,915	4,33,815	47,918	5,15,469	1,40,802
October ...	1,33,606	3,98,430	5,79,118	2,73,147	4,75,872	91,873
November ...	2,47,657	1,50,606	8,56,814	67,300	4,74,015	84,170
December ...	6,59,861	3,16,198	7,95,869	77,470	2,38,215	13,32,212
January ...	1,12,276	5,09,695	12,22,370	3,01,455	8,50,335	8,54,608
February ...	1,38,825	3,02,926	2,30,651	26,662	59.386	2,86,814
March ...	4,23,104	2,82,443	3,67,793	18,42,581	3,97,350	8,08,183
April... ...	4,79,394	7,‚3,662	4,23,268	486,3 12	1,10,435	14,43,351
Total...	45,16,663	44,64,999	60,11,231	40,05,172	61,88,427	53,7ε,582

Mint receipts and expenditure.

256. The charges for sèignorage and refinage on merchants' silver bullion received for coinage, with the gain on the coinage of copper' and sale of copper scissel,˙ the excess of silver found in the different departments of the Mint, and of cash received into the Mint for work done for private parties, and charges for articles made for other departments amounts to Rupees 7,15,456-0-6. The expenses of the Mint and of the Assay Department, with the amount written off on account

of loss on the re-melting of copper scissel is Rupees 2,10,518-8-7. The sum left in favor of the Mint is Rupees 5,04,937-7-11, as shewn in the following statement :—

RECEIPTS.

	RS.	A.	P.	RS.	A.	P.
Seignorage and refining charges on silver bullion	1,12,986	4	9			
Gain on copper coins, after deducting value of the copper...	5,53,021	0	6			
Gain on copper scissel sold ...	957	10	8			
Excess of silver found in the different departments	6,795	0	1			
Amount of cash received for work done for private parties, acids and unserviceable articles sold at the Mint ...	19,865	8	0			
Amount of articles made and supplied for other departments for which cash payments have not been received, as per order of Government, No. 822, 19th December 1863	21,830	8	6			
				7,15,456	0	6

DISBURSEMENTS.

Mint Master's salary	12,600	0	0			
Mint Establishment...	45,385	11	5			
Contingent servants...	65,792	6	8			
Gram, straw, &c., and purchased articles...	19,513	7	2			
Coal...	14,500	0	0			
Coke	3,932	6	4			
Store articles	18,384	2	2			
Amount of loss on the re-melting of copper scissel	996	10	9			
Total Assay Office Establishment	29,413	12	1			
				2,10,518	8	7

Net gain as exhibited by the Mint Books... 5,04,937 7 11

257. The total amount of cash received on bills on the sale of gold, copper scissel, &c., and for articles made and supplied to other public departments, and private parties, is shewn in the following statement.

MINT.

RECEIPTS.	RS.	A.	P.	RS.	A.	P.

To gold sold at the Mint   40,338   9   5

To Copper scissel, &c., &c.   1,82,357   12   2

To Iron castings and other articles for private parties, nitric and sulphuric acid, and unserviceable articles sold ... ...   19,865] 8   0

                              2,42,561   13   7

By cash remitted to the Bank of Madras   2,33,003   3   6

By deductions from the contingent abstracts on account of cash received for work done for private parties...   9,558   10   1

                              2,42,561   13   7

Castings from the Mint foundry.

258. The weight of castings from the Mint foundry has been—

For the Mint   ...   .   46 Tons.

For public departments   ...   .   109 do.

For private parties   ...   .   15 do.

                                      170 do.

Coinage for the past ten years.

259. The following statement exhibits the coinage of the past ten years :—

Years.	Silver.		Copper.		Total silver and copper pieces.	Total value.
	Pieces.	Value.	Pieces.	Value.		
		RS.		RS.		RS.
1856-57	1,51,31,526	86,78,139	1,51,29,884	2,59,435	3,02,61,410	89,37,574
1857-58	1,63,38,249	96,21,933	3,48,95,280	6,50,791	5,12,33,529	1,02,72,724
1858-59	67,63,524	48,53,440	3,05,25,947	5,64,131	3,72,89,471	54,17,571
1859-60	1,10,78,847	56,62,073	6,54,68,832	9,02,991	7,65,47,679	65 65,064
1860-61	66,18,433	51,34,699	7,23,50,400	10,22,420	7,89,68,833	61,57,119
1861-62	60,59,977	43,99,290	7,09,49,760	10,76,750	7,70,09,737	54,76,040
1862-63	1,20,54,231	67,32,540	6,27,65,760	9,93,280	7,48,19,991	77,25,820
1863-64	1,60,06,926	1,27,76,765	9,53,21,280	17,69,630	11,13,28,206	1,45,46,395
1864-65	93,72,918	64,48,285	7,96,80,000	13,27,500	8,90,52,918	77,75,785
1865-66	55,05,318	54,49,943	5,41,01,760	9,56,440	5,96,07,078	64,06,383

Department of Issue of Paper Currency.

Notes issued.

260. The total number of notes issued to the Madras Bank was 38,550, representing a total value of Rupees 45,50,000 ; details of this issue are given below :—

Notes issued to the Madras Bank in exchange for cash—

    300 Notes of 500 Rupees in value   1,50,000

    200   do   of 1,000   do   do   2,00,000

    500   3,50,000

Notes issued to the Madras Bank in exchange for cancelled Notes—

10,000	Notes	of	10	Rupees	in value	1,00,000
5,000	do	of	20	do	do	1,00,000
8,000	do	of	50	do	do	4,00,000
7,000	do	of	100	do	do	7,00,000
1,200	do	of	500	do	do	6,00,000
1,450	do	of	1,000	do	do	14,50,000

32,650   33,50,000

Notes issued to the Madras Bank for Circle Notes of Calicut, Trichinopoly, and Vizagapatam—

2,500	Notes	of	20	Rupees	in value	50,000
2,000	do	of	100	do	do	2,00,000
600	do	of	500	do	do	3,00,000
300	do	of	1,000	do	do	3,00,000

5,400   8,50,000

261. The total number of good Notes returned by the Bank of Madras was 14,625, representing Rupees 27,00,000; of these, 2,800 from the Madras Circle, the value of which was Rupees 15,00,000; 6,284 from the Calicut Circle, representing Rupees 4,97,020; 5,309 from the Trichinopoly Circle, representing Rupees 6,82,980; and 232 from the Vizagapatam Circle, aggregating Rupees 20,000, were returned in exchange for cash and other Notes, and subsequently re-issued. 3,660 old Notes, representing Rupees 3,00,000, were returned by the Bank in exchange for cash.

262. The following table shews the number and value of Notes issued and received, by the three Circles, in exchange for cash or other Notes—

Notes issued.

	Number.	Value Rupees.
By the Calicut Circle	16,697	13,72,690
Trichinopoly do	9,472	8,74,550
Vizagapatam do	5,983	5,32,580
Total ...	32,152	27,79,820

71

Notes Received.

	Number.	Value Rupees.
By the Calicut Circle	14,018	12,29,250
Trichinopoly do	5,354	7,39,330
Vizagapatam do	4,690	4,45,380
Total...	24,062	˙24,13,960

Notes cancelled.　263. The number and value of Notes cancelled in the year is subjoined—

	10 Rs.	20 Rs.	50 Rs.	100 Rs.	500 Rs.	1,000 Rs	Total.	
							No.	Value Rs.
Madras Circle ...	16,240	10,730	8,600	7,130	1,660	1,300	44,660	36,50,000
Calicut do ...	10	4	1	1	...	...	16	330
Trichinopoly do	732	720	1	9	...	...	1,462	22,670
Vizagapatam do	351	374	50	57	26	13	871	45,190
Total...	17,333	1 828	8,652	7,197	1,686	1,313	48,009	37,18,190

Notes in circulation.　264. The circulation of Notes, at the end of last official year, in the Madras and other Circles, amounted to Rupees 66,36,710, and that on the 30th April 1866, Rupees 64,02,570,* shewing a decrease of Rupees 2,34,140.

The total value of Notes cancelled in the Madras and other Circles, during the year, was Rupees 37,18,190, and of those cancelled in the previous year amounted to Rupees 41,58,780, shewing a decrease of Rupees 4,40,590.

Securities and Cash in deposit.　265. The investment in Government Securities from the Currency Reserve at the end of the year is as follows :—

Madras Circle	Rupees 30,02,969	1	0
Calicut do	,, 1,00,058	14	3
Trichinopoly do	,, 1,00,058	14	3
Vizagapatam do	,, 1,00,058	14	3
Total Rupees	33,03,145	11	9

These securities are held by the Head Commissioner to the credit of their respective Circles.

---

* Madras Circle	Rupees. 51,00,000
Calicut do	,, 4,38,180
Trichinopoly do	,, 4,64,130
Vizagapatam do	,, 4,10,260
	64,02,570

Cash in deposit on the 30th April 1866—

Madras	Circle	... ...	Rupees	19,47,030 15	0
Calicut	do	... ...	„	3,28,121 1	9
Trichinopoly	do	... ...	„	3,64,071 1	9
Vizagapatam	do	... ...	„	3,10,201 1	9

Total Rupees ... 29,49,424 4 3

Trichinopoly Circle Notes availed for issue at the Madras Office, on the 30th April 1866, amounted to Rupees 1,50,000. These Notes were treated as cash.

The total of investment, and that of cash in deposit, added with the Trichinopoly Circle Notes on hand, amounted to Rupees 64,02,570, the value of Notes in circulation in the Madras and other Circles on the 30th April 1866.

266. A supply of 92,000 Notes of the following denominations was received from England during the year :— Particulars and value of Notes received from England.

27,000 Notes of 10	Rupees in value	Rupees	2,70,000
24,000 do	of 20	do	do	„	4,80,000
29,000 do	of 50	do	do	„	14,50,000
12,000 do	of 100	do	do	„	12,00,000
92,000				„	34,00,000

267. During the year the Mint obtained from the Currency Re- Advance on account of Bullion. serve an advance of Rupees 6,50,000, in exchange for Bullion, received and remitted the same to the Government Treasury to meet Assay Certificates, and after the coinage of the Bullion the said sum of six and a half lacs was refunded to the Currency Treasury.

268. Under orders from the Government of India, the offices of Abolition of Assistants to Deputy Commissioners. Assistant to the Deputy Commissioner for the Issue of Paper Currency in the circles of Calicut, Trichinopoly, and Vizagapatam have been abolished, and the Deputy Collectors in charge of the Treasuries at the abovementioned places have been placed in charge of the Currency Departments, with an extra allowance of Rupees 100, paid by the Currency Department in addition to their present pay.

269. Receipts and Disbursements of the Department during the Receipts and Disbursements. year—

RECEIPTS.	RS.	A.	P.	RS.	A.	P.
Profit by Interest calculated upon Government Securities of the Madras and other Circles				1,81,819	15	3
DISBURSEMENTS.						
Salary of the Commissioner and Assistant Commissioner of Issue...	24,082	15	11			
Establishment including Circles	13,734	3	4			
Contingent charges do ...	4,588	6	10			
Commission paid to the Bank of Madras on daily average circulation under Clause XVII of its agreement with Government...	45,860	6	0			
Cost of Note Forms received from England during the year, including Freight and Landing charges	1,511	12	8			
				89,777	12	9
Saving...				92,042	2	6

Section VIII—POLITICAL.

270. The following resumé of the administration of these States is based, in great measure, on the detailed information contained in the Reports of the Dewans of Travancore and Cochin. The statements in the Appendix refer to the Malabar year, ending on the 14th August 1865; but this report is brought up to the close of the official year.

TRAVAN-
CORE AND
COCHIN.

271. The reforms and improvements, initiated during the previous year, in the administration of justice, have been steadily persevered in, and the whole system of the Judicial administration has felt their beneficial effect. Justice has been more carefully and satisfactorily administered, and the Courts have risen in the confidence of the public. A detailed statement of the operations of the Courts is given in the Appendix. Important enactments, based upon those of British India, were passed in the year under review, relating to criminal breach of trust; the appointment of qualified vakeels to plead in the several Courts; the adjudication of claims to waste lands on their sales under the recent rules; and the limitation of suits. Subsequently, an Act was passed for improving the constitution of the Zillah Courts, by reducing the number of Judges, and rendering it competent for a single Judge to sit in Civil and Criminal cases, and also extending the jurisdiction of the Moonsiff's Courts, and rendering their decisions final within a limited amount.

TRAVAN-
CORE.
Civil and Cri-
minal Justice.

272. The Police statistics shew that considerable energy has been displayed in the supervision of this important department. Its efficiency is much improved, and business is carried on with greater despatch, though its organization is still far from perfect. The number of serious offences has been decreasing of late years.

Police.

273. The continued influence of the sanitary improvements in Jails, is manifested by the continuance of the reduced rate of mortality noticed in last year's Report. The two great epidemics which periodically thinned the Jails in former times, were scarcely felt, there being no cases of small pox, and only four of cholera. Under these circumstances, the project of a new Central Jail has been allowed to remain in abeyance, and to give place to the not less urgent undertaking of the erection of new public offices, and a large Civil Dispensary.

Jails.

274. The land revenue retains its usual standard of about 16½ lacs of Rupees. A highly important measure in this branch deserves to

Land Revenue.

75

TRAVAN-
CORE.

be noticed, as fraught with the hope of the most beneficial results, viz., the enfranchisement of the crown lands of the State, which are of a very considerable extent. As described more fully in the Dewan's report, which is given at length in the Appendix, the State, as landlord, had arbitrary right over these lands, and was not bound to respect possession or any right accruing from it to the tenant. These arbitrary rights have been relinquished by His Highness the Maha Rajah, and the lands are declared to be "private, heritable, saleable, and otherwise transferable property," subject only to the declared assessment, as in Ryotwary districts. They are thus placed upon a satisfactory footing which at once immensely enhances their value, and gives a stimulus to their improvement, which will tend largely to develope the agricultural resources of this extensive property. Reduction of taxation has taken place on the irrigated lands in South Travancore, by lowering all excessive rates to a certain maximum standard. Upwards of one hundred petty and vexatious taxes have been abolished, and a considerable amount of outstanding arrears has been remitted. The observation made by the Dewan, that under the influences of "moderate taxation, improved tenure, high prices, and reduced duties," " the landholders, as a body, were never before more contented and prosperous," is fully borne out by experience. The re-assessment of garden lands has been initiated, though little progress has yet been made in carrying out this important measure.

Customs.

275. In this branch there is a considerable falling off, occasioned, in a great measure, by the serious depression of trade, extending to the European as well as the Indian markets, and also by the effects of reduced taxes in operation for a portion only of the previous year. The tariff value of the total exports for the year was Rupees 46,47,829 as compared with Rupees 52,13,823, for the previous year. A similar table of imports is not obtainable. The excess of exports over imports is considerable ; it is balanced by large importation of the precious metals, especially gold.

The interportal arrangements, which, with a few exceptions, freed the trade between British India and the Travancore and Cochin States, by placing it on the same footing as that of British India generally, were in operation little more than two months of the Malabar year, and it is too early to trace results, particularly under the circumstance of the great stagnation of trade above alluded to, though there can be no doubt that considerable relief has been afforded by the removal of the restrictions on the trade of these States.

Particulars of these interportal arrangements, given in the Dewan's report, will be found in the Appendix. TRAVAN-CORE.

276. The tobacco revenue very nearly retains the standard of Tobacco. the previous year, notwithstanding the reduction of the import duty on this article towards the close of the present year, under the terms of the convention above noticed, to the extent of about one lac of rupees a year. The consumption increased by thirteen per cent.

277. Under the convention, the selling price of salt is now Salt. equivalent to that in British India, thus affording an increase of revenue, though the consumption remained the same.

278. Some progress has been made in working the forests, though Forests. the results are not manifest in the returns of this year. Under a proper system of Forestry, and a liberal outlay at starting, the Travancore forests may be expected to yield a large annual revenue of several lacs of rupees.

279. This enterprise still continues to extend itself, both in Coffee. Travancore and Cochin, more particularly in the former. Considerable progress has been made in Travancore in the survey of these lands.

280. The experimental Tea and Chinchona plantations, on the Tea and Chinchona. Peermade hills, were visited lately, and the experiment pronounced by competent authorities successful, and most promising of future results. A few Tea and Chinchona plants have been distributed gratis to each of the planters in that locality, and the sale of further supplies is commencing.

281. Considerable advance has been made in Educational insti- Education. tutions, and the effect is being felt in the different branches of the administration in the supply of better qualified servants. The High School at Trevandrum has sustained its important position ; the standard in the highest class being the subjects prescribed for the Matriculation Examination at the Madras University. The increasing demand for education, in accordance with the progress of the times, rendered it desirable to raise the standard still higher; and another European Master has recently arrived from England, to constitute an upper department, for which the B. A. Examination will form the standard.

An English Law Class, as mentioned in last year's report, and also a Vernacular Law Class, have been most valuable additions to the

TRAVAN-
CORE.

school, in training persons for the Judicial and Police departments. The standard of the former is the examination for District Moonsiffs in British India.

The number of District Schools has been increased, and the importance of extending vernacular education has been recognized by His Highness the Maha Rajah, in recently assigning an annual grant of Rupees 20,000 for this object.

The London and Church Missionary Societies continue their valuable and unremitting efforts in the cause of education.

The progress that is now being made has enabled the State to impose tests of examination for appointments in several branches of the administration, and it will probably be able shortly to make this condition of employment general.

Female education has by no means been overlooked, and is now gaining a footing among the higher classes at the capital.

Public lectures, in a popular form, have contributed their aid to the other sources of knowledge, and it is gratifying to observe, with reference to this Native State, that some of the most able of these lectures have been delivered by His Highness the First Prince, the Dewan, Sir T. Madava Row, and Sadasiva Pillay, first Judge of the Sudder Court.

Medical.

282. In this department may be noticed the opening of the new and commodious Dispensary at Trevandrum, and the appointment of an able Superintendent of Vaccination. A Medical class of stipendiary students has been in training to supply Medical subordinates for the department.

His Highness the Maha Rajah has liberally assigned a grant of Rupees 20,000, per annum, for establishing Hospitals throughout Travancore, suitable buildings being erected from the surplus funds of the State.

The Medical Mission at Neyoor, has contributed its valuable aid in the relief of sickness and suffering in that locality, and is expanding its benevolent influence.

In Cochin, and the northern part of Travancore, a very severe epidemic of cholera broke out in the the hot weather. In Cochin, the cases reported amount to nearly three per cent. of the whole population, and the number of those that were fatal was about 10,000, or eighty per cent. The disease seems to have prevailed generally in the country, without reference to any local peculiarities of site or climate.

283. The public gardens, recently formed in connection with the TRAVAN-
Museum at Trevandrum, are beginning to be thoroughly appreciated CORE.
by the people as a healthy source of recreation ; the successful culture Public Gardens.
in these gardens of the Victoria Regia, which, it is believed, has only
flowered in two other places in India, is not undeserving of notice.

284. Public Works have been vigorously pressed on under the Public Works.
able superintendence of the Engineer, Mr. Barton. The expenditure has
been not far short of five lacs of rupees, or upwards of one-tenth of the
income of the State. Of this sum, one lac of rupees was spent on the
Victoria canal, and the granite barriers, which presented such formidable difficulty in this section under operation, have now been
removed.

The Peermade ghaut has received considerable attention. A
distance of seven miles is open for carts ; a permanent line has been laid
out for the remainder on an easy gradient.

The hill tracts at Augusteer and Asamboo, where extensive lands
have been taken up for coffee and other cultivation, have been opened
out by roads to the foot of the ghauts.

285. The new Civil Dispensary, above alluded to, was formally New Public
opened by His Highness the Maha Rajah in November last. It con- Buildings.
tains four wards, dispensary, lecture, and waiting rooms, and other
conveniences.

The foundation stone of a handsome pile of buildings for public
offices was laid by His Highness in December. This accommodation
is much needed, and will greatly contribute to the convenience of
public business. The address delivered by His Highness the Maha
Rajah on this occasion, declaring the policy of His Highness' Government, which received the commendatory notice both of the Government
and of the Secretary of State for India, will be found in the account
of the proceedings on that occasion, given in Appendix.

The project for removing the only barrier in the water communication between Travancore and Cochin, has been matured, and is likely
soon to be commenced.

Much has not been done in the repair and restitution of irrigation
works, but the subsequent appointment of a professional Assistant to
the Engineer, and the enlargement of the establishment, will enable
this important branch to be taken in hand in earnest in the ensuing
year.

TRAVAN-
CORE.
Finances.

286. The finances of the Travancore State continue in a flourishing condition, and notwithstanding the increased expenditure in largely augmenting the pay of public servants, in the remission of customs duties under the recent convention, the reduction of land assessment, the further abatement of the duty on tobacco, the greater outlay on public works, and the provision of retiring pensions, the balance sheet still shews a considerable surplus. The full effect, however, of the above and other measures will not be felt till the ensuing year, for the whole period of which they will be in operation, but the prospective estimate of its finances affords the expectation of continued prosperity in the revenues of the State. A comparative statement of the revenue collections and expenditure of this State during the past two years, is given in the Appendix. The collections during the past year amounted to Rupees 42,11,140, the expenditure to Rupees 40,47,734.

The remarks recorded in last year's report, that this "State was in a more favorable position than it ever had been for extending its reforms and improving the administration," and the anticipation that there would be " every disposition manifested on its part to avail itself of the opportunity thus afforded for the advancement of the prosperity of the State, and the welfare of His Highness' subjects," have been fully borne out in the administration of the present year.

In connection with the prosperous administration of this State, must be here noticed the recognition of His Highness the Maha Rajah's enlightened policy, in the grant of Her Most Gracious Majesty to His Highness of the distinguished honor of Knight Grand Commander of the Most Exalted Order of the Star of India ; and also the recognition of the services of His Highness' able Dewan, T. Madava Row, in the conduct of the administration, by the grant to him of the honor of Knight Commander of the same Most Exalted Order.

COCHIN.
Civil and Cri-
minal Justice.

287. Some progress has been made in the reform of Judicial administration, and occasion has been taken, by the removal of some of the Zillah Judges for corruption and incompetency, to introduce able and trustworthy officers from the British service.

Arrangements for the improvement of the Highest Court of Appeal are in progress, consequent on which results similar to those obtained in Travancore may be looked for in this important depart. ment.

The introduction of the Code of Civil Procedure has already . COCHIN. produced a beneficial result, by facilitating the progress of Civil Justice. Enactments, similar to those introduced in Travancore, have been passed for constituting authorized Pleaders in the Courts, and for the punishment of criminal breach of contract in certain cases.

There is little that calls for remark in the administration of Criminal Justice.

288. The health of the prisoners was generally very good, Jails. notwithstanding the presence of epidemics in the surrounding country.

289. The land revenue, which is the main source of wealth, Land Revenue. shews a trifling decrease; this is merely nominal; there has been in fact an increase, owing to increased cultivation and resumption of rent free tenures.

290. There is a decrease in customs, owing to the interportal Customs. convention between the British, and Cochin and Travancore Governments, and to the receipts being only given for ten months and a half, previous to the date of introduction of the new rules.

291. The Salt Revenue fell below the ordinary level, owing Salt. chiefly to the merchants having large stores of salt on hand when the price was raised.

292. A Sanscrit School has been opened at Trichoor. Improve- Education. ments have been effected in the Government School at Ernacollum; the number of students in His Highness' School rose from thirty to 150, the demand for education being in no way checked by the introduction of school fees.

293. The expenditure on public works was considerable, amount- Public Works. ing to about one-sixth of the revenues. The principal outlay was upon a large bridge over the Ponany river at Shoranoor. There is every prospect of this bridge being open for traffic in the ensuing dry season. Considerable progress has been made in the water communication between Trichoor and Cochin; when this is effectually completed, it is expected that steam communication may be established between the two places.

It is proposed to substitute a tramway, instead of the contemplated railway, between Shoranoor and Cochin.

K   81

COCHIN.　294. The port of Narakal is increasing in reputation as a safe
Narakal.　harbour during the monsoon, when all the other ports on this coast,
Alleppy excepted, are closed; fifteen steamers, besides other vessels
touched there during the monsoon, and on one occasion the advantage
of this port was particularly felt in the facility it afforded for throwing
in a supply of rice to the country, when it was threatened with famine
prices. The facilities for shipment are being improved.

Finances.　295. The finances of this State may be regarded as prosperous.
The income slightly exceeded that of the previous year, but was a trifle
short of the expenditure, as shewn in Appendix A. There was, however,
a considerable surplus available in the treasury. The State was
enabled to continue its large outlay on public works, to increase
further the salaries of public servants, and to introduce rules for
retiring pensions to its servants.

CARNATIC.　296. The payments to stipendiaries (including Jaghiredars)
amounted, during the official year 1865-66, to Rupees 7,07,160; of
which Rupees 1,46,000 were drawn by His Highness Prince Azeem
Jah Bahadoor, as arrears of stipend.

The number of persons receiving pensions on the 1st May 1866,
was 1,561. The lapses by death, &c., in 1865-66, exclusive of those
who commuted their stipends, were 104, and amounted in the aggregate to Rupees 15,422.

Bonuses to the amount of Rupees 24,958 were granted in com-
mutation of forty-three stipends, not exceeding ten Rupees each per
mensem, aggregating Rupees 3,009 per annum.

Petty claims against the estate of the late Nabob were settled to
the extent of Rupees 4,998, and arrears of salary and pension, amounting to Rupees 3,452, were paid.

Section IX.—MILITARY.

297. The average strength of the Army, during the year under review, was 16,077 Europeans, and 32,986 Natives. The increase in the European force is accounted for by the arrival of relieving Regiments before the departure of others. Average strength of the Army.

298. The system of organization in force in the Bengal and Bombay Presidencies was introduced into the Native Army of this Presidency, on the 1st November 1865, with an establishment of six European Officers to each Regiment of Cavalry and Infantry, as specified below, and a second Doing Duty Officer (to each corps) to provide a reserve for the staff corps, and for the various departments in which Military Officers are employed. Re-organization of the Native Army.

For the Cavalry.

A Commandant.
A Second in command, also Commanding a Squadron.
A Senior Squadron Officer.
A Junior   do.
An Adjutant, and
A Doing Duty Officer.

For the Infantry.

A Commandant.
A Senior wing Commandant.
A Junior   do. ·
An Adjutant.
A Quarter Master, and
A Doing Duty Officer.

No change has been made in respect of the pay of Troopers in the Cavalry, or in the system under which they are armed and clothed, nor as to the provision, &c., of horses, or the supply and repair of saddlery, &c. The only change in this branch has been similar to that made in the Infantry, namely, that Native Officers should command Troops, and European Officers perform the duties of Squadron Officers, &c., under the new organization. In view, however, to the early introduction of the Silladar system, the enlistment of recruits for the Cavalry has been stopped. Provision has been made for transferring

83

RE-ORGANI-ZATION. recruit boys, already on the establishment, to the ranks, on the usual conditions ; future admissions to the boy establishment being restricted to the pension class only, the establishment will be gradually reduced, in rateable proportion to the decrease in the effective combatant ranks.

Effects of re-organisation. 299. These changes, which are attended with increased emoluments to Officers on the strength of the new Regiments, involve at present an additional expenditure of about Rupees 4,05,864 per annum, to be gradually counterbalanced by the absorption of the supernumerary Officers in the cadres of the old Regiments.

Reductions.

Reduction of Divisional command. 300. The arrangement which had been determined upon in the official year 1864-65, of converting the Divisional command of the Northern Division in this Presidency into a District command, under a Brigadier General of the first class, on the occurrence of a vacancy in the former, was carried into effect in September 1865, at an annual saving of Rupees 18,264.

Reduction of European Force. 301. The strength of the British force in this Presidency has been reduced from ten to nine Regiments of Infantry, by the transfer of H. M.'s 105th Foot to Bengal, resulting in an annual saving of about Rupees 6,24,658.

Native Horse Artillery. 302. It having been considered desirable, on financial grounds, finally to break up the Battery of Madras Native Horse Artillery, special advantages were offered to the Native Officers and men, to induce them to accept of pension and discharge.

East Indian Drivers attached to Royal Artillery. 303. The services of the East Indian Drivers attached to two Batteries of Royal Artillery in this Presidency, have also been dispensed with.

Dooly Bearers. 304. By the introduction of light sick carts, as a substitute for doolies, the allotment of dooly bearers, for the several stations south of Secunderabad, has been reduced from 15th May 1865 to the extent indicated below :—

Head Maistries, from	9	to	6
Petty do.	25	to	18
Bearers, from	765	to	540

305. The number of commissioned grades in this department, Commissioned Commissariat which was shewn in the Administration Report of 1863-64 to be Officers. twenty-six, of all grades, has been reduced to twenty-two, viz., by one Deputy Assistant and three Sub-Assistants Commissary General, the Supernumeraries being absorbed as vacancies occur. A saving of about Rupees 15,600 per annum will accrue from this measure.

306. The system of audit and account, established in 1860, Pay Department. with some slight modifications, which have been effected during the year, System of audit and account. still continues.

307. The expenditure in connection with the pay of British Pay of British Troops for thir- Troops for thirteen months, will, however, be included in the accounts teen months in- cluded in the of 1865-66, consequent on the establishment of the system of adjusting accounts of the year 1865-66. the pay of such troops within the month for which it is due, instead of in arrears, as has hitherto been the practice.

308. The working of the system is reported to be very satisfactory, System work- ing satisfac- being characterized by promptitude and accuracy in adjustment and torily. accounting.

309. The outstanding balances have, as hitherto, been narrowly Outstanding balances nar- watched. rowly watched.

310. In the Pay department the outstanding retrenchments on Outstandings. the 30th April last, amounted to only Rupees 2,673-13-8, with an annual expenditure of 254 lakhs. The outstanding advances to Rupees 4,01,987-4-11:

311. The outstanding retrenchments of the Commissariat depart- Outstanding of Commissariat ment amounted only to Rupees 10,403-12-10, the outstanding advances Department. to Rupees 1,08,082-11-9.

312. The audit in all branches is current. Audit.

313. The prices of supplies generally have continued and still Increase. continue to rise, and the Commissariat expenditure, which is chiefly affected by the enhanced rates, has increased.

314. The establishment of good service pensions in the Indian Good service Army, as notified in G. O. G. 29th March 1866, No. 129, involves, on pensions. account of Officers of the Madras Army, an expense of Rupees 7,000 per annum,

FINANCIAL.
Expense under new passage Warrant.

315. The new Warrant, published in G. O. G. No. 209, of 2nd June 1865, extending the grant of passage money to all British Officers who may embark for service in India, and to Officers quitting India involves an extra expense of about 40,000 Rupees per annum.

Reductions effected in 1865-66 amount to Rupees 7,54,196.

316. The reductions of Military expenditure effected during the past year amount to Rupees 7,54,196.

Cost of the Army.

317. The estimated cost of the Army for 1866-67 is Rupees 3,28,84,269. The Budget estimate of last year was only Rupees 3,15,91,290; but in consequence of many unanticipated changes, involving expense, the regular estimate of the year rose to Rupees 3,26,27,700. The actual expenditure of 1864-65 was Rupees 3,17,78,543.

Modification of the constitution of the Sanitary Commission.

318. The constitution of the Sanitary Commission in this Presidency (noticed in the Administration Report of 1863-64) has been modified; the duties hitherto performed by that body being now carried on, so far as the Military department is concerned, by a Sanitary Commissioner, aided by a Medical Officer as Secretary. Officers, Civil, Military, or Medical, may however be associated with the Sanitary Commissioner, as Committees at stations where it may be desirable to form such a body to consider any particular subject.

Health of Troops.

Comparative freedom of the Army from epidemics.

319. The Madras Army, European and Native, has been, on the whole, healthy during the past year, notwithstanding that the civil population in many parts of Southern India has suffered severely from epidemic cholera and small pox. The comparative exemption of the Military, from diseases affecting the surrounding population, may be held in some degree to testify to the care and attention bestowed upon the sanitary condition of the troops.

Prevalence of cholera in certain parts.

Extent to which the troops have suffered from cholera.

320. Cholera has been prevalent in the Northern Division, Ceded Districts, and northern parts of Mysore; also on the Western Coast, and in and about Trichinopoly; but compared with its very general prevalence, very few of the troops have been attacked by, or have died of, the malady. The casualties amongst European troops from cholera were only twenty-six, and of Natives seventy-one.

Small-pox amongst the Native troops at Bangalore.

321. A few cases of small pox have occurred amongst the Native troops at Bangalore, but chiefly of a mild character.

322. In illustration of the comparative healthiness of the Military during the past year, it may be noted that there has been a considerable diminution in the proportion of hospital admissions to strength.

HEALTH.
Decrease of admissions into Hospital.

323. The proportion of those treated to strength in 1864-65 was 159·9 per cent., and in 1856-66 only 111·6. The rate of mortality too has been lower in the past year.

Proportion of treated to strength for 1864-65 and 1865-66.

324. The diminution in the number of admissions into Hospital has been due, to some extent, to the decrease of venereal disorders at some of the large Military stations. The low rate of mortality is due to the absence of epidemic outbreaks of cholera. Five men died of cholera in Bellary, five at Secunderabad, six at Nagpore, and four in Burmah ; but in none of the stations did the disease assume a real epidemic character amongst the European troops.

Causes of the less number of admissions and of mortality.

325. The average strength of the European Army has been raised, during the past year, by the arrival of relieving Regiments before the departure of others. The strength was 16,077 ; deaths 247. Mortality to strength at the rate of fifteen per thousand. These figures may be regarded as satisfactory evidence in favor of the health of the European portion of the Madras Army.

Increase of the average strength of the European Army.
Strength and mortality, and the proportion of strength.

326. The Native troops, with a few exceptions, have also been healthy. Fever prevailed to a considerable extent at the new Cantonment of Mysore, but by the close of the year it had disappeared. Epidemic cholera caused some mortality at Trichinopoly in November and December 1865, and in some of the stations of the Northern Division.

State of health of the Native troops. ·
Considerable prevalence of Fever at Mysore.
Mortality caused by cholera.

327. The average strength of the Native Army was 32,986, the number treated in Hospital 20,441, and the total of deaths 304. The death rate to strength was only nine per 1,000.

Strength, admissions, and deaths in the Native Army.
Rate of mortality.

The table appended gives detailed information regarding the extent and effect of sickness among the troops on the Madras Establishment.

HEALTH.

DIVISIONS.	EUROPEANS.							NATIVES.						
	Average strength.	Treated.	Died.	Average daily sick.	Per-centage of — Treated to strength.	Deaths to strength.	Deaths to treated.	Average strength.	Treated.	Died.	Average daily sick.	Per-centage of — Treated to strength.	Deaths to strength.	Deaths to treated.
Presidency..	2,196	2,330	48	214	147·08	2·1	1·4	4,366	1,936	39	106	44·3	0·8	2·01
Southern..	1,125	1,263	19	67	112·1	1·6	1·5	2,978	1,037	32	37	34·8	1·07	3·08
Mysore	4,489	3,692	39	213	80·8	0·8	1·07	7,177	4,555	64	190	63·4	0·8	1·4
Ceded Districts	1,780	1,733	22	197	97·3	1·2	1·2	2,642	1,655	12	84	62·6	0·4	0·7
Hyderabad Subsidiary Force. ..	3,951	3,840	61	259	97·1	1·5	1·5	6,596	2,115	36	196	32·06	0·5	1·7
Nagpore Force ...	1,866	2,384	24	84	174·5	1·7	1·006	3,718	4,948	42	141	132·9	1·1	0·6
Northern ...	35	2	...	...	5·7	...	...	3,796	2,558	61	78	66·3	1·6	2·4
Pegu (for eight months) ..	1,135	1,870	34	68	164·7	2·9	1·8	1,711	1,662	18	73	97·1	1·05	1·08
Total ...	16,077	17,949	247	1082	111·6	1·5	1·3	32,986	20,441	304	835	61·9	0·9	1·4

Decrease in the number treated in Lock Hospitals. Decrease of venereal diseases at some stations occupied by European Troops. Effect of Lock Hospital in checking venereal affections.

328. The number of females treated in these institutions has somewhat diminished in the past year; but as there has been a marked decrease in the proportion of venereal diseases, at the larger stations occupied by European troops, the smaller number is probably to be accounted for by supposing that the Lock Hospitals have been to some extent, effectual in reducing the virulence and prevalence of these disorders in Military cantonments.

Introduction of the provisions of the health of Cantonment's Act.

329. The provisions of the health of Cantonment's Act of 1864, for the registration and supervision of the class of prostitutes inhabiting Military bazaars, have not yet come into operation.

Table shewing the number of persons who were treated, and died in Lock Hospitals, during the past official year 1865-66.

	Bangalore.		Bellary.		Cannanore.		Kamptee.		St. Thomas' Mount.		Secunderabad.		Trichinopoly.		Vizagapatam.		Wellington.		Total.		Per-centage of deaths to treated.
	Treated.	Died.	Treated.	Died.	Treated.	Died.	Treated.	Died.	Treated.	Died	Treated.	Died.	Treated.	Died.	Treated.	Died.	Treated.	Died.	Treated.	Died.	
1865-66.	385	4	192	3	31	3	250	...	70	...	463	...	112	...	88	...	50	...	1,641	10	0·6

Wellington converted into a convalescent Depôt.

330. On the vacation of the Barracks at Wellington (on the Neilgherries), by the transfer of H. M.'s 105th Regiment from that station to the Bengal Presidency, those buildings were appropriated for

88

use as a general convalescent depôt for the Army, and adapted to accommodate 500 men.

331. Buildings are now in progress at Madras, Bangalore, and Secunderabad, in which the machinery recently received from England will be set up, and the intended bakeries established. *Government Bakeries.*

332. In June 1865, Government sanctioned the adoption of a suggestion from the Inspector General of Ordnance, for making the Gun Carriage Manufactory at Madras available for the instruction of the pupils of the Military Male Orphan Asylum, and other similar Educational establishments, in trades and the use of machinery, the number under instruction being limited, experimentally, to twenty. The measure is regarded as one which will eventually effect much public good at very slight, if at any, extra expense. *Pupils of Orphan Schools instructed in trades.*

333. A General Order by the Commander-in-Chief in India, (dated 17th April 1865,) laying down rules for the award of prizes for work done in European Regimental workshops, has been made applicable to this Presidency. *Prizes for work done in Regimental Workshops.*

L   89

SECTION X.—EDUCATIONAL.

Number of Schools and Pupils.

334. The number of Colleges and Schools connected with the Department of Public Instruction on the 30th April 1866 was 1,261, with an attendance of 45,056 pupils, exhibiting an increase of 278 schools and 5,936 pupils, as compared with the returns of the previous year. This numerical increase belongs entirely to private schools. The number of Government Institutions was less by one than the number in operation on the 30th April 1865. The chief increase was in the Districts of Coimbatore and Tinnevelly, forming part of the fifth Educational Division. In the latter district, the numbers rose from 173 aided schools, with 6,171 pupils, and sixty-six unaided schools, with 1,422 pupils, at the close of 1864-65, to 276 aided schools, with 7,863 pupils, and thirty-eight unaided schools, with an attendance of 578 pupils. The large increase in the number of schools in this district qualified to receive aid from Government is very satisfactory.

Classification of Schools.

335. The following is a classification of the schools with reference to the Agency by which they are managed :—

	No. of Schools.	No. of Pupils.
Government Schools	109	9,434
Schools supported by a rate ...	79	1,951
Aided Schools...	896	27,351
Schools under simple inspection ...	377	6,320

or, with reference to the standard of instruction imparted in them—

	No. of Schools.	No. of Pupils.
First Class Schools	28	6,651
Middle Class do.	237	15,821
Lower Class do.	842	16,909
Girls' do.	139	3,816
Normal do.	11	1,428
Schools and Colleges for Special or professional instruction ...	4	431

Of the 45,056 pupils—

410	were	Europeans.
3,031	,,	East Indians.
7,617	,,	Native Christians.
32,412	,,	Hindus.
1,576	,,	Mahomedans.

Of the entire number—

4,111	were	girls, of whom
131	„	Europeans.
1,011	„	East Indians.
2,149	„	Native Christians.
815	„	Hindus.
5	„	Mahomedans.

336. The number of Inspecting Officers employed at the close of the year was twenty-nine, viz. :— Inspecting Officers.

     5 Inspectors of Schools.
   15 Deputy Inspectors of Schools.
     8 Inspecting School Masters.
     1 Superintendent of Hill Schools.

337. The aggregate expenditure was Rupees 7,16,384-11-11, distributed as follows :— Expenditure.

Direction	Rupees	32,846 4 7
Inspection	„	91,106 10 4
Instruction, including all Educational expenditure not coming under "Direction" or "Inspection"	„	5,92,431 13 0

Of the last mentioned item, Rupees 4,96,717-2-10 were disbursed from the public treasury, and Rupees 95,714-10-2 from local funds.

The expenditure may be further classified as follows :—

		RS.	A.	P.
	Direction	32,846	4	7
	Inspection	91,106	10	4
	Government Colleges and Schools ...	3,34,100	0	10
Expenditure met from Imperial Revenue.	Grants-in-aid of the current expenses of Private Schools charged to Imperial Revenue	1,16,876	4	8
	Grant to the Madras School Book Society	2,000	0	0
	Public Instruction Press... ...	2,550	15	1
	Preparation and purchase of School Books	20,724	3	9
	Central Book Depôt	4,548	0	0
	University of Madras ...	15,917	10	6
Expenditure met from Educational Building Fund.	Building Grants to Government Schools	51,064	1	7
	Do. to Private Schools ...	4,725	0	1
School Fee Fund.	Charges in Government Institutions borne by School fees... ...	32,970	12	0
Donations, &c.	Charges in Government Institutions borne by Donations and Subscriptions.	6,954	12	6
		*7,16,384	11	11

* These figures do not include the expenditure, amounting to Rupees 3,06,433-15-8, incurred from other sources than the Government grants, by the Managers of Private Schools under Government inspection.

EXPENDI-
TURE.

It will be seen from the above that the Imperial expenditure amounted to Rupees 6,20,670-1-9. From the above the following items, viz.:—

	RS.	A.	P.
University Fees paid to the credit of Government	5,425	0	0
School Fees do. do. ...	5,423	11	1
Proceeds of the sale of Books	29,372	9	3
	40,221	4	4

have to be deducted, which reduces the net expenditure from the public treasury to Rupees 5,80,448-13-5. If to this sum be added Rupees 3,06,433-15-8, the expenditure incurred from other sources than the Government grants by the Managers of Private Schools under inspection, the aggregate net expenditure incurred in this Presidency on account of schools connected with Government, and for other educa-. tional objects in which the Government took a part, may be put down at Rupees 8,86,832-13-1 or £88,688-5-9.

University Ex-
amination.

338. The following is an abstract statement of the numerical results of the several examinations held by the University :—

	No. of Candidates examined.	No. of Passed Candidates.		Total passed.
		From Government Institutions.	From Private Institutions.	
Matriculation Examination	555	120	109	229
First Examination in Arts ...	214	53	23	76
Bachelor of Arts Examination	8	6	0	6
Bachelor of Laws Examination	2	2	0	2

Owing, apparently, to a change which was made in the time at which the Matriculation and First Arts Examination were held, there was a slight falling off in the number of candidates for Matriculation, as compared with the previous year. The number of passed candidates at this examination was, however, slightly in excess of the corresponding number for 1864-65, and the proportion of those who were educated at Private Schools was considerably higher. In 1864-65, the number of Private Schools which sent up successful candidates to the Matriculation Examination was nineteen. In 1865-66, the number was twenty-nine. The increase in the number of students who passed the First Arts Examination is satisfactory. This examination has only been in operation for the last three years. In 1863-64, the number of passed candidates was twenty-three. In 1864-65, fifty, and in 1865-66, seventy-six.

The Matriculation Examination and the First Examination in Arts are at present, and it is probable will continue, for some time to come, to be, the two examinations which in this Presidency exercise the greatest influence over education. As yet, the Presidency College is the only Institution which annually sends up successful candidates for the Degree of Bachelor of Arts. On the last occasion, only eight candidates were examined for the Degree, of whom six passed, against twenty-nine candidates and ten graduates for the previous year. The number of candidates for the B. A. Degree in 1864-65 was, however, exceptionally high, owing to that year being the last in which a matriculated student could go up for the Degree without having passed the First Examination in Arts.

The names of the Institutions which sent up successful candidates to the several Examinations in Arts held during the year under review, are given in the following tables :—

MATRICULATION EXAMINATION.
Government Institutions.

	Number in both classes.
Presidency College	28
Provincial School, Combaconum	32
Do. Calicut	5
Do. Bellary	10 .
Zillah School, Rajahmundry ..., ...	1
Do, Cuddalore	2
Do. Chittoor	6
Do. Salem	6
Do. Madura	3
Normal School, Madras	12
Do. Vizagapatam	4
Do. Vellore	1
Do. Trichinopoly	2
Do. Cannanore	1
Madrissa-i-azam	4
Anglo-Vernacular School, Ellore	1 .
Normal Class, Nursapur	1
Anglo-Vernacular School, Tripatore	1
	120

EXAMINA- TIONS.	*Private Institutions.*	Number in both classes.
	Church Mission School, Masulipatam	4
	Hindu School, Masulipatam	4
	Do. Vizagapatam	3
	Church Mission School, Ellore	1
	Free Church Mission School, Nellore	2
	Do. Institution, Madras	9
	London Mission Institution, Madras	3
	Doveton College	11
	Patcheappah's Central Institution	8
	Bishop Corrie's Grammar School	3
	Mission Seminary, Sullivan's Gardens	1
	St. Mary's Seminary, Madras	1
	Wesleyan Mission Institution, Royapettah	7
	Harris School, Madras	1
	Anglo-Vernacular School, Sydapett	2
	High School, Bangalore	7
	Patcheappah's School, Chedumbaram	1
	St. Joseph's College, Negapatam	1
	Vediarpuram Seminary	2
	Gospel Society's High School, Tanjore	7
	Gospel Society's School, Trichinopoly	4
	Ootacamund Grammar School	4
	Sawyerpuram Seminary	1
	Nagercoil Seminary	1
	Church Mission Society's Native English School, Palamcottah	1
	H. H. the Rajah's High School, Trevandrum	1
	Church Mission Society's College, Cottyam	6
	Chudderghat Protestant School	2
	Battercotta School, Jaffna	1
	Private Tuition	10
		109

FIRST ARTS EXAMINATION. Government Institutions.	Number in both classes.	EXAMINA-TIONS.

FIRST ARTS EXAMINATION.
Government Institutions.

	Number in both classes.
Presidency College	29
Provincial School, Combaconum	8
Do. Bellary	4
Do. Calicut	2
Zillah School, Madura	1
Do. Chittoor	1
Normal School, Madras	7
Do. Vizagapatam	1
	53

Private Institutions.

Church Mission Society's School, Masulipatam	4
Free Church Mission Institution, Madras	1
Wesleyan Mission Institution, Royapettah	1
Doveton College	1
Mission Seminary, Sullivan's Gardens	1
Ootacamund Grammar School, ...	4
Gospel Society's High School, Tanjore	1
H. H. the Rajah's High School, Trevandrum	1
King William's College, Isle of Man	1
Private Tuition	8
	23

BACHELOR OF ARTS EXAMINATION.
Government Institution.

Presidency College	6

The following table shews the several classes of the community to which the Candidates belonged :—

CLASSES OF THE COMMUNITY.	MATRICULATION EXAMINATION.		FIRST ARTS EXAMINATION.		BACHELOR OF ARTS EXAMINATION.	
	Examined.	Passed.	Examined.	Passed.	Examined.	Passed.
Brahmins	257	124	134	46	7	5
Other Hindus	161	44	45	13	...	...
East Indians	41	19	7	3	...	...
Europeans	26	14	8	6	...	...
Mahomedans	17	8	4	...	...	...
Native Christians ...	53	20	16	8	1	1

Presidency College. 239. The annual Report on the Presidency College is favorable. The most satisfactory feature in the working of this Institution is the steady increase which has taken place of late years in the number of students attending the Senior Department, which has risen gradually from forty-seven in 1862-63, to eighty-one in 1865-66. It should also be mentioned that the College is now largely resorted to by youths from the Provinces. Of the eighty-one students forming the Senior Department, fifty-one have come from Districts other than Madras; Of these, the District of Tanjore alone contributed sixteen, and •Malabar eight, students. In the Junior Department 126, out of 285 students, have come from the Provinces. Since the close of the year, the Secretary of State has sanctioned the appointment of a Professor of Sanscrit to the College. The new building has been commenced.

Medical College. 240. At the commencement of the Session, the Senior Department contained only eight students, of whom only two had completed the prescribed course at its close, and were awarded the Diploma of the College. Eight students, forming the Senior class of the second Department, were found qualified for the grade of Assistant Apothecary, and twenty-two pupils of the Junior Department were passed as Hospital Assistants. The conduct of the students generally is reported to have been good, and their progress in their studies appears to have been very much on a par with that which has characterized the working of the College of late years. The changes in the several curricula of study, which were ordered in the Proceedings of Government of the 29th March 1865, have been carried into effect, as far as circumstances would admit. Some time, however, must still elapse before the rule, that candidates for the grade of Assistant Apothecary and of Hospital Assistant shall have two years' preliminary training in a Hospital, previous to their admission into the College, can have any effect on the preliminary attainments of students entering the College. The present Report furnishes additional evidence that such a preliminary training is greatly needed, to enable the students in the second and junior Departments to follow with intelligence and ease the lectures of the Professors ; and in regard to the Senior Department, the Professor o Surgery describes two of the students as being " the only youths in th class that are sufficiently acquainted with English to derive the fu benefit from attending lectures." Certain rules, however, have latel been sanctioned with the view of improving the position of, and exac ing higher preliminary attainments from, the holders of scholarships this department of the College, which, it is to be hoped, will remove the defect above adverted to.

96

341. The number of students in the Civil Engineering College, at Civil Engineering College. the close of the year, was ninety-seven, of whom

    5 belonged to the 1st Department.
   57 do. to the 2nd do.
   35 do. to the Special Surveying, Drawing and Estimating classes.

Three students of the first Department obtained certificates as Assistant Engineer at the close of the Session, and eleven of the second Department passed as Taluk Overseers, while five others passed the minor test required for the Bengal Public Works Department. The result of the annual examination was, on the whole, satisfactory, and the conduct of the students was generally good. The small number of students who resort to the first Department of this Institution is attributed to the great difficulty which the members of that Department at present experience in obtaining employment at all commensurate with the time, labor, and expense, which their professional education entails.

342. The report on the Government Normal School at Madras Madras Normal Schools. is again unfavorable. The Director of Public Instruction states that the arrangements have been defective, and the management faulty; that in the general examination for Certificates, the students shewed to disadvantage when tested in method and teaching power, and proved, in many instances, in these subjects, to be inferior to the untrained candidates. The Government await the receipt of a detailed report, which the Director has been instructed to furnish, before determining what steps it will be necessary to take with the view of restoring this important Institution to the condition of efficiency which it maintained under the management of its first Principal.

343. The Normal Schools at Vizagapatam, Trichinopoly, Vellore, Normal Schools in the Mofussil. and Cannanore, are all doing fairly. That at Trichinopoly is in a very satisfactory condition. Owing, to the difficulty which is experienced in inducing Canarese Candidates for training, to resort to the Normal School at Cannanore, which is situated in the District of Malabar, it is proposed to form a Normal Class in connexion with the Provincial School which is about to be established at Mangalore, in the District of Canara. The reports on the Training Institutions supported by the Church Missionary Society at Palamcottah, by the Society for the Propagation of the Gospel in Foreign Parts at Sawyerpuram and at Tanjore, and by the Christian Vernacular Education Society at Madura, are all, more or less, favorable.

M   97

Teachers' certificate Examination.

344. At the annual examination for Teachers' Certificates, 283 male candidates, and eighteen female candidates obtained Certificates of qualification.

School of Arts.

345. The School of Industrial Arts was carried on as usual during the year. The work turned out consisted of cuts in wood and metal, drawings, engravings, designs, sketches, photographs, ornamental vases, bricks, tiles, water-pipes, plaster casts, models (comprising those of a bridge, a house, a sawing machine, and water wheels), ploughs, harrows, scythes, and other agricultural implements. Remunerative employment was found for some of the pupils. Several students of the Civil Engineering College received practical instruction in the manufacture of bricks, tiles, &c., and assistance was afforded to other Schools of Art. The value of the work executed during the year amounted to Rupees 7,381-7-4.

Provincial Schools.

346. The three Government Provincial Schools are all doing well.

Name of School.	Number of Pupils.
Combaconum.	851
Bellary...	246
Calicut	845

The attendance, at the close of the year, is noted in the margin. Judged of by the results of the University examinations, the Combaconum School is considerably in advance of those at Bellary and Calicut. Thirty-two of its students passed at the last Matriculation Examination, and eight at the First Arts Examination. Sanction has recently been granted for raising the position of this School to that of a Provincial College, but owing to the temporary withdrawal of the Head Master to act as Principal of the Presidency College, this change cannot be carried out immediately. A fourth Provincial School will shortly be opened at Mangalore in South Canara, the inhabitants of which district have raised the munificent sum of Rupees 67,000, as an endowment for the projected school.

Zillah Schools.

347. Of the Zillah Schools, that at Chittoor is the most advanced,

Name of School.	Number of Pupils.
Chittoor	332
Salem	274
Rajahmundry	191
Berhampore	111
Cuddapah	173
Kurnool	116
Cuddalore	218
Madura	262
Madrissa-i-Azam ...	297

in respect both of the number and attainments of the pupils. This school sent up six successful candidates to the last Matriculation Examination, and one to the First Arts Examination. The Schools at Madura, Salem, and Rajahmundry have improved. Those at Cuddalore and Berhampore are not in a satisfactory condition. The Schools at Kurnool and Cuddapah appear to be doing fairly. The report on the Madrissa-i-Azam, a School in Madras for the instruction of

Mahomedans, which is on a level with the Zillah Schools in the Provinces, is not altogether favorable.

348. The following statement shews the number of middle class Anglo-Vernacular Schools supported by Government in the several districts, under the designation either of Anglo-Vernacular or Taluk Schools, and the attendance in each :—

	Number of Schools.	Number of Pupils.
Ganjam	6	216
Vizagapatam	6	300
Godavery	2	97
Kistna	1	28
Bellary	3	179
Madras District ...	6	427
South Arcot	9	435
North Arcot	5	516
Salem	5	376
Trichinopoly	1	100
Tanjore	6	572
Coimbatore	6	392
Madura	2	192
Malabar	3	159
South Canara... ...	4	176
	65	4,165

There has been no increase in the number of Government Schools of this class. Indeed, the number of schools supported by Government has diminished by one during the year under review, owing to the Taluk School at Mulki, in South Canara, having been converted into a Rate School. This result is in accordance with the policy which has for some time past been adopted by the Madras Government of developing the grant-in-aid system. The reports on the Anglo-Vernacular Schools at Chicacole in the Ganjam District, at Berhampore in the District of Vizagapatam, at Mayaveram in Tanjore, at Tripatur in Salem, and on the Taluk Schools in Vizagapatam, Salem, Coimbatore, Malabar, and Canara, are, for the most part, favorable.

349. The only schools of the lower class which are now supported directly by Government, are the Hill Schools in Ganjam, and the School for Yanadis at Sriharicotta, near Madras. The former are sixteen in number, and, at the close of the year, numbered 487 pupils, or 80

less than is shewn in the returns for the previous year. Four of the schools are favorably reported on. The condition of the others was more or less unsatisfactory. Hitherto, owing to the unhealthiness of the Hill tracts, there has been great difficulty in providing adequate supervision for these schools. Their immediate supervision is entrusted to an officer, under the designation of Superintendent of Hill Schools, at Rupees 30 per mensem, but both the Deputy Inspector of Schools for the District, and the Divisional Inspector are expected to inspect them once a year. During the year under review, the Schools were not visited by the Inspector, in consequence of his having been obliged to leave his division, on urgent private affairs, at the time when the schools should have been inspected ; and, in the course of the year, two officers who filled the situation of Superintendent of Hill Schools, died. The unsatisfactory condition of the majority of the schools is doubtless attributable, partly to these circumstances, and partly to the insurrections of the Khonds, which took place in November and December last, and which were not entirely suppressed until February. It should, however, be mentioned, that eight of the masters passed for Certificates at the last Certificate Examination, and as, under recent orders, the Assistant Agent and the Assistant Superintendent of Police are to reside on the Hill Tracts for a considerable part of each year, it may be hoped that the schools will, in future, have the advantage of more effective supervision than has hitherto been possible. The schools for the Yanadis is reported to have advanced, both in ordinary school intruction, and in basket making, the industrial work pursued by the pupils.

Private Schools.   350. It has already been stated that there was a considerable increase in the number of private schools under inspection during the year under review. The number of private schools connected with the Department, which at the commencement of the year was 873, had risen at its close to 1,152. The increase was chiefly in schools of the middle and lower classes, the first of which rose from 210 to 237, and the second from 658 to 842. The number of schools in the receipt of grants rose from 501 to 896. This is exclusive of the Rate Schools, seventy-nine in number, most of which receive grants. The number of schools under simple inspection was 297 in 1864-65, and 377 in 1865-66.

As regards the standard of instruction, the results of the University examinations and the reports of the Inspectors shew that there is a gradual, but steady, improvement. Among the Institutions ranked in the first class, the Doveton College, and the Central Institution of the Free Church Mission at the Presidency ; and in the Provinces, the Church Mission School at Masulipatam, the Tanjore High School, supported by the Gospel Society, and the Hindu School, at Vizagapatam, are all favorably reported on. The Church Mission School at Masulipatam, which for many years has been the most advanced school in the Northern Circars, has lately suffered a very severe loss in the death of the Rev. Mr. Noble, whose devoted exertions in the cause of Native education will long be remembered in this Presidency.

351. The establishment of schools under the provisions of the Madras Education Act. Madras Education Act has not made much progress during the year under review. According to the Returns appended to the last Report, the number of schools supported by a rate at the close of the official year 1864-65 was seventy-five, including seventy-two schools of this class in the Godavery District. At the end of 1865-66, that number had only risen to seventy-nine. Of the four new Rate Schools, one is in South Canara, and three in Malabar; the first mentioned being the Taluk School of Mulki, which, at the request of the inhabitants has been converted from a Government School into a Rate School. The working of the Act in the Godavery District has not been satisfactory. The Inspector states that the machinery of the Act is "ill-adapted to the purpose to which it has been applied in the Godavery District," viz., the maintenance of elementary schools in villages, the population of which is chiefly agricultural. " The Commissioners," Mr. Bowers observes, " are ignorant ryots, who care nothing for the schools, and neglect their " duties." " The only way," he writes, " in which they can be prevented " from causing the abolition of the schools by simple inaction, is to place " them, in their capacity of school Commissioners, as they are in their " capacity of Village Curnums, under the authority of the Sub-Collector, " but in that case the Act becomes a dead letter and a superfluity. " This would be virtually a return to the ante-Act state of things, and " would be an admission that these schools could never have been " voluntarily maintained. Up to a very recent date, many of the Mas- " ters had received no salaries for months." From the returns appended to the Director's report, it appears that, in two of the Taluks in which these schools are in operation, the amount of the collections under the Act was somewhat less than the Government grant.

The difficulty of obtaining competent School Commissioners for the management of the Rate Schools is also adverted to by the Deputy Inspector of Schools in Malabar and Canara, in which Districts, however, the Act appears likely to work well. In the latter District, five Middle Class Schools have been established, and the preliminary measures for the establishment of five more, under the provisions of the Act, had been carried out before the close of the year. One of the latter, an Anglo-Vernacular School at Palghat, has been opened since the close of the year, with an attendance of 400 pupils. The Deputy Inspector reports that for this school a building, capable of accommodating 500 boys, is to be provided, at an estimated cost of Rupees 16,000, and the school is to be eventually placed under a gradu-ate of an English University. He adds that the introduction of the Act would succeed as well in Canara, as in Malabar, were trained teachers available. In Coimbatore, the inhabitants of fifty-four villages had placed themselves under the Act, and in twenty-four of them Com-missioners had been appointed; but in none had any schools been opened before the close of the year. In only two had the Commissioners com-menced to levy taxes, and even in these they had not ventured to employ any coercive processes, but had collected only from those who paid, if not willingly, at least without legal pressure. From what is stated by the Inspector, it is to be feared that, in this District, the applications for the introduction of the Act can hardly have been voluntary in the true sense of the term. The Director has been instructed to proceed to the District, and, in concert with the Collector and the Educational Inspector of the Division, ascertain and report in what cases it is desir-able to cancel the application of the Act to particular villages, either in consequence of its not being really in accordance with the wishes of the inhabitants, or being inexpedient for other reasons. The Director has been requested to institute a similar inquiry in the Godavery District, and has been informed the Government do not wish the Act to be applied to any town or village, its application to which is not clearly in accordance with the wishes of a considerable majority of the inhabitants, or where competent School Commissioners are not available.

Grant-in-aid Rules.
352. The working of the grant-in-aid rules issued in January 1865, may be regarded as tolerably satisfactory. The number of aided schools rose during the year under review from 502, with an atten-dance of 22,351 pupils, to 876, with an attendance of 27,351 pupils, and the amount disbursed in grants in aid of the current expenses of the schools (chiefly in aid of the salaries of the Teachers) from Rupees 89,802, to Rupees 1,16,876-4-8. These figures, however, include the indigenous Village Schools in the Districts of Vizagapatam, Nellore, North Arcot, Coimbatore, and Madura, numbering 498, with an atten-

dance of 8,493 pupils, which received grants, amounting to Rupees 3,777-12-0, on the 'payment for results' system,' which, though similar in principle, is not identical in detail with the system provided for in Rule IV of the grant-in-aid rules. Since the close of the year, sanction has been granted for the extension of this system to every District in the Presidency, and the Director of Public Instruction has been requested so to re-cast the Schedules appended to the grant-in-aid rules, as to make them applicable to indigenous schools.

It would appear from the reports from some of the leading Managers of schools, that the late revision of the grant in-aid rules has resulted in effecting a considerable improvement in many of the existing schools, but that it has not contributed as much as might have been expected to the establishment of additional schools. This result is, doubtless, to be traced to the comparative inefficiency or inadequacy of the agency previously employed, and which induced the Managers of schools to apply such aid as they could obtain from the State to strengthening the establishments of schools already in operation, in preference to organizing new schools. But there is nothing in the rules, as they now stand, which can be said to impose undue checks on the extension of education, or to render the grant-in-aid system less applicable to elementary schools than to schools of a more advanced grade. The latter is a point on which considerable misconception appears to exist. The only Inspectors who, in the reports for the year under review have expressed any opinions on the success or otherwise of the grant-in-aid system, as now administered, are Mr. Bowers and Mr. Marden. The former, contrasting its working with that of the Madras Education Act, remarks that, " as now " administered, in connection with Educational Certificates," the grant-in-aid system has " the advantage of greater simplicity, and is proving " the more effectual instrument of popular education, chiefly through " the medium of Middle-Class Schools." Mr. Bowers states that "Teach- " ers who have obtained Certificates are fast re-placing those who " have not," and he observes that, " although in individual instances it " will sometimes be found that an uncertificated Teacher is much superior " to certificated teachers of the same grade, in the majority of cases " the benefit of the rule which exacts some certificate of qualifications " will be apparent." Mr. Marden, while admitting that the present rules have " somewhat stimulated education," does not look " for any rapid extension of education under the present arrangements," and advocates the abolition of that part of the present system which makes

103

the grants dependent on the Certificates held by the Teachers, and the substitution for it of a system of payment for results, under rules better adapted to the requirements of elementary Native School, than those now in force. The Government see nothing in the reports before them that would justify so radical an alteration of the existing rules. In the discussions which took place regarding the grant-in-aid system in 1864, and in which several of the leading educational authorities in this Presidency took a part, there was a considerable preponderance of opinion in favor of the maintenance of the Certificate system, and against the feasibility of carrying out effectively, and on an extensive scale, the system of payment for results. The Government, on full consideration, determined not to abandon the Certificate system, but, at the same time, embodied in the rules a provision which it was hoped would afford to such Managers of schools as might prefer the ' payment for results' system,' the means of obtaining aid in that form. It has lately been brought to the notice of Government that the standards of examination in arithmetic prescribed for Native Schools seeking aid under the latter system are too high, and that the scale of grants offered is too low. The first objection has been met by a reduction of the standard, and the Director of Public Instruction has been directed further to revise the Schedules, in such manner as he may deem best calculated to promote the successful working of the system. It remains to be seen which of the two systems of grant-in-aid will be found the more effective, viz., first, that of making monthly payments in aid of the salaries of Teachers who have afforded evidence of their qualifications, or, second, that of making grants on the results of periodical examinations of the pupils ; but, in the meantime, it is the desire and intention of the Governor in Council that each of these two systems shall have a full and fair trial, and he trusts that, under their operation, considerable progress will be made in the extension, as well as in the improvement, of Education in this Presidency, in the course of the next few years. Much, of course, must depend on the exertions of the leading Educational Societies, and of private persons interested in the cause, but much may be effected by the judicious efforts of the Inspectors of Schools, whose duties should embrace, not only the inspection of those schools which are placed under Government inspection, but the promotion generally of all such measures as have for their object the improvement and extension of education in the Districts under their charge.

104

353. During the year 1865-66, four Examinations were held, namely, a Special Test Examination in October 1865, a General Test Examination in February 1866, and two modified Special Test Examinations, one in October 1865, the other in February 1866.

Uncovenanted
Civil Service Ex-
amination Com-
mission.
Examination held
during the year.

354. The Special Test has been considerably modified in accordance with the recommendation of the Commissioner, the Tests being arranged with reference to the different subjects in which the Examination is held, and not with regard to the offices for which candidates propose to qualify.

Special Test.

For the Special Test, 1,178 candidates were registered: of the 1,052 who presented themselves for examination, 511 were successful. There was a considerable increase in the number of candidates, and in the proportion of successful to unsuccessful examinees, as compared with those in the previous year. The number of those who qualified for the higher grades was unusually large, and it is satisfactory to find that the number of well-educated and duly qualified candidates for public employment is rapidly increasing.

355. There was a slight decrease in the number of candidates presenting themselves at the General Test Examination, but there was a marked improvement in the number of successful, compared with that of unsuccessful, examinees.

General Test.

356. The modification of the Special Test for Tahsildars, Deputy Tahsildars, Sub-Magistrates, and Taluk Sheristadars, sanctioned by Government in April 1865, by which any unpassed officer, who, on the 1st January 1865, may have served ten years in the grades of the Revenue Department entitled to pension, and who may be selected by a Collector in certain cases, is permitted to qualify by passing an appropriate examination in the Vernacular in such portions of the Penal and Procedure Codes, and in Taluk and Village Accounts, as it is absolutely necessary that he should be acquainted with, was found to be necessary both in fairness to public servants of long standing, whose only disqualification was that of not having passed an examination, and in order that public business might not come to a stand-still. These modifications are temporary and provisional, to terminate on the 1st July 1867.

Modified Special
Test.

The greatest care and precaution has been taken to prevent the possibility of the question papers being dishonestly procured before the Examinations: the General Test Examination, held at Salem in

N   105

1865, was quashed by order of Government in consequence of packets having been opened, and papers obtained beforehand by some of the candidates: the precautions taken, with regard to the papers set in February 1866, were perfectly successful: and it may be presumed that such malpractices will be rendered impossible for the future.

Receipts and Expenditure.

357. From the statement of receipts and expenditure, it appears that there is a net balance of Rupees 1,360 in favor of Government.

SECTION XI.—ECCLESIASTICAL.

358.   There were 157 Clergymen in the Diocese at the close of the Number of Clergymen in the Diocese. year under report, shewing a diminution of five on the number in the preceding year.   Of these, thirty-eight were Chaplains on the Madras Establishment, and fourteen received stipends from Government for ministering to congregations not supplied with Chaplains.   The European and Eurasian Missionaries numbered fifty-four, and the Native Clergymen forty-five.   Six Clergymen were engaged in scholastic duties.

Six vacancies occurred during the year among the Chaplains, and were filled up by an equal number of new appointments.

359.   The Bishop held three Ordinations at the following Stations, Ordinations. and ordained thirteen Priests, and seven Deacons.

Stations.	PRIESTS.		DEACONS.		Date.
	European.	Native.	European.	Native.	
Kotteyam	2	1	...	1	26th November 1866.
Palamcottah ...	...	3	...	6	7th January 1866.
Madras...	3	4	...	...	25th March 1866.
Total...	5	8	...	7	

360.   The number of persons confirmed during the past year Confirmations. was—

Of Males	2,704
„ Females ...	2,315
	5,019

of whom 4,463 were Native Christians.

361.   Two Churches were consecrated during the year.   Christ Consecrations. Church at Kurnool, and St. Bartholomew's at Mysore, the latter of which the residents at that place have lately given over to the Government. An addition made to the burial ground at Tanjore was also consecrated.

362.   The Bishop, in pursuance of his visitation of the Diocese, Visitation Tour. proceeded from Madras towards the end of June to Kurnool, Bellary, Hurryhur, Shimoga, and Bangalore.

363.   Later in the year he visited Cannanore, Calicut, Cochin, Quilon, Trevandrum, Palamcottah ; all the principal Mission Stations in Cochin, Travancore, and Tinnevelly, and returned by Madura and Trichinopoly to Madras, early in February.

Church Build-
ings.

364.   Efforts are being successfully made to increase the Church accommodation at Ootacamund, by raising funds for the erection of a new Church, the Government having promised a conditional grant-in-aid.

A fund has been raised for re-building the Church at Cuddapah.

Section XII.—MISCELLANEOUS.

Medical.

365. The public health in the Madras Presidency has not been Public health. satisfactory during the past year.

366. Epidemic cholera prevailed to a great extent on the Mala- *Prevalence of cholera and ma- larious fevers.* bar coast during June, July, and August 1865. Cholera and malarious fevers have been unusually frequent on the table lands of Mysore ; and the long continued drought since the termination of the north- east monsoon, in December, seems, in many places, to have caused such *Scarcity and dearness of arti- cles. Their ef- fects on the poorer classes.* a scarcity of grain, that all the evil effects of famine, as regards the poorer classes, may be anticipated. At the close of the official year famine and cholera prevailed to a considerable extent in the Northern Sircars, and the high cost of the necessaries of life in many other parts of the country told unfavorably upon the public health.

367. Notwithstanding the prevalence of epidemic disease in *Healthy state of the town of Madras.* many districts of the Presidency, the population of the town of Madras remained healthy up to the close of the official year. Cholera and small-pox were much less frequent than usual.

368. These institutions continue to afford material benefit to *Working of the Civil Dis- pensaries.* the sick of the several districts in which they are placed. There has been a slight increase in the number of sick treated over the former year.

1864-65...	...	...	...	...	...	275,643
1865-66...	...	...	...	...	...	278,107

Increase in the latter year...   2,464

369. The funded capital which stood at Rupees 2,34,780-12-4 on *Increase of funded capital.* the 31st December 1864, had increased to 3,00,306.4-6 at the end of 1865.

370. The Raneepett Dispensary in North Arcot, which had been *Re-opening of the Raneepett Dispensary.* closed, was re-opened during the year, and is supported by the surplus funds of an old local charitable endowment.

MEDICAL.   371. This department has been in a transitional state during
Vaccine Department. nearly one-half of the year under report, but nevertheless the results
of the new system are more satisfactory than those obtained under the
former arrangements.

Method of working.   372. The staff of Vaccinators work in a group, leaving large
portions of a circle temporarily unattended, but every village and ham-
let is in turn visited, and the observations are correctly and efficiently
carried out. The number of insertions has been increased from four to
six punctures ; an intercommunication of lymph is constantly kept up
by the different Deputy Superintendents, and an exchange of lymph
has been effected with Calcutta.

The total number of operations, during the period under
review, amounted to 190,989 ; of this number 159,755 were successful,
and 31,234 failed ; the per-centage of successful cases being 83·59.

Efficacy, as febri-fuges, of Chin-chona alkaloids.   373. In accordance with · the suggestions conveyed in the
Secretary of State's despatch, No. 27, under date 30th September 1865,
a Commission, consisting of the officers noted below,* has been
appointed to conduct enquiries with a view to test the efficacy, as febri-
fuges, of the Chinchona alkaloids, other than quinine, and of the
preparations of quinium, &c.

Fourteen Medical officers, holding appointments in localities where
fever is prevalent, have been directed to conduct experiments, and to
submit monthly tables of the result of their investigations.

Mr. J. Dougall, of the Madras Medical Service, has been specially
selected to visit the hilly districts of the Northern Division, where
fever of every variety prevails, and to remain at the different stations
a sufficient length of time to enable him to test the effects of the
alkaloids both relatively and positively.

EMIGRATION.

Emigrants des-patched.   374. The total number of emigrants despatched to British
Colonies, during the year under review, was 5,192, as against 4,773
during the previous year. The number of men was less by nearly 150,
but there was an increase in the number of women and children.

---

* President.

Officiating Principal Inspector General, Medical Department, JAMES SHAW, F.R.C.S.

MEMBERS.

Deputy Inspector General of Hospitals, W. MACKENZIE, C.B.
Deputy Inspector General J. G. INGLIS, C.B.
Surgeon Major J. KENNEDY, M.D.

The following table gives the numbers that have left for all
British Colonies, exclusive of Ceylon, during the past seven years :—

	Men.	Women.	Boys.	Girls.	Infants.	Total.
1859-60...	8,001	3,374	1,165	929	588	14,057
1860-61...	3,966	1,603	399	324	187	6,479
1861-62...	4,120	1,531	499	401	253	6,804
1862-63...	3,082	1,155	401	323	157	5,118
1863-64...	3,109	1,172	408	351	189	5,229
1864-65...	2,923	1,147	313	276	123	4,773
1865-66...	2,779	1,277	506	485	145	5,192

375. There has been no increase in irregularities connected with   Recruiting.
the recruiting of laborers ; generally the operations of the Agencies
have been conducted satisfactorily.

376. The mortality on the passage to the Mauritius, from which   Mortality.
Colony only returns are received, has been trifling. Reports have
been received of eleven vessels despatched with 3,917 emigrants
of all ages. In one vessel only, the " Cashmere," did cholera break out,
carrying off four persons. Four vessels reached without any casualty ;
and the entire number of deaths was only fifteen, being a ratio of 0·35
per cent. on the number embarked, a result, considering the unhealthiness of the past season, which speaks well for the arrangements
made.

377. The only other Colonial Agency that has been in operation   Natal Emigration.
at Madras, is that of Natal, to which place four vessels have been despatched, carrying 1,245 persons. No regular reports of their arrival
have been received.

378. The Depôts have not been so healthy as usual ; this is to be   Depôts.
attributed to the season, and to the fact that very many who presented
themselves for registry were half-starved, and consequently more liable
to disease. The following table shews the number provided for in the
Mauritius Depôt in each month, the number of cases treated, and the
number of deaths. In the Natal Depôt only one death occurred.

EMIGRA-
TION.

Mauritius Depôt.

Months.	No. in Depôt.	No. of		Remarks.
		Cases.	Deaths.	
1865.				
May	266 to 340	36	...	
June	82 to 430	33	...	
July	182 to 539	30	7	Cholera broke out on the 4th and ceased on the 7th. Four died of the disease.
August... ...	188 to 661	33	...	
September ...	44 to 234	30	...	
October... ...	157 to 224	11	4	
November ...	28 to 81	6	1	
December ...	234 to 301	6	5	Cholera appeared on the 11th and ceased on the 15th. Three cases were fatal.
1866.				
January ...	385 to 444	6	4	Two fatal Cholera cases.
February ...	100 to 138	4	1	One do. do.
March	177 to 717	38	2	
April	221 to 323	26	2	

Proportion of women to men.

379. The proportion of women to men, embarked for the Mauritius, was fifty per cent., and to Natal nearly thirty-six per cent.

Returned Emigrants.

380. Only 400 emigrants, including women and children, have returned from the Mauritius during the year, of whom three died on the voyage. None have returned from Natal or the West Indies.

Receipts and disbursements.

381. The collections for fees and licenses at Madras and in the districts amounted to Rupees 9,199-14-2, and the disbursements to Rupees 6,181-6-0.

French Agencies.

382. The French Agencies have continued their operations at Pondicherry, Karikal, and Yanam. It is understood that Madras is to be finally abandoned as an embarking port. The total number of emigrants sent during the year to French Colonies is 2,155, namely, 1,166 from Pondicherry, 672 from Karikal, and 317 from Yanam. Of these, 1,077 went to Reunion, 412 to Guienne, 338 to Martinique, and 328 to Guadaloupe.

The proportion of women to men is as follows :—

To Reunion ... ... 33 per cent.
„ Guienne... ... ... 32 „
„ Martinique ... ... 32 „
„ Guadaloupe ... ... 48 „

The authorities at Pondicherry complain of the impediments thrown in the way of their obtaining emigrants ; these restrictions are simply those imposed on recruiting carried on by this Government.

The returned emigrants from all the French Colonies number 792, of whom 177 were from Guadaloupe, 375 from Martinique, and 240 from Reunion.

The receipts are Rupees 8,174-0-3, and the disbursements Rupees 12,135-8-7.

383. The Medical Inspector of emigrants, during the year 1865, passed 3,582 coolies for the Mauritius, 1,274 for Natal, and forty-nine for Bourbon.

Emigration to the French Colonies, from the port of Madras, ceased in January, since which month shipment of coolies has taken place only to the British Colonies of Mauritius and Natal.

The Officers in medical charge of the depôts, examine emigrants before they are submitted for examination by the Medical Inspector of Emigrants, and it is owing to the care and vigilance which those Officers exercise, that it has been found necessary to reject so few during the past year. The number so rejected has been only seven.

The numbers mentioned in paragraph 377 do not represent the actual numbers embarked. No less than 250 of those passed for Mauritius, had deserted or disappeared before embarkation, leaving only 3,332 as the number actually shipped for that island. 1,274 persons were furnished with pass-tickets for Natal, and 266 remained in the depôt from 1864, making a total of 1,540 ; of these, only 1,347 actually embarked for that Colony.

The schedules of medicines for emigrant ships, in respect of disinfectants, have been improved, and either Burnett's disinfecting fluid or Norton's carbolic acid is substituted for chloride of lime.

On two occasions cholera appeared in the Mauritius Depôt, necessitating the postponement of embarkation not only from that depôt, for some days, but also, on the last visitation, from the Natal Emigration Depôt.

The annual return of disease in the depôts abundantly testify to the necessity of placing the depôts under the charge of fully qualified Surgeons, a necessity foreseen and provided for by Government. During the year, depôts for Emigrants to Ceylon, Assam, and Cachar were opened, and the Medical Inspector was authorized by Government to exercise supervision over all such depôts, on receiving information from the Commissioner of Police of such depôts being opened.

EMIGRA-
TION.

The Cachar and Assam depôts have been closed, but that of Ceylon continues open in Tondiarpet; there are seldom more than thirty or forty emigrants in this latter depôt at a time.

Presidency Municipality.

Receipts,

384. The Receipts of the Presidency Municipal Commissioners during the year 1865, amounted to Rupees 3,75,450-8-4 ; the balance in hand on the 31st December being 2,40,568-12-8 ; this latter sum consisted chiefly of arrears due, investments, and value of office premises. The chief items of income were Assessment, Rupees 2,47,083-3-7 ; Wheel-tax, 52,024-15-10 ; and maintenance of Government roads, 49,794.

Disbursements,

385. The Expenditure was Rupees 3,56,750-9-3, the principal charges being Road-works, Rupees 1,13,879-12-10 ; Scavenging, Rupees 74,406-2-0 ; Salaries and Expenses, Rupees 62,330-3-0. Government Works, Rupees 15,460-6-11 ; and construction, repairs, and improvements of works, Rupees 57,780-5-8. A full statement of the receipts and disbursements will be found in the Appendix. The total length of roads re-formed was 147 miles : the total amount spent on the maintenance of roads was Rupees 1,11,865-10-4 ; the average cost per mile for roads repaired and re-formed was Rupees 760-15-0. 126 Drainage Works were built, re-built, improved or extended. It would be premature to express a decided opinion upon the working of the Madras Municipal Act (No. IX of 1865,) which came into force on the 1st November 1865 ; but the special attention of Government has been directed to remedying certain difficulties which have been found to attend on the collection of the tax on Professions and Callings.

Electric Telegraph.

386. The changes consequent upon the re-organization of the Department, at the commencement of the present calendar year, by which Divisions were substituted for the former Madras Circle, and several new Offices attached to the different Divisions which are no longer conterminous with the Presidential limits, render it impossible to give an account which should be generally intelligible, or which should fairly represent the expenditure, income, and increase of communication, as compared with that of previous years.

The lines in the Presidency have, generally, been maintained in fair order ; interruptions have not been frequent, and when occurring were repaired with as little delay as was practicable.

Observatory.

Proceedings of
Madras Ob-
servatory,

387. Notwithstanding the continued urgent want of European assistance, the proceedings of the Madras Observatory may be pronounced,

upon the whole, more satisfactory than for several past years. The
work accomplished has been, throughout, above the average amount in
quantity, and when submitted to the test of publication, will, it is
hoped, be found equal in quality to any reasonable expectations on
the part of the astronomical public. That great desideratum, however,
publication, remains a matter of impossibility with the present insufficient establishment.

388. The construction of a convenient and suitable room, with a *Buildings and Instruments.*
revolving dome, for the new Equatoreal, has at last been accomplished
by Messrs. Leggett and Broomhall of Madras, in a most creditable
and efficient style. The interior diameter of the dome is sixteen feet.
Its rotation is effected by means of eight six-inch rollers or wheels,
the axles of which are connected by a ring of hard wood, as in the
much larger domes employed by Mr. Lassell of Liverpool, described
in the twelfth volume of the Memoirs of the Royal Astronomical Society.
Notwithstanding the size and weight of the new dome, its motion is
so smooth and perfect, that the pressure of a finger, or the single-handed
force of a child of eight years of age, suffices to start it, while it stops
dead wherever required. Two sliding shutters, easily opened, expose
an observing slit three feet in aperture, and extending over nearly two-
thirds of the dome, or from the horizon to about twenty-five degrees
beyond the zenith. The new Equatoreal, by Messrs Troughton and
Simms of London, has been erected, and worthily sustains the high
reputation of its makers. It is supported by a central iron pillar, on
what is known as the German plan of mounting; and for steadiness,
perfect equilibrium, and convenience in its mechanical details, it is all
that the most fastidious could desire. Owing to the prevalence of bad
weather since its very recent erection, no opportunity has yet occurred
for finally adjusting or critically examining its eight-inch object glass;
but as this was duly tested and approved by the Astronomer Royal at
Greenwich, before the instrument left England, it may be justly expected that it will prove as satisfactory in this important point as it has
already been found in its mechanism. It is liberally equipped with
all the usual appliances in the way of eye-pieces, &c., and is also provided
with an excellent parallel wire micrometer and a double image micrometer of Mr. Airy's construction.

The former Equatoreal, by Messrs. Lerebours and Secretan, is in
fair working order. Other extra-meridional instruments belonging to
the Observatory are, a five-foot telescope, with a zodiacal portable stand
far from steady, and a good universal equatoreal stand, provided with three
different telescopes, viz., two of three feet, and one of five feet focal length,

OBSERVA-   the latter having been made up in Madras by Mr. F, Doderet, Mathe-
TORY.   matical Instrument maker to the Public Works Department, with the
object glass (by Dolland) formerly used in the old, and now discarded,
transit instrument. In the meridional department, the transit circle,
also by Messrs. Troughton and Simms, continued to yield unexception-
able results from June 1862, the commencement of its career, until the
end of March 1866, when symptoms of unsteadiness in the circle clamps
suddenly appeared, which have given much trouble and anxiety during
the last month of the official year. It is now undergoing repair in Mr.
Doderet's hands, and will, it is confidently hoped, soon regain the former
high character for permanence of adjustment and general excellence
which it has so worthily maintained during the past four years. The
old arrangement of shutters, most objectionable and inconvenient,
opening in four sections, and never weather-proof, has been superseded
by a single flap, twenty-three feet in length by two in breadth, counter-
poised, and opening from within by means of ropes and pullies in the
usual manner. The magnetical and meteorological instruments are in
fair working order, but those of the former class, in use since 1841, are
by no means equal to those now constructed and used in European
Observatories. The Anemograph, by Mr. Adie of London, is in satisfactory condition, and stood the test of two tolerably severe gales,
in 1865, without injury or failure.

Astronomical   389. The observations with the transit circle have been made
Observations, Re-
ductions, and Dis- throughout the year by the two Head Native Assistants, as usual, and
coveries.   it may be remarked, with pleasure, that their care and assiduity have
secured results highly creditable to themselves, and of great value to
science. The steady progress of the meridian observations will be
best shewn by the subjoined tabular statement of work done since the
erection of the instrument, in May 1862. The number of observations
taken, stands thus for the successive official years :—

Observations of	Moon.	Planets.	Stars.	Total.
1862-63	54	85	1,723	1,862
1863-64	70	77	2,272	2,419
1864-65	64	119	2,409	2,592
1865-66	55	91	2,599	2,745

We have, therefore, 9,618 complete observations of Right Ascension
and Polar distance, taken in three years and eleven months (1862-63),
awaiting publication, averaging 2,443 per year ; a large per-centage
of which refers to stars in the Southern hemisphere, the positions of
which have not been previously determined at any other Observatory. Reductions of standard stars and all instrumental corrections

are kept rigorously up to date. Those of other objects are but little OBSERVA-
behind being completed up to December 31st, 1863, and very nearly TORY.
so up to October 1865.

The old Equatoreal . has been employed chiefly in the construction and revision of the Atlas of variable stars, in hand for several
years past. Twenty-three observations have been taken of the five
planets, Isis, Ariadne, Hestia, Asia, and Sappho, and numerous com-
parisons of variable stars have been made throughout the year. The
periodical comets of Faye and Biela were sought for unsuccessfully,
the former being much too faint for the telescope, and the latter
having, doubtless for the same reason, eluded the pursuit of Astrono-
mers generally, even when provided with instruments of the largest
size. None of the equatoreal observations of planets or comets are
yet ready for publication, but it is hoped that this year will be the
last in which such will be the case.

390. Two small telescopic variable stars and one new minor New Discoveries.
planet have been discovered since the last report was written; of these,
Z. Virginis had been previously mapped as an ordinary star of the
tenth magnitude, but was found to have vanished entirely in 1865.
The other new variable X. Capricorni was first seen and observed as
a supposed new planet on July 26th 1865. Neither the periodic time
between two successive maxima, nor yet the range in regard to
brilliancy of either of these objects can yet be decided. Another
new planet was discovered on May 16th, 1866, in the constellation
Scorpio, extremely faint, being but little brighter than a twelfth magnitude. The name selected for this 87th member of the asteroidal
group is Sylvia, one suggested by Sir J. F. W. Herschel a few years
back as suitable for a future new planet. From its slower apparent
motion than that of most others when similarly situated, it has
evidently a considerable mean distance from the sun, but its orbital
elements have yet to be calculated.

391. The records in these subjects continue to be made three Magnetism and
Meteorology.
times daily, as formerly ; and the results of the latter are published
in the Fort Saint George Gazette, and in one local newspaper. The
arrears of the twenty years' series of hourly observations have been
nearly worked up, and printing has been proceeded with, so as to
ensure publication at no distant period. The curves of hourly corrections
for the barometer and dry and wet bulb thermometers will be of great
service throughout India, as it is evident that they must be far more
fairly applicable to tropical registers than those derived from observations made in the widely different climate of Europe. The early and

OBSERVA-
TORY.

remarkable heat of 1866 exceeded any previously recorded at Madras. The thermometer reached 110·6 in the shade on May 28th, the depression of the wet bulb being 35·8, and the per-centage of humidity so low as sixteen. A scheme for meteorological registrations is now under the consideration of Government, which, if sanctioned, will greatly extend our knowledge of the climate of Southern India, and its important bearing upon the statistics of health, mortality, and the cultivation of the staple productions of the country.

Rain Returns.

392. The rain returns, maintained with more or less regularity at upwards of 350 stations since 1852, under the control of the Revenue Board, are under discussion, and though many will doubtless have to be rejected as untrustworthy, sufficient will remain to furnish an interesting rain map of the Presidency, shewing the comparative influences of elevation above sea level, and proximity to the coast, in a marked and highly instructive manner. New gauges of an improved and uniform pattern are about to be issued, and it is hoped that the increased accuracy of future returns will amply compensate for the additional outlay involved thereby.

Time Signals
for the Shipping.

393. The Madras mean time of the flash of the 8 P. M. gun has been carefully noted, and published as formerly, to facilitate the rating of chronometers in the Roads. It is intended, as early as possible, to carry out the long contemplated telegraphic discharge of the Fort and Mount guns, and the erection of three sympathetic electrical clocks, for the convenience of the public in various parts of Madras.

GOVERNMENT CENTRAL MUSEUM.

Specimens
added.

394. The total number of specimens added during the year is 8,678, of which the following are the most important.

Birds.

395. From the North West Provinces, A. O. Hume, Esq., C.B., sent sixty birds; 187 British birds, and thirty American humming-birds were obtained, in exchange, from London ; 160 from the Brunswick Museum, and 202 Indian birds were purchased.

Reptiles.

396. Captain Beddome contributed twenty-one snakes; and fifty-five other reptiles have been brought in by Collectors.

Fish.

397. A collection of 328 British fish, including a few from America, were received from the Derby Museum, Liverpool ; 208 have been added, by purchase, and the Brunswick Museum sent sixty-five.

Mollusca and
Corals.

398. His Excellency Sir William Denison presented 362 shells, and fifty-eight specimens of Australian corals; 271 shells were presented

by Miss Mitchell; 256 were received, in exchange, from Monsieur MUSEUM.
Robillard of Port Louis; and 3,627 were brought in by Collectors.

399. 136 Insects were presented by Miss Mitchell; 227 were Insects.
brought in by the Collectors; and 602 Burmah insects, chiefly Lepidoptera, were obtained by purchase from the men of the 60th Rifles; 251
species of British, and 167 species of European and exotic Lepidoptera
were obtained in London by exchange. A small but very excellent
collection of sixty-three species of European Lepidoptera was received,
in exchange, from F. Moore, Esq., London. A very fine collection of
British Coleoptera, containing upwards of 4,000 specimens, has been
purchased in London, but has not yet arrived.

400. Several skeletons of mammals and birds have been mounted Skeletons.
during the year, and others are in course of preparation.

401. The Government of Bombay have sent specimens of eighteen Coins.
gold, 123 silver, and sixty-two copper coins from the Western Provinces
of India. The Museum is indebted to the liberality of Mr. Maneckjee
Sorabjee, a Parsee gentleman of Pandora, in the Tannah Collectorate,
for sixty ancient copper coins, Bactrian, Hindoo, and Mahomedan;
208 coins of various kinds were transferred from the Madras Mint.

402. A complete collection of Indian War Medals is in the course Medals.
of formation, but only those issued to the Madras Army have yet been
received.

403. A fine collection of (thirty) stone implements, found in the Stone Imple-
Madras Presidency, was presented by R. B. Foote, Esq., of the Geolo- ments.
gical Survey.

404. The number of visitors during the year was 78,067.   Visitors.

Local Museum at Rajahmundry.

405. The Museum building was appropriated from May 1862 to
February 1865, to supply the wants of the Educational Department,
and during that time, of necessity, little has been done to forward the
legitimate objects of the Institution. Since the removal of the Zillah
School to a house built for it, the Museum has been repaired, and some
additions have been made to the collection of specimens.

406. The number of visitors in the year under report has been Visitors.
7,070.

APPENDIX I.

A.

List of Bills pending before the Council of the Governor of Fort Saint George, for the purpose of making Laws and Regulations, on the 30th April 1866.

No.	Title.	What stage Bill has reached.
No. 9 of 1862.	A Bill for organizing a popular form of Municipal Corporation, in lieu of the present Municipal Board, for the Town of Madras.	In accordance with the recommendation of the Select Committee, contained in their Report of the 16th December 1863, it was ordered that this Bill should remain in abeyance for the present.—Vide Proceedings of the Council, dated 16th January 1864.
No. 10 of 1863.	A Bill to make better provision for the protection and due appropriation, for the purposes for which they were made, of all Hindu and Mahomedan religious endowments.	Introduced on the 20th December 1862. First reading postponed till the sanction of the Governor General, for taking the Bill into consideration, has been received under the provisions of Section 43 of the Indian Councils Act.—Vide Proceedings of the Council, dated 20th December 1862.
No. 4 of 1863.	A Bill to declare more precisely the legal efficacy of Wills among Hindus, and to legalize the alienations of self-acquired property of Hindus in land.	Read a first time on the 28th February 1863, and referred to a Select Committee, now consisting of The Honorable T. PYCROFT, Do. A. J. ARBUTHNOT, and Do. G. LUTCHMENARASU CHETTI GARU.
No. 6 of 1865.	A Bill to exempt enfranchised Village or other Service Inams, whether Revenue or Police, from the operation of Regulation VI of 1831.	Introduced on the 1st July 1865, and referred to a Select Committee, now consisting of The Honorable T. PYCROFT, Do. H. D. PHILLIPS, Do. C. PELLY, and Do. G. LUTCHMENARASU CHETTI GARU. Vide Proceedings of Council, dated 1st July 1865.
No. 9 of 1865.	A Bill to make provision for improving the sanitary condition of places in the immediate vicinity of Railway Stations.	Introduced on the 9th August 1865, and referred to a Select Committee, now consisting of The Honorable T. PYCROFT, Do. H. D. PHILLIPS, and Do. C. PELLY, with instructions to make their Report in a month.—Vide Proceedings of the Council, dated 24th February 1866.

APPENDIX I.

A.

**BILLS
PENDING.**

A.—*(Concluded.)*

*List of Bills pending before the Council of the Governor of Fort
Saint George, for the purpose of making Laws and Regulations,
on the 30th April 1866.*

No.	Title.	What stage Bill has reached.
No. 10 of 1865.	A Bill to enable land-holders in certain localities to make provision for the construction, repair, and maintenance of Cross Roads in the District in which their lands are situated.	Introduced on the 12th August 1865, and referred to a Select Committee, now consisting of The Honorable T. Pycroft, Do. C. Pelly, Do. A. J. Arbuthnot, and Do. A. F. Brown. Vide Proceedings of the Council, dated 12th August 1865.
No. 14 of 1865.	A Bill to enable the Government to prescribe Rules for regulating the navigation of rivers, canals, and other inland waters, and for the management of ferries, and for the levying of tolls and license fees.	Introduced on the 16th December 1865, and referred to a Select Committee, now consisting of The Honorable T. Pycroft, Do. H. D. Phillips, Do. C. Pelly, Do. G. Lutchmenarasu Chetti Garu, and Do. A. F. Brown. Vide Proceedings of Council, dated 16th December 1865.

APPENDIX I.
B.

List of Petitions received and disposed of during the year 1865-66.

No.	Date of Petitions.	From whom received.	Substance of Petitions.	How disposed of.
No. 7 of 1865.	15th May.	Mr. J. D'Silva and others, residing in the Town of Calicut, in the District of Malabar.	Submitting observations on some of the provisions of the Towns Municipal Improvement Bill, No. 4 of 1865.	Communicated to the Members of the Select Committee.
No. 8 of 1865.	23rd May.	C. Bunga Charlu, Assistant Commissioner, Paper Currency Department, Calicut Circle.	Submitting observations on the "Towns Municipal Improvement Bill," No. 4 of 1865.	Do. do.
No. 9 of 1865.	30th June.	Nangiah and others, Vakeels of the Civil and Sessions Court of Chittoor.	Praying that Vakeels may be exempted from the tax proposed to be levied on them by the Towns Improvement Bill No. 4 of 1865, inasmuch as they will have to pay Rupees 25 annually for obtaining Certificates to practice under the Pleaders' and Mookhtars' Act No. XX of 1865, passed by the Government of India.	Ordered to be recorded.—Vide Proceedings of the Council, dated 12th July 1865.
No. 10 of 1865.	1st July.	G. L. Narsing Row and 52 others, residing in Vizagapatam.	Submitting observations on some of the provisions of the Towns Improvement Bill, and objecting to the levy of taxes on the inhabitants for the maintenance of the Police.	Ordered to be recorded.—Vide Proceedings of the Council, dated 26th July 1865.
No. 11 of 1865.	13th July.	K. Basavalinga and 119 others, residing in Jaganadapooram, in the Taluk of Cocanada, in the District of Godavery.	Objecting to the tax proposed to be levied on houses, buildings, and lands by Bill No. 4 of 1865.	Do. do.

APPENDIX I.

B.—(*Continued.*)

List of Petitions received and disposed of during the year 1865-66.

No.	Date of Petitions.	From whom received.	Substance of Petitions.	How disposed of.
No. 12 of 1865.	31st July ...	G. Vencatakistnama Chetty and 133 others, residing in the Town of Madras and its suburbs.	Submitting observations on some of the provisions of the Madras Municipal Bill No. 5 of 1865.	Ordered to be recorded. —Vide Proceedings of Council, dated 2nd August 1865.
No. 13 of 1865.	7th August. ...	J. G. Coleman, Esq., and 143 others, East Indians and Native inhabitants of the Town of Madras.	Praying that Section 3 of the Madras Municipal Bill may be amended, so as to give the inhabitants of Madras a share in the management of their Municipal affairs.	Considered in Council. —Vide Proceedings of Council, dated 9th August 1865.
No. 14 of 1865.	5th September....	Ayathooray Mudali of Chikavalum in Negapatam Taluk, in Tanjore Zillah.	Referring to his former petition of 7th July last, prays that his suggestions therein made may be included in the Bill lately published.	Petition returned to petitioner (to be re-transmitted with copy of his former petition, dated 7th July last), on the 18th September 1865.
No. 15 of 1865.	14th September....	A. Colundavaloo Pillay, house-holder in Theroovadagramam in the Taluk of Madura, in the Zillah of Madura.	States that he had brought to the notice of the Collector that the Curnum of the village has not, for the last 40 or 50 years, included (in his accounts) about an acre of land with those liable to be taxed, that he, therefore, requested him either to lease out to him the said land for 20 years, or give him on Durkast, and that the Collector refused his application, alleging that all the house-holders in the said village have their interest	Transferred to Petition Department of Government.

No. 16 of 1865.	13th October. ...	Chinnasawmy Naidu, son of Bommookistnama Naidu, Meerasidar of the Village of Authoor, attached to the Zillah of Chingleput.	to the land in question. Prays, therefore, that his claim may be taken into .... Bringing to ... that, from time ... memorial, the village of Authoor was left in Zemin and without the ... that the Collector has lately introduced the puttah; ... begun to the great disadvantage of the ryots, Izarah ... and that under the present ... there is a loss of Revenue. Praying, therefore, that puttahs may be ordered to be granted to the ryots, and the Izarah system abolished.	Petition rejected as not being in ... ity with Rule No. XII.—Vide Proceedings of ... ... dated 2nd ... 1865.
No. 17 of 1865.	10th November. ...	Chinnasawmy Naidu, son of Bommookistnama Naidu, Meerasidar of the Village of Authoor, attached to the Zillah of Chingleput.	States that he had ... no reply to a petition of the 13th October ..., anent the granting of puttahs to ryots in ... Village.	Petition returned to the Petitioner.
No. 18 of 1865.	20th November....	C. Ayathooray Mudali of Negapatam, in the Zillah of Tanjore.	Referring to the order passed on his former petition, No. 2207 of 1865, brings to notice the desirability of embodying, in one enactment, all the Laws relating to the realization of the Sircar Revenues, and states that he is in ... sion of certain Regulations, and requests to ... him within what ... the the Government would ... require him to submit his views on the ... of the said consolidating Act, as also on the new Bill relating to Municipal ... tion. Requests also that he may be furnished with certain ... ords from the Taluks, and that ... tains to him may be written in Tamil and sent free of postage.	Transferred to Petition Department of Government.
No. 1 of 1866.	27th January. ...	T. Streenevassa Rao, B. Ramiah, and others, Inamdars of the Vizagapatam Zemindary, Zillah of Vizagapatam.	Submitting, for the ... tion of the Select Committee, copy of a ... tion ... aid to the Governor in ... cil, praying that the proposed District Road Cess may not be levied on Inam lands.	Ordered to be recorded.—Vide Proceedings of Council, dated 24th February 1866.

B.
LIST OF
PETITIONS.

APPENDIX I.

B.—*(Concluded.)*

List of Petitions received and disposed of during the year 1865-66.

No.	Date of Petitions.	From whom received.	Substance of Petitions.	How disposed of.
No. 2 of 1866.	30th January. ...	A. Narasuppah, T. Naraina Rauz, and others, inhabitants of Gudivada Village, in the Vizagam Zemindary, in the Zillah of Vizaga-pam.	Objecting to the levy of the District Road Cess proposed by Bill No. 13 of 1865, and suggesting, in substitution thereof, the imposition of a general duty, similar to land custom duties, on all grains and other produce of the land.	Ordered to be recorded.—Vide Proceedings of Council, dated 24th February 1866.
No. 3 of 1866.	1st February. ...	uBka Naidu, N Pohiáh, and Mrs, habitants of 1 Iddiia Village, in the Vizianagram Zemindary, in the Zillah of Vizagapatam.	Objecting to the levy of the District Road Cess proposed by Bill No. 13 of 1865, and suggesting, in substitution thereof, the imposition of a general duty, similar to land custom duties, on all grains and other produce of the land.	Do. do.
No. 4 of 1866.	30th January. ...	K. Seetharamiah and others, inhabitants of Gudivada Village, in the Vizianagram Zemindary, in the Zillah of Vizagapatam.	Objecting to the levy of the District Road Cess proposed by Bill No. 13 of 1866, and suggesting, in lieu thereof, the imposition of a general duty, similar to land custom duties, on all grains and other produce of the land.	Do. do.
No. 5 of 1866.	2nd February. ...	B. Chinniah, P. Narasimmooloo, and others, inhabitants of Gudivada	Objecting to the levy of the District Road Cess proposed by Bill No. 13 of 1865, and suggesting, in lieu thereof, the imposition of a general duty, similar to	Do. do.

No.	Date	Petitioner	Subject	Remarks
No. 6 of 1866.	1st February. ...	Village, in the Vizianagram Zemindary, in the Zillah of Vizagapatam.	land custom duties, on all grains and other produce of the land.	Ordered to be recorded.—Vide Proceedings of Council, dated 24th February 1866.
No. 7 of 1866.	2nd February. ...	G. Pothiah, T. Appiah, and others, inhabitants of Gudivada Village, in the Vizianagram Zemindary, in the Zillah of Vizagapatam.	Objecting to the levy of the District Road Cess proposed by Bill No. 13 of 1865, and suggesting, in lieu thereof, the imposition of a general duty, similar to land custom duties, on all grains and other produce of the land.	Do. do.
		S. Veerunnah, T. Appadoo, and others, inhabitants of Gudivada Vilge, in the Vizianagram Zemindary, in the Zilh of Vizagapatam.	Objecting to the levy of the District Road Cess proposed by Bill No. 13 of 1865, and suggesting, in lieu thereof, the imposition of a general duty, similar to land custom duties, on all grains and other produce of the land.	
No. 8 of 1866.	19th February. ...	Merchants and other Mants in Chittoor Zillah.	Bringing to notice that, in the Rules relating to the examination of Pleaders and Mookhtars, published on the 3rd January last, nothing has been said about Pleaders of District Moonsiffs' Courts, and requesting information upon the subject.	Petition rejected as not being in conformity with Rule XII.—Vide Proceedings of Council, dated 24th February 1866.
No. 9 of 1866.	4th February. ...	Suriyaprakasam and others, Inamdars of Anakapalli Hoonda, Vizagapatam.	State that the Inam lands they possess are very small; that two sorts of quit-rent having been made payable to ... ... them, they find it very difficult to live with what they get from the Inams; and that now they hear that an additional tax, termed "District Road Cess," is to be imposed on their lands. Pray that as they are utterly unable to pay any more tax, and as they do not require any road for their use, Government will kindly issue orders exempting them from paying the Road Cess.	...ered to be recorded.—Vide Proceedings of Council, ...il, dated 24th February 1866.

APPENDIX II.

A.

Statement shewing the Number of Suits instituted and disposed of by the High Court of Judicature at Madras, on its Ordinary Original Jurisdiction during the year 1865.

Suits		Disposed of on Merits.		Dismissed for default.	Withdrawn		Adjusted		Otherwise disposed.	Depending on 31st December 1865.	Cases remaining from the late Supreme Court disposed of.
Remaining from 1864.	Instituted in 1865.	At settlement of Issues.	On final disposal.		With leave to bring fresh suit.	Absolutely.	Before hearing.	At hearing.			
98	358	162	84	28	9	73	...	...	...	100	14

B.

GENERAL ABSTRACT STATEMENT.

CIVIL.

No. 1.—Punchayets.

	1861.	1862.	1863.	1864.	1865.
Depending 1st January	49	69	58	47	71
Instituted during the year. ...	88	95	122	348	582
Total...	137	164	180	395	653
Decided on merits	28	43	59	67	400
Dismissed on default	7	8	22	15	33
Adjusted or withdrawn	25	36	33	111	77
Otherwise disposed of	8	19	19	131	42
Total...	68	106	133	324	552
Depending 31st December ...	69	58	47	71	101

No. 2.—*Village Moonsiffs.*

	1861.	1862.	1863.	1864.	1865.
Depending 1st Jan.	7,557	20,523	15,341	14,503	11,885
Instituted during the year	64,520	49,824	42,910	38,181	40,222
Total...	69,077	70,347	58,251	52,684	52,107
Decided on merits...	17,945	20,876	16,946	15,859	18,290
Dismissed on default	6,518	9,685	8,213	8,153	6,919
Adjusted or withdrawn	21,706	21,045	15,399	15,685	13,671
Otherwise disposed of	2,385	3,400	3,190	1,602	1,286
Total...	48,554	55,006	43,748	40,799	40,166
Depending 31st Dec.	20,523	15,341	14,503	11,885	11,941

No. 3.—*District Moonsiffs.*

	1861.	1862.	1863.	1864.	1865.
Depending 1st Jan.	58,471	1,40,146	1,09,345	73,173	47,062
Instituted during the year	2,05,741	1,12,860	75,823	99,988	1,11,433
Remanded	772	592	447	376	1,908
Received by transfer	4,083	18,405	18,315	6,590	3,185
Total...	2,69,067	2,72,003	2,03,930	1,80,127	1,63,588
Decided on merits	58,072	64,555	61,555	72,336	74,264
Dismissed on default	9,768	16,065	13,620	12,548	6,677
Adjusted or withdrawn	49,241	51,591	33,799	34,107	29,669
Otherwise disposed of	11,840	30,447	21,783	13,074	5,779
Total...	1,28,921	1,62,658	1,30,757	1,33,065	1,16,389
Depending 31st Dec.	1,40,146	1,09,345	73,173	47,062	47,199

No. 4.—*Cantonment Small Cause Courts.*

	1861.	1862.	1863.	1864.	1865.
Depending 1st Jan.	...	...	...	...	....
Instituted during the year	...	...	...	...	331
Remanded	..·	...	...	...	...
Received by transfer	...	...	...	...	...
Total...	...	...	...	...	331
Decided on merits...	...	...	...	...	183
Dismissed on default	...	...	...	...	14
Adjusted or withdrawn...	...	...	...	...	36
Otherwise disposed of	...	...	...	...	1
Total...	...	...	...	...	234
Depending 31st Dec.	...	...	...	...	97

No. 5.—*Principal Sudder Ameens.*

	1861.		1862.		1863.		1864.		1865.	
	Original.	Appeal.	Original.	Appeal.	Original.	Appeal.	Original.	Appeal.	Original.	Appeal.
Depending 1st January.	262	1,349	680	1,232	2,117	1,047	1,203	1,329	1,365	1,841
Instituted during the year	470	2	653	24	1,125	16	2,439	50	4,034	22
Remanded	12	34	12	47	17	20	29	21	20	55
Received by transfer ...	581	3,905	2,019	3,121	79	3,404	162	3,503	59	2,627
Total...	1,325	5,290	3,364	4,424	3,338	4,487	3,833	4,903	5,478	4,545
Decreed for Plaintiff or Appellant	268	1,398	571	986	747	982	1,142	1,000	2,130	1,010
Decreed for Defendant or Respondent... ...	110	2,102	207	1,657	307	1,758	338	1,723	514	1,615
Remanded	...	92	...	122	...	83	...	80	···.	84
Dismissed on default ...	25	110	117	136	288	151	186	115	197	121
Adjusted or withdrawn.	184	173	259	94	457	119	652	86	1,063	81
Otherwise disposed of...	58	183	93	382	336	65	150	58	147	105
Total...	645	4,058	1,247	3,377	2,135	3,158	2,468	3,062	4,051	3,016
Depending 31st Dec. ...	680	1,232	2,117	1,047	1,203	1,329	1,365	1,841	1,427	1,529

No. 6.—*Judges of the Court of Small Causes.*

	1861.	1862.	1863.	1864.	1865.
	Original.	Original.	Original.	Original.	Original.
Depending 1st January ...	...	...	1,439	706	671
Instituted during the year	...	7,084	10,033	8,251	10,205
Received by transfer ...	...	...	...	...	...
Total...	...	7,084	11,472	8,957	10,876
Decreed for Plaintiff or Appellant	...	2,598	6,103	4,967	6,158
Decreed for Defendant or Respondent	...	418	894	573	937
Dismissed on default ...	...	401	1,005	539	512
Adjusted or withdrawn ...	...	2,228	2,764	9,207	2,586
Otherwise disposed of ...	...	...	...	...	...
Total...	...	5,645	10,766	8,286	10,193
Depending 31st December.	...	1,439	706	671	683

No. 7.—*Assistant Agents.*

	1861.		1862.		1863.		1864.		1865.	
	Original.	Appeal.	Original.	Appeal.	Original.	Appeal.	Original.	Appeal.	Original.	Appeal.
Depending 1st January ...	653	1,026	1,060	437	891	115	1	...	5	...
Instituted during the year ...	1,275	45	893	26	286	24	32	...	12	...
Remanded	16	2	14	...	8	...	...	...	...	...
Received by transfer	161	791	287	414	18	19	2	...	19	...
Total...	2,105	1,864	2,254	874	703	158	35	...	36	..
Decreed for Plaintiff or Appellant	461	275	608	100	287	18	19	...	9	...
Decreed for Defendant or Respondent	73	587	140	368	22	72	4	...	2	...
Remanded	...	55	...	25	1	5	...	...	...	...
Dismissed on default	41	43	203	27	34	4	...	...	12	...
Adjusted or withdrawn ...	350	41	430	16	46	1	6	...	2	...
Otherwise disposed of	120	426	482	223	313	53	1	...	1	...
Total...	1,045	1,427	1,863	759	702	158	30	...	26	...
Depending 31st December ...	1,060	437	891	115	1	...	5	...	10	...

B.
CIVIL.
ABSTRACT.

No. 8.—Judges of Small Causes with the powers of a Principal Sudder Ameen.

	1861.		1862.		1863.		1864.		1865.	
	Original.	Appeal.	Original.	Appeal.	Original.	Appeal.	Original.	Appeal.	Original.	Appeal.
Depending 1st Jan.	...	...	...	...	...	...	...	...	...	...
Instituted during the year	...	...	...	...	...	...	...	...	348	...
Remanded	...	...	...	...	...	...	...	...	5	2
Received by transfer.	...	...	...	...	...	...	...	...	1	474
Total...	...	...	...	...	...	...	...	...	354	476
Decreed for Plaintiff or Appellant.	...	...	...	...	...	...	...	...	103	86
Decreed for Defendant or Respondent.	...	...	...	...	...	...	...	...	47	153
Remanded	...	...	...	...	...	...	...	...	...	17
Dismissed on default	...	...	...	...	...	...	...	...	7	32
Adjusted or withdrawn.	...	...	...	...	...	...	...	...	46	16
Otherwise disposed of	...	...	...	...	...	...	...	...	5	56
Total...	...	...	...	...	...	...	...	...	208	360
Depending 31st Dec.	...	...	...	...	...	...	...	...	146	116

No. 9.—Civil Judges.

	1861.		1862.		1863.		1864.		1865.	
	Original.	Appeal.	Original.	Appeal.	Original.	Appeal.	Original.	Appeal.	Original.	Appeal.
Depending 1st January.	317	4,488	345	4,363	434	3,989	503	3,755	582	3,782
Instituted during the year	354	7,144	457	5,726	455	5,677	532	6,053	962	6,263
Remanded	4	19	5	14	15	16	2	13	15	49
Received by transfer ...	2,593	411	7,682	412	8,127	320	2,469	62	1,777	159
Total...	3,268	12,062	8,489	10,515	9,031	10,002	3,506	9,883	3,336	10,253
Decreed for Plaintiff or Appellant	63	944	87	863	147	612	170	711	446	670
Decreed for Defendant or Respondent ...	47	1,708	64	1,649	88	1,333	120	1,491	135	1,266
Remanded	...	125	...	133	...	118	...	112	...	80
Dismissed on default ..	10	151	17	149	30	132	40	128	35	129
Adjusted or withdrawn.	78	175	106	160	110	153	143	161	198	122
Otherwise disposed of..	2,725	4,596	7,781	3,572	8,153	3,699	2,451	3,498	1,805	3,128
Total...	2,923	7,699	8,055	6,526	8,528	6,247	2,924	6,101	2,619	5,335
Depending 31st Dec...	345	4,363	434	3,989	503	3,755	582	3,782	717	4,918

No. 10.—*High Court.*

	1861.		1862.		1863.		1864.		1865.	
	Regular.	Special.	Regular.	Special.	Regular.	Special.	Regular.	Special.	Regular.	Special.
Depending 1st Jan.	21	592	63	770	76	552	63	252	48	156
Admitted during the year...	67	869	58	642	76	526	83	487	87	661
Total...	88	1,461	121	1,412	152	1,078	146	739	135	817
Dismissed on default	...	57	6	104	6	57	5	30	...	22
Adjusted or withdrawn...	1	16	1	5	2	4	2	5	...	3
Confirmed	15	513	27	626	55	690	68	498	52	456
Amended	2	10	4	9	6	11	7	9	5	18
Reversed	4	88	6	108	11	49	10	31	19	28
Remanded	2	5	1	8	9	15	4	8	8	13
Otherwise disposed of	1	2	...	...	...	...	2	2	3	4
Total...	25	691	45	860	89	826	98	583	87	544
Depending 31st Dec.	63	770	76	552	63	252	48	156	48	273

No. 11.—*Aggregate of Original Jurisdiction.*

	1861.	1862.	1863.	1864.	1865.
Depending 1st January ...	68,855	1,66,180	1,,9 125	90,136	61,641
Instituted during the year...	2,82,976	2,02,813	1,87,780	1,59,401	1,68,129
Remanded or re-admitted (not including suits received by transfer)... ...	...	...	...	...	1,948
Total...	3,51,831	3,68,993	2,86,905	2,49,537	2,31,718
Decided on merits	78,872	91,413	87,155	96,095	1,03,618
Dismissed on default	16,804	26,962	23,212	21,481	14,406
Adjusted or withdrawn ...	72,557	76,390	52,608	52,911	47,348
Otherwise disposed of (not including suits merely transferred)	17,418	45,103	33,794	17,409	4,025
Depending 31st December .	1,66,180	1,29,125	90,136	61,641	62,321
Decided by European Judges	3,968	15,563	19,679	11,536	11,740
Do. by Native Judges...	1,81,615	2,24,199	1,76,957	1,76,036	1,57,105
Do. by Punchayets ...	68	106	133	324	552
Total decided...	1,85,651	2,39,868	1,96,769	1,87,896	1,69,397

B.
CIVIL.
ABSTRACT.

No. 12.—*Aggregate of Appellate Jurisdiction.*

APPEALS FROM.

CIVIL JUDGES.

	1861 Reg.	1861 Spec.	1862 Reg.	1862 Spec.	1863 Reg.	1863 Spec.	1864 Reg.	1864 Spec.	1865 Reg.	1865 Spec.
Suits appealable	107	2,652	136	2,512	213	2,145	219	2,302	280	1,876
Appealed	67	427	58	350	76	289	83	801	87	878
Appeals depending on the 1st January	21	297	63	876	76	337	63	143	48	80
Total	88	724	121	726	152	626	146	443	135	458
Affirmed	15	254	27	307	55	409	68	312	52	236
Modified	2	7	4	5	6	7	7	6	5	8
Reversed	4	48	6	45	11	28	10	18	19	90
Remanded	2	4	1	6	9	11	4	5	8	10
Dismissed on default	…	23	6	42	6	25	5	16	…	13
Adjusted or withdrawn	1	12	1	4	2	4	2	4	…	3
Otherwise disposed of	1	…	…	…	…	…	2	2	…	4
Total	25	348	45	409	89	484	98	363	87	294
Depending 31st December	8	376	76	817	8	142	48	80	48	164

ASSISTANT AGENTS.

	1861 Reg.	1861 Spec.	1862 Reg.	1862 Spec.	1863 Reg.	1863 Spec.	1864 Reg.	1864 Spec.	1865 Reg.	1865 Spec.
Suits appealable	289	79	435	88	182	62	17	19	…	…
Appealed	85	58	89	46	101	31	…	…	…	…
Appeals depending on the 1st January	134	55	124	54	95	31	28	3	…	…
Total	219	113	213	100	196	31	28	8	…	…
Affirmed	56	42	64	58	43	23	9	9	…	…
Modified	6	3	4	…	6	…	8	…	…	…
Reversed	17	7	15	6	13	1	7	1	…	…
Remanded	4	…	6	1	2	4	7	…	…	…
Dismissed on default	…	6	14	…	8	…	1	…	…	…
Adjusted or withdrawn	6	1	7	…	8	…	1	…	…	…
Otherwise disposed of	8	…	8	…	93	…	…	1	…	…
Total	95	59	118	69	168	28	28	8	…	…
Depending 31st December	124	54	95	31	28	8	…	…	…	…

B.
CIVIL.
ABSTRACT.

No. 12.—*Aggregate of Appellate Jurisdiction.*—(Concluded.)

APPEALS FROM

	PRINCIPAL SUDDER AMEENS										COLLECTORS					SUDDER AMEENS					DISTRICT MOONSIFFS				
	1861		1862		1863		1864		1865		1861	1862	1863	1864	1865	1861	1862	1863	1864	1865	1861	1862	1863	1864	1865
	Reg.	Spl.	Reg.	Spl.	Reg.	Spl.	Reg.	Spl.	Reg.	Spl.	Reg.	Reg.	Reg.	Reg.	Reg.	Reg.	Reg.	Reg.	Reg.	Reg.	Reg.	Reg.	Reg.	Reg.	Reg.
Suits appealable...	324	91	573	125	755	159	528	250	713	324	98	97	214	186	179	1,139	748	14	2	6	25,583	25,182	27,419	24,099	21,249
Appealed	136	384	185	246	315	237	244	186	231	283	80	29	141	53	117	589	535	11	1	...	11,463	8,943	8,928	9,404	9,303
Appeals depending on 1st January	91	339	112	340	159	184	292	107	234	76	60	53	59	184	28	479	574	587	127	27	6,099	5,169	4,301	4,508	5,834
Total...	227	633	297	586	474	421	536	293	465	359	140	82	200	187	145	1,068	1,109	548	128	27	17,562	14,112	13,229	13,907	14,637
Affirmed	66	216	93	281	103	258	167	184	155	220	23	11	32	106	29	213	270	178	59	10	8,988	8,141	2,746	2,798	2,684
Modified	11	..	12	4	18	4	38	8	42	10	3	1	4	6	7	66	58	86	7	1	854	518	405	508	572
Reversed	14	33	20	57	88	21	45	12	27	8	9	5	16	13	25	106	139	63	19	...	1,528	1,277	1,279	1,145	1,188
Remanded	15	1	6	1	13	..	22	3	12	3	4	1	1	9	...	17	24	15	2	...	232	243	177	152	169
Dismissed on default...	4	28	5	58	2	28	12	14	11	9	1	...	..	11	...	11	24	13	5	18	285	249	272	214	258
Adjusted or withdrawn	4	8	9	1	4	..	15	1	8	..	1	2	5	12	2	23	22	6	9	2	353	230	245	208	207
Otherwise disposed of	1	2	..	...	4	..	3	..	..	..	46	8	8	2	3	58	35	115	...	...	5,097	4,181	3,602	3,553	3,286
Total...	115	283	145	402	182	314	302	217	255	280	87	23	66	159	66	494	572	421	101	26	12,893	9,804	8,726	8,573	8,864
Depending 31st December	112	340	159	184	292	107	284	76	210	109	53	59	184	28	79	574	587	127	27	1	5,169	4,301	4,503	7,334	6,273

No. 13.—*Description of Original Suits instituted.*

	1861.	1862.	1863.	1864.	1865.
Connected with land revenue	5,388	3,549	2,852	3,420	5,646
Otherwise connected with land	13,010	11,560	10,442	12,111	13,395
For houses or other fixed property ...	4,981	3,813	3,845	4,484	5,192
Connected with debts and wages, &c ...	2,43,673	1,51,780	1,11,837	1,27,328	1,41,156
Do. do caste, religion, &c. ...	449	380	421	420	458
Do. do. Indigo, Sugar, Silk, &c.	5,735	2,143	1,357	1,757	2,282
Total...	2,73,236	1,73,225	1,30,754	1,49,771	1,68,129

No. 14.—*Results of Original Suits.*

In favor of Plaintiff.	In favor of Defendant.
82,304	21,314

No. 15.—*Average duration of Suits.*

	1861.			1862.			1863.			1864.			1865.		
	Years.	Months.	Days.	Years.	Months.	Days.	Years.	Months.	Days.	Years.	Months.	Days.	Years.	Months.	Days.
High Court, Appellate Side	...	4	20	...	9	2	...	8	1	...	6	10	...	4	...
Civil Judges	1	...	16	1	4	2	1	3	5	1	2	23	1	2	27
Assistant Agents	1	2	9	1	3	1	...	9	13	...	...	23	...	9	18
Judges of the Small Cause Courts	...	...	...	...	...	17½	...	...	19	...	...	23	...	...	22
Do. with the powers of a Principal Sudder Ameen	...	...	...	...	...	...	...	...	...	...	...	...	...	9	10
Principal Sudder Ameens.	...	10	20	...	10	24	...	9	25	...	10	2	1	4	7
Cantonment Small Cause Courts...	...	...	...	...	...	...	...	...	...	...	...	...	...	...	12¼
District Moonsiffs	...	6	25	...	9	29	...	10	28	...	10	17	...	9	29

No. 16.—*Total value of Suits depending.*

	1861.	1862.	1863.	1864.	1865.
Before the High Court, Appellate Side	1,643,722	2,173,202	2,461,493	1,519,437	1,401,125
Do. other Courts—Original	14,285,591	15,486,761	12,018,282	12,777,335	15,022,438
Do. do. Appeal	1,603,052	1,473,585	1,476,546	1,364,234	1,508,287
Total..	17,532,365	19,133,548	15,956,321	15,661,006	17,931,850

C.

POLICE ESTABLISHMENT AND COST FOR THE OFFICIAL YEAR 1865-66.

DISTRICTS.	Area.	Population.	Sanctioned Strength.	Strength of Force on 30th April 1865.	Supervising Staff.	Superintendents.	Assistant Supts.	Inspectors.	Constables—general duty.	Salt Guards.	Jail Guards.
Inspr. Genl., Asst. Inspr. Genl. of Police and Establishment.	...	...	42	42	2	...	...	26	16	...	...
Dy. Inspector Genl. of Police	...	...	...	...	1	...	..	...	...	...	...
Ganjam	7,757	1,136,926	1,412	1,301	...	1	2	22	1,181	175	60
Vizagapatam..	9,935	1,415,652	1,446	1,361	...	1	1	25	1,281	100	62
Jeypore... ...	9,000	300,000	424	345	...	1	...	6	340	...	...
Godavery	7,534	1,366,831	1,447	1,404	...	1	1	22	1,232	95	84
Kistna... ...	8,353	1,194,421	1,516	1,487	...	1	1	20	1,178	138	48
Nellore... ...	8,341	999,254	1,429	1,382	...	1	1	23	1,109	210	39
Total...	50,920	6,413,084	7,674	7,280	1	6	6	118	6,321	718	293
Dy. Inspector Genl. of Police	...	...	...	...	1	...	...	...	...	...	...
Kurnool... ...	7,470	725,768	1,072	1,032	...	1	1	21	1,010	...	50
Bellary	11,496	1,234,674	1,392	1,384	...	1	2	30	1,276	...	75
Cuddapah.. ...	9,177	1,050,104	1,276	1,229	...	1	2	28	1,119	...	53
North Arcot..	7,526	1,654,557	1,361	1,338	...	1	1	26	1,226	...	78
Madras... ..	3,100	675,390	960	948	...	1	...	17	600	262	52
Total...	38,769	5,340,493	6,061	5,931	1	5	6	122	5,231	262	308
Dy. Inspector Genl. of Police	...	...	...	...	1	...	...	...	...	...	...
South Arcot..	4,765	1,128,430	1,217	1,184	...	1	1	21	899	145	52
Tanjore.... ...	3,736	1,652,170	1,416	1,438	...	1	1	23	1,147	178	54
Trichinopoly...	3,097	939,400	729	719	...	1	...	13	671	...	48
Madura	8,790	1,856,406	1,366	1,305	...	1	2	21	1,109	67	50
Tinnevelly ...	5,144	1,670,262	1,169	1,049	...	1	1	19	952	51	38
Total...	25,532	7,246,668	5,897	5,695	1	5	5	97	4,778	441	242
Dy Inspector Genl. of Police.	...	...	..	...	1	...	...	...	...	...	...
Salem	7,617	1,493,221	1,178	1,185	...	1	2	22	1,058	...	76
Coimbatore ...	8,417	1,215,920	1,160	1,084	...	1	2	25	922	...	202
South Malabar	6,259	1,709,081	{ 993	992	...	1	1	20	896	...	60
North Malabar			563	567	...	1	...	12	457	...	54
South Canara.	4,205	788,042	899	810	...	1	...	11	632	107	41
Total...	26,498	5,206,264	4,793	4,638	1	5	5	90	3,965	107	433
Grand Total...	141,719	24,206,509	24,467	23,586	6	21	22	453	20,311	1,528	1,276

3

C.
POLICE.

POLICE ESTABLISHMENT AND COST FOR THE OFFICIAL YEAR 1865.66.—(*Continued.*)

Ranges	DISTRICTS.	Land Custom Guards.	Total Strength.	Local or Village Police.	Pay and Allowances.	Clothing and Accoutrements.	Rent, Stationery, and other Charges.	Total.	Village Police.	Grand Total.
					RS.	RS.	RS.	RS.	RS.	RS.
	Inspector Genl., Asst. Inspector Genl. of Police, and Establishment	...	44	...	55,802	573	5,030	61,405	...	61,4
Northern Range.	Dy. Inspr. Genl. of Police	...	1	...	9,469	...	171	9,640	...	9,6
	Ganjam	...	1,441	162	1,73,700	18,045	8,895	2,00,640	2,753	2,03,3
	Vizagapatam ...	...	1,470	49	1,62 004	19,188	9,956	1,91,148	1,150	1,92,2
	Jeypore	...	347	78	43,200	4,298	1,400	48,898	1,810	50,7
	Godavery... ...	13	1,448	35	1,67,772	21,387	3,979	1,93,138	838	1,93,9
	Kistna	...	1,386	20	1,63,455	21,284	3,784	1,88,523	720	1,89,2
	Nellore	...	1,383	99	1,69,557	19,306	4,427	1,93,290	3,528	1,96,8
	Total...	13	7,476	443	8,89,157	1,03,508	32,612	10,25,277	10,799	10,36,0
Central Range.	Dy. Inspr. Genl. of Police	...	1	...	12,476	...	...	12,476	...	12,4
	Kurnool	...	1,083	12	1,48,448	16,013	3,198	1,67,659	413	1,68,0
	Bellary	...	1,384	...	1,89,003	21,047	4,300	2,14,350	...	2,14,3
	Cuddapah ...	...	1,203	...	1,65,724	15,850	4,182	1,85,756	...	1,85,7
	North Arcot ...	...	1,332	...	1,74,411	18,453	4,366	1,97,230	...	1,97,2
	Madras	...	932	...	1,17,218	13,850	3,232	1,34,300	...	1,34,3
	Total...	...	5,935	12	8,07,280	85,213	19,278	9,11,771	413	9,12,1
Southern Range.	Dy. Inspr. Genl. of Police ...	...	1	...	13,677	...	117	13,794	...	13
	South Arcot ...	63	1,182	2,570	1,52,220	16,654	4,875	1,73,749	21,861	1,95
	Tanjore	30	1,434	...	1,69,628	20,946	5,096	1,95,670	...	1,95
	Trichinopoly ...	...	733	...	89,617	10,252	3,099	1,02,968	...	1,03
	Madura	...	1,250	...	1,63,306	16,350	3,548	1,83,204	...	1,83
	Tinnevelly ...	...	1,062	...	1,37,452	14,113	3,460	1,55,025	...	1,55
	Total...	93	5,662	2,570	7,25,900	78,315	20,195	8,24,410	21,861	8,46
Western Range.	Dy. Inspr. Genl. of Police ...	...	1	...	14,072	...	217	14,289	...	14
	Salem	...	1,159	...	1,53,028	15,562	5,518	1,74,108	...	1,74
	Coimbatore ...	...	1,152	...	1,58,000	15,673	5,993	1,79,666	...	1,79
	South Malabar..	...	978	9	1,33,819	13,671	10,684	1,58,174	533	1,58
	North Malabar...	28	552	8	73,603	7,012	2,923	83,538	459	83
	South Canara ...	...	792	...	98.303	9,859	2,788	1,10,950	...	1,10
	Total...	28	4,634	17	6,30,825	61,777	28, 13	7,20,725	992	7,21
	Grand Total..	134	23,751	3,042	31,08,964	3,29,386	1,05,238	35,43,588	34,065	35,77

C.—(*Continued.*)

Ranges.	DISTRICTS.	STRENGTH OF FORCE, ENLISTMENTS, AND CASUALTIES DURING THE OFFICIAL YEAR 1865-66.								
		Sanctioned strength of Force.	Actual strength of Force on 30th April 1865.	Actual strength of Force on 30th April 1866.	CASUALTIES DURING THE YEAR.					Enlisted during the year 1865-66.
					Dismissed and discharged or reduced.	Resigned and deserted.	Died.	Total.	Per-centage.	
1	2	3	4	5	6	7	8	9	10	11
Northern Range.	Ganjam...	1,412	1,301	1,438	330	87	60	477	33·1	657
	Vizagapatam ...	1,446	1,361	1,468	137	90	46	273	18·5	417
	Jeypore...	424	345	346	28	25	8	61	17·6	57
	Godavery	1,447	1,404	1,446	88	78	37	203	14·0	246
	Kistna...	1,516	1,487	1,384	106	41	22	169	12·2	91
	Nellore...	1,429	1,382	1,381	96	60	19	175	12·6	174
	Total...	7,674	7,280	7,463	785	381	192	1,358	18·1	1,642
Central Range.	Bellary...	1,392	1,384	1,381	102	69	12	183	13·2	193
	Kurnool..	1,072	1,032	1,081	53	64	10	127	11·7	176
	Cuddapah	1,276	1,229	1,200	96	70	14	180	15·0	165
	North Arcot ...	1,361	1,338	1,330	67	61	11	139	10·4	131
	Madras...	960	948	931	106	51	9	166	17·8	151
	Total...	6,061	5,931	5,923	424	315	56	795	13·4	816
Southern Range.	South Arcot ...	1,217	1,184	1,180	91	57	9	157	13·3	153
	Tanjore ..	1,416	1,438	1,432	88	43	11	142	9·9	140
	Trichinopoly ...	729	719	732	56	76	6	138	18·8	149
	Madura...	1,366	1,305	1,247	87	159	21	267	21·4	210
	Tinnevelly ...	1,169	1,049	1,060	52	82	8	142	13·3	153
	Total...	5,897	5,695	5,651	374	417	55	846	14·9	805
Western Range.	Salem ...	1,178	1,185	1,156	61	80	13	154	13·3	161
	Coimbatore ...	1,160	1,084	1,149	87	111	25	223	19·4	313
	South Malabar...	993	992	976	56	33	41	130	13·3	92
	North Malabar..	563	567	551	46	8	17	71	12·8	5t
	South Canara...	899	810	791	69	86	9	164	20·7	145
	Total...	4,793	4,638	4,623	319	318	105	742	16·0	766
	Grand Total...	24,425	23,544	23,660	1,902	1,431	408	3,741	15·8	4,029

C.—*(Continued.)*

Ranges.	DISTRICTS.	STATE OF EDUCATION ON 31st DECEMBER 1865.			INSTRUCTION DURING THE YEAR 1865.		
		Cannot read and write.	Can read and write.	Passed General Test.	Number who have been in District Head Quarter School.	Passed prescribed Test of Rank.	Passed Police Special Test.
1	2	3	4	5	6	7	8
Northern Range.	Ganjam	449	839	3	999	112	6
	Vizagapatam... ...	685	676	1	153	112	...
	Jeypore	151	179	12	43	...	...
	Godavery	781	784	1	256	101	15
	Kistna	700	716	3	208	60	5
	Nellore	765	575	1	263	153	...
	Total...	3,531	3,769	21	1,922	538	26
Central Range.	Bellary	725	652	10	319	71	4
	Cuddapah	676	542	1	122	57	1
	Kurnool	860	220	...	167	65	8
	North Arcot... ...	576	767	6	193	50	4
	Madras	197	711	3	124	113	3
	Total...	3,034	2,892	20	925	356	20
Southern Range.	South Arcot... ...	578	576	3	114	76	1
	Tanjore	336	1,061	3	82	43	...
	Trichinopoly... ...	25	686	2	60	20	1
	Madura	108	1,152	6	110	69	2
	Tinnevelly	273	804	3	95	86	3
	Total...	1,320	4,279	17	461	294	7
Western Range.	Salem...	283	883	...	100	35	...
	Coimbatore	407	737	2	169	169	5
	North Malabar ...	67	499	...	54	43	1
	South Malabar ...	305	700	3	92	29	7
	South Canara ...	458	363	8	81	56	4
	Total...	1,520	3,182	13	496	332	17
	GrandTotal...	9,405	14,122	71	3,804	1,520	70

C.—(*Continued.*)

C.
POLICE.

POLICE OFFICERS CONVICTED IN 1865.

CONVICTED BY MAGISTRATES.

Ranges	Districts	House-breaking and Theft	Theft and Receiving, &c.	Assault and Criminal force.	Criminal Breach of Trust and Misappropriation.	Extortion and Bribery.	Negligent escape.	False evidence and causing disappearance of evidence.	Causing Hurt.	Furnishing false information to a Public Servant.	Cheating.	Miscellaneous.	Total.
Northern Range.	Ganjam			1		4			3			12	20
	Vizagapatam		3	4	1	7	13	2				6	36
	Jeypore		2	5		5	7					6	25
	Godavery		1	1		1	5					8	16
	Kistna		2	2		6	4		2	1		1	18
	Nellore		5	7	1	3	2		1			13	32
	Total		13	20	2	26	31	2	6	1		46	147
Central Range.	Kurnool		2	1	1		2						6
	Bellary		2	1	4	5	12					8	32
	Cuddapah		3		2	3	5					4	17
	North Arcot		2			3	1		1			1	8
	Madras		3	4		3						14	24
	Total		12	6	7	14	20		1			27	87
Southern Range.	South Arcot		3	3	1	2	4				1	4	18
	Tanjore		1	1		3	3					3	11
	Trichinopoly		1	1			1				1	8	12
	Madura	1	3			6	1					12	23
	Tinnevelly		3		1	3	3					6	16
	Total	1	11	5	2	14	12				2	33	80
Western Range.	Salem		2	1		5	4			1		15	28
	Coimbatore		7	2		3	8					21	41
	South Malabar			3		3	5					7	18
	North Malabar											2	2
	South Canara		1		1				2				4
	Total		10	6	1	11	17		2	1		45	93
	Grand Total	1	46	37	12	65	80	2	9	2	2	151	407

C.
. POLICE.

C.—(Continued.)

POLICE OFFICERS CONVICTED IN 1865.—(Continued.)

CONVICTED BY COURTS.

Ranges.	DISTRICTS.	Murder.	Culpable Homicide.	Dacoity.	House-breaking and Theft.	Theft.	Causing Hurt.	False Evidence.	Taking Bribe.	Forgery.	Adultery.	Miscellaneous.	Total.
Northern Range.	Ganjam ...	1	...	...	...	...	...	1	...	...	...	...	2
	Vizagapatam ...	...	...	...	...	...	1	...	...	...	...	...	1
	Jeypore ...	...	...	...	...	...	...	...	...	...	...	...	...
	Godavery ...	...	...	...	...	...	...	...	...	...	...	...	...
	Kistna ...	...	...	...	...	...	...	1	...	...	1	1	3
	Nellore ...	...	...	...	...	...	1	...	...	1	...	...	2
	Total...	1	...	...	...	1	1	2	...	1	1	1	8
Central Range.	Kurnool ...	...	...	...	...	...	...	...	...	...	...	...	...
	Bellary ...	...	...	1	...	...	...	1	...	...	...	...	2
	Cuddapah ...	...	...	...	...	...	...	2	...	...	...	1	3
	North Arcot ...	...	...	...	...	...	...	...	...	...	...	...	...
	Madras ...	...	...	...	...	2	...	...	...	...	...	...	2
	Total...	...	...	1	...	2	...	3	...	...	...	1	7
Southern Range.	South Arcot ...	...	...	...	...	...	...	...	...	...	...	...	...
	Tanjore ...	...	1	...	1	...	...	...	...	...	...	...	2
	Trichinopoly ...	...	...	...	...	...	...	...	...	...	...	...	...
	Madura ...	...	1	...	...	...	...	...	...	...	...	...	1
	Tinnevelly ...	...	...	...	...	...	2	...	...	...	...	...	2
	Total...	...	1	1	1	...	2	...	...	...	...	...	5
Western Range.	Salem ...	...	...	...	...	...	...	...	...	...	...	1	1
	Coimbatore ...	...	...	...	...	...	...	...	...	...	...	...	...
	South Malabar ...	...	...	...	...	...	...	...	...	...	...	1	1
	North Malabar ...	...	...	...	...	...	...	...	...	...	...	...	...
	South Canara ...	1	...	...	...	...	...	...	1	...	...	2	4
	Total...	...	1	...	...	...	...	...	1	...	...	4	6
	Grand Total...	1	2	2	1	3	3	5	1	1	1	6	26

C.—(*Continued.*)

Ranges.	DISTRICTS.	Europeans.	East Indians.	Foreigners not British Subjects.	Brahmins.	Rajaputs and Mahrattas.	Naidoos.	Mnodeliars.	Sattanies.	Chetties.	Commaties.	Vunniers.	Weavers.	Yadiers.	Conicapolies.	Nairs.	Moplas.	Teers.	Oryas.	Christians.	Mahomedans.	Pariahs, &c.
		1	2	3	4	5	6	7	8	9	10	11	12	13	14	15	16	17	18	19	20	21
Northern Range.	Ganjam ...	1	4	...	1	1	7	...	...	...	...	...	...	...	...	...	...	...	3	...	5	...
	Vizagapatam ...	2	4	...	5	2	8	...	...	...	...	...	...	...	...	...	...	..	1	...	3	...
	Jeypore ...	...	1	...	...	...	2	...	...	2	...	...	...	...	...	...	...	...	1	...	...	...
	Godavery ...	7	4	...	2	...	7	...	...	...	...	...	...	...	...	...	...	...	...	...	2	...
	Kistna ...	3	1	...	4	1	10	...	...	...	...	...	..	...	...	...	..	...	..	...	1	..
	Nellore ...	3	2	...	8	2	3	3	...	...	...	...	..	...	...	...	...	...	...	1	...	1
	Total ...	16	16	...	20	6	37	3	...	2	...	...	..	...	...	...	...	··	5	1	11	1
Central Range.	Kurnool ...	1	1	...	5	1	6	2	..	...	1	...	...	...	...	...	...	...	...	...	5	...
	Bellary ...	1	5	...	15	4	2	..	...	...	1	...	...	...	...	...	...	...	...	...	2	..
	Cuddapah ...	1	7	..	6	2	7	5	...	...	...	...	...	...	...	...	··	...	...	...	...	...
	North Arcot ...	4	2	...	8	1	3	4	...	...	...	...	...	...	...	...	··	...	··	...	4	...
	Madras ..	2	5	...	4	..	2	1	...	...	..	...	...	...	...	...	...	...	...	2	1	..
	Total ...	9	20	...	38	8	20	12	...	...	1	...	...	...	...	...	...	...	...	2	12	...
Southern Range.	South Arcot ...	4	3	1	6	...	1	5	...	...	...	...	...	...	...	...	...	...	...	...	1	...
	Tanjore ...	6	3	...	1	...	3	6	...	...	...	1	...	..	...	...	...	...	...	2	1	...
	Trichinopoly ..	2	3	...	1	..	1	3	1	...	...	..	1	...	...	...	...	...	...	1	..	...
	Madura ...	3	2	...	5	...	1	10	...	...	...	...	..	...	...	...	...	...	...	..	..	...
	Tinnevelly ...	4	2	...	3	...	2	6	...	...	...	...	..	...	...	...	·	...	...	...	2	...
	Total ...	19	13	1	16	...	8	30	1	...	...	1	..	1	...	...	...	··	··	3	4	...
Western Range.	Salem ...	4	2	...	6	..	5	3	..	...	...	...	...	...	...	...	...	...	...	1	1	..
	Coimbatore ...	1	11	...	2	2	4	2	..	...	...	...	...	...	...	...	...	...	··	1	2	...
	South Malabar ...	4	4	...	1	...	...	...	...	...	...	...	...	...	10	1	...	...	...	...	...	...
	North Malabar ..	1	2	...	...	...	...	...	...	...	...	...	...	...	5	..	4	...	..	...	...	...
	South Canara ...	...	...	...	8	...	..	...	...	...	...	...	...	...	...	...	...	...	...	1	...	...
	Total ..	10	19	...	17	2	9	5	...	...	...	...	...	...	15	1	4	...	..	3	3	2
	Grand Total ...	54	68	1	91	16	74	50	1	2	1	1	..	1	...	15	1	4	5	9	30	3

C.
POLICE.

C.—(Continued.)

Ranges.	DISTRICTS.	CASTES AND RACES ON 30TH APRIL 1866.—(Continued.) CONSTABULARY.								
		Europeans.	East Indians.	Brahmins.	Rajaputs and Mahrattas.	Naidoos.	Modeliars.	Sattanies.	Chetties.	Commaties.
		1	2	3	4	5	6	7	8	9
Northern Range.	Ganjam...	...	2	1	15	816	1	...	...	...
	Vizagapatam	1	4	38	13	941	1	...	...	1
	Jeypore	...	...	4	3	67	...	...	...	...
	Godavery	2	2	47	52	696	2	...	...	...
	Kistna	...	1	26	67	640	2	...	...	...
	Nellore...	1	3	30	69	534	26	...	...	...
	Total ...	4	12	146	219	3,694	32	...	...	1
Central Range.	Kurnool...	...	...	69	157	65	3	...	...	...
	Bellary	3	3	52	80	291	67	...	...	1
	Cuddapah	...	2	33	87	370	20	...	...	...
	North Arcot... ...	2	1	35	159	309	125	...	...	...
	Madras	6	5	12	37	269	92	...	...	...
	Total...	11	11	201	520	1,304	307	...	...	1
Southern Range.	South Arcot	3	11	11	41	259	198	...	...	...
	Tanjore	6	10	23	192	417	321	3	...	...
	Trichinopoly	6	5	8	34	220	6	2	1	...
	Madura...	2	1	18	57	283	323	...	...	...
	Tinnevelly	2	5	8	41	279	329	...	...	...
	Total ...	19	32	68	365	1,458	1,176	5	1	...
Western Range.	Salem	2	5	91	80	214	254	...	...	...
	Coimbatore	4	9	40	76	284	175	...	...	...
	South Malabar ...	...	4	1	23	27	...	...	9	...
	North Malabar ...	1	5	4	15	3	...	...	5	...
	South Canara... ...	...	..	45	11	398	...	...	...	...
	Total ...	7	23	181	205	926	429	...	14	...
	Grand Total...	41	78	596	1,309	7,382	1,944	5	15	2

C.—*(Continued.)*

CASTES AND RACES ON 30TH APRIL 1866.—*(Continued).*

CONSTABULARY.

Vunniers.	Weavers.	Yadiers.	Conicapolies.	Nairs.	Moplas.	Teers.	Oryas.	Christians.	Mahomedans.	Pariahs, &c.
10	11	12	13	14	15	16	17	18	19	20
...	..	...	...	...	...	...	475	1	102	6
...	...	...	...	..	...	...	212	3	184	93
...	...	...	...	...	...	...	216	...	20	26
...	29	42	...	4	...	...	...	...	409	140
...	...	...	...	...	...	...	...	2	518	108
...	...	.	...	...	...	...	...	10	628	57
...	29	42	...	4	...	...	903	16	1,861	430
...	...	...	...	...	...	...	...	...	750	16
...	...	...	...	...	...	...	...	6	751	97
...	...	...	...	...	...	...	...	...	659	1
...	...	...	...	...	...	...	...	16	514	143
...	...	...	...	...	...	...	...	29	400	64
...	...	1	...	...	...	...	...	51	3,074	321
...	185	...	...	...	...	...	...	24	399	28
28	...	10	...	...	...	...	...	15	209	140
...	...	207	...	...	...	...	...	11	206	13
183	...	...	...	...	...	...	...	39	252	69
...	28	40	..	...	...	...	...	29	247	33
211	213	257	...	...	...	...	...	118	1,313	283
...	...	...	...	...	...	...	...	11	440	37
...	...	...	...	...	...	...	...	35	404	97
...	...	11	...	510	88	...	...	22	180	77
...	...	...	...	307	16	125	...	4	38	23
...	...	...	...	...	...	...	...	117	162	47
...	...	11	...	817	104	125	...	189	1,224	281
211	242	311	...	821	104	125	903	374	7,472	1,315

C.
POLICE.

C.—(*Continued.*)

Range.	DISTRICTS.	WARRANTS AND SUMMONS ISSUED BY MAGISTRATES, SUB-MAGISTRATES, AND COURTS IN 1865.						
		GRAVE CASES.						
		WARRANTS.		SUMMONS.		TOTAL.		
		Number of Processes.	Number of Persons.	Number of Processes.	Number of Persons.	Number of Processes.	Number of Persons.	Proportion to Population.
Northern Range.	Ganjam	566	599	3,321	3,350	3,837	3,949	288
	Vizagapatam	1,402	1,890	3,514	3,514	4,916	5,404	261
	Jeypore	29	45	32	33	61	78	3,846
	Godavery	525	531	2,547	2,548	3,072	3,079	444
	Kistna	811	1,043	1.990	2,317	2,801	3,360	355
	Nellore	463	519	2,656	2,656	3,119	3,175	315
	Total..	3,796	4,627	14,060	14,418	17,856	19,045	336
Central Range.	Kurnool	102	168	536	536	638	704	1,031
	Bellary	402	596	2,402	2,418	2,804	3,014	409
	Cuddapah	323	325	1,363	1,363	1,686	1,688	622
	North Arcot	1,484	1,484	5,348	5,352	6.832	6,836	242
	Madras	319	319	773	773	1,092	1,092	618
	Total...	2,630	2,892	10,422	10,442	13,052	13,334	400
Southern Range.	South Arcot	902	928	3,564	3,564	4,466	4,492	251
	Tanjore	1,328	1,328	8.303	8,314	9,631	9,642	171
	Trichinopoly	420	420	1,454	1,454	1,874	1,874	501
	Madura	903	912	4,602	4,603	5,505	5,515	373
	Tinnevelly	1,128	1,141	7,323	7,323	8,451	8,464	197
	Total..	4,681	4,729	25,246	25,258	29,927	29,987	241
Western Range.	Salem	1,047	1,092	3,624	3,624	4,671	4,716	316
	Coimbatore	567	567	3,073	3,073	3,640	3,640	334
	North Malabar	303	326	941	847	1,244	1,173	} 454
	South Malabar	877	1,007	1,577	1,582	2,454	2,589	
	South Canara	340	340	1,931	1,929	2,271	2,269	347
	Total...	3,134	3,332	11,146	11,055	14,280	14,387	361
	Grand Total...	14,241	15,580	60,874	61,173	75,115	76,753	315

C.—(*Continued.*)

	DISTRICTS.	WARRANTS AND SUMMONS ISSUED BY MAGISTRATES, SUB-MAGISTRATES, AND COURTS IN 1865.—(*Continued.*)						
		MINOR CASES.						
		WARRANTS.		SUMMONS.		TOTAL.		
Ranges.		Number of Processes.	Number of Persons.	Number of Processes.	Number of Persons.	Number of Processes.	Number of Persons.	Proportion to Population.
Northern Range.	Ganjam	405	410	3,191	3,212	3,596	3,622	313
	Vizagapatam ...	843	1,715	11,731	11,732	12,574	13,447	105
	Jeypore	83	109	397	397	480	506	592
	Godavery... ...	1,168	1,170	11,530	11,530	12,698	12,700	107
	Kistna	2,285	2,550	17,465	21,492	19,750	24,042	49
	Nellore	1,090	1,162	11,071	11,083	12,161	12,245	81
	Total...	5,874	7,116	55,385	59,446	61,259	66,562	96
Central Range.	Kurnool	863	1,312	9,230	9,230	10,093	10,542	68
	Bellary	892	1,638	7,912	8,773	8,804	10,411	118
	Cuddapah ...	1,059	1,096	12,102	12,102	13,161	13,198	79
	North Arcot ...	678	678	6,574	6,580	7,252	7,258	227
	Madras	2,743	2,749	13,746	13,747	16,489	16,496	40
	Total...	6,235	7,473	49,564	50,432	55,799	57,905	92
Southern Range.	South Arcot ...	1,573	1,601	23,018	23,021	24,591	24,622	45
	Tanjore	633	634	14,866	14,885	15,499	15,519	106
	Trichinopoly ...	732	732	10,864	10,864	11,596	11,596	81
	Madura	655	660	18,383	18,385	19,038	19,045	97
	Tinnevelly ...	1,346	1,346	12,449	12,449	13,795	13,795	121
	Total...	4,939	4,973	79,580	79,604	84,519	84,577	85
Western Range.	Salem ...	1,076	1,085	13,506	13,506	14,582	14,591	102
	Coimbatore ...	940	940	13,165	13,165	14,105	14,105	86
	North Malabar...	398	403	4,454	4,455	4,852	4,858	} 132
	South Malabar...	960	1,045	6,973	7,036	7,933	8,081	
	South Canara ..	271	271	2,804	2,804	3,075	3,075	256
	Total...	3,645	3,744	40,902	40,966	44,547	44,710	116
	Grand Total...	20,693	23,306	225,431	230,448	246,124	253,754	95

C.
POLICE.

C.—*(Continued).*

Ranges.	DISTRICTS.			MISCELLANEOUS PROCESSES ISSUED IN 1865.			
				NUMBER OF MISCELLANEOUS PROCESSES INCLUDING REMAND WARRANTS, LEVY OF DISTRESS, COMMITTALS, &c.			
				Number of Processes.	Number of Persons.	Number of Search Warrants.	Number of Houses searched.
Northern Range.	Ganjam ...	...	...	3,081	3,943	114	120
	Vizagapatam	...	...	2,986	6,137	131	221
	Jeypore ...	...	...	219	298	8	8
	Godavery	...	...	2,427	3,754	172	347
	Kistna ...	...	...	1,584	2,740	173	261
	Nellore ...	...	...	1,492	2,356	57	84
		Total...		11,789	19,228	655	1,041
Central Range.	Bellary ...	...	...	2,580	4,285	136	284
	Kurnool...	...	...	1,340	2,137	74	105
	Cuddapah	...	...	1,731	2,139	85	94
	North Arcot	...	...	2,041	2,652	349	367
	Madras ...	...	...	735	1,140	48	57
		Total...		8,427	12,353	692	907
Southern Range.	South Arcot	...	...	4,147	5,853	243	267
	Tanjore ...	...	...	1,207	1,478	322	322
	Trichinopoly	...	...	1,723	2,312	95	100
	Madura ...	...	...	1,105	1,414	83	120
	Tinnevelly	...	...	2,660	4,280	103	173
		Total...		10,842	15,337	846	982
Western Range.	Salem ...	...	...	4,086	5,374	188	221
	Coimbatore	...	...	2,782	3,705	152	185
	South Malabar	...	...	2,702	4,054	43	47
	North Malabar	...	...	1,762	2,470	61	173
	South Canara	...	...	1,140	1,491	68	87
		Total...		12,472	17,094	512	712
		Grand Total..		43,530	64,012	2,705	3,642

C.—*(Continued.)*

Ranges.	DISTRICTS.	SHORT-SENTENCED PRISONERS IN SUBSIDIARY JAILS DURING 1865			
		Number of Jails.	Total number of convicts during the year.	Total number of days.	Average duration of confinement.
		1	2	3	4
Northern Range.	Ganjam	5	655	8,013	12·23
	Vizagapatam	16	963	7,815	8 11
	Jeypore	4	66	1,317	19·95
	Godavery	11	431	6,222	14·43
	Kistna	20	493	3,063	6 21
	Nellore	18	271	1,430	5·28
	Total	74	2,879	27,860	9·68
Central Range.	Kurnool	13	820	7,240	8·83
	Bellary	11	901	9,704	10·77
	Cuddapah	13	563	4,525	8·04
	North Arcot	18	492	3,017	6·13
	Madras	10	596	5,101	8·56
	Total	65	3,372	29,587	8·77
Southern Range.	South Arcot	17	1,570	13,399	8·53
	Tanjore	9	967	11,460	11·85
	Trichinopoly	6	510	3,720	7·29
	Madura	17	367	3,545	9·65
	Tinnevelly	19	983	7,804	7·94
	Total	68	4,397	39,928	9·08
Western Range.	Salem	13	1,368	12,938	9·45
	Coimbatore	10	1,188	13,693	11·52
	North Malabar	10	556	6,957	12·51
	South Malabar	12	1,219	10,048	8·24
	South Canara	9	233	2,331	10·00
	Total	54	4,564	45,967	10·07
	Grand Total	261	15,212	143,342	9·42

C.
POLICE.

C.—*(Continued.)*

Ranges.	DISTRICTS.		PRISONERS ESCAPED DURING THE YEAR 1865.							
			FROM JAILS.		FROM SUBSIDIARY JAILS.		FROM OTHER CUSTODY.		TOTAL.	
			Escaped.	Re-captured.	Escaped.	Re-captured.	Escaped.	Re-captured.	Escaped.	Re-captured.
			1	2	3	4	5	6	7	8
Northern Range.	Ganjam	...	...	...	...	...	25	18	25	18
	Vizagapatam ...	..	3	3	.	...	13	8	16	11
	Jeypore ...	..	...	...	4	3	8	5	12	8
	Godavery ...	..	...	...	4	2	15	10	19	12
	Kistna ...	..	3	3	3	3	12	7	18	13
	Nellore ...		...	...	...	...	15	6	15	6
	Total....		6	6	11	8	88	54	105	68
Central Range.	Kurnool ...	...	...	...	7	5	4	2	11	7
	Bellary ...	...	..	...	1	1	53	36	54	37
	Cuddapah ...	...	...	.	9	6	8	4	17	10
	North Arcot ...	..	1	1	2	1	23	16	26	18
	Madras ...	...	...	...	...	...	12	6	12	6
	Total...		1	1	19	13	100	64	120	78
Southern Range.	South Arcot ...	...	1	...	4	3	22	11	27	14
	Tanjore ...	...	...	...	...	...	18	10	18	10
	Trichinopoly ...	...	details not received.				...	...	5	4
	Madura ...	...	2	2	1	...	20	18	23	20
	Tinnevelly ...	...	...	..	4	4	4	3	8	7
	Total...		3	2	9	7	64	42	81	55
Western Range.	Salem ...	...	5	4	8	6	21	12	34	22
	Coimbatore ...	..	24	6	2	2	14	9	40	17
	North Malabar...	...	6	6	14	13	23	22	43	41
	South Malabar...	...	...	...	5	4	32	16	37	20
	South Canara ...	..	..	...	7	7	...	...	7	7
	Total...		35	16	36	32	90	59	161	107
	Grand Total..		45	25	75	60	342	219	467	308

XXX

C.—(*Continued.*)

Ranges.	DISTRICTS.		FALL OF RAIN AND PRICE OF FOOD DURING THE YEAR 1865, AS COMPARED WITH THE LAST FIVE YEARS.			
			Average fall of rain during past five years.	Fall of rain during present year.	Staple articles of food and average price during past five years.	Price during present year.
			1	2	3	4
Northern Range.	Ganjam		46·63	21·		160
	Vizagapatam		33·72	30·53		154
	Jeypore		34·65	30·60		114
	Godav·ry		34·65	30·60		114
	Kistna		25·31	24·39		104
	Nellore		25·88	22·57		113
	Average, Northern Range.		33·24	25·82		129
Central Range.	Kurnool		27·34	19·17		123
	Bellary		18·67	14·44		123
	Cuddapah		19·35	15·35		119
	North Arcot		21·38	24·58		110
	Madras		29·66	20·64		110
	Average, Central Range...		23·28	18·83	Taken at 100	117
Southern Range.	South Arcot.		67·06	25·05		105
	Tanjore		44·88	21·42		130
	Trichinopoly		36·50	45·64		133
	Madura		35·19	20·27		125
	Tinnevelly		28·60	24·10		133
	Average, Southern Range...		42·44	27·29		125
Western Range.	Salem.		27·10	25·48		116
	Coimbatore		28·26	23·07		126
	North Malabar		116·05	82·33		122
	South Malabar		173·91	140·48		113
	South Canara.		173·91	140·48		113
	Average, Western Range...		86·33	67·84		120
	Average, throughout the Presidency		46·32	34·94		123

C.
POLICE.

C.—(Continued.)

DEPREDATORS, OFFENDERS, AND

NUMBER OF DEPREDATORS, OFFENDERS, AND SUSPECTED PERSONS AT LARGE ON 31ST DECEMBER 1865.

Ranges.	DISTRICTS.	Known Thieves & Depredators.		Receivers of stolen goods.		Prostitutes.	Suspected persons.		Vagrants and wandering gangs.		Total.	
		Males.	Females.	Males.	Females.		Males.	Females.	Males.	Females.	Males.	Females.
Northern Range.	Ganjam	315	12	46	7	630	265	5	16	...	642	654
	Vizagapatam...	874	33	135	29	524	1,039	47	139	47	2,187	680
	Jeypore... ...	...	...	...	...	Not received.			...	...	...	...
	Godavery ...	212	12	50	6	80	411	21	6	6	679	125
	Kistna... ...	542	8	110	15	...	888	54	312	248	1,852	325
	Nellore ...	534	28	138	16	...	1,437	20	315	300	2,424	364
	Total...	2,477	93	479	73	1,234	4,040	147	788	601	7,784	2,148
Central Range.	Bellary ...	1,591	43	265	38	224	2,519	134	2,082	1,233	6,457	1,672
	Kurnool ...	229	1	26	...	15	298	42	15	2	568	60
	Cuddapah ...	1,550	56	177	23	...	1,127	79	68	28	2,922	186
	North Arcot...	1,074	10	104	8	15	979	46	1,056	319	3,213	398
	Madras ...	39	...	24	1	85	419	5	41	9	523	100
	Total...	4,483	110	596	70	339	5,342	306	3,262	1,591	13,683	2,416
Southern Range.	South Arcot...	875	3	135	36	30	1,444	22	195	108	2,649	199
	Tanjore ...	1,022	23	162	19	498	2,223	43	614	15	4,021	598
	Trichinopoly...	441	3	10	...	...	797	11	28	2	1,276	16
	Madura ...	567	1	54	2	288	474	2	31	1	1,126	294
	Tinnevelly ...	..	...	...	...	...	...	...	...	...	...	...
	Total...	2,905	30	361	57	816	4,938	78	868	126	9,072	1,107
Western Range.	Salem ..	320	12	69	4	1	438	5	93	...	920	22
	Coimbatore ..	270	10	49	10	11	523	6	281	8	1,123	45
	South Malabar	77	1	1	...	67	433	...	11	...	522	68
	North Malabar.	353	2	40	7	114	282	8	30	...	705	131
	South Canara..	87	...	1	...	....	4	...	...	....	92	...
	Total...	1,107	25	160	21	193	1,680	19	415	8	3,362	266
	Grand Total...	10,972	258	1596	221	2,582	16,000	550	5,333	2,326	33,901	5,937

C.—*(Continued.)*

SUSPECTED PERSONS.				ACCIDENTAL DEATHS IN 1865.					
NUMBER OF HOUSES OF BAD REPUTE.				ACCIDENTAL DEATHS.					
Toddy-shops resorted to by thieves, &c.	Prostitutes in Cantonments.	Receivers of stolen goods.	Notorious Gambling Houses.	By drowning.		By other causes.		Total.	
				Males.	Females.	Males.	Females.	Males.	Females.
87	84	12	80	56	59	125	68	181	127
216	16	81	113	98	47	137	39	235	86
...	...	...	...	14	4	56	16	70	20
192	56	69	155	145	93	90	32	235	125
280	...	126	33	109	94	70	38	179	132
66	...	44	19	117	150	85	21	202	171
841	156	33	400	539	447	563	214	1,102	661
84	199	90	130	148	143	102	52	250	195
18	...	12	10	50	86	49	14	99	100
220	72	94	140	164	225	54	21	218	246
126	34	78	57	252	340	57	25	309	365
23	39	10	12	93	85	48	21	140	106
471	344	284	349	706	879	310	133	1,016	1,012
94	...	144	44	166	149	66	20	232	169
363	...	125	61	125	114	58	13	183	127
40	41	9	9	63	58	34	18	97	76
32	124	36	9	112	90	43	7	155	97
...	...	...	...	90	89	65	12	155	101
529	165	314	123	556	500	266	70	822	570
63	...	11	44	191	212	48	7	239	219
8	1	16	73	219	203	58	10	277	213
...	48	1	10	103	128	11	17	214	145
1	48	1	16	43	41	38	1	81	42
...	...	...	...	102	98	203	70	305	168
72	97	29	143	658	682	453	105	1,116	787
1,913	762	959	1,015	2,459	2,508	1,597	522	4,056	3,030

Ranges	DISTRICTS	By drowning.		By hanging.		By poison.		By lethal weapons.		By other causes.		Total.	
		Males.	Females.	Males.	Females.	Males.	Females.	Males.	Females.	Males.	Females.	Males.	Females.
Northern Range.	Ganjam... ...	11	16	31	17	...	...	1	...	1	1	44	34
	Vizagapatam...	11	35	9	8	...	...	2	...	...	...	22	43
	Jeypore... ...	3	2	4	4	...	...	...	...	...	...	8	8
	Godavery ...	26	73	6	7	...	...	1	...	2	1	35	81
	Kistna... ...	20	54	2	2	1	...	...	...	..	...	23	56
	Nellore	20	54	8	2	1	1	1	...	...	1	30	58
	Total...	91	234	60	40	2	1	6	2	·3	3	162	280
Central Range.	Bellary... ...	18	59	16	4	..	2	9	1	...	...	43	66
	Kurnool... ...	8	42	5	2	1	1	1	...	1	...	16	45
	Cuddapah ...	14	43	3	2	...	...	3	...	2	6	22	51
	North Arcot ...	25	80	11	3	4	1	1	...	...	1	41	85
	Madras... ...	8	18	3	...	...	...	...	...	...	...	11	18
	Total...	73	242	38	11	5	4	14	1	3	7	132	265
Southern Range.	South Arcot ...	4	18	9	5	...	...	1	...	..	1	14	24
	Tanjore... ...	4	6	6	2	...	1	1	...	...	...	11	9
	Trichinopoly ...	1	9	2	2	...	...	...	...	...	...	3	11
	Madura... ...	12	29	5	7	...	...	...	...	...	...	17	36
	Tinnevelly ...	9	11	6	7	..	3	1	...	...	2	16	23
	Total...	30	73	28	23	...	4	3	...	...	3	61	103
Western Range.	Salem... ..	2	12	10	3	1	...	...	...	...	...	13	15
	Coimbatore ...	12	39	16	19	...	...	...	...	...	...	28	58
	North Malabar	7	7	12	1	..	...	...	...	...	...	19	8
	South Malabar,	8	7	27	7	...	...	2	...	2	1	39	15
	South Canara...	3	7	23	5	1	4	...	...	...	...	27	16
	Total...	32	72	88	35	2	4	2	...	2	1	126	112
	Grand Total.	226	621	214	109	9	13	2^5	3	8	14	482	760

AND SUICIDES IN 1865.

SUICIDES.

C.—(*Continued.*)

Ranges.	DISTRICTS.	FIRES AND PROPERTY LOST IN 1865.				CONVICTS GUARDED IN JAILS IN 1865-66.		
		Number of Fires.	Number of houses, &c., burnt.	Value of property destroyed.	Number of lives lost.	Average number of Prisoners.	POLICE GUARDS	
							No.	Cost.
		1	2	3	4	5	6	7
								RS.
Northern Range.	Ganjam ...	368	3,653	50,996	7	353	50	5,628
	Vizagapatam ..	433	6,073	38,569	7	343	49	5,532
	Jeypore ...	17	19	159	...	...	...	...
	Godavery ...	1,039	5,564	69,046	24	288	41	4,560
	Kistna ...	444	2,612	108,018	6	353	50	5,628
	Nellore ...	243	602	23,225	2	346	49	5,532
	Total...	2,544	18,523	290,013	46	1,683	239	26,880
Central Range.	Bellary... ...	442	780	12,093	8	488	70	7,896
	Cuddapah ...	77	365	23,265	...	395	56	6,288
	Kurnool ..	146	1,078	25,514	7	278	40	4,464
	North Arcot ...	445	724	23,691	11	661	94	10,668
	Madras... ...	195	2:9	11,449	...	332	47	5,328
	Total...	1,305	3,166	96,012	26	2,154	307	34,644
Southern Range.	South Arcot ...	242	415	16,816	3	384	55	6,180
	Tanjore ...	623	925	8,019	6	387	55	6,180
	Trichinopoly ...	300	1,864	35,719	9	326	47	5,328
	Madura	415	3,319	58,275	8	377	54	6,084
	Tinnevelly ...	517	2,545	43,269	4	308	44	4,860
	Total...	2,097	9,068	162,098	30	1,782	255	28,632
Western Range.	Salem... ...	318	611	16,965	...	521	74	8,472
	Coimbatore ...	307	1,111	17,502	7	962	160	19,296
	North Malabar ...	88	103	7,098	...	278	46	5,244
	South Malabar ...	210	321	34,658	1	490	82	9,312
	South Canara ..	281	373	39,015	6	271	39	4,368
	Total...	1,204	2,519	115,238	14	2,522	401	46,692
	Grand Total...	7,150	33,276	663,361	116	8,141	1,202	1,36,848

D.

Annual Return of Criminal Statistics in the four Ranges of the

DESCRIPTION OF OFFENCES.	NORTHERN RANGE.		
	Cases		
	Reported.	Detected.	Per-centage.
No. 1. *Offences against the person.*			
Murder...	72	27	37·5
Attempt to murder	15	10	66·6
Culpable homicide	25	16	64
Attempt to commit do.	..	...	...
Attempt to commit and abetment of suicide... ...	78	39	50
Causing miscarriage	14	6	42·8
Concealment of birth, exposure of children... ...	16	7	43·7
Causing grievous hurt and hurt to extort confession...	38	20	56·6
Kidnapping and abducting ... ... :··	12	3	25
Prostitution of minors	...	...	...
Rape...	16	5	37·2
Total of No. 1...	286	133	46·5
No. 2. *Offences against property with violence.*			
Robbery in houses...	28	3	10·7
Do. in fields	95	14	14 7
Do. on highways and thoroughfares	83	16	19·2
Dacoities in houses	25	9	36
Do. in fields	34	5	14·7
Do. on highways ... ... ·.·	20	4	20
Lurking house-trespass, house-breaking, and house-breaking by night	3,038	539	17·7
Do. with violence	1	...	...
Breaking open closed receptacle of property ...	183	32	17·4
Total of No. 2 ..	3,507	622	17·7
No. 3. *Offences against property without violence.*			
Theft...	4,685	1,800	38·4
Petty theft under Regulation IV of 1821	1,813	1,624	89·5
Extortion	121	39	32·2
Criminal breach of trust and misappropriation ...	578	275	47·5
Receiving, &c., stolen property	136	81	59·5
Cheating	126	35	27·7
Frauds relating to weights and measures	23	12	52·1
Total of No. 3...	7,482	3,866	51·6

D.—(*Continued.*)

Madras Presidency, for the year ending 31st *December* 1865.

RANGES.

| NORTHERN RANGE. | | | | | | CENTRAL RANGE. | | | | | |
| Persons | | | Property | | | Cases | | | Persons | | |
Summoned and arrested.	Convicted.	Per-centage.	Lost.	Recovered.	Per-centage.	Reported.	Detected.	Per-centage.	Summoned and arrested.	Convicted.	Per-centage.
167	62	37·1	179	34	18·9	77	28	36·3	162	31	19·1
19	10	52·6	19	...	...	10	3	30	17	3	17·6
32	18	56·2	41	21	51·2	14	7	50	28	11	39·2
...						1	...	...	2	...	...
73	39	53·4	...	...	...	59	23	38·9	57	23	40·3
23	9	39·1	...	...	...	22	4	18·1	30	4	13·3
21	7	33·3	...	...	...	16	6	37·5	10	7	70
101	36	35·6	...	...	...	64	23	35·9	146	45	30·8
27	10	37	...	...	...	13	3	23	14	5	35·7
...	...	...	...	...	...	7	1	14·2	17	3	17·6
17	6	35·2	...	...	...	16	4	25	16	4	25
480	197	41	239	55	23	299	102	34·1	499	136	27·2
13	4	30·7	537	8	1·4	52	9	17·3	56	18	32·1
83	25	30·1	750	89	11·8	195	24	12·3	118	41	34·7
56	28	50	1,300	134	10·3	137	20	14·6	105	37	35·2
274	64	23·3	7,023	623	8·8	67	21	31·3	470	131	27·8
66	15	22·7	727	78	10·7	125	19	15·2	203	51	25·1
64	14	21·8	1,140	219	19·2	76	14	18·4	143	48	33·5
1,352	863	63·8	62,187	7,964	12·8	2,103	327	15·5	1,122	461	41
...	...	...	...	...	...	3	1	33·3	8	1	12·5
133	69	51·8	2,073	740	35·6	28	4	14·2	23	4	17·4
2,041	1,082	53	75,737	9,855	13	2,786	439	15·7	2,248	792	35·2
5,342	3,358	63·0	60,243	15,344	25·4	4,467	1,550	34·6	3,995	2,385	59·6
2,908	2,690	92·5	573	450	28·5	1,549	1,396	90·1	2,362	2,162	91·5
228	56	24·5	894	525	58·7	38	3	7·9	80	5	6·2
1,035	412	39·8	18,088	3,691	20·4	527	230	43·6	1,166	373	31·9
201	115	57·2	791	918	...	113	55	48·6	197	73	37·0
188	36	19·1	823	332	40·3	200	18	9	168	34	20·2
27	12	44·4	...	...	...	27	19	70·3	33	23	69·7
9,929	6,679	67·2	81,412	21,260	26·1	6,921	3,271	47·2	8,001	5,055	63·1

D
POLICE.

D.—(*Continued.*)

Annual Return of Criminal Statistics in the four Ranges of the

DESCRIPTION OF OFFENCES.	CENTRAL RANGE.		
	Property		
	Lost.	Recovered.	Per-centage.
No. 1. *Offences against the person.*			
Murder	327	11	3·3
Attempt to murder	...	...	...
Culpable homicide	...	...	...
Attempt to commit do	...	...	...
Attempt to commit and abetment of suicide... ...	...	...	...
Causing miscarriage	...	...	...
Concealment of birth, exposure of children	...	...	...
Causing grievous hurt and hurt to extort confession ...	...	...	...
Kidnapping and abducting	...	...	...
Prostitution of minors	...	...	...
Rape...	...	...	...
Total of No. 1...	327	11	3·3
No. 2. *Offences against property with violence.*			
Robbery in houses	1,244	207	16·6
Do. in fields	2,656	611	23·0
Do. on highways and thoroughfares	4,021	859	21·3
Dacoities in houses	23,450	4,969	21·1
Do. in fields	6,277	603	9·6
Do. on highways	6,940	143	2·0
Lurking house-trespass, house-breaking, and house-breaking by night	1,42,325	19,559	13·7
Do. with violence	15	4	26·6
Breaking open closed receptacle of property... ...	164	34	20·7
Total of No. 2...	1,87,092	26,989	14·4
No. 3. *Offences against property without violence.*			
Theft...	86,218	23,024	26·7
Petty theft under Regulation IV of 1821	464	408	87·9
Extortion	392	186	47·4
Criminal breach of trust and misappropriation ...	10,242	3,210	31·3
Receiving, &c., stolen property	667	1,943	...
Cheating	539	88	16·3
Frauds relating to weights and measures	...	...	...
Total of No. 3...	98,522	28,859	29·2

D.—(*Continued.*)

Madras Presidency, for the year ending **31st December** 1865.

RANGES.

	SOUTHERN RANGE.								WESTERN RANGE.		
Cases			Persons			Property			Cases		
Reported.	Detected.	Per-centage.	Summoned and arrested.	Convicted.	Per-centage.	Lost.	Recovered.	Per-centage.	Reported.	Detected.	Per-centage.
32	21	65·6	96	35	36·4	113	10	8·8	51	33	64·7
8	3	37·5	8	3	37·5	...	...	...	14	10	71·4
15	6	40	38	8	21	...	...	...	22	13	59
1	...	...	1	...	...	...	...	...	2	2	100
31	14	45·1	32	14	43·7	...	...	...	34	13	38·2
12	1	8·3	23	1	4·3	...	...	...	10	2	20
14	7	50	9	8	88·8	...	...	...	8	4	50
59	22	37·3	151	38	25·1	...	...	...	61	30	49·1
23	2	8·7	54	9	16·6	58	...	...	17	2	11·7
3	1	33·3	4	1	25	...	...	...	...	...	...
17	4	23·5	23	5	21·7	...	...	...	11	4	36·3
215	81	37·6	439	122	27·7	171	10	5·8	230	113	49·1
50	16	32	62	32	51·6	2,672	129	4·8	47	24	51
67	5	7·4	44	9	20·4	894	100	11·1	88	20	22·7
43	14	32·5	49	28	57·1	2,253	237	10·5	40	15	37·5
59	27	45·7	377	143	37·9	43,198	2,618	6·06	41	27	65·8
53	11	20·7	121	41	33·8	1,155	177	15·3	36	11	30·5
12	2	16·6	37	9	24·3	1,858	87	4·6	23	8	34·7
1,946	224	11·5	701	321	45·7	1,07,953	10,737	9·9	1,205	305	25·3
...	...	...	...	...	...	...	...	...	...	...	...
7	2	28·5	7	4	·57·1	96	9	9·3	24	...	...
2,237	301	13·4	1,398	587	41·9	1,60,079	14,094	8·8	1,504	410	27·2
4,438	1,502	33·8	4,366	2,312	52·9	86,752	22,570	26·01	4,091	1,653	40·4
3,456	3,091	89·4	5,149	4,708	91·4	792	625	78·9	1,633	1,536	94
85	13	15·2	278	21	7·5	270	40	14·8	56	7	12·5
266	134	50·3	447	160	35·7	12,161	1,261	10·3	386	165	42·7
134	67	50·	239	89	37·2	1,750	4,831	...	105	61	58
61	19	31·1	88	20	22·7	1,750	681	38·9	134	34	25·3
12	9	75	65	55	84·6	...	...	...	15	10	66·6
8,452	4,835	57·2	10,632	7,365	69·2	1,03,475	30,008	29	6,420	3,466	53·9

D. —(*Continued.*)

Annual Return of Criminal Statistics in the four Ranges of the

DESCRIPTION OF OFFENCES.	WESTERN RANGE.		
	Persons		
	Summoned and arrested.	Convicted.	Per-centage.
No. 1. Offences against the person.			
Murder	113	49	43·3
Attempt to murder	25	14	56
Culpable homicide	42	18	42·8
Attempt to commit do	2	2	100
Attempt to commit and abetment of suicide... ...	30	13	43·3
Causing miscarriage	20	3	15
Concealment of birth, exposure of children	10	5	50
Causing grievous hurt and hurt to extort confession ...	127	49	38·5
Kidnapping and abducting	32	2	6·2
Prostitution of minors	...	...	...
Rape	11	4	36·3
Total of No. 1 ..	412	159	38·5
No. 2. Offences against property with violence.			
Robbery in houses	92	49	53·2
Do. in fields	87	33	37·9
Do. on highways and thoroughfares	36	22	61·1
Dacoities in houses	272	154	56·6
Do. in fields	69	33	47·8
Do. on highways	58	35	60·3
Lurking house-trespass, house-breaking, and house-breaking by night	823	465	56·5
Do. with violence	...	...	...
Breaking open closed receptacle of property ...	16	...	...
Total of No. 2...	1,453	791	54·4
No. 3. Offences against property without violence.			
Theft...	3,642	2,528	69·4
Petty theft under Regulation IV of 1821	2,367	2,187	92·3
Extortion	89	13	14·6
Criminal breach of trust and misappropriation ...	510	206	40·3
Receiving, &c., stolen property	165	78	47·2
Cheating	155	40	25·8
Frauds relating to weights and measures	36	21	58·3
Total of No. 3 ..	6,964	5,073	72·8

D.—(*Continued.*)   D.
                            POLICE.

Madras Presidency, for the year ending 31st December 1865.

RANGES.

WESTERN RANGE.			TOTAL.								
Property			Cases			Persons			Property		
Lost.	Recovered.	Per-centage.	Reported.	Detected.	Per-centage.	Summoned and arrested.	Convicted.	Per-centage.	Lost.	Recovered.	Per-centage.
1,113	192	17·2	232	109	46·9	538	177	32·9	1,732	247	14·2
...	...	...	47	26	55·3	69	30	43·4	19	...	...
...	...	...	76	42	55·2	140	55	39·2	41	21	51·2
...	...	...	4	2	50	5	2	40	...	...	...
...	...	...	202	89	44	192	89	46·3	...	...	...
...	...	...	58	13	22·4	96	17	17·7	...	...	...
...	...	...	54	24	44·4	50	27	54	...	...	...
...	...	...	232	95	42·7	525	168	32	...	...	...
485	128	26·3	65	10	15·3	127	26	20·4	543	128	23·5
...	...	...	10	2	20	21	4	19	...	...	...
...	...	...	60	17	28·3	67	19	28·3	...	...	...
1,598	320	20	1,030	429	41·6	1,830	614	33·5	2,335	396	16·9
1,829	528	28·8	177	52	29·3	223	103	46·1	6,282	872	13·8
1,192	223	18·7	445	63	14·1	332	108	32·5	5,492	1,023	18·6
2,335	305	13	303	65	21·4	246	115	46·7	9,909	1,535	15·4
10,530	2,250	21·3	192	84	43·7	1,393	492	35·3	84,201	10,460	12·4
762	54	7	248	46	18·5	459	140	30·5	8,921	912	10·2
2,260	52	2·3	131	28	21·3	302	106	35	12,198	501	4·1
49,045	13,001	26·5	8,292	1,395	16·8	3,998	2,110	52·7	3,61,510	51,261	14·1
..	...	...	1	25	...	8	1	12·5	15	4	26·6
107	6	5·6	242	38	15·7	179	77	43	2,440	789	32·3
68,060	16,419	24·1	10,034	1,772	17·6	7,140	3,252	45·5	4,90,968	67,357	13·7
62,059	14,595	23·5	17,681	6,505	36·7	17,345	10,583	61	2,95,272	75,533	25·5
550	455	82·7	8,451	7,647	90·4	12,786	11,747	91·8	2,379	1,938	81·4
145	...	...	300	62	20·6	675	95	14	1,701	751	44·1
10,572	2,026	19·1	1,757	804	45·7	3,158	1,151	36·1	51,063	10,188	19·9
2,552	1,496	58·6	488	264	54·09	802	355	44·2	5,760	9,188	...
8,127	415	5·1	521	106	20·3	599	130	21·7	11,239	1,516	13·4
1	...	...	77	50	64·9	161	111	69	1	...	...
84,006	18,987	22·6	29,275	15,438	52·7	35,526	24,172	68	3,67,415	99,114	26·9

D.—(*Continued.*)

Annual Return of Criminal Statistics in the four Ranges of the

DESCRIPTION OF OFFENCES.	NORTHERN RANGE.		
	Cases		
	Reported.	Detected.	Per-centage.
No. 4. Malicious Offences against property.			
Mischief with aggravating circumstances	76	29	38·1
Do. by fire...	41	4	9·7
Total of No. 4...	1·17	33	28·2
No. 5. Forgery and Offences against Currency.			
Forgery	16	2	12·5
Counterfeiting coins ... •••	1	1	100
Uttering coins	28	9	32·1
Frauds relating to stamps	3	3	100
Total of No. 5...	48	15	31·2
No. 6. Offences not included in the above Classes.			
Unlawful assembly ... ••.	22	19	86·3
Riot... ..-	24	17	70·8
Affray ... ... ·.. ...	56	52	92·8
Harbouring escape and rescue of offenders	12	7	58·3
Return from transportation	...	...	...
Negligent escape ́	26	24	92·3
False evidence	14	8	57·1
Nuisances and offences against public health, safety, and decency	82	47	57·3
Offences against Police Act by Policemen, Act XXIV of 1859	67	52	77·6
Nuisances and other offences under Police Act XXIV of 1859 ... ́	1,237	1,148	92·8
Breach of Post Office Act ... ••• •••	6	3	50
Railway Act ... ... ••• ... ` ...	...	...	...
Total of No. 6...	1,546	1,377	89
No. 7. Offences against Revenue.			
A bkari ••• ... ... ••• ...	182	126	69·2
Salt ... ••• ... ••• ••• •••	472	421	89·1
Total of No. 7...	654	547	83·6
Grand Total...	13,640	6,593	48·3

D.—(*Continued.*)

Madras Presidency, for the year ending 31st December 1865.

RANGES.

| NORTHERN RANGE. | | | | | | CENTRAL RANGE. | | | | | |
| Persons | | | Property | | | Cases | | | Persons | | |
Summoned and arrested.	Convicted.	Per-centage.	Lost.	Recovered.	Per-centage.	Reported.	Detected.	Per-centage.	Summoned and arrested.	Convicted.	Per-centage.
284	88	30·9	...	...	...	44	15	34	142	47	33
51	6	11·7	991	...	...	50	2	4	39	2	5·1
335	94	28	991	...	...	94	17	18	181	49	27
39	14	35·8	10	10	100	65	19	29·2	147	28	19
1	1	100	...	...	...	...	...	...	...	...	...
34	10	29·4	...	...	...	39	15	38·4	58	23	39·6
3	3	100	...	...	...	1	1	100	1	1	100
7	28	36·3	10	10	100	105	35	33·3	206	52	25·2
227	154	67·8	..	...	...	35	20	57·1	300	153	51
335	167	49·8	...	...	...	41	34	82·9	373	226	60·5
207	170	82·1	...	...	...	82	73	89	322	235	72·9
15	7	46·6	...	...	...	10	4	40	13	5	38·4
...	...	...	...	...	...	...	...	...	...	...	...
43	32	74·3	...	...	...	37	31	83·7	52	39	76·8
19	10	52·6	...	...	...	44	30	68·1	73	48	65·7
212	111	52·3	...	...	...	58	45	77·5	95	67	70·5
93	67	72	...	...	...	94	83	88·3	170	142	83·5
4,852	4,256	87·7	417	1	·2	1,691	1,562	92·3	6,298	5,595	88·8
5	3	60	...	...	...	4	3	75	5	4	80
...	...	...	...	...	...	33	27	81·8	51	42	82·3
6,008	4,977	82·8	417	1	·2	2,126	1,912	89·8	7,752	6,556	84·7
331	192	58	86	86	100		30	57·6	73	40	54·7
2,110	2,011	95·3	633	451	71·2		44	81·4	210	170	80·9
2,441	2,203	90·2	719	537	74·6	106	74	69·8	283	210	74·2
21,311	15,260	71·6	1,59,525	31,718	74·6	12,440	5,850	47	19,170	12,850	67

D.—(*Continued.*)

Annual Return of Criminal Statistics in the four Ranges of the

DESCRIPTION OF OFFENCES.	CENTRAL RANGE. Property		
	Lost.	Recovered.	Per-centage.
No. 4. Malicious Offences against property.			
Mischief with aggravating circumstances	...	...	...
Do. by fire...	6,230	...	...
Total of No. 4...	6,230	...	...
No. 5. Forgery and Offences against Currency.			
Forgery.	25	8	32
Counterfeiting coins	...	...	...
Uttering coins...	11	...	...
Frauds relating to stamps..	..	...	...
Total of No. 5...	36	8	22·2
No. 6. Offences not included in the above Classes.			
Unlawful assembly	...	...	...
Riot	...	...	...
Affray.	...	...	...
Harbouring escape and rescue of offenders	...	...	...
Return from transportation	...	...	...
Negligent escape	...	...	...
False evidence	...	...	...
Nuisances and offences against public health, safety, and decency	...	...	...
Offences against Police Act by Policemen, Act XXIV of 1859.	21	4	19·0
Nuisances and other offences under Police Act XXIV of 1859	...	...	...
Breach of Post Office Act	...	...	...
Railway Act	...	...	...
Total of No. 6...	21	4	19
No. 7. Offences against Revenue.			
Abkari.	6	6	100
Salt	...	...	...
Total of No. 7...	6	6	100
Grand Total...	2,92,234	55,877	19·1

D.—(*Continued.*)

Madras Presidency, for the year ending 31st December 1865.

RANGES.

	SOUTHERN RANGE.									WESTERN RANGE.		
	Cases			Persons			Property			Cases		
	Reported.	Detected.	Per-centage.	Summoned and arrested.	Convicted.	Per-centage.	Lost.	Recovered.	Per-centage.	Reported.	Detected.	Per-centage.
	50	18	36	161	58	36·02	72	...	...	71	45	63·3
	39	3	7·6	35	3	8·5	658	...	...	38	8	21·
	89	21	23·5	196	61	31·1	730	...	...	109	53	48·6
	40	12	30	97	19	19·5	153	...	...	33	8	24·2
	8	2	25	9	2	22·2	...	...	...	...	...	...
	15	8	53·3	19	9	47·3	...	...	...	25	15	60
	1	...	...	...	...	...	...	...	...	1	1	100
	63	22	34·9	125	30	24	153	...	...	59	24	40·6
	22	11	50	170	74	43·5	...	...	...	19	10	52·6
	44	25	56·8	314	149	47·4	...	...	...	47	27	57·4
	42	39	92·8	116	107	92·2	...	...	...	83	78	93·9
	16	7	43·1	28	15	53·5	...	...	...	13	7	53·8
	...	...	...	...	...	...	...	...	...	...	...	...
	20	16	80	24	18	75	...	...	...	18	15	83·3
	31	13	41·9	43	14	32·5	...	...	...	71	48	67·6
	86	48	55·8	273	193	70·6	...	...	...	113	62	54·8
	27	19	70·3	30	22	73·3	...	...	...	44	42	95·4
	1,800	1,680	93·3	5,368	4,820	89·8	...	...	...	860	808	93·9
	4	2	50	3	2	66·6	1,328	...	...	1	1	100
	55	50	90·9	75	66	88	...	...	...	171	157	91·8
	2,147	1,910	88·9	6,439	5,480	85·1	1,328	...	...	1,440	1,255	87·1
	51	44	86·2	160	65	40·6	...	5	...	103	66	64
	126	114	90·4	328	327	99·6	62	59	95·1	28	21	75
	177	158	89·2	488	392	80·3	62	64	...	131	87	66·4
	13,380	7,328	54·7	19,717	14,037	71·1	2,65,998	44,176	16·6	9,893	5,408	54·6

D.—(*Continued.*)

Annual Return of Criminal Statistics in the four Ranges of the

DESCRIPTION OF OFFENCES.	WESTERN RANGE.		
	Persons		
	Summoned and arrested.	Convicted.	Per-centage.
No. 4. Malicious Offences against property.			
Mischief with aggravating circumstances	232	159	68·5
Do. by fire...	33	13	39·3
Total of No. 4...	265	172	64·9
No. 5. Forgery and Offences against Currency.			
Forgery.	63	19	30·1
Counterfeiting coins	...	...	...
Uttering coins	30	19	63·3
Frauds relating to stamps.	1	1	100
Total of No. 5...	94	39	41·4
No. 6. Offences not included in the above Classes.			
Unlawful assembly	153	80	52·2
Riot	312	203	65
Affray... ... ... ,...	270	231	85·5
Harbouring escape and rescue of offenders	22	15	68·1
Return from transportation	...	...	...
Negligent escape	36	20	55·5
False evidence	91	59	64·8
Nuisances and offences against public health, safety, and decency	33	135	57·9
Offences against Police Act by Policemen, Act XXIV of 1859.	48	47	97·9
Nuisances and other offences under Police Act XXIV of 1859.	1,541	1,428	92·6
Breach of Post Office Act. ... ... · ...	1	1	100
Railway Act	221	185	83·7
Total of No. 6...	2,928	2,404	82·1
No. 7. Offences against Revenue.			
Abkari...	162	95	58·6
Salt	82	60	73·1
Total of No. 7...	244	155	63·5
Grand Total...	12,360	8,793	71·3

D.—(*Continued.*)

Madras Presidency, for the year ending 31st December 1865.

RANGES.

| WESTERN RANGE. | | | TOTAL. | | | | | | | | |
| Property | | | Cases | | | Persons | | | Property. | | |
Lost.	Recovered.	Per-centage.	Reported.	Detected.	Per-centage.	Summoned and arrested.	Convicted.	Per-centage.	Lost.	Recovered.	Per-centage.
225	...	...	241	107	44·4	819	352	43	297	...	...
413	...	...	168	17	10·1	158	24	15·2	8,292	...	...
638	...	...	409	124	30·3	977	376	38·4	8,589	...	...
1,009	30	2·9	154	41	26·6	346	80	26·1	1,197	48	4
...	...	...	9	3	33·3	10	3	30	...	...	...
...	...	...	107	47	43·9	141	61	43·2	11	...	...
...	...	...	5	5	100	5	5	100	...	...	...
1,009	30	2·9	275	96	34·9	502	149	29·6	1,208	48	3·9
...	...	...	98	60	61·2	850	461	54·2	...	...	...
...	...	...	156	103	66	1,334	745	55·8	...	...	...
...	...	...	263	242	92	915	743	81·2	...	...	...
...	...	...	51	25	49	78	42	53·8	...	...	...
...	...	...	...	...	...	...	...	...	...	...	...
...	...	...	101	86	85·1	155	109	70·3	...	...	...
...	...	...	160	99	61·8	226	131	57·9	...	...	...
120	...	...	339	202	59·5	813	506	62·2	120	...	...
13	11	84·6	232	196	84·4	341	278	81·5	34	15	44·1
...	...	...	5,588	5,198	93	18,054	16,099	89·1	417	1	·2
...	...	...	15	9	60	14	10	71·4	1,328	...	...
33	30	90·9	259	234	90·3	347	293	84·4	33	30	90·9
166	41	24·6	7,262	6,454	88·8	22,127	19,417	87·4	1,932	46	2·3
...	...	...	388	266	68·5	726	392	53·9	92	97	...
9	9	100	680	600	88·2	2,730	2,568	94	704	519	73·7
9	9	100	1,068	866	81	3,456	2,960	85·6	796	616	73·7
1,55,486	35,806	23	49,353	25,179	51	72,558	50,940	70·2	8,73,243	1,67,577	19·1

E.

From the Chief Secretary to the Government of Fort St. George,
Judicial Department, to the Secretary to the Government of
India, Home Department, dated 9th December 1865, No. 1,760.

1. I am directed to submit, for the consideration of His Excellency
the Viceroy and Governor
General in Council, the
accompanying papers, re-
lating to the measures which have been, and are being, taken by this
Government, with the view of increasing the amount of Jail accommodation, and improving the system of Jail management and discipline,
in this Presidency.

Proceedings, 16th June 1865, Nos. 156—162.
Do. 8th Sept. „ „ 83—110.
Do. 9th Dec. „ „ 76—79 & 81, 82.

2. The letter from Messrs. Rohde and Ellis, recorded in the Proceedings of Government, under date the 16th June last, paragraphs 16
to 30, contains a tolerably full report on the accommodation afforded
in the existing Jails, and on the additional accommodation which is
required. It will be seen that, while the existing Jails are capable,
according to the standard recently laid down by the Government of
India, of containing only 4,492 prisoners, the number actually in confinement at the date of the report in question was 6,802, and at times
the latter number has been considerably exceeded. Indeed the average
daily number during the last official year was 7,855, and on the 30th
April last, the actual number of prisoners in confinement was 8,120.
Two Central Jails are now in course of erection at Rajahmundry and
Coimbatore, which will be finished in the course of a few months;
and it is proposed to erect additional Central Jails at Bellary, Cannanore, and Trichinopoly, so as to provide altogether for about 4,500
prisoners sentenced to periods of imprisonment in excess of one year.
Adding this to the accommodation available for 4,492 short-sentenced
prisoners in the existing Jails, there will eventually be prison accommodation for some 9,000 prisoners, which, it is hoped, will be ample to
meet the requirements of this Presidency. The proposals of Messrs.
Rohde and Ellis included the erection of a Central Jail at Vellore, in
addition to those to be provided at Bellary, Cannanore, and Trichinopoly, but the Governor in Council is of opinion that, for the present
at all events, six Jails of this description, including the two at Coimbatore and Salem, which are to serve the purposes of both Central and
District Jails, will be sufficient.

xlviii

3. Orders have been issued for the preparation of estimates of the cost of constructing the new Cetral Jails on the plan submitted by the Commitee appointed in June last, and of the improvements which are required to the existing District Jails ; and adverting to the letter of the Suprme Government, under date the 23rd June 1864, No. 952, to the effect that the Government of India would be prepared to make the necessary provision of funds for giving early effect to any carefully considered proposals for increasing Jail accommodation, wherever it may be manifestly insufficient, I am directed to request that a special grant of Rupees (2,00,000) two lakhs may be sanctioned for this purpose, as an addition to the amount of the Publc Works Budget grant for the current official year, as it will not be possible to meet the additional expenditure which will have to be incurred on Jail buildings from that grant, which, under the orders of the Government of India, was reduced to an amount quite inadequate to meet even the ordinary demands upon it. The estimates which have been received for the completion of the Jails at Coimbatore and Rajahmnndry, for the erection of new Jails at Tanjore and Madura, and for improving the Jails at Tanjore, Vizagapatam, and Guntoor, amount to upwards of Rupees 3,00,000, and it is very desirable that one, at all events, of the three additional Central Jails which it is proposed to erect should be commenced during the present season.

4. Among the papers now submitted are the orders which have been passed by this Government regarding the superintendence of the several Jails, from which it will be seen that Zillah Surgeons have been placed in charge of nineteen of the District Jails, including, as a temporary measure, the Central Jail at Salem ; while at Bellary and Cannanore, the Cantonment Magistrates have been placed in charge of the Jails, and at Cuddapah the Magistrate has been instructed to place one of his Assistants in charge, acting under his general supervision.

8th September 1865, Nos. 88—110.

5. I am directed to request that authority may be granted to pass the salaries sanctioned in the Resolution of the Government of India, in the Financial Department, under date the 22nd February last, No. 912, to the Cantonment Magistrates at Bellary and Cannanore, and that the enforcement of the rule laid down in that Resolution, that the salaries in question are only to be given in Jails where intramural labor is the rule, and not the exception, may be postponed

E.
JAILS. until the necessary arrangements for the working of prisoners within the walls of the Jails are carried out. Sanction is also requested for the salaries proposed in the Report made by Messrs. Rohde and Ellis for Jailers, viz. :—

Jailers of Central Jails ... ... Rupees 150
    Do.   1st Class District Jails ... ... „ 100
    Do.   2nd Class   do. ... ... „ 50

and for the salary proposed in paragraph 12 of the Proceedings of this Government, under date the 16th June 1865, for the Superintendents of the Central Jails at Salem and Coimbatore, viz., Rupees 600 per mensem.

6. I am also to inquire, with reference to the question raised in the correspondence noted in the margin, whether the Resolution of the Government of India in the Financial Department, of the 13th March 1865, No. 1,425, precludes the grant of salary for the charge of a Jail to a Zillah Surgeon who has been allowed to draw his Military pay and allowances in lieu of his Civil salary.

From the Inspector General of Jails, 16th November 1865.

From the Inspector General of Jails, and the President of the Sanitary Commission, to the Chief Secretary to Government, Fort Saint George ; dated Madras, 10th April 1865, No. 654A.

In compliance with the Orders of Government, dated 7th February last, we have the honor to submit a Report on the additional Jail accommodation required in the Madras Presidencey, and the measures to be taken for improving existing Jails.

2. We also submit a Manual of Jail Rules.

Report on the additional Jail accommodation required in
the Madras Presidency, and the measures to be taken
for improving existing Jails.

1. In calculating the Jail accommodation required, the standard adopted is that prescribed by the Government of India, in the Office Memerandum from the Home Department, No. 128, dated 6th January

1865, and communicated by the order of Madras Government, dated 16th February, No. 464.

2. According to this standard, each prisoner is to have for his accommodation a minimum superficial area of 36 square feet, and 648 cubic feet.

3. This standard differs somewhat from that recommended by the Calcutta Jail Committee, which gave to each prisoner a minimum superficial area of 54 square feet and 648 cubic feet.

4. We have received from each Jail in the Presidency, a return shewing the accommodation which each is capable of affording at the latest standard. Before entering upon a detailed statement regarding each of these Jails, we may state that, supposing all the Jails at present existing to be retained, and we shall afterwards shew that this is not desirable, they afford not much more than half the accommodation required, if each prisoner is to have the area considered absolutely necessary.

5. The necessity of Central Jails of moderate size has been recognized by the Calcutta Jail Committee, and, before that Committee was appointed, this necessity was admitted by the Madras Government, who ordered Central Jails to be built at Coimbatore and Rajahmundry, and who had had it in contemplation, so far back as 1857, to build five Central Jails.

6. The Calcutta Committee recommended, 1st, that all persons whose sentences exceed the period of one year should be confined in Central Jails, and that no Central Jail should contain more than one thousand Prisoners—(in the arrangements proposed for the Bengal Presidency, this principle is somewhat relaxed, and it is provided that prisoners sentenced to more than six months' rigorous imprisonment may also be imprisoned in Central Jails); 2nd, that in the District Jails those prisoners only should be confined, whose sentences do not exceed one year. The District Jails are divided into 1st and 2nd Class.

The 1st Class Jails to contain 500 prisoners.
The 2nd Class Jails to contain 300 prisoners.

7. We concur generally in these recommendations, and we have, therefore, considered how many Central Jails will be necessary to meet the requirements of this Presidency.

8. In this and in other estimates regarding the probable number of prisoners of different classes requiring prison accommodation, we do not pretend to have arrived at strictly accurate results. The necessity of collecting careful judicial statistical information has only recently

E.
JAILS.

attracted the attention it deserves, and there are other circumstances, such as the introduction of the New Police and the Indian Penal Code, which have had a tendency to render less reliable the averages which can be calculated from the Criminal and Jail returns of the last ten years.

Central Jails.

9. Making allowances for the variations in the number of convictions, as shewn by a comparison of the annual Judicial returns of the last few years, we think we may safely state that Central Jail accommodation is required for about 5,000 prisoners, whose sentences exceed one year's imprisonment. Had nothing been done in this Presidency towards the construction of Central Jails, we should have proposed *six* Central Jails: four to contain one thousand prisoners, and two to contain eight hundred prisoners.

10. The places which seem most suitable for these Central Jails are,

		Prisoners.			Prisoners.
1.	Rajahmundry...	1,000	4'	Vellore ...	1,000
2.	Bellary	1,000	5.	Trichinopoly...	800
3.	Coimbatore ...	1,000	6.	Cannanore ...	800,

and we should have recommended that, except upon an emergency, the rule should be maintained that prisoners whose sentences exceed one year should be confined in these Central Jails, while prisoners whose sentences are for less than one year should be detained in District Jails.

11. But we are met by the difficulty that there has already been completed at Salem a Jail that is capable, at the new standard, of containing 426 prisoners; while a large Jail at Coimbatore, calculated at the new standard to contain 554 prisoners, is far advanced in construction. Under these circumstances, we think the Jails at Coimbatore and Salem must unite the characters of Central and District prisons, instead of following out entirely the recommendation of the Calcutta Jail Committee, according to which Central and District prisons are completely separated. In reality, this will not be an abandonment of the principle involved of separating entirely these two great classes of convicts; for, owing to the construction of the Jails at Coimbatore and Salem, the convicts sentenced to long terms of imprisonment, and the prisoners whose sentences do not exceed one year, can be kept quite distinct. This arrangement will obviate the necessity of building a District Jail at Coimbatore, which, under the circumstances detailed, would involve an unnecessary expense. The

total number of prisoners which these two Jails would accommodate, as at present planned, is 980.

Accommodation is required at Coimbatore and Salem for 1,134 prisoners, thus classified :—

	Prisoners for more than one year.	Prisoners for less than one year.	Total.
Coimbatore	564	111	675
Salem	303	156	459
	867	267	1,134

All that need be done to meet these requirements is to complete the ground-floor of the Coimbatore Jail as planned, and to add upper stories to two of the blocks.

12. With this modification, the Central Jails would be as follows :—
Central Jails to contain 1,000 prisoners.
Rajahmundry.
Trichinopoly.
Vellore.
Central Jails to contain 800 prisoners.
Bellary.
Cannanore.
Jails to serve both as Central and District Jails.
Coimbatore.
Salem.

13. The Central Jails at Bellary, Trichinopoly, and Cannanore, will have the important advantage of being at stations where there are European Troops. Bellary and Cannanore have already been approved by Government as proper positions for Central Jails. At Rajahmundry the proposed Central Jail has been sanctioned by Government, and is already under construction. As above explained, the Jail at Salem is finished, and that at Coimbatore is almost completed.

14. We now proceed to detail the Districts which will supply the inmates of each of the proposed Central Jails.

The Central Jail at Rajahmundry will supply accommodation for all convicts sentenced to more than one year's imprisonment from the Districts of Ganjam, Vizagapatam, Godavery, and Kistna, and for a portion of Nellore. We do not propose transferring Khond convicts, although their sentences exceed one year, to the Rajahmundry Central Jail, experience having shewn that they cannot be imprisoned away from their own country, without serious risk of life. The Khond convicts should, we think, as hitherto, continue to be imprisoned in a separate Jail at Russelcondah (the old Barracks).

The Central Jail at Bellary will supply accommodation for all convicts sentenced to more than one year's imprisonment, from the Districts of Bellary, Cuddapah, and Kurnool.

The Central Jail at Trichinopoly will afford accommodation for the convicts sentenced to more than one year's imprisonment, from the Districts of Trichinopoly, Madura, Tinnevelly, and Tanjore.

The Central Jail at Cannanore will receive the convicts sentenced to more than one year's imprisonment from Malabar, South Canara, and Cochin.

The Central Jail at Vellore will receive the convicts sentenced to more than one year's imprisonment from North and South Arcot, and the Madras and Nellore Districts.

As explained above, the Jails at Coimbatore and Salem will contain the convicts from these Districts, sentenced both to long and short terms of imprisonment.

District Jails.

15. As shewn above, we propose to accommodate in the Central Jails an average number of 5,000 prisoners, whose sentences exceed one year. It remains to provide prison accommodation for convicts sentenced to less than one year's imprisonment ; for prisoners kept in confinement, in consequence of failing to give security ; for prisoners under trial ; and for Civil Debtors.

16. These* represent a total number of 3,059, of which the following is the detail :—

Prisoners for one year and under ...	...1,766
Prisoners, in default of giving security	... 186
Prisoners under trial	... 740
Civil Debtors	... 355
State Prisoners	... 12
	3,059

These prisoners, we propose, should be confined in the under-mentioned District Jails :—

Berhampore ...	... 148	Nellore... ...	... 118
Vizagapatam ...	... 172	Bellary... ...	... 275
Rajahmundry...	... 94	Kurnool.. ...	... 92
Masulipatam ...	... 63	Cuddapah ...	... 276
Guntoor.. ...	... 169	Coimbatore ...	... 111

* This is exclusive of seventy-two Hill Prisoners of all classes, in the Russelcondah Jail.

Ootacamund ...	... 87	Tanjore ...	...	... 86
Salem ...	... 156	Madura ...	...	... 220
Chittoor...	... 143	Tinnevelly	...	... 114
Chingleput	... 130	Mangalore	...	... 77
Cuddalore	... 120	Tellicherry	...	... 85
Trichinopoly ...	... 83	Calicut ...	...	... 126
Tranquebar	... 69	Cochin ...	...	... 45

17. The following tabulated statement shews the capacity of each Jail according to the new standard, which allows 36 superficial feet and 648 cubical feet to each prisoner, the probable number of prisoners who will be confined in each Jail, and the number of all classes at present confined in these Jails. When the prisoners sentenced to more than one year's imprisonment have been removed to the proposed Central Jails, the District Jails, as recommended by us, will afford accommodation for 4,492 prisoners, being 1,433 more than are actually requiring accommodation at present. But the maximum accommodation required varies much in particular Districts, and in some Jails the apparent accommodation will be considerably reduced by the conversion of wards into workshops.

	JAILS.	1. No. of Prisoners Jail is capable of containing, according to mini-mum standard of 648 cubic and 36 superficial feet to each.	2. No. to be imprisoned in District Jails, including under trial Pri-soners and Civil Debtors.	3. No. of Prisoners of all classes at present confined in each Jail.	4. No. of Prisoners sentenced to above 1 year, and to be trans-ferred to Central Jail.	REMARKS.
RAJAHMUNDRY CIRCLE.	Berhampore	168	148	247	139	
	Vizagapatam	156	172	332	193	VIZAGAPATAM.—This is a new Jail nearly completed. The accommodation provided, according to the original plan, is for 156 prisoners. The total number for whom accommodation is required is 172, or 16 in excess. Allowance must be made for sick prisoners in Hospital. This building has not yet been provided, but must be constructed. This will pro-vide the necessary accommodation for the average number of prisoners, 172. Any excess over that number can be provided by the transfer of prisoners sentenced to more than six months' rigorous imprison-ment to the Central Jail at Rajahmundry.

E.
JAILS.

JAILS.	1 — No. of Prisoners Jail is capable of containing, according to minimum standard of 648 cubic and 36 superficial feet to each.	2 — No. to be imprisoned in District Jails, including under trial Prisoners and Civil Debtors.	3 — No. of Prisoners of all classes at present confined in each Jail.	4 — No. of Prisoners sentenced to above 1 year, and to be transferred to Central Jail.	REMARKS.
RAJAHMUNDRY CIRCLE. Rajahmundry ...	77	94	121	54	**RAJAHMUNDRY.**—It will be observed that there is an estimated excess of 17 prisoners above the accommodation, which can be provided in this Jail. A per-centage of prisoners sentenced for more than six months' rigorous imprison- ment can be sent to the Central Jail, which will be in close proximity to the District Jail.
Masulipatam... ...	98	63	103	14	
Guntoor...	117	169	347	186	**GUNTOOR.**—It will be observed that at present the District Jail at Guntoor can only contain 117 prisoners at the new standard. If, however, as recom- mended in this report, the Jail walls are raised four feet, this Jail will accom- modate 175 prisoners, which will be amply sufficient.
BELLARY CIRCLE. Nellore	160	118	478	336	
Bellary	203	275	501	250	**BELLARY.**—In order to afford the necessary accommodation in the District Jail at Bellary, it will be necessary to construct two new wards, for 35 prisoners in each ward. There is sufficient avail- able space within the Jail enclosure, for the erection of these additional wards.
Kurnool ...	53	92	195	127	**KURNOOL.**—We would refer to the remarks on this Jail in the portion of our Report headed "Alterations and Im- provement of existing Jails." It will be necessary to build a new District Jail either at Kurnool or Nundial, for the accommodation of 100 prisoners.
Cuddapah	175	276	49 9	328	**CUDDAPAH.**—An addition must also be made to this Jail. Further accommoda- tion, at the prescribed standard, is re- quired for about 100 prisoners. We would propose the construction of three new wards, to contain each 32 pri- soners.
VELLORE CIRCLE. Chittoor ...	270	143	473	484	Any excess in the transfers to the Cen- tral Jail can be met by making transfers from Cuddalore to the Central Jail of Trichinopoly.
Chingleput ...	166	130	241	296	
Cuddalore ...	366	120	318	224	
TRICHINOPOLY CIRCLE. Trichinopoly ...	246	83	296	255	
Tranquebar ...	139	69	207	160	
Tanjore New Jail...	309	86	105	44	**TANJORE.**—It had been proposed to build a District Jail for 309 prisoners at Tanjore; but if the sanction of Govern- ment is accorded to the provision of a Central Jail at Trichinopoly, a small Dis- trict Jail for 100 prisoners will be suffi- cient.

JAILS.		1 No. of Prisoners Jail is capable of containing, according to minimum standard of 648 cubic and 36 superficial feet to each.	2 No. to be imprisoned in District Jails, including under trial Prisoners and Civil Debtors.	3 No. of Prisoners of all classes at present confined in each Jail.	4 No. of Prisoners sentenced to above 1 year, and to be transferred to Central Jail.	REMARKS.
TRICHINOPOLY CIRCLE.	Madura New Jail...	309	220	243	244	MADURA.—A new District Jail for 309 prisoners has been proposed at Madura. The estimated number for whom accommodation will be required is 220. A reduction of 1 block, ¼th of the proposed Jail might with advantage be made for the present.
	Tinnevelly... ...	66	114	238	171	TINNEVELLY.—For the reasons stated in that portion of the report headed, "Alterations and Improvements in existing Jails," we have recommended that a new small District Jail be built at Tinnevelly, the present District Jail not admitting of improvement or addition.
CANNANORE CIRCLE.	Mangalore	309	77	252	212	MANGALORE.—Although this Jail is of superior construction, the place itself is unhealthy, and the mortality in this Jail has always been large. Mangalore is therefore not suited to a Central Jail, and when a Central Jail is built at Cannanore, accommodation will only be required for between 70 and 80 prisoners. The remaining space in this Jail can only be utilised as workshops and will then be in excess of what is required.
	Tellicherry	134	85	153	170	
	Calicut	260	126	319	337	
	Cochin...	48	45	53	...	
COIMBATORE CIRCLE.	Coimbatore	172	111	330	562	COIMBATORE.—As explained in a previous part of this report, the Coimbatore and Salem Jails will have to contain all classes of prisoners. In completing the Coimbatore Jail it will be necessary to build upper stories on two of the blocks.
	Ootacamund...	65	87	201	...	
	Salem...	426	156	550	303	
	Total...	4,492	3,059	6,802	5,089	

18. From this statement it will be seen that in Jails affording proper accommodation for 4,492 prisoners, there are at present confined 6,802 prisoners, and these Jails have at certain periods of the year been much more crowded. We need make no comment on the urgent necessity for reform in this respect, for it has been recognized by the Government, and will be remedied when the new Jails are built; but we beg to bring the present condition of these prisoners, whose lives are undoubtedly exposed to serious risk from over-crowding, to the prominent notice of Government, and we trust that the proposal

which we have made in another portion of this report, for the immediate employment of gangs of prisoners in the construction of the new Jails, will be approved.

Additions and alterations required in District Jails.

19. We now proceed to detail the various improvements required in each of those District Jails which we propose to retain.

Berhampore.—Subsoil drainage should be introduced. The surface drainage also requires improvement, especially in the neighbourhood of interior walls and cook-houses.

The water of the well within the Jail is of inferior quality, as in that of the neighbourhood ; the well might with advantage be deepened. A Jail garden is required ; there is no difficulty in getting the necessary ground.

Palisades, as originally designed, should be erected, parallel to the outer walls, at a distance of eight feet from the outer wall, so as to secure separation of yards, without interfering with ventilation of yards now impeded by the cross walls.

Two solitary cells are required.

Russelcondah.—Subsoil drainage should be introduced. The water for the use of the prisoners is drawn from the river, which is likely to fail in hot weather. To supply this defect a well is required. There is no suitable spot for a Jail garden in the neighbourhood.

Vizagapatam.—Subsoil drainage is required in this new Jail which is under construction ; a well is also necessary.

The same improvement as regards palisades, as recommended for Berhampore, is required in this Jail, and sun shades should be added to the doors and windows. There is no available space for a garden for this Jail.

The Hospital is, like that at Berhampore, placed in a ward of the Jail which will be required for the accommodation of the prisoners.

Two solitary cells are required.

Rajahmundry.—Subsoil drainage is required. The lateral ventilation in this Jail requires improvement. A Jail Garden should be established, and there is no difficulty in obtaining the ground required for this purpose.

Two solitary cells are also wanted.

Masulipatam.—Subsoil drainage will be required if this Jail is retained ; but as this prison is notoriously unhealthy, it is proposed to transfer prisoners sentenced to more than one month's imprisonment to the District Jail at Guntoor. It has not been thought necessary to recommend any alterations in the Masulipatam Jail.

Guntoor.—Jail requires subsoil drainage. Floors of the wards require to be raised one foot, and the walls of the wards must be raised at least four feet, to afford the cubical space required. The present Jail garden requires extension.

Two solitary cells are also wanted.

Nellore.—This Jail requires subsoil drainage. When the long-sentenced prisoners are removed to a Central Jail, the old part of the Jail should be altogether removed. In the newer part of the Jail, the roof requires complete repair, spaces being left open between the rafters and walls to secure ventilation. A sufficient plot of ground must be purchased for a Jail garden.

Two solitary cells are also wanted.

Kurnool.—There has been great uncertainty as to whether the District Jail is to be built here or at Nundial. The present building used for the confinement of prisoners does not deserve the name of a Jail; it is an enclosure in the middle of the town, with common sheds of no value.

If Kurnool is to be retained as the station for the Court and for the District Jail, a new Jail should be built without delay. At present, prisoners are often kept in tents in consequence of the insufficiency of the Jail accommodation.

Cuddapah.—Subsoil drainage is required in this as in other Jails ; saucer drains for carrying off the surface drainage should be substituted for the present deep drains.

A Jail garden is required in this Jail.

Bellary.—Subsoil and surface drainage are both required in this Jail.

Iron-barred doors and windows are required to insure the ventilation of the building. A piece of land has been appropriated for conversion into a Jail garden.

Two solitary cells are also wanted.

Chittoor.—This Jail is surrounded by a moat, and there may be difficulty in providing, as in other Jails, for subsoil drainage.

Lateral ventilation should be improved by the substitution of iron-grated doors and windows, for the wooden batten doors. The Hospital drainage should be improved by both subsoil and surface drainage, as there is not the same difficulty in doing this, as in the case with the Jail ; a granite platform for washing should be built in the Hospital yard. A Jail garden should be made.

E.
JAILS.

Vellore.—This Jail will not be retained when the long-sentenced prisoners are removed. But in the meantime, some improvement might be made in the ventilation of this Jail. The prisoners are at present over-crowded in narrow wards, and although the Jail has been healthy, any epidemic would prove unusually fatal in this Jail.

Chingleput.—This Jail requires subsoil and surface drainage, and an enclosing wall. Two solitary cells are also wanted. The lateral ventilation requires improvement. The moats should be filled in, and a new entrance to the Fort made so as to prevent the public road intersecting the Jail as at present. Cooking sheds should be built within the enclosing wall.

Guindy.—If the gang of prisoners is to be kept at Guindy, as at present, considerable improvements must be made in the lateral ventilation, and an enclosing wall should be built; but if out-of-door labor is to be discontinued, it seems unnecessary to retain a gang of prisoners at Guindy.

Cuddalore.—This Jail requires subsoil drainage. The ventilation of the Jail should be improved by substituting iron-grated doors and windows for the present wooden batten doors and windows. The lateral ventilation should also be greatly increased. There is no available ground for a Jail garden.

Two solitary cells are wanted.

Tranquebar.—The Jail is situated in an old Dutch Fort. Some of the cells in the case-mate have defective ventilation, but the prisoners are generally healthy, and from the position of this Jail and its peculiar construction no important improvement can be made to the buildings. A Jail garden should be made, and for this purpose there is ground available.

Two solitary cells are wanted.

Tanjore.—No alteration is required in the present Jail, which is temporary, and is in a hired building. A new Jail has been sanctioned.

Trichinopoly.—This Jail requires subsoil and surface drainage. For the latter purpose saucer drains should be substituted for the present deep drains. Palisades should be substituted for the dwarf walls at the end of the courts between the wards, except the division wall separating the Hospital from the wards, which should remain as at present. The well should be deepened but not widened, as has been proposed by the Officer in charge of the Jail. A Jail garden should be formed in the walled enclosure at the back of the Jail.

Two solitary cells are also wanted.

lx

Madura.—The present Jail will be abandoned, and a new Jail constructed. No alterations which would entail expense can be recommended.

. *Paumbum.*—This Jail will be discontinued when intramural labor is general. The wards are thatched, which is objectionable, and if the Jail is retained, even temporarily, this ought to be remedied.

Tinnevelly.—It will be difficult to make the necessary additions and improvements to this building. On the new standard this Jail can only accommodate sixty six prisoners. It is an old Choultry which has been added to. It will be necessary to build a new District Jail here to contain about 120 prisoners.

Salem.—This is a new Jail which is not entirely completed. A separate building for a Hospital, properly enclosed, must be provided. A deep well to supply drinking water for the use of the prisoners must be sunk.

Coimbatore.—The present Jail is so unhealthy that it should not be retained. A Central Jail has been commenced. It is proposed also to provide in a portion of this Jail accommodation for prisoners sentenced to short terms of imprisonment.

Ootacamund.—The number of prisoners will be greatly reduced as regards Native prisoners. The Jail requires both surface and subsoil drainage, and the ventilation should be improved. The Jail garden should be enclosed and improved. Plans for a new Civil Jail have been submitted.

Two solitary cells are also wanted.

Calicut.—This Jail has always been subject to outbreaks of epidemic disease, and should be abandoned. The site is admirably suited for store-houses, &c., as it is close to the sea. The Jail ought to be moved to high ground ; the sale of the present Jail would pay for the construction of a new building.

Mangalore.—This Jail requires subsoil drainage, and a garden which has been commenced should be completed. The supply of water must also be increased by deepening the well.

Two solitary cells are also wanted:

Cochin.—This small Jail for short-sentenced prisoners will be continued ; all that is required is to put it in thorough repair.

. *Tellicherry.*—All but the wards on the sea face are unfit for the use of prisoners ; but when the long-sentenced prisoners are removed, sufficient and proper accommodation can be provided for prisoners under short sentences.

E.
JAILS.

Additional wards will be required for prisoners under trial, and for the Civil debtors. A garden should be made.

Two solitary cells are also wanted.

Cannanore.—No District Jail is required here; a new Central Jail has been proposed at this station.

20. As shewn above, new District Jails are required at Kurnool, Madura, Tanjore, and Tinnevelly. These Jails have from the first been so defective and are in such a condition, that they are incapable of being rendered by alteration or addition suitable for the confinement of prisoners.

We propose to abandon the use of the Vellore, Guindy, Paumbum, and Cannanore Jails, which are now occupied temporarily by gangs of laboring convicts.

21. When the alterations and additions which we have suggested are made to the District Jails, when the Central Jails are completed, and when proper superintendence has been secured, we may reckon on the introduction of a well organized system of intramural labor, and with this a more complete enforcement of Jail discipline. This has been hitherto impossible in our over-crowded Jails, the condition of which made out-of-door labor imperative.

Jail Statistics.

22. We would beg to press upon the attention of the Government the urgent necessity of greater attention being paid to the maintenance of Jail Statistics. This will be attended by some expense, but will secure advantages which will more than justify the expenditure entailed. Owing to the absence of complete Judicial Statistics this report is much less accurate and less complete than it would otherwise have been, and this same difficulty will again recur whenever the Government desire information on the condition of Jails in this Presidency and the effect of Jail discipline, unless some uniform and complete system of Judicial Statistics is introduced.

23. We can do no more in the present report than allude to this important subject, and to provide in the Manual of Jail Rules for the more necessary statistical forms to be kept in Jails. Jail Statistics form only a branch of Judicial Statistics, and the whole subject requires much consideration before a complete form of Jail Returns can be devised.

24. It will remain for the Inspector General of Jails to address the Government departmentally on any increase in the Jail Establish-

ments, and in the Central Office, which will be required to insure the accurate preparation and punctual submission of Jail Statistics.

Superintendence.

25. The Calcutta Indian Jail Committee have, with justice, attached great importance to the selection of competent officers for the charge of both Central and District Jails, and have pointed out the Medical service as peculiarly qualified to furnish this class of officers.

26. We attach the greatest importance to the Superintendent of every Jail, whether Central or District, being regarded as the *sole officer in charge* of such Jail, and as being in that capacity directly responsible to the Inspector General of Jails for the good order and discipline of the Jail and the welfare of the prisoners.

27. We would, therefore, respectfully suggest an alteration in the arrangement at present sanctioned by Government, whereby the Magistrates of Districts are *nominally* in charge of Jails, while the Superintendents, whether they be the Assistant Magistrates or the Civil Surgeons, have *really the management* of the Jails. This divides responsibility, and will not, we believe, be found useful. We recommend that the Sessions Judges and District Magistrates should be ex-officio visitors of Jails—checking by their presence and by occasional inspections, (reports of which will be submitted to the Inspector General of Jails,) the conduct of the Jail Superintendents.

28. A separate officer should, as recommended by the Calcutta Jail Committee, be appointed as Superintendent of each Central Jail, on a salary of 800 Rupees a month consolidated allowance, with free quarters. For the charge of 1st and 2nd Class District Jails, Superintendents at 150 Rupees and 80 Rupees per mensem respectively, should be appointed. For these appointments there are two classes of officers generally available in Districts : the Assistant Magistrates and the Civil Surgeons.

29. Where qualified Civil Surgeons are available, we would recommend that they should be selected as Superintendents of District Jails, both because they are generally well qualified for the office, and because they are less liable to be absent from the locality of the Jails than the Assistant Magistrates. Where there are no Civil Surgeons stationed at the place where a District Jail is located, it would remain for the Government to select as Superintendent of such District Jail the Assistant Magistrate or other public officer. We recommend that officers appointed as Superintendents of Jails should be required within

a reasonable time to pass an examination testing their colloquial knowledge of the vernacular language of the District.

Jailers.

30. It is of great importance for the enforcement of Jail discipline that respectable men should be selected as Jailers, whether European, East Indian, or Native, and we therefore concur in the recommendation of the Calcutta Jail Committee that the salaries assigned to these officers should be respectively,

Jailers of Central Jails, 150 Rupees per mensem.

Jailers of 1st Class District Jails, 100 Rupees per mensem.

Jailers of 2nd Class District Jails, 50 Rupees per mensem.

Jail Rules.

31. In accordance with the instructions of the Government, we beg to submit a revised Code of Rules for the management of Jails ; we have embodied in these Rules the draft Rules relating to the duties of Medical Officers, which accompanied the Government Proceedings of the 7th March last.

32. We have been guided, in preparing this Manual, by the Rules recently sanctioned by the Government, and which are based on the recommendations of the Calcutta Jail Committee.

33. We do not pretend that these Rules can be enforced in their entirety until the new Central Jails are built, and until it is possible to confine prison labor to the interior limits of Jails. We have decided, however, to prepare as complete a Manual of Jail Rules as possible, and to add a set of Rules for the guidance of officers in charge of prisoners who, for the present, are employed on out-door labor. We have also prepared instructions for the guidance of officers in charge of Jails and Medical Officers, both when epidemic sickness appears in the neighbourhood of Jails, and also when such sickness declares itself in the Jails. In submitting the Manual of Jail Rules we may add that, except to simplify some of the details, and to make such alterations as would render the Rules applicable to this Presidency, the draft now presented to Government differs but little from the Rules prepared by the Sub-Committee of the Calcutta Jail Committee, and which have been adopted in Bengal. In all important respects the appended Manual contains, fully explained and detailed, for the use of the Jail officers, all the principles laid down and the recommendations made by the Calcutta Jail Committee, regarding the health of prisoners, prison discipline, labor, and classification.

Dietary.

34. As instructed by Government we have included in our inquiry the question of Jail dietary, and on this subject we have had the advantage of conferring with the Principal Inspector General of the Medical Department, and Dr. Cornish. We have also carefully examined the returns made on this subject by the Medical Officers in charge of Jails, who have submitted proposals for reformed Jail dietaries.

35. After a careful consideration of this important subject, we recommend that the several Jails should, as regards the prisoners' diets, be divided into three classes :—

1*st.*—Jails where Rice is the principal staple of diet.

2*nd.*—Jails where " Dry grains" are the principal staple of diet.

3*rd.*—Where mixed grains are used.

36. The diet to be used for each of these classes is detailed in the following table, which also exhibits the Jails to be included in each of the several classes.

When a gang is working within any of the Districts classified below, it will observe the diet of the Jail of the District in which it is located.

37. We recommend that the following Rules regarding diet should be strictly observed :—

1*st.*—When prisoners are employed on out-door labor, they shall have a warm meal before starting for their labor.

2*nd.*—They shall carry with them to their work a small quantity of Raggee cake to be eaten at mid-day, and they shall have a third meal at 6 P. M., on returning from work.

3*rd.*—When the prisoners are employed on in-door labor, a small meal shall be given at 6 A. M., before commencing work.

4*th.*—They shall have a meal at noon with an hour's rest, and they shall have their last meal at the close of their day's labor or about 6 P. M.

5*th.*—A reduction of one-fifth shall be made in the scale of diet in the case of women and juvenile prisoners.

38. The proper recipe for curry powder is given in the Diet Table, and equivalents have been given in the marginal notes when, on account of local peculiarities, any change is made in articles of diet prescribed for any class.

39. These dietaries have been specially prepared, at our request, by Dr. Cornish, with the approval of the Principal Inspector General, Medical Department, after an examination of the recommendations made by the Medical Officers in charge of the Jails throughout the Presidency. We believe that they are well suited to maintain the health and strength of the prisoners in Jail.

E.
JAILS.

Scale of Diet for Prisoners where Rice is the principal staple (No. 1.)

	Monday.	Tuesday.	Wednesday.	Thursday.	Friday.	Saturday.	Sunday.	NOTE.
	oz.	oz.	oz.	oz.	oz.	oz.	oz.	
Rice........................(a)	26	26	26	26	26	26	26	(a) 3 oz. of Rice to be made into Hoppers and eaten in the mid-day.
Dholl.......................	2	4	2	4	2	4	2	
Mutton or Fish.......(b)	3	0	5	0	5	0	0	b) When dried or Salt. fish is used 2½ ounces to be considered equiva. lent to 5 ozs. of fresh fish.
Buttermilk or Tyre...	0	10	0	10	0	10	10	
Ghee or Oil..........(c)	½	½	½	½	½	½	½	(c) In Districts where Cocoanut is plentiful 2 ozs. of coprah may be given in lieu of oil or ghee.
Tamarind.............(d)	¼	¼	¼	¼	¼	¼	¼	(d) Mango pickle may be substituted for tamarind when procurable.
Salt.......................	1	1	1	1	1	1	1	
Curry powder.......(e)	½	½	½	½	½	½	½	(e) Curry powder to be made according to for- mula in the Medical Code. (Appended.)
Vegetable...............	0	6	0	6	0	0	6	
Onions	½	½	½	½	½	½	½	
Garlick..................	30 grs.	0	30 grs.	0	30 grs.	0	0	
Firewood...............	2 lbs.	2 lbs.	2 lbs.	2 lbs.	2 lbs.	2 lbs.	2 lbs.	

No. 1. Scale of Diet will be applicable to the undermentioned Jails:—

Chingleput.   Trichinopoly.
Cuddalore.   Mangalore.
Tanjore.   Calicut.
Tranquebar.   Tellicherry.

Scale of Diet where " Dry grains" are the staple (No. 2).

	Monday.	Tuesday.	Wednesday.	Thursday.	Friday.	Saturday.	Sunday.	NOTE.
	oz.	oz.	oz.	oz.	oz.	oz.	oz.	
Veragoo...	22	22	22	22	22	22	22	Any of these quanti- ties may be consi- dered equivalent to 26 ozs. of rice.
Raggee....	24	24	24	24	24	24	24	
Cholum...	24	24	24	24	24	24	24	
Cumboo...	25	25	25	25	25	25	25	
Dholl......	2	4	2	4	2	4	2	
Mutton or Fish ...	5	0	5	0	5	0	0	
Buttermilk or Tyre ...	0	10	-0	10	0	10	10	
Ghee or Oil ...	½	½	½	½	½	½	½	
Tamarind ...	¼	¼	¼	¼	¼	¼	¼	
Salt ...	1	1	1	1	1	1	1	
Curry powder ...	½	½	½	½	½	½	½	
Vegetable ...	0	6	0	6	0	0	6	
Onions... ...	½	½	½	½	½	½	½	
Garlick... ...	30 grs.	0	30 grs	0	30 grs.	0	0	
Firewood ...	2 lbs.	2 lbs	2 lbs	2 lbs.	2 lbs.	2 lbs.	2 lbs.	Raggee or Cholum cakes (2½ ounces) in mid- day in lieu of hoppers.

No. 2. Scale of Diet will be applicable to the undermentioned Jails :—

    Guntoor.   Cuddapah.

    Nellore.   Coimbatore.

    Kurnool.   Salem.

    Bellary.

Scale of Diet where mixed grain is used (No. 3).

	Monday.	Tuesday.	Wednesday.	Thursday.	Friday.	Saturday.	Sunday.	NOTE.
	oz.	oz.	oz.	oz.	oz.	oz.	oz.	
Rice	12	12	12	12	12	12	12	
Dry grain	13	13	13	13	13	13	13	
Dholl	2	4	2	4	2	4	2	
Mutton or Fish	5	0	5	0	5	0	0	
Buttermilk or Tyre ...	0	10	0	10	0	10	10	
Ghee or Oil	½	½	½	½	½	½	½	
Tamarind	¼	¼	¼	¼	¼	¼	¼	
Salt	1	1	1	1	1	1	1	
Curry powder	¼	¼	¼	¼	¼	¾	¼	
Vegetable	0	6	0	6	0	0	6	Raggee cake or rice hopper may be given at mid-day.
Onions...	¼	¼	¼	¼	¼	¼	¼	
Garlick...	30 grs.	0	30 grs	0	30 grs.	0	0	
Firewood	2 lbs.	2 lbs.	2 lbs.	2 lbs.	2 lbs.	2 lbs.	2 lbs.	

No. 3. Scale of Diet will be applicable to the undermentioned Jails :—

        Berhampore.   Chittoor.

        Russelcondah.   Madura.

        Vizagapatam.   Tinnevelly.

        Masulipatam.

Curry powder used in Jails shall be composed of

	oz. dr.		oz. dr.
Chillies	3 6	Cummin seeds	0 6
Black pepper	1 4	Mustard seeds	0 6
Coriander seeds	0 6	Vendeum	0 6
Turmeric	1 1		

Employment of prisoners in the constructions of Jails.

40. We beg, in conclusion, to bring to the special notice of Government, the great mortality that at present prevails in some of the over-crowded Jails of this Presidency.

41. This will undoubtedly be remedied when the Central Jails, which we have recommended, are built and occupied by prisoners. Although many of the present Jails are ill-designed, badly situated, and badly built, many of them not having been originally intended for

Jails, it is to the excessive crowding of prisoners that the lamentable mortality that has prevailed in the Jails must principally be attributed. How great this mortality has been for many years past is well known to the Government ; and that this mortality, arising from over-crowding, continues, is sufficiently evidenced by the recent outbreak of cholera at Nellore, where up to the date at which we are writing, 178 prisoners had been attacked, of whom 84 have died.

42. A considerable time must elapse before the new prisons can be built, and it is to guard against the over-crowding of Jails and its certain consequence, a heavy death rate, that we beg to suggest that the most over-crowded Jails should be relieved of their prisoners, by the formation of special gangs of able-bodied convicts, carefully selected who should be employed in the construction of the new Central Jails.

43. If the workshops which will. be required for these Jails be first constructed, they will serve as temporary barracks for the prisoners employed in building the Jail. The Jail enclosure should be the next portion of the building completed, and when this is finished the prisoners can be effectually guarded, and all escapes prevented until the Jail is completed.

44. While the workshops and enclosures are under construction, the prisoners must be hutted. This will no doubt somewhat add to the expense of the construction of these Central Jails, and will perhaps allow of occasional escapes. But we respectfully suggest that outbreaks such as that which has recently taken place at Nellore, and in previous years at Salem and Calicut, make it a matter of the most urgent necessity to obviate, even in an incomplete and defective manner, the certain results of deficient Jail accommodation.

45. The mortality that took place at Lovedale, near Ootacamund is not, we believe, any valid argument against the course we have recommended of hutting prisoners employed on public works. If the prisoners are carefully selected, well hutted, in climates which are not uncongenial to them, we believe that the unskilled labor necessary for the construction of new Jails may be safely furnished by convicts, to the great and immediate relief of the over-crowded District Jails.

(Signed) J. ROHDE,
Inspector General of Jails.

(„) R. S. ELLIS,
President of the Sanitary Commission.

MADRAS, 10*th April* 1865.

lxviii

ORDER THEREON, 16th June 1865, No. 877.

In the Proceedings of Government, under date the 7th February last, the Inspector General of Jails and President of the Sanitary Commission were directed to form themselves into a Committee, for the purpose of collecting, and placing before Government, the information which is requisite to enable the Government to determine what additional Jail accommodation is required in this Presidency, and what measures should be taken for improving each of the existing Jails, or otherwise carrying out the measures suggested in the Report of the Indian Jail Committee which assembled at Calcutta in March last year, or any others that may be deemed advisable. The Committee were instructed to include in the scope of their inquiry the question of a Jail dietary, and to prepare a revised code of Rules for the management of Jails.

2. The Government have now before them the Report prepared by the Committee in accordance with the foregoing instructions, and also a letter from the Inspector General of Jails, submitting his own views, and those of several of the local officers, as to the best arrangement to be made for the superintendence of the Jails. A letter on the latter subject from the Session Judge of Cuddapah, is also recorded at the head of these Proceedings.

3. Orders will be passed hereafter on the draft code of Rules, which has been referred to the Principal Inspector General of the Medical Department, and to the Inspector General of Police, for their remarks on such of the rules as relate in any way to their respective Departments. The Governor in Council will now dispose of what are the most pressing matters treated of in the Committee's Report, viz:—

(a).—The number and location of the additional Central Jails to be erected.

(b).—The steps to be taken for improving the existing Jails.

(c).—The means to be adopted for affording early relief to over-crowded Jails; and

(d).—The officers to be selected for the charge of each Jail.

4. *Central Jails.*— On the first point, the Governor in Council approves of the recommendation of the Commissioners. Additional Central Jails will be built at Bellary, Cannanore, Vellore, and Trichinopoly; the two former to contain 800 prisoners each, and the two latter 1,000 prisoners each. The Jail now under construction at Coimbatore, and the Jail at Salem which has been completed, will, for the reasons assigned by the Committee, be used both as Central and

E.
JAILS.

District Jails. In planning the new Jails, and in determining the number of prisoners to be kept in the existing Jails, when sufficient additional accommodation shall be available, due regard will be paid to the rule laid down by the Government of India, that each prisoner is to be allowed a minimum superficial area of 36 square feet, and a cubical space of 648 feet. The Central Jails will be for the imprisonment of persons whose sentences exceed one year. All persons sentenced to one year or less, will be confined in the District Jails, except at Coimbatore and Salem, where provision will be made for both classes of convicts in one Jail, with the view of avoiding the additional expense of new District Jails at those stations. When the new Central Jails are ready, convicts will be sent to them, respectively, from the Districts specified in the 14th paragraph of the Committee's Report. An exception, however, will be made in the case of Khond convicts who will, as hitherto, be imprisoned in the Jail at Russelcondah. A similar exception will be made in the case of the other tribes inhabiting the hill tracts of Ganjam and Vizagapatam.

5. *Arrangements to be made for improving existing Jails.*—The recommendations of the Committee, in regard to the steps to be taken for improving the existing Jails, appear to His Excellency in Council to require further consideration and examination on the spot. From what came under the observation of His Excellency, in the course of his late tour in the Northern Circars, when he inspected the new Jail at Berhampore, and the Jail now being built at Waltair, he is satisfied that in two cases, at all events, the remedies proposed by the Committee are not sufficient to correct the existing defects. He, accordingly, directs that at each station a Committee be at once formed, composed of the Officer in charge of the Jail, the Medical Officer, and an Officer of the Public Works Department, who will report how far the suggestions made by the Inspector General of Jails, and the President of the Sanitary Commission, are, in their opinion, sufficient to meet the requirements of the Jail, and whether any other improvements are requisite, submitting in each case, plans and estimates of the proposed alterations and additions, which will be forwarded to the Superintending Engineer, if he be not a member of the Committee, for submission to Government in the Department of Public Works.

6. The several Committees will refer to the remarks of His Excellency the Governor, on the Berhampore and Waltair Jails, and to the report of the Inspector General of Hospitals on the former; both of which are recorded in these Proceedings. They will also be fur-

nished with copies of the draft code of Rules, in order that they may obtain a clear insight into what are likely to be the actual requirements of the several Jails. Whenever the Superintending Engineer can conveniently act on the Committee, he will do so. If not, he will depute one of his best executive officers for the duty.

7. *Means to be adopted for affording early relief to over-crowded Jails.*—It is of the greatest importance, as the Inspector General of Jails and the President of the Sanitary Commission justly observe, that something should be done, as speedily as possible, to relieve the present over-crowded Jails, the number of convicts in which is more than 50 per cent. in excess of that which, according to the standard laid down by the Government of India, ought to be confined in them. The expedient which is suggested in the report now under consideration, that large gangs of convicts should be hutted on the sites selected for the new Central Jails, and should then be employed in building the Jails, is probably the best that, under the circumstances could be adopted. The first work on which the convicts should be employed is the outer wall of the Jail. They should then build the workshops, in which they can live, pending the completion of the Jail buildings. Before, however, anything can be done, the sites of the new Jails must be fixed on, and then plans and estimates must be prepared. The Inspector General of Jails is probably well acquainted with the various sites available; but before settling them, the Government would wish to have the opinions of the local officers. The Principal Inspector General of the Medical Department will, accordingly,

depute a Medical officer at each of the four

Bellary.
Cannanore.
Vellore.
Trichinopoly.

stations named in the margin, to confer with the District Magistrate and the Superintending Engineer of the Division as to the best site for the projected Central Jail; and these officers will submit a report on the subject through the Inspector General of Jails, who, if he thinks fit, will place himself in communication with them previous to the preparation of their Report, and will forward it to Government, with such remarks as he may deem proper. Each Report should be accompanied by a plan of the proposed site, shewing the position and relative distances of any villages, tanks, rivers, topes, or hills that may be in its immediate neighbourhood. The direction of the prevailing winds should be specified, and the nature of the soil. The reports should be prepared so as to reach the Inspector General of Jails not later than the 1st August, and should be laid before Government by the 10th of that month.

E.
JAILS.

8. The duty of settling the plans of the Jails in question will be best performed by a Central Committee at the Presidency, composed of the Inspector General of Jails, a Medical officer, and an Engineer officer, who will carefully examine the plans of the Jails now being built at Rajahmundry, and at Coimbatore, and will adapt them, with such modifications as they may deem necessary, to the requirements of the new Jails; sketch plans being sent in each case to the Superintending Engineer, for such alterations as the nature of the site and other local circumstances may render necessary. For this duty, the Governor in Council resolves to associate Dr. Mackenzie, Inspector General of Hospitals, and Lieutenant Colonel Anderson, Consulting Engineer for Railways, with the Inspector General of Jails. This Committee will report, with as little delay as possible, the number of prisoners they would propose to locate on the site of each of the projected Central Jails, and the cost of hutting them; and in preparing the estimates, due allowance will be made by the Superintending Engineer for the labor of the convicts. Government attach great importance to the speedy and careful preparation of the plans and estimates now ordered. As soon as they are furnished, an application for a special grant will be made to the Government of India, who have stated that they " will be prepared to make the necessary provi-
" sion of funds for giving early effect to any carefully considered
" proposal for increasing Jail accommodation, wherever it is manifestly
" insufficient."

9. *Superintendence of Jails.*—The only question which remains to be determined is, that of the arrangements to be made for the superintendence of the Jails in future. It is recommended in the Report of Messrs. Ellis and Rohde, now under consideration, that in supersession of the arrangement ordered by Government in their Proceedings of the 5th October last, but which has not yet been carried out, of placing each District Jail under the general supervision of the Magistrate of the District, who is to nominate from time to time, for the approval of Government, an officer for the immediate management of the Jail, who is to be either one of his Assistants, Covenanted or Uncovenanted, or the Zillah Surgeon of the station, that, as a general rule, the Zillah Surgeon be appointed the sole Superintendent of the District Jail, directly responsible to the Inspector General, the Session Judge and Magistrate of the District being ex-officio visitors of the Jail.

10. On further consideration, the Governor in Council is disposed to concur in the opinion expressed in the 26th paragraph of the Report

above alluded to, that " the Superintendent of every Jail, whether Cen-
" tral or District, should be regarded as the sole officer in charge of
" such Jail, and as being, in that capacity, directly responsible to the
" Inspector General of Jails for the good order and discipline of the
" Jail, and the welfare of the prisoners ;" the Session Judge and Magistrate being in each case ex-officio visitors of the Jail, except in those
cases in which the Session Judge may desire to retain the charge, and
it may be considered advisable that he should do so.

11. So many changes, however, have taken place since the
reports forwarded with Mr. Rohde's letter of the 18th February last,
that in many cases the recommendations made in them cannot now be
acted on. Moreover, those recommendations were made on the understanding that the selection was to be confined to Zillah Surgeons and
Assistant Magistrates, and that the general supervision of the Jail was
to be vested in the Magistrate. The Governor in Council directs
that each Magistrate will submit, not later than the 15th proximo,
the name of the officer whom he would recommend for the charge
of the District Jail, with a brief statement of his qualifications. The
Superintendents should, as a general rule, be Europeans, holding
appointments which do not take them away from the Jail station,
men of good business habits, and possessing energy and firmness of
character. Zillah Surgeons, Military Staff Officers, whose duties keep
them stationary, Cantonment Magistrates, Deputy Collectors in charge
of the Treasury, if Europeans, may all be considered eligible. It is not
advisable that a Joint Magistrate, Head Assistant or Assistant Magistrate, whose Revenue work takes him into the Taluks during a portion
of the year, should be put in charge of the Jail. For each Jail Superintendent, the Government of India have sanctioned an allowance of
Rupees 100 for the charge of a 1st Class Jail, and Rupees 50 for the
charge of a 2nd Class Jail, subject, however, to the proviso that when
the charge is held by an officer employed in the Civil administration
Covenanted or Uncovenanted, this allowance is not to be given. The
recommendation of the Session Judge of Cuddapah, that the charge of
the Jail should be entrusted to an Assistant Superintendent of Police
is quite inadmissible.

12. The salaries proposed by the Inspector General of Jails and
President of the Sanitary Commission for the Superintendents of Central Jails, and for the Jailers, are approved, subject, however, to an
exception in the case of the Salem and Coimbatore Jails, the Superintendents of which will, in the opinion of the Governor in Council, be
sufficiently remunerated by a salary of Rupees 600 per mensem, the
number of prisoners to be confined in each of these Jails being much

below the number proposed for the other Central Jails. A reference in regard to the salaries to be assigned to the Superintendents of these Jails, and also regarding the salaries of the Jailers, will be made to the Supreme Government.

Telegram from the Secretary to the Government of India, Public Works Department, Calcutta, to the Secretary to the Government of Madras, Public Works Department, dated 12th January 1866.

Your telegram to Home Department, dated eleventh. No special grant can be given; but any arrangement the Government of Madras may be able to make within its Budget grant will be sanctioned.

From the Chief Secretary to the Government of Fort Saint George, Judicial Department, to the Secretary to the Government of India, Public Works Department, dated 4th August 1866, No. 1,209.

1. Adverting to the 1st paragraph of Colonel Orr's letter of the 12th ultimo, No. 2,182, I am directed to submit, for the consideration of His Excellency the Viceroy and Governor General of India in Council, the annexed copy of a Minute by His Excellency Lord Napier, in which His Lordship has reviewed at length the requirements of this Presidency, in the matter of Jail accommodation, as well as the necessity of providing better accommodation for lunatics. I am directed to state that the other Members of the Government entirely concur in His Lordship's views and recommendations, and to request that, under the circumstances, and, adverting to the promise given in Mr. Secretary Bayley's letter, of the 23rd June 1864, No. 952, to the effect that the Government of India would be prepared to make the necessary provision of funds for giving early effect to any carefully considered proposals for increasing Jail accommodation, wherever it may be manifestly insufficient, the Governor General in Council will be pleased to reconsider the decision conveyed in your telegram of the 12th January last, and to sanction a special grant of Rupees 2,00,000, or such sum as the state of the finances may admit of, to be expended on Jail buildings in the course of the present official year, in order that the erection of the projected Central Jails at Vellore and Trichinopoly may be at once proceeded with.

2. I am to explain, with reference to the remarks made in the 25th paragraph of Lord Napier's Minute, that the sums therein referred to, amounting to Rupees 1,95,000, cannot now be obtained by transfers from the Budget, the greater part of the reserve having been expended, while expenditure has been already incurred on many of the items forming the sum of Rupees 95,000. The buildings, however, to which His Lordship proposed to appropriate the sums in question will be

proceeded with, and their cost will be met from savings in the General Budget.

Minute by the Right Honorable the President, dated 10th July 1866.

1. The defective condition of the Jails in this Presidency has long been attested by a death-rate which might well touch the conscience of a Government which admits its duties in reference to the life, welfare, and reformation of criminals.

2. Measures for the correction of abuses, which constituted a reproach to civilized administration, have been for years past contemplated, and in part embraced, by the Government of Madras ; nor has their solicitude been unshared by the Supreme Government, which pledged itself, in Mr. Secretary Bayley's letter, of June 23rd, 1864, " to " make the necessary provision of funds for giving early effect to any " carefully matured proposals for increasing Jail accommodation, " wherever it is now manifestly insufficient."

3. Conformably to the principles thus avowed, the construction of six Central Jails has been sanctioned in this Presidency at the following places : Salem, Coimbatore, Rajahmundry, Cannanore, Vellore, and Trichinopoly. At the same time, it has been determined to repair, develope, and improve almost all the District Jails in the country, and to rebuild several. The local lock-up houses and places of preliminary detention, though most insufficient, have necessarily been left for after consideration. From time to time, some palliatives are sanctioned for evils which it is impossible at present radically to remedy.

4. When the construction of the projected six Central Jails has been completed, it is estimated that these establishments, in connection with the improved District Jails, will afford proper and sufficient accommodation for about 9,000 prisoners, the number which the Presidency may probably furnish, but which, as a yearly average, has not yet been attained.

5. The perspective of Jail improvement which is thus opened would be satisfactory if there was any security that the end desired would be certainly and rapidly attained ; but this is not the case. The design, which was pushed forward at first with benevolence and ardour, is in some danger of being arrested.

Little has been sanctioned for the present year. It becomes my duty once more to record the wrongs and sufferings of the prisoners

E.
JAILS.

in our charge ; to point out what can be effected for their partial relief from local resources ; and to urge the Supreme Government to redeem its promise by sanctioning a larger expenditure than that which we can independently undertake.

6. The Central Jail at Salem is alone completed. That of Coimbatore is nearly terminated. The buildings at Rajahmundry are about half finished. At Cannanore, Vellore, and Trichinopoly nothing has been done.

7. It would be unjust to deny the benefits which have been already conferred even by the works commenced. The pressure on certain District Jails has been materially lightened by the drafts of prisoners employed on the construction of the new buildings, or transferred to them for confinement. Many lives have probably been saved in this way. In some places the mortality, which had attained disastrous proportions, has sunk to something like a normal death-rate.

8. It would, however, be an error to suppose that the relief hitherto procured is such as to justify the Government in relaxing its efforts to obtain Jail accommodation fully commensurate for the wants of the Presidency. On the contrary, the two last years have witnessed in the Jails of Madras both a continuous loss of life from various maladies indigenous to neglected prisons, and sudden out-bursts and ravages of epidemic disorders in these institutions, which cannot be recorded without deep concern, and which are certainly susceptible of being restrained.

9. With the view of illustrating these evils, the accompanying return has been prepared with reference to nine Jails which seem most subject to a high death-rate, either chronic or occasional. It shews the rates of mortality during the last four years, calculated on the average daily number of prisoners; the classes in which such mortality has occurred ; and the diseases by which it has been caused.

10. It will here be seen that for these four successive years, respectively, the average annual death-rate in these nine Jails has been eleven, fifteen, twenty, and twenty-one per cent. The highest death-rate reached in any year in any single Jail was at Calicut, where the loss was nearly fifty-five per cent. on the daily average. The same Jail shews the highest average death-rate in the four years, upwards of thirty-one per cent. It is, however, followed at no great distance by Tellicherry, with a culminating death-rate of forty-one, and a mean death-rate of twenty-four per cent.; by Rajahmundry, with forty-two and twenty-

two in the same categories; and by Madura, with twenty-eight and eighteen per cent.

The mean annual death-rate in the nine Jails struck on the four years is nearly seventeen per cent.*

11. In instituting a comparison between the death-rate in Jails, and that of other classes of men, it would not, however, be strictly correct to adopt, as the basis of comparison, the death-rate calculated on the daily average number of prisoners; for the population of a Jail is a transitory and fluctuating quantity, and on the whole year many more than the daily average are brought under the influence of Jail life and discipline, for good or evil.

I do not possess any scientific formula for calculating the rate of mortality under these circumstances, so as to bring it accurately into juxta-position with that of other bodies of a more stable, though not of an absolutely stationary, character, such as a Regiment, or the inhabitants of a parish, or the population of a country. I conceive, however, that if to the daily average number about one-third be added, in consideration of those who come and go, and if, consequently, the same proportion be subtracted from the death-rate calculated on the daily average number, it would be a liberal allowance. I will, therefore, as the basis of comparison, assume the average annual death-rate in the nine Jails under consideration not to be seventeen per cent., but, in round numbers, to be twelve per cent. This rate of mortality is seven times greater than the mortality of a European Regiment in the Madras Presidency; it is twelve times greater than that of a Native Regiment in Cantonments; it is fifteen times greater than the death-rate in a well-managed Jail in England; it is fifteen times greater than that of the common civil population in England. The death-rate among the miscellaneous inhabitants of an Indian city has not been very exactly ascertained. It is estimated, on returns little worthy of confidence, to be rather more than ten per thousand; if we assume it to be twelve per thousand, the death-rate of the Jail is still ten times greater than that of the Town.

12. Such being the actual and comparative death-rate in the bad Jails of the Madras Presidency, we may naturally inquire what the normal death-rate ought to be in a Native Jail under a good system

---

* Note.—In the year 1864-65, the death-rate on the average daily number of prisoners in *all* the Jails of the Presidency was 12¼ per cent., 998 deaths on 7,855 prisoners; but the average daily strength is not a proper basis for *comparative* statements.

of management. The reply may be deduced from analogy, or supplied from experience.

13. In England, the death-rate in prisons does not exceed that of the general population of the most favorable age. It is less than in the Army. Prisoners have considerable advantages with regard to the maintenance of health compared with other men. Good lodging, sufficient food, light work, regular medical assistance, enforced sobriety, protection against contagion from without, and the power of removal in case of necessity, ought to place them in a superior sanitary position to the lower orders of the general population : on the other hand, the depression of spirits incidental to confinement is a predisposing cause of sickness, and the pressure of numbers in a limited area may render the progress of infectious disease at first more rapid and fatal if it once breaks out. The influences favorable to prisoners ought not to be less operative in India than in Europe. If the effects of change of climate and diet* be narrowly observed, I cannot see speculatively why the death-rate among this class need be higher than that of the miscellaneous population, viz., twelve per thousand. Yet, as the Native constitution may possibly be more susceptible of deterioration by confinement than the European, as our experience is of short date, as the means of organization and control are less perfect here than in Europe, and as, with the best intentions in the superior authorities, there will still be errors and abuses in the subordinate management, I am willing to concede that the mortality in a Native Jail might rise to an average of twenty per thousand, or two per cent. As in the Jails under consideration it is twelve per cent., if the basis of my argument be sound, ten per cent. are destroyed by the neglect of Government.

14. The same conclusion is warranted by experience, that is, by the results exhibited in the healthiest Jails of the Madras Presidency. In the prisons at Guindy, Tanjore, and Vellore, the mortality in the years 1863-64 and 1864-65, was from one to two per cent. There are examples of the same low rate in other places; yet no exceptional intelligence or care seems to have been exercised in those places, nor do they enjoy any extraordinary privileges of position.

*Note.—A gang of nearly 500 convicts was employed at the Lawrence Asylum Works on the Neilgherry Hills in the year 1864.65. Of this number, 123 died in the year, chiefly of scurvy and ulcers caused by bad food, by an uncongenial climate, by exposure, and, I suspect, by labor in irons. This shocking mortality lies at the door of those who selected the drafts from the Jails in the plains, and of those who made no sufficient preparation for their reception on the Hills. After this sacrifice of life, proper measures were taken for the diet, protection, and treatment of the convicts. The gang is now very healthy.

15. The causes of the great sacrifice of life in the Madras Jails are defects in the buildings, attacks of epidemic diseases, and a general inadequacy of space.

16. Defects of position and construction are so numerous and general, that it would be superfluous to analyze and enumerate them. They are set forth in detail in the report addressed by the Inspector General and the Sanitary Commissioner to Government, under date the 10th April 1865, and in previous communications on the same subject. In some places the Jail is placed in the casemates of an old fort, or it is in the centre of a town, or it is intersected by a public road, or it is the adaptation of a barrack or of a Native rest-house, or of a private dwelling. In all the old, and in some of the recent buildings, provisions for ventilation have been neglected; in almost all, subsoil drainage has been deficient; in some, there has been no hospital; at some there is no garden or recreation ground; in some the soil is so tainted by excretions, and the walls so saturated with disease, that the place is incurable, and must be abandoned; in some there is a mysterious liability to sickness, that cannot be explained by apparent material facts. The death-rate is not always highest where the locality or the structure is most objectionable.

17. If epidemic disease were a powerful agency in raising the death-rate, that might be in a measure consolatory to Government; for the apparition and destructive power of cholera are sometimes beyond human anticipation and control. But an inspection of the return will not wholly justify this reflection. There are undoubtedly occasions on which cholera suddenly breaks out, claims its victims, and as promptly vanishes.

In the years 1862-63 and 1863-64, there was not one single death from cholera in the Jail at Nellore, and in other respects it was unusually healthy; in 1864-65, ninety-five persons were swept off by the disease; in 1865-66, the mortality from the same cause declined to four. At Calicut, in 1862-63, there were eighty-six deaths by cholera; in 1865-66, forty deaths; in the two intervening years none at all. At Tellicherry there were for three years no deaths by cholera; in the fourth year there were twenty-two. As a general rule, however, when cholera does come, it is most fatal in Jails which are otherwise unhealthy, and it is often found, as at Calicut and Tellicherry, in its greatest virulence, associated with dysentery, fever, and anasarca, which is the result of Jail diarrhœa. Jail reform will not extirpate cholera; but the locality

E.
. JAILS.

will be less congenial to the malady, and the sufferer will be better able to resist it.

18. After all, it is satisfactory to observe that the defects of construction and situation, and the deadly visitations of epidemic disorders, are mere auxiliary forces in producing the death-rate. The main agency is over-crowding. The prisoners perish by impure air. If this cause implies most reproach to Government, it is also the cause most easy to subdue. Government has only to build more Jails, and the prisoners will be saved. It is a simple question of arithmetic : we can redeem so much life with so much money. At the close of the year 1864-65, 8,120 persons were confined in Jails which, according to the standard of the Supreme Government, contained accommodation for 4,492. There was, therefore, an excess of 3,628 prisoners, who were doing injury to each other and to the normal number. The pressure may not have been quite so great during the past year, for prisoners have been placed in the Central Jail at Coimbatore, and there are gangs of convicts established for labor at various points of the Neilgherry range. The death-rate of 1865-66 was, however, rather larger than the death-rate of the preceding year ; the number of prisoners has increased, and it will probably increase still more under the pressure of the prevailing scarcity of food. At certain periods of the current year, there will probably be not less than 3,000 prisoners thrust into habitations already full. I need not add that the general excess of prisoners over the general capacity of the Jails affords no accurate picture of the local mischief occasionally inflicted. In particular Jails, at particular moments, the actual number of inmates, compared with the legitimate space, is much higher than the general disproportion, and the distressing effects may easily be conceived. There is an example of 195 being confined where the proper number would be fifty-three ; another of 499 being lodged in the room adapted for 175; another of 347 being received where 117 was the normal strength. It would be idle to multiply instances. The deadly effect of crowding is not a mere speculative inference. It is practically demonstrated by the salutary result obtained by thinning over-peopled Jails. The Jail at Rajahmundry is calculated to hold seventy-seven. The average number confined in it, during the last quarter of 1865-66, was 120. There were fourteen deaths in ten months and ten days. On the 10th of April, sixty were drafted out to the works at the Central Jail, and vigorous measures were embraced for purifying the building. The mortality instantly disappeared. For six weeks there was not a single death, and on the

29th of May the report shewed a strength of 102 with one man sick. At Calicut the average number confined during the same quarter in a prison adapted for 260 was 328. In the three months thirty-four died without a single case of cholera. In April, however, 128 prisoners were transferred elsewhere. In May, and the first half of June, there were only two deaths. The buildings, however, of this notorious prison are bad, and the position is condemned.

I must add that both these prisons will be rapidly filled up again unless extensive works are undertaken elsewhere, and hundreds of convicts are hutted out.

19. In contemplating measures for the acceleration of Jail reform, we ought not to lose sight of any branch of the general undertaking. The correction of defects in District Jails which are to be preserved, the construction of new District Jails, and the expansion of general Jail accommodation by the construction of Central Prisons, should all go hand in hand.

20. During the present financial year, the sum of Rupees 50,000 might be advantageously laid out in the improvement of District Jails, in conformity with the plans submitted by the Inspector General, and approved by Government, selecting the most urgent cases for prior execution.

21. Plans and estimates have been prepared for rebuilding the Jails at Madura and Calicut, both of which have long since been condemned as among the worst in the Presidency. It is hoped that the cost of the Jail at Madura, estimated at above one lakh, may not exceed Rupees 70,000, if a cheaper style of construction be adopted, and if convict labor be vigorously applied, in conformity with the strict injunctions of the Supreme Government and the example of Northern India.

The Jail at Calicut will be rather more expensive. The outlay on each during the remaining portion of the present year may, however, be limited to Rupees 30,000.

22. In the Budget of the current year, sums have been already appropriated to the completion of the Central Jails at Rajahmundry and Coimbatore, according to the amount of the estimates for those buildings respectively. Rupees 43,679 have been awarded to the former, Rupees 50,000 to the latter.

I do not propose, at present, to add any thing to these appropriations, though they will doubtless prove insufficient. I would, however, respectfully suggest that the Central Jail at Cannanore, for

J1　　　　　　　　　　　　　　　　　　　lxxxi

E.
JAILS.

which a site has been selected and a plan prepared, should be immediately advanced with energy. Rupees 60,000 might be expended on this work during the present season.

23.　To these appropriations, we must add about Rupees 5,000 for the expense of hutting the convicts, and their guards, in connection with the new works.

24.　I also submit the expediency of setting apart Rupees 20,000 for the commencement of a Lunatic Asylum at Madras, a subject to which I shall return at the end of this minute.

25.　The projected expenditure would, therefore, be as follows :—

	RS.
For improvements in the old District Jails	50,000
For a new District Jail at Madura	30,000
For a new District Jail at Calicut	30,000
For the new Central Jail at Cannanore	60,000
For hutting Convicts and Guards	5,000
For the Lunatic Asylum at Madras	20,000
	1,95,000

The sum of Rupees 1,95,000 can be obtained from our local resources by the application of one lakh from the Reserve Fund, and by the transfer of Rupees 95,000 from other appropriations on the Budget of Public Works in the Civil Department.

26.　According to the present scheme, the convicts at Madura and Calicut would be hutted on the locality of their future prisons, and build themselves in. They would thus be withdrawn from the influences which have made the old prisons so obnoxious to health and life. Three or four hundred convicts could be employed on the Central Jail at Cannanore. As the Jails at Rajahmundry and Coimbatore approach completion, they will be gradually filled up. In this way, before the end of the current year, about 1,000 prisoners may be eliminated from the existing Jails, leaving the excess at the reduced, but still formidable, amount of 2,000.

27.　It is for the extrication and employment of these 2,000 prisoners, or of a large portion of them, that this Government is, in my humble judgment, constrained once more to appeal to the Supreme Government. In the letter addressed to the Governor General of India in Council by this Government, on the 9th March 1865, the Government of India was earnestly requested to appropriate the sum of two lakhs, as an addition to the amount of the Public Works' grant in this Presidency for the current year, with a view to the commence.

ment of the New Central Jails. To this appeal, concerning a question of the highest social importance, and based on a distinct engagement on the part of the Supreme Government, no reply has, after the lapse of seven months, been received ; for, though a communication in general terms has been recently transmitted to this Government on the subject of Public Works, the question of prisons and the application regarding them has not been so much as adverted to. It is no doubt repugnant to natural feeling to reiterate arguments which remain unanswered, and solicitations which remain unnoticed, nor can we be insensible to the numerous demands which beset the Supreme Government in all the departments of public expenditure ; but the cause in which this Government has spoken, and is now asked to speak, is one in which the moral character of the English administration in India is plainly at stake. It will not do for us to be silent, nor can the Supreme Government seriously intend to close its eyes and its ears. If the Supreme Government cannot heal these wrongs of ancient standing all at once, it can, at least, recognize and discuss them when its attention and assistance are respectfully invoked, and afford some imperfect help. I cannot do less than advise a new application for the sum set down in the letter of December last. With a grant of two lakhs, the Central Jails at Rajahmundry and Coimbatore could be more rapidly completed, and a considerable advance might be made in those of Vellore and Trichinopoly. But the sum of one lakh even would enable us to make a commencement at the two last mentioned places in the current year, and thus relieve the existing prisons from the deadly pressure under which they labor. From the limited resources of the local Budget, no more can, at present, be supplied. In the higher interest of prison reform, sums would even, according to my present proposal, be withdrawn from works of considerable material utility.

28. It now remains for me to justify the proposal that the sum of Rupees 20,000 should be at once applied to the commencement of a Lunatic Asylum at Madras. This question is closely allied to the question of prison discipline and organization.

29. There are, in this Presidency, about 23,000 persons of unsound mind if the proportion of lunatics to the general population is approximatively the same in India as in Europe, namely, one to 1,000. I am not enabled to state what per-centage of insane persons urgently requires supervision and restraint. It would, of course, be idle at present to contemplate the application of European principles of treatment to the

mass of insane persons in this country. We are very far from that. The expenditure involved in such a project would far exceed any means at the command of Government. If we assume, however, that only one in ten of this unfortunate class is a perfectly helpless idiot, or a dangerous maniac, without any provision for his sustenance, protection, and control, on the part of the relatives or other charitable persons, then the Government would lie under an obligation to provide places of habitation and restraint for 2,300 persons.

Let us see how far this obligation has been recognized and acted on.

30. The public provision for insane persons in this Presidency is, as far as I can learn at this moment, as follows :—

(1). The Asylum at Madras, with accommodation for forty-six persons of both sexes and all conditions.

(2). The so-called Idiot Asylum at the Monegar Choultry, containing about eighty individuals.

(3). An Asylum at Vizagapatam, in a hired house, for twenty persons.

(4). A similar èstablishment at Trichinopoly, in some old Government building.

(5). In the District Jails, accommodation afforded to seventeen lunatics.

(6). At the General Hospital at Madras, occasional accommodation for European Lunatics.—I conceive, however, that others are not excluded, for I recently saw a native lunatic lying in the corner of a dark shed attached to that establishment in charge of some one.

31. The provision systematically made by the State for lunatics, is thus for 183 out of a general estimated total of 23,000, and a presumable destitute or dangerous class of 2,300.

32. If we turn from the number of persons to the nature of the accommodation and treatment, there is not much reason for satisfaction. All that is good in the existing Asylums, depends on the intelligence and benevolence of those who direct them. The Government has no share in it ; it only votes a little money—that is all.

33. The Lunatic Asylum is a collection of very humble buildings —I had almost said hovels—scrupulously clean, in which the patients are managed with the utmost humanity and solicitude, by an estimable East Indian Director. But the Asylum has no bath-rooms, no infirmary, no padded cells for frantic patients, and no department for the convalescent ; no space walled in for recreation or exercise ; no place of labor; no place of instruction ; no division in the grounds for the separation of the sexes, so that the male and female patients are walked

out alternately in gangs to take the air, the former twice, the latter once a day. The Government have paid for many years a high rent for this place. It cannot be improved, because it is not State property.

34. The Idiot Asylum at the Monegar Choultry is not properly termed an Idiot Asylum ; for clamorous and fretful lunatics of the milder sort are mixed up with the idiots. The sexes are divided, and that is the only division. The men on their side, and the women on their side, are penned up, each in their respective common room at night, with what results may be conceived ; however, there are night latrines, to which they can repair if they please. They are unlocked in the morning. The women sit together all day, and mope or chatter in the verandah or in the sun ; the men make some attempts at ordinary, and even at skilled, labor. The dietary is good, and the discipline humane. This establishment, even in its primitive shape, reflects credit on Dr. vanSomeren, the Visiting Physician, and on the Warders, by whom it is controlled. It cannot be seen without sympathy and approval.

35. Nothing is known here of the Asylums at Vizagapatam and Trichinopoly, if such they may be called. The District Jails and the General Hospital are not fit places for the confinement of lunatics. It is obvious that their presence must be embarrassing to the authorities of these establishments, and that no proper system can be carried out for the separate lodging and treatment of the insane. Insane criminals should be placed in an appropriate department of a General Lunatic Asylum. They are often refused at the present Lunatic Asylum of Madras, for want of room. The only justification for the reception of lunatics at the General Hospital is to be found in the reflection, that there is not fitting accommodation at the Lunatic Asylum for Insane Europeans of the superior class, and that space is often wanting there for East Indians or for Natives of the lower orders. If they were not received at the General Hospital, they would be abandoned in the streets. ·

36. The facts which I here submit to the Council are not discoveries. They are well known to the Council, and have often engaged its attention. The evils complained of have been debated, and remedies have been designed. There are reports and plans of remote and recent date ; but nothing has been done—nothing effectual will, perhaps, ever be done until some small beginning is set on foot. Adopting, as my basis, the judicious letter addressed by Dr. Shaw, the Inspector General of Hospitals, to the Chief Secretary, under date March 24th, 1864, I would suggest that Government should call for plans for a Lunatic Asylum of a very modest character, calculated to accommodate 200 persons, but susceptible of eventual expansion, and place it on the Government estate called Locock's Gardens. The Idiot Asylum might

E.
JAILS.

remain where it is for the present, in connection with the Monegar Choultry, but it should be restricted to idiots properly so called, and be relieved from the disturbing association of lunatics.

37. If the design which I here advocate be carried out, ample provision would be made for the reception and treatment of all the lunatic criminals in the Presidency; better accommodation and discipline would be provided for the lunatics of the capital and the adjoining Provinces; and the General Hospital would be relieved of the care of European Lunatics of the superior class. The expenditure of Rupees 20,000 in the present year would effect little in a work which would probably cost about Rupees 1,50,000, but the Government would stand committed to the prosecution of an indispensable undertaking.

(Signed) NAPIER.

From the Secretary to the Government of India, Public Works Department, (Account,) to the Secretary to the Government of Madras, Public Works Department, dated Simla, 31st August 1866, No. 783 A.

* No. 1,209,~ dated 4th August 1866, from Chief Secretary to Government of Madras, Judicial Department, to Secretary to Government of India, Public Works Department.

1. I am directed to acknowledge receipt of the letter, as per margin,* forwarding copy of a Minute by His Excellency the Governor of Madras, regarding the requirements of the Madras Presidency in the matter of Jail and Lunatic accommodation, and the additional Budget grants required for this purpose.

2. In reply, I am to say that, as from paragraphs 27 and 28 of His Lordship's Minute, it would appear that the immediate necessities of the case during 1866-67 would be met by an additional grant of one lakh for Jails, and Rupees 20,000 for a Lunatic Asylum at Madras, or Rupees 1,20,000 in all, the Governor General in Council, having regard to the representations brought forward in respect to the urgency of making a commencement in this matter, agrees to the case being met by an extra grant, and authorizes an additional Public Works Budget Grant to Madras for 1866-67 to that extent, on the understanding that the estimates for the works to which it is to be applied are sanctioned by competent authority. A telegram to this effect was despatched on the 23rd instant.

3. I am at the same time to notice that the statement made in paragraph 27 of the Minute, regarding a letter of the *9th March* 1865, on the subject of Jail accommodation, not having been acknowledged by the Government of India, seems to have been founded on a misapprehension, since the communication on this subject, No. 1,760,

dated *9th December* 1865, was duly replied to by my telegram of the   E.
12th January 1866, and my letter, No. 130 C, dated 7th February 1866.   JAILS.

4. With reference to the remark made in the concluding portion of the second paragraph of your letter, to the effect that the additional expenditure on certain Jails will be met from savings in the General Budget, I am to enquire whether by this is meant the Budget estimate of the Civil Department, or that of the Public Works Department.

ORDER THEREON, 24th September 1866, No. 3,060.

Account, No. 58.   1. A sum of Rupees 1,20,000 having now been placed at the disposal of this Government as an addition to the Budget grant for the current official year, the Right Honorable the Governor in Council sanctions the following appropriations from that source :—

	RS.
To Central Jail at Cannanore, Malabar District	30,000
To do. at Vellore, North Arcot District	40,000
To District Jail at Madura, Madura District	30,000
To Lunatic Asylum at Madras, Presidency	20,000

2. It is also the intention of Government, in conformity with the terms of their letter* to the Government of India of August 4th, No. 1,209, to supple-

* Judicial Department.

ment these appropriations by the sum of Rs. 1,95,000 from savings in the general Public Works assignment of the year, to be applied to the amelioration and enlargement of Jail accommodation conformably to the tenor of the Minute of His Excellency the Governor, dated July 10th, 1866.

3. The plans and estimates for the Central Jail at Cannanore are now under the consideration of Government ; those for the Central Jail at Vellore should be submitted with as little delay as practicable in accordance with the Order of the 19th instant, No. 3,014. The Superintending Engineer of the 8th Division will expedite the preparation of the revised estimate for the District Jail at Madura, with reference to the Orders which were communicated to him in the Proceedings of Government, No. 1,996, dated 25th June 1866. The Superintending Engineer of the 7th Division will take immediate measures for pushing on the construction of the District Jail at Calicut from the funds at his disposal, leaving the expenditure to be adjusted from savings later in the year. Measures will be prosecuted with a view to the selection of a site for the Central Jail at Trichinopoly, and Captain Oakes will expedite the submission of estimates for the work on the standard designs, adhering to the instructions conveyed to the Superintending Engineer

E.
JAILS.

of the 4th Division, in Proceedings of Government, No. 3,014 of 19th instant, relative to the preparation of estimates for the proposed Central Jail at Vellore.

4. Plans and Estimates for a new Lunatic Asylum at Madras were called for in G. O. No. 1,103, dated 11th April 1866, and the Superintending Engineer of the 4th Division will be requested to report, in compliance with a Memorandum from this office, No. 277, dated 19th September 1866, what progress has been made with the preparation of those documents.

5. The Governor in Council is particularly anxious that the additional allotments sanctioned and contemplated in these Orders should be fully utilized ; and, as this result can be obtained only by the prompt submission of the plans and estimates, and by the speedy commencement and vigorous prosecution of the several works, His Lordship confidently looks for the hearty co-operation of the Superintending Engineers, and for the unremitting exertions of the Officers who may be placed in executive charge.

6. Arrangements have already been made for the location of convicts for employment on the Jail at Cannanore, and as the Government are desirous that, in the construction of all the new Jails, convict labor should be utilized to the fullest extent to which that description of labor can be employed, in order to reduce the cost of those buildings as much as possible, the Inspector General of Jails will be requested to detach all available convicts for employment on the new Central Jail at Vellore and the District Jail at Calicut. The Superintending Engineers of the 4th and 7th Divisions will take immediate measures for locating the men on the sites of those buildings, and for employing them in the preparation of materials, as well as in the actual execution of the works. In connection with this subject, the Superintending Engineers will give their particular attention to providing suitable accommodation for the Police force engaged in guarding the several gangs of convicts employed. The lodging of the Police and Convicts must be completely provided for before any other work is undertaken, and the charge for this item will be exclusive of the estimate for the Jail buildings. The Superintending Engineers will also be careful to make a reduction in the estimates which they are now about to submit equivalent to the full value of the convict labor that can be employed.

Proceedings of Government, No. 3,014, of 19th September 1866.

Do. do. No. 1,536, of 14th May 1866.

7. The construction of the Central Jails at Rajahmundry and Coimbatore, upon which the outlay up to the 31st July last amounted

to Rupees 3,811, and 18,628, against the Budget assignments of Rupees 43,679 and 50,000, respectively, should be pushed on as rapidly as possible, and, in the event of additional allotments of funds being required for those buildings during the current official year, they will be placed at the disposal of the Superintending Engineers concerned from savings on the General Grant for Public Works.

E. JAILS.

MINUTE BY HIS EXCELLENCY THE GOVERNOR.

1. In paragraph 27 of a Minute communicated by me to Government, under date of the 10th of July last, I adverted to a letter from the Chief Secretary to this Government, to the Secretary to the Government of India, under date of December* 9th, 1865, soliciting a special grant of two lakhs for Jail buildings, and I stated that the letter in question had not received any reply from the Supreme Government.

* NOTE.—By a clerical error *March* was printed in 'the Minute instead of *December.*

2. In a letter from the Secretary to the Government of India, Public Works Department, to the Secretary to the Government of Madras, Public Works Department, dated August 31st, the above statement has been corrected, and Lieutenant-Colonel Dickens has recorded that the above-mentioned letter of the Madras Government was duly replied to, first by a telegram of the 12th of January 1866, and, secondly, by letter No. 130 C., dated the 7th of February of the same year·

3. The statement of the Secretary to the Government of India, Public Works Department, being perfectly correct, I have to express my regret that I should have committed the inaccuracy referred to, and that I should have imputed to the Government of India an omission which did not occur.

4. In making the erroneous statement in question, without reference to documents, I had, no doubt, in my mind the letter addressed by the Secretary of the Department of Public Works in Madras, to the Secretary for the same Department in the Government of India, No. 406, under date of February 1st, 1866, accompanying the Madras Budget of Public Works for 1866-67, in which, among other matters, Colonel Orr urged, in paragraph 13, the pressing necessity of an extraordinary appropriation for the improvement and development of Jail accommodation, and in which he suggested, with reference to Mr. Secretary Bayley's letter, dated Simla, June 23rd, 1864, that the Supreme Government should add to the general assignment for the Public Works of this Presidency the sum of at least four lakhs of Rupees, to be exclusively expended in the construction of new Jails.

E.
JAILS.

5. To this letter from the Secretary for the Department of Public Works a reply was received, under date of March 27th, 1866, No. 344 A., containing the orders passed on the Madras Public Works Budget Estimate ; but while several of the questions submitted by Colonel Orr were fully commented on, it was merely stated, with reference to paragraphs 11, 12, and 13 of Colonel Orr's letter, that they would be answered separately.

6. The promised reply to paragraphs 11, 12, and 13, subsequently reached the Government of Madras, embodied in a letter under date of May 26th, addressed by the Secretary to the Government of India, Public Works Department, to the Secretary for the same Department in this Presidency ; but while paragraphs 11 and 12 were duly noticed, no specific reference was made to paragraph 13 of Colonel Orr's letter, and the whole question of improved and increased Jail accommodation, so earnestly urged by this Government, was passed over in silence.

7. The silence of the Secretary to the Government of India, Public Works Department, was alluded to, by the desire of this Government, in the letter addressed to that Officer by Colonel Orr, under date of July 12th, 1866, and it was to this incident that I ought to have referred in my Minute prepared about the same time.

8. In recording a rectification of my mistake, it is not in the least my desire to enter upon any controversy, or to impute to the Supreme Government any indifference to the wishes expressed by this Government in regard to the question of prison development and reform. I wish, on the contrary, to avail myself of this occasion to express my gratitude for the additional grant of Rupees 1,20,000, which the Supreme Government have recently made with a view to the prosecution of Jail buildings in this Presidency, and the commencement of a Lunatic Asylum. The amount is not a large one, but in consequence of the prevailing scarcity the calls on the Supreme Government for extraordinary disbursements both for Bengal and Madras have been incessant and irresistible. Under these circumstances, the sum referred to might be ill-afforded, and, in conjunction with other available funds, it can be made highly instrumental in advancing the work which we have at heart, now more than ever urgent on account of the increase of crime caused by famine and high prices.

9. I request that a copy of this Minute may be imparted to the Supreme Government.

OOTACAMUND,   (Signed)   NAPIER.
16th October 1866.

F.

Return of Mortality in the undermentioned Jails for the Official years 1862-63, 1863-64, 1864-65, and 1865-66.

NAMES OF JAILS.	Daily average number of Convicts in confinement.	NUMBER OF CONVICTS WHO DIED DURING THE YEAR FROM				
		Cholera.	Jail Diarrhœa or Dysentery.	Fever.	Scurvy.	Other diseases.
1862-63.						
Rajahmundry	180·25	...	9	3	...	2
Nellore	336·5	...	...	...	...	9
Trichinopoly	414·7	2	15	1	...	21
Madura	241·25	4	17	1	...	8
Tinnevelly	157	...	11	...	...	11
Coimbatore	464	2	21	1	...	15
Calicut	380·75	86	20	3	1	27
Mangalore	238	...	10	2	...	8
Tellicherry	121·25	...	6	3	...	11
1863-64.						
Rajahmundry	134	...	2	...	...	15
Nellore	416·66	...	5	...	...	10
Trichinopoly	397·8	3	8	2	...	10
Madura	219·75	20	26	1	...	25
Tinnevelly	202	...	20	...	...	15
Coimbatore	264	35	22	...	...	17
Calicut	321·5	...	17	1	3	54
Mangalore	256	...	18	...	...	13
Tellicherry	120·75	...	5	2	...	9
1864-65.						
Rajahmundry	132	...	14	2	...	28
Nellore	416·16	94	6	...	...	5
Trichinopoly	341·2	...	40	...	...	14
Madura	244·25	26	20	...	...	14
Tinnevelly	195	...	15	...	...	23
Coimbatore	322	...	54	3	...	24
Calicut	343·75	...	28	5	...	21
Mangalore	258	4	9	1	...	17
Tellicherry	136·5	...	21	1	1	12
1865-66.						
Rajahmundry	109	3	5	...	...	41
Nellore	310·18	4	13	...	...	12
Trichinopoly	322·1	1	7	1	...	3
Madura	188	6	14	...	...	5
Tinnevelly	288·18	1	28	1	...	4
Coimbatore	354·58	1	14	2	...	5
Calicut	349·25	40	25	9	9	114
Mangalore	258·40	2	19	...	...	16
Tellicherry	127·18	13	22	5	...	7

F.
JAILS

F.—(*Continued.*)
Return of Mortality in the undermentioned Jails for the Official

NAMES OF JAILS.	Daily average number of Prisoners under trial	No. of Prisoners under trial who died during the year from					Daily average number of Debtors.
		Cholera.	Jail Diarrhœa or Dysentery.	Fever.	Scurvy.	Other diseases.	
1862-63.							
Rajahmundry	21	...	...	...	...	...	·75
Nellore	12·75	...	...	...	...	...	2·5
Trichinopoly	44	...	...	...	...	...	1·7
Madura	31·75	2	...	...	...	...	16·25
Tinnevelly	32	...	...	...	...	...	2
Coimbatore	33	...	...	...	...	...	5
Calicut	18·75	4	1	...	...	1	11·5
Mangalore.	8	...	1	...	...	1	17
Tellicherry	10	...	1	...	...	2	8
1863-64.							
Rajahmundry	11·75	...	...	...	...	...	1·25
Nellore	14·75	...	...	...	...	...	3·55
Trichinopoly	10·5	...	...	...	...	...	2·7
Madura	15·25	1	...	...	...	...	22·5
Tinnevelly	23·25	...	1	...	...	...	5·75
Coimbatore	12	...	...	...	...	...	·4
Calicut	20	...	...	...	...	3	9
Mangalore.	20	...	...	...	...	1	11
Tellicherry	7·5	...	1	...	...	...	7
1864-65.							
Rajahmundry	7·5	...	...	...	...	...	2·5
Nellore	12·83	...	...	...	...	...	2·66
Trichinopoly	2·7	...	...	...	...	...	2·3
Madura	15·25	1	...	...	...	1	31·75
Tinnevelly	18	...	...	...	...	2	5·75
Coimbatore	12	...	...	...	...	...	1
Calicut	11·5	...	...	1	...	...	19·25
Mangalore.	12	...	1	...	...	...	8
Tellicherry	6·5	...	...	...	...	...	8
1865-66.							
Rajahmundry	8·5	...	...	...	...	1	1·5
Nellore	7·44	...	1	...	...	...	1·67
Trichinopoly	6·83	...	...	...	...	...	3·06
Madura	13·25	...	...	...	...	...	33·25
Tinnevelly.	19·73	...	...	...	...	...	3·98
Coimbatore	13	...	...	...	...	...	2·75
Calicut	19·75	8	3	1	4	...	16·5
Mangalore...	10·94	...	2	...	...	2	3·84
Tellicherry	9·68	11	1	...	...	1	17·3

F.—(*Continued.*)
years 1862-63, 1863-64, 1864-65, and 1865-66.

F.
JAILS.

No. OF DEBTORS WHO DIED DURING THE YEAR FROM					Daily average number of State Prisoners.	NUMBER OF STATE PRISONERS WHO DIED DURING THE YEAR FROM				
Cholera.	Jail Diarrhœa or Dysentery.	Fever.	Scurvy.	Other diseases.		Cholera.	Jail Diarrhœa or Dysentery.	Fever.	Scurvy.	Other diseases.
...	...	...	...	...	2	...	...	...	...	...
...	...	...	...	...	6·5	...	...	...	...	...
...	...	...	...	...	...	...	...	...	...	...
...	...	...	...	...	...	...	...	...	...	...
...	...	...	...	...	...	...	...	...	...	...
...	...	...	...	...	...	...	...	...	...	...
2	...	...	...	1	...	...	...	...	...	...
...	...	...	...	...	...	...	...	...	...	...
...	...	...	...	...	...	...	...	...	...	...
...	...	...	...	...	2	...	...	...	...	...
...	...	...	...	...	2·5	...	...	...	...	1
...	...	...	...	...	...	...	...	...	...	...
...	...	...	...	...	...	...	...	...	...	...
...	...	...	...	...	...	...	...	...	...	...
...	...	...	...	...	...	...	...	...	...	...
...	...	...	...	...	...	...	...	...	...	...
...	...	...	...	...	...	...	...	...	...	...
...	...	...	...	...	...	...	...	...	...	...
...	1	...	...	...	1·75	...	...	...	...	1
...	...	...	...	...	2	...	...	...	...	...
...	...	...	...	...	...	...	...	...	...	...
1	2	...	...	...	...	...	...	...	...	...
...	...	...	...	...	...	...	...	...	...	...
...	1	...	...	1	...	...	...	...	...	...
1	...	...	...	...	...	...	...	...	...	...
...	...	...	...	...	...	...	...	...	...	...
...	...	...	...	...	1	...	...	...	...	1
...	...	...	...	...	2·41	...	...	...	...	...
3	...	...	...	...	...	...	...	...	...	...
...	...	...	...	...	...	...	...	...	...	...
...	...	...	...	...	1	...	...	...	...	...
...	...	...	...	...	...	...	...	...	...	...
...	...	1	...	3	...	...	...	...	...	...

F.—*(Continued.)*
Return of Mortality in the undermentioned Jails for the

NAMES OF JAILS.	Daily average number of Insane Prisoners.	No. of Insane Prisoners who died during the year from				
		Cholera.	Jail Diarrhœa or Dysentery.	Fever.	Scurvy.	Other diseases.
1862-63.						
Rajahmundry	...	...	...	...	...	...
Nellore	·41	...	...	...	...	...
Trichinopoly	...	...	...	...	...	...
Madura	...	...	...	...	...	...
Tinnevelly	...	...	...	...	...	...
Coimbatore	1	...	...	...	...	...
Calicut	...	...	...	...	...	...
Mangalore...	...	...	...	...	...	...
Tellicherry	4	...	...	...	...	1
1863-64.						
Rajahmundry	...	...	...	...	...	...
Nellore	·75	...	...	...	...	...
Trichinopoly	...	...	...	...	...	...
Madura	...	...	...	...	...	...
Tinnevelly	...	...	...	...	...	...
Coimbatore	1	...	...	...	...	...
Calicut	...	...	...	...	...	...
Mangalore	...	...	...	...	...	...
Tellicherry	3	...	...	...	...	4
1846-65.						
Rajahmundry	·25	...	...	...	...	...
Nellore	1·08	...	...	...	...	...
Trichinopoly	...	...	...	...	...	...
Madura	...	...	...	...	...	...
Tinnevelly	...	...	...	...	...	...
Coimbatore	1	...	...	...	...	...
Calicut	·5	...	...	...	...	...
Mangalore	...	...	...	...	...	...
Tellicherry	·75	...	...	...	...	2
1865-66.						
Rajahmundry	...	...	...	...	...	...
Nellore	·34	...	...	...	...	...
Trichinopoly	...	...	...	...	...	...
Madura	...	...	...	...	...	...
Tinnevelly	...	...	...	...	...	...
Coimbatore	1	...	...	...	...	...
Calicut	1	...	...	...	...	...
Mangalore	...	...	...	...	...	...
Tellicherry	1	...	...	...	...	1

F.—(*Concluded.*)　　　　　　F.

official years 1862-63, 1863-64, 1864-65, *and* 1865-66.　　JAILS.

Daily average of Prisoners on security.	DEATHS FROM.					Per-centage of deaths on the mean daily average of all classes of Prisoners.
	Cholera.	Jail Diarrhoea or Dysentery.	Fever.	Scurvy.	Other diseases.	
1.5	...	...	...	...	...	6·81
15·5	...	...	...	...	...	2·40
...	...	...	...	...	...	9·26
...	...	...	...	...	...	11·06
...	...	...	...	...	...	11·51
12	...	...	...	...	1	7·76
7·5	...	...	...	...	...	34·88
...	...	...	...	...	...	8·36
7	...	...	...	...	...	15·97
5·5	...	...	...	...	...	11
10·83	...	...	...	...	...	3·56
...	...	...	...	...	...	5·59
...	...	...	...	...	...	28·35
...	...	...	...	...	...	15·58
10	...	...	...	...	...	25·42
4·75	...	1	...	...	1	22·51
...	...	...	...	...	...	11·15
3·5	...	1	...	...	...	15·52
1	...	...	...	...	...	31·72
8·66	...	...	...	...	...	23·63
...	...	...	...	...	...	15·59
...	...	...	...	...	...	22·31
...	...	...	...	...	...	19·2
3	...	...	...	...	...	23·89
3·5	...	...	...	...	...	15·05
...	...	...	...	...	...	11·87
1·5	...	...	...	...	...	24·14
...	...	...	...	...	...	42·5
2·63	...	...	...	...	...	9·24
...	...	...	...	...	...	3·61
...	...	...	...	...	...	11·94
...	...	...	...	...	...	10·9
1	...	...	...	...	...	5·89
1·5	...	...	...	...	...	54·89
...	...	...	...	...	...	15
1·56	...	...	...	...	...	41·47

A.
CULTIVA-
TION.

APPENDIX III.

A.

Statement shewing the cultivation in the several Districts of

DISTRICTS.	DRY.		WET·	
	Extent.	Assessment.	Extent.	Assessment.
1	2	3	4	5
	Acres.	Rupees.	Acres.	Rupees.
I. Ganjam	1,04,729	1,32,057	1,78,513	5,10,924
2. Vizagapatam... ...	52,207	58,027	21,549	1,15,196
3. Godavery	2,43,846	8,76,188	1,72,470	6,04,314
4. Kistna	14,07,161	21,34,481	1,59,190	7,36,551
5. Nellore	5,63,632	7,79,783	1,43,858	7,69,425
6. Cuddapah	11,11,137	8,16,097	1,45,343	11,09,105
7. Bellary	21,35,737	13,00,198	1,71,265	7,95,751
8. Kurnool	11,25,624	11,07,588	27,991	2,23,243
9. Madras	1,16,830	1,90,457	2,31,353	9,81,851
10. North Arcot... ...	3,91,299	5,81,130	1,85,398	11,17,107
11. South Arcot... ...	8,17,883	15,90,479	2,76,137	15,44,319
12. Tanjore	1,69,864	2,25,600	7,16,618	35,55,761
13. Trichinopoly... ...	7,06,692	6,60,453	1,24,479	5,82,602
14. Madura	5,59,875	7,97,141	1,22,472	5,75,498
15. Tinnevelly	7,38,343	6,12,910	2,11,700	15,59,711
16. Coimbatore	17,53,565	15,75,726	83,763	5,17,701
17. Salem...	9,89,553	12,93,307	76,599	4,76,760
18. South Canara	...	...	...	...
19. Malabar	...	5,80,008	...	12,46,486
Total...	1,29,87,977	1,53,11,630	30,48,698	1,70,13,304

N. 1.—In the Kistna, Kurnool, and South Arcot Districts the extent and assessment entered for
figures entered in the present Return representing the actual transactions, while those in the Statement of

A.—(*Continued.*)

the Madras Presidency for the official year 1865-66.

TOTAL, 1865-66.		1864-65.		COMPARISON.			
				INCREASE.		DECREASE.	
Extent.	Assessment.	Extent.	Assessment.	Extent.	Assessment.	Extent.	Assessment.
6	7	8	9	10	11	12	13
Acres.	Rupees.	Acres.	Rupees.	Acres.	Rupees.	Acres.	Rupees.
2,83,242	6,42,981	2,80,706	6,38,535	2,536	4,446	...	...
73,756	1,73,223	65,605	1,52,707	8,151	20,516	...	...
4,16,316	14,80,502	3,95,378	14,70,077	20,938	10,425	...	...
15,66,351	28,71,032	15,94,437	28,90,851	...	...	28,086	19,819
7,07,490	15,40,208	6,74,784	15,63,343	32,706	...	...	23,135
12,56,480	19,25,202	12,52,633	18,91,025	3,847	34,177	...	...
23,07,002	20,95,949	24,66,777	21,78,960	...	...	1,59,775	83,011
11,53,615	13,30,830	11,59,855	13,55,421	...	...	6,240	24,591
3,48,183	11,72,308	3,57,304	12,16,138	...	...	9,121	43,830
5,76,697	16,98,237	5,88,449	17,16,704	...	...	11,752	18,467
10,94,020	31,34,798	10,97,255	31,60,803	...	...	3,235	26,005
8,86,482	37,81,361	8,96,908	37,80,600	...	761	10,426	...
8,31,171	12,43,055	7,81,840	12,15,447	49,341	27,608	...	...
6,82,347	13,72,639	6,62,211	13,28,593	20,136	44,046	...	...
9,50,043	21,72,621	9,17,399	21,13,122	32,644	59,499	...	...
18,37,328	20,93,427	16,01,689	21,45,457	2,35,639	...	...	52,030
10,66,152	17,70,067	10,56,433	17,48,984	9,719	21,083	...	...
...	...	...	...	...	...	...	...
...	18,26,494	...	17,94,542	...	31,952	...	...
160,36,675	323,24,934	158,49,663	323,61,309	4,15,647	2,54,513	2,28,635	2,90,888
			Net. .	1,87,012	...	...	36,375

1864-65, will be found to differ from those given in the similar Return of that year, in consequence of the
1864-65, were only estimates,

B.

Statement shewing the prices of grain and other chief articles of produce in the several Districts under the Madras Presidency, for the official year 1865-66, compared with 1864-65.

DISTRICTS.	RICE, 1st sort, per garce.		RICE, 2nd sort.		PADDY, 1st sort.		PADDY, 2nd sort.		CHOLUM.		CUMBOO.		RAGGY.		VARAGOO.		HORSE GRAM.	
1	2	3	4	5	6	7	8	9	10	11	12	13	14	15	16	17	18	19
	1864-65.	1865-66.	1864-65.	1865-66.	1864-65.	1865-66.	1864-65.	1865-66.	1864-65.	1865-66.	1864-65.	1865-66.	1864-65.	1865-66.	1864-65.	1865-66.	1864-65.	1865-66.
	Rs.	Rs.	Rs.	Rs.	Rs.	Rs.	Rs.	Rs.	Rs.	Rs.	Rs.	Rs.	Rs.	Rs.	Rs.	Rs.	Rs.	Rs.
1. Ganjam ...	278	480	257	437	107	188	102	177	161	301	123	220	127	151	...	...	128	232
2. Vizagapatam	335	486	303	443	143	215	131	201	171	227	142	215	154	235	106	204	139	228
3. Godavery ...	316	320	298	299	145	144	137	136	175	175	139	148	162	166	151	140	163	196
4. Kistna ...	432	408	403	376	201	178	179	169	232	196	224	189	182	173	213	153	259	263
5. Nellore ...	404	387	409	362	194	182	193	164	212	197	190	191	186	174	129	127	233	245
6. Cuddapah ...	560	559	497	496	255	256	231	230	294	290	264	288	260	264	222	235	311	298
7. Bellary ...	649	594	584	517	278	247	253	224	348	345	334	344	287	302	229	...	401	396
8. Kurnool ...	586	557	521	506	269	252	243	230	320	295	334	313	294	281	209	180	347	340
9. Madras ...	382	413	355	391	179	193	160	177	218	258	191	229	212	230	177	191	281	322
10. North Arcot.	375	423	350	379	171	182	163	169	215	236	199	226	183	218	278	297	250	264
11. South Arcot.	392	417	363	382	170	185	157	162	174	222	170	223	167	192	138	130	243	239
12. Tanjore ...	371	496	352	386	170	188	162	180	207	247	171	217	168	195	107	125	254	258
13. Trichinopoly.	413	456	394	426	197	220	183	203	190	218	186	219	174	209	103	117	224	245
14. Madura ...	544	588	516	562	256	284	243	269	251	323	206	246	256	297	99	118	221	251
15. Tinnevelly ...	594	603	520	535	275	301	239	251	255	360	212	337	284	317	...	145	294	339
16. ....re ...	520	554	468	498	237	260	218	232	248	288	203	245	207	256	205	217	225	290
17. Salem ...	415	445	385	417	192	206	179	190	190	237	169	212	163	213	104	121	116	232
18. South Cnara.	453	395	404	362	...	...	195	179	...	...	...	...	283	269	...	...	304	341
19. alabar ...	489	497	432	446	226	227	199	212	...	...	...	...	219	252	...	...	272	335
Average...	443	478	411	431	203	229	189	198	227	260	209	237	210	231	161	164	246	280

B.—(Concluded.)

Statement shewing the prices of grain and other chief articles of produce in the several Districts under the Madras Presidency, for the official year 1865-66, compared with 1864-65.

B. PRICES OF GRAIN, &C.

DISTRICTS.	ULUNDU		WHEAT		GINGELY-OIL SEED		LAMP-OIL SEED		SALT		COTTON, per candy.		INDIGO, per candy.		SUGAR, per candy.	
	1864-65	1865-66	1864-65	1865-66	1864-65	1865-66	1864-65	1865-66	1864-65	1865-66	1864-65	1865-66	1864-65	1865-66	1864-65	1865-66
	20	21	22	23	24	25	26	27	28	29	30	31	32	33	34	35
	Rs.	Rs.	Rs.	Rs.	Rs.	Rs.	Rs.	Rs.	Rs.	Rs.	Rs.	Rs.	Rs.	Rs.	Rs.	Rs.
1. Ganjam	231	312	379	536	395	372	269	323	240	244	198	131	860	856	103	89
2. Vizagapatam	200	368	317	412	354	374	286	268	246	261	137	142	816	821	82	83
3. Godavery	202	344	417	465	317	349	258	324	217	236	220	160	800	800	35	30
4. Kistna	293	380	518	645	319	385	243	296	252	251	203	149	920	960	60	40
5. Nellore	371	360	609	689	422	449	280	292	234	234	233	158	1,047	972	98	98
6. Cuddapah	476	538	719	840	502	504	340	388	341	325	267	190	1,165	1,116	90	110
7. Bellary	605	720	866	990	...	...	403	440	499	462	240	172	1,270	1,342	85	90
8. Kurnool	438	422	769	1,021	...	...	...	...	370	345	223	166	1,144	1,172	94	97
9. Madras	375	507	633	601	403	490	...	...	226	240	211	209	926	938	...	...
10. North Arcot	341	493	685	672	541	537	383	390	228	228	314	219	1,057	1,079	81	77
11. South Arcot	344	388	957	840	522	552	315	451	261	250	263	112	615	633	43	48
12. Tanjore	317	369	805	753	468	614	333	405	216	216	206	165	231	222	38	45
13. Trichinopoly	340	382	770	674	406	581	320	437	269	267	264	170	840	937	40	42
14. Madura	293	379	705	711	714	647	284	491	247	249	187	80	720	660	56	52
15. Tinnevelly	417	465	822	832	637	582	419	511	275	266	272	188	760	760	80	80
16. Coimbatore	398	500	734	706	...	...	296	400	324	314	232	142	600	443	44	46
17. Salem	308	387	671	645	...	...	...	...	267	267	272	190	822	755	...	...
18. South Canara	383	413	632	638	...	...	...	...	218	218	320	171	...	...	...	...
19. Malabar	410	482	556	626	618	574	...	...	290	293	...	...	...	...	...	...
Average...	357	427	668	700	467	501	311	387	276	272	227	161	858	851	68	68

C.
COLLEC-
TIONS.

C.

Statement shewing the Collections of all sources of Revenue
official year 1865-66,

DISTRICTS.	LAND REVENUE.			
	1864-65.	1865-66.	Increase.	Decrease.
1	2	3	4	5
	Rupees.	Rupees.	Rupees.	Rupees.
1. Ganjam	10,78,943	10,08,597	...	70,346
2. Vizagapatam	13,36,974	12,56,425	...	80,549
3. Godavery	35,38,604	41,37,003	5,98,399	...
4. Kistna	28,01,004	33,78,312	5,77,308	...
5. Nellore	21,97,328	21,68,653	...	28,675
6. Cuddapah	19,26,614	20,35,253	1,08,639	...
7. Bellary	23,88,112	22,66,123	...	1,21,989
8. Kurnool	15,02,165	14,18,563	...	83,602
9. Madras	15,81,946	16,71,391	89,445	...
Do. Town	...	...	...	...
10. North Arcot	23,43,094	22,94,094	...	49,000
11. South Arcot	31,70,729	28,53,587	...	3,17,142
12. Tanjore	41,69,417	40,64,444	...	1,04,973
13. Trichinopoly	13,35,666	13,82,494	46,828	...
14. Madura	22,59,825	22,59,625	...	200
15. Tinnevelly	25,01,227	26,53,245	1,52,018	...
16. Coimbatore	23,70,022	25,60,397	1,90,375	...
17. Salem	21,69,571	21,47,326	...	22,245
18. South Canara	13,61,577	15,56,849	1,95,272	...
19. Malabar	17,78,802	18,05,283	26,481	...
Madras Sea Customs.	...	...	...	...
Total...	4,18,11,620	4,29,17,664	19,84,765	8,78,721
		Net.	11,06,044	
Stoppages made by Ex-Officio Asses-sors from the salary of the Public Servants at the Presidency, and interest on Promissory Notes........	...	...	...	...
Total...	...	...	...	...

C.—*(Continued.)*

in the several Districts of the Madras Presidency, for the
compared with 1864-65.

ABKARRY.				INCOME TAX.		
1864-65.	1865-66.	Increase.	Decrease.	1864-65.	1865-66.	Decrease.
6	7	8	9	10	11	12
Rupees.	Rupees.	Rupees.	Rupees.	Rupees.	Rupees.	Rupees.
86,603	87,175	572	...	30,727	7,010	23,717
67,155	62,614	...	4,541	69,884	36,704	33,180
1,81,149	1,78,490	...	2,659	47,878	22,629	25,249
82,800	1,40,009	57,209	...	42,953	23,315	19,638
53,644	53,983	339	...	34,430	31,758	2,672
1,21,328	1,18,432	...	2,896	43,382	16,880	26,502
5,09,647	4,88,438	...	21,209	1,21,996	55,342	66,654
1,68,561	1,63,824	...	4,737	47,238	18,085	29,153
10,41,426	11,85,235	1,43,809	...	17,687	1,23,792	53,083
...	...	...	...	...	...	...
2,92,189	2,87,286	...	4,903	47,243	18,079	29,164
1,69,373	1,96,843	27,470	...	27,168	22,885	4,283
3,20,206	3,20,570	364	...	64,005	27,899	36,106
1,15,333	1,07,488	...	7,845	18,502	8,985	9,517
1,01,044	98,958	...	2,086	89,229	37,534	51,695
53,890	43,185	...	10,705	49,316	23,052	26,264
1,68,650	1,65,792	...	2,858	35,297	14,887	20,410
1,84,515	1,87,961	3,446	...	32,041	8,782	23,259
61,618	85,766	24,148	...	17,060	5,402	11,658
1,81,359	1,70,756	...	10,603	75,244	48,612	26,632
...	...	...	...	1,893	520	1,373
39,60,490	41,42,805	2,57,357	75,042	10,72,361	5,52,152	5,20,209
		1,82,315				5,20,209
...	...	...	...	3,93,291	1,18,396	2,74,895
...	...	...	...	14,65,652	6,70,548	7,95,104

C.—*(Continued.)*

Statement shewing the Collections of all sources of Revenue

DISTRICTS.	MOTURPHA.			SEA CUSTOMS.	
	1864-65.	1865-66.	De-crease.	1864-65.	1865-66.
	13	14	15	16	17
	Rupees.	Rupees.	Rupees.	Rupees.	Rupees.
1. Ganjam	...	...	...	50,576	33,081
2. Vizagapatam ...	...	...	...	51,638	39,409
3. Godávery	...	...	...	33,991	44,353
4. Kistna...	...	...	...	4,776	1,912
5. Nellore...	...	...	...	357	50
6. Cuddapah	...	...	...	...	...
7. Bellary...	411	...	411	...	...
8. Kurnool	...	...	...	...	...
9. Madras...	23	...	23	...	...
Do. Town	...	...	...	...	...
10. North Arcot ...	...	...	...	33,787	41,007
11. South Arcot ...	2,084	...	2,084	2,86,482	3,31,106
12. Tanjore...	...	...	...	...	...
13. Trichinopoly ...	...	...	...	25,053	29,332
14. Madura...	...	...	...	59,548	54,732
15. Tinnevelly	...	...	...	...	...
16. Coimbatore... ...	...	...	...	...	...
17. Salem	...	...	...	...	...
18. South Canara ...	...	...	...	44,010	58,832
19. Malabar	...	...	...	1,16,426	1,20,101
Madras Sea Customs.	...	...	...	11,03,402	11,97,104
Total...	2,518	...	2,518	18,10,046	19,51,019
			2,518		Net...
	...	...	...	...	...
Total...	...	...	...	...	...

C.—*(Continued.)*

in the several Districts of the Madras Presidency, &c.

SEA CUSTOMS.— (Concluded.)		LAND CUSTOMS.			
Increase.	Decrease.	1864-65.	1865-66.	Increase.	Decrease.
18	19	20	21	22	23
Rupees.	Rupees.	Rupees.	Rupees.	Rupees.	Rupees.
...	17,495	...	...	...	...
...	12,229	...	...	...	...
10,362	...	660	811	151	...
...	2,864	...	...	...	...
...	307	...	...	...	...
...	...	...	...	...	...
...	...	...	...	...	...
...	...	...	...	...	...
...	...	...	...	...	...
...	...	...	...	...	...
7,220	...	...	...	...	...
44,624	...	55,519	62,002	6,483	...
...	...	68,776	61,876	...	6,900
4,279	...	...	...	...	...
...	4,816	449	104	...	345
...	...	1,01,439	4,468	...	96,971
...	...	...	...	...	...
...	...	...	...	...	...
14,822	...	...	...	...	...
3,675	...	1,890	5,204	3,314	...
93,702	...	...	...	...	...
1,78,684	37,711	2,28,733	1,34,465	9,948	1,04,216
1,40,973				Net...	94,268
...	...	...	...	...	...
...	...	...	...	...	...

C.
COLLEC-
TIONS.

C.—*(Continued.)*

Statement shewing the Collections of all sources of Revenue

DISTRICTS.	SALT.			
	1864-65.	1865-66.	Increase.	Decrease.
	24	25	26	27
	Rupees.	Rupees.	Rupees.	Rupees.
1. Ganjam	13,20,307	13,35,256	14,949	...
2. Vizagapatam ...	2,84,884	3,22,740	37,856	...
3. Godavery	4,17,088	8,91,721	...	25,367
4. Kistna	7,24,024	7,31,478	7,454	...
5. Nellore	12,28,665	10,69,344	...	1,59,321
6. Cuddapah... ...	...	...	...	...
7. Bellary	...	...	...	...
8. Kurnool	...	...	...	...
9. Madras	23,21,396	20,55,829	...	2,65,567
Do. Town ...	...	...	...	...
10. North Arcot ...	...	...	...	...
11. South Arcot ...	5,11,062	5,53,922	42,860	...
12. Tanjore	9,91,831	9,93,278	1,447	...
13. Trichinopoly ...	...	...	...	...
14. Madura	5,74,237	6,14,889	40,652	...
15. Tinnevelly ...	6,39,074	6,45,072	5,998	...
16. Coimbatore ...	...	...	...	...
17. Salem	...	...	...	...
18. South Canara ...	5,49,965	6,07,359	57,394	...
19. Malabar	7,83,440	7,91,601	8,161	...
Madras Sea Customs.	...	...	...	...
Total...	103,45,973	101,12,489	2,16,771	4,50,255
				2,33,484
	...	...	...	...
Total...	...	...	...	...

c

C.—*(Continued.)*

in the several Districts of the Madras Presidency, &c.

STAMPS.			
1864-65.	1865-66.	Increase.	Decrease.
28	29	30	31
Rupees.	Rupees.	Rupees.	Rupees.
67,794	73,369	5,575	...
1,01,504	1,15,273	13,769	...
1,28,627	1,41,944	13,317	...
73,511	1,06,956	33,445	...
57,746	64,576	6,830	...
1,12,873	1,14,291	1,418	...
1,27,697	1,44,731	17,034	...
85,164	1,00,665	15,501	...
1,76,641	1,95,546	18,905	...
1,19,502	1,28,754	9,252	...
1,01,252	98,639	...	2,613
82,987	94,779	11,792	...
3,27,690	4,31,772	1,04,082	...
68,959	86,550	17,591	...
2,06,192	2,08,194	2,002	...
1,59,054	1,95,143	36,089	...
98,740	1,20,869	22,129	...
99,576	1,29,661	30,085	...
1,20,042	1,37,202	17,160	...
3,68,367	3,77,644	9,277	...
...	...	...	...
26,83,918	30,66,558	5,85,253	2,613
		3,82,640	
...	...	...	...
...	...	...	...

C.
COLLEC-
TIONS.

C.—*(Concluded.)*

Statement shewing the Collections of all sources of Revenue, &c.

DISTRICTS.	TOTAL.			
	1864-65.	1865-66.	Increase.	Decrease.
	32	33	34	35
	Rupees.	Rupees.	Rupees.	Rupees.
1. Ganjam	26,34,950	25,44,488	...	90,462
2. Vizagapatam ...	19,12,039	18,33,165	...	78,874
3. Godavery	43,47,997	49,16,951	5,68,954	...
4. Kistna	37,29,068	43,81,982	6,52,914	...
5. Nellore ...	35,72,170	33,88,364	...	1,83,806
6. Cuddapah... ...	22,04,197	22,84,856	80,659	...
7. Bellary	31,47,863	29,54,634	...	1,93,229
8. Kurnool	18,03,128	17,01,137	...	1,01,991
9. Madras	52,98,307	52,31,793	...	66,514
Do. Town ...	1,19,502	1,28,754	9,252	...
10. North Arcot ...	27,83,778	26,98,098	...	85,680
11. South Arcot ...	40,52,709	38,25,025	...	2,27,684
12. Tanjore	62,28,407	62,30,945	2,538	...
13. Trichinopoly ...	15,38,460	15,85,517	47,057	...
14. Madura	32,56,029	32,48,636	...	7,393
15. Tinnevelly ...	35,63,548	36,18,897	55,349	...
16. Coimbatore ...	26,72,709	28,61,945	1,89,236	...
17. Salem	24,85,703	24,73,730	...	11,973
18. South Canara ...	21,54,272	24,51,410	2,97,138	...
19. Malabar	33,05,528	33,19,201	13,673	...
Madras Sea Customs...	11,05,295	11,97,624	92,329	...
Total...	6,19,15,659	6,28,77,152	20,09,099	10,47,606
		Net...	9,61,493	
Stoppages made by Ex Officio Assessors from the salary of the Public Servants at the Presidency, and interest on Promissory Notes.........	3,93,291	1,18,396	..	2,74,895
Total...	623,08,950	629,95,548	6,86,598	Net

N. B.—The total collections for 1864-65, as entered in column 34 of this Statement will be found to differ from those in the Statement of that year owing to the exclusion of Forest Revenue.

D.

ARTICLES.	VALUE.		ARTICLES.	VALUE.	
	1864-65.	1865-66.		1864-65.	1865-66.
IMPORTS.	Rs.	Rs.	EXPORTS.	Rs.	Rs.
Millinery and Wearing Apparel	7,85,083	8,84,190	Bones	23,386	43,360
Gold and Silver Lace and Thread	4,99,969	3,54,290	Coffee	76,84,938	78,13,813
Books and Stationery	4,19,627	5,55,771	Cotton Wool	4,04,18,937	4,84,16,848
Twist and Yarn	61,76,796	71,61,022	Cotton Goods	15,60,671	20,43,953
Piece Goods, dyed.	15,25,616	11,13,489	Dregs of Gingely	4,67,679	5,09,441
Do. printed	10,62,440	15,59,476	Drugs	1,70,522	2,35,750
Do. plain	69,96,720	85,72,175	Indigo	33,35,915	34,57,070
Drugs	2,94,557	3,90,960	Dyes of Sorts	1,11,995	1,01,293
Dyes	86,406	1,37,579	Feathers	33,511	21,326
Betel-nut, boiled	3,63,000	4,60,523	Fishmaws	19,894	14,519
Do. raw	2,78,082	3,29,036	Fruits and Nuts	40,31,784	24,34,011
Glass-ware	2,26,842	1,69,108	Paddy	8,57,101	6,97,629
Paddy	6,17,849	12,69,036	Rice	60,64,255	65,88,482
Rice	40,33,597	25,12,203	Wheat	1,00,628	39,055
Wheat	3,79,330	3,94,733	Grain of sorts	7,48,394	5,04,238
Grain of sorts	1,99,481	1,94,033	Hides	19,39,459	19,81,107
Gunnies and Gunny Bags	4,30,227	5,55,447	Horns	1,37,906	1,35,440
Jewellery	4,72,299	3,85,390	Ivory and Ivory-ware	7,628	16,076
Machinery	2,53,193	2,42,625	Jewellery	14,279	14,748
Malt Liquors	7,56,838	6,66,830	Mats	30,365	28,524
Metals	37,51,840	31,83,255	Molasses	9,28,059	14,08,928
Naval Stores	3,91,685	5,19,941	Coir and Coir Rope	9,50,206	12,27,560
Oilman's Stores	2,30,964	2,24,718	Hemp	15,746	10,538
Porcelain and Earthenware	1,30,215	1,31,727	Naval Stores of Sorts.	22,570	18,586
Pipe Staves and Casks	1,54,922	1,09,303	Oil	25,07,457	15,43,435
Provisions	2,18,995	2,19,161	Perfumery	1,27,459	1,26,901
Railway Stores	15,34,102	33,98,924	Precious Stones	45,675	28,956
Seeds	2,13,535	3,03,791	Provisions	4,22,954	5,25,419
Silk, raw	1,46,152	6,768	Salt	1,39,491	1,35,216
Silk Piece Goods	2,14,626	5,25,000	Saltpetre	61,249	1,39,450
Spices	2,96,481	2,94,897	Seeds	27,57,558	22,69,161
Spirits	3,91,840	6,10,344	Shawls, Cashmere	5,817	1,230
Tea	1,29,989	2,50,857	Silk Piece Goods	54,489	37,013
Timber and Planks	11,79,332	19,57,739	Spices	21,65,854	23,59,650
Wines	5,82,430	7,59,121	Spirits	2,188	2,082
Woollens	6,19,268	5,14,069	Sugar	22,40,991	13,36,872
Sundries*	57,57,212	68,96,489	Timber and Woods	15,96,845	16,35,447
			Tobacco	5,73,074	4,63,104
			Wax and Wax-Candles.	75,653	1,02,368
			Sundries†	12,36,957	15,45,358
Total	1,18,02,487	4,79,87,412	Total	8,36,71,790	9,00,15,155
£	41,80,248	47,98,741	£	83,67,179	90,01,515

*Includes Government Stores	13,72,600	19,78,544	†Includes Government Stores	24,391	17,926
Do. do. Salt (on the Western Coast.)	3,41,523	5,79,293	Do. do. Salt	24,693	152

E.

Value of the trade in food-grains.

Items.	1863-64.	1864-65.	1865-66.
	Rupees.	Rupees.	Rupees.
Imports	50,00,512	51,39,145	43,33,953
Exports	68,88,717	74,50,654	76,93,003

F.

Imports and Exports of Bullion and Specie.

YEARS.	IMPORTS.			EXPORTS.		
	By Government.	By Individuals.	Total.	By Government.	By Individuals.	Total.
	Rupees.	Rupees.	Rupees.	Rupees	Rupees.	Rupees.
1860-61......	...	2,07,25,887	2,07,25,887	3,00,000	59,88,632	62,88,632
1861-62......	...	2,22,85,900	2,22,85,900	3,00,000	-36,58,486	39,58,486
1862-63......	51,02,833	2,52,84,057	3,03,86,890	35,40,000	26,50,551	61,90,551
1863-64......	44,30,000	3,16,45,985	3,60,75,985	1,60,03,000	63,36,284	2,23,39,284
1864-65......	...	3,03,13,958	3,03,13,958	89,52,000	91,98,942	1,81,50,942
1865-66......	...	3,66,42,492	3,66,42,492	62,00,600	64,09,623	1,26,10,223

APPENDIX IV.

A.

*Statement shewing the Expenditure on Public Works in 1865-66,
from Imperial Funds as compared with the allotment for
that year and with the outlay in 1864-65.*

DISTRICTS.	Allotment for 1865-66 including private contributions.	Expenditure in 1865-66.	Expenditure in 1864-65.
	RS.	RS.	RS.
Ganjam	1,48,585	1,48,029	1,21,886
Vizagapatam	1,26,349	1,09,090	2,05,448
Godavery	3,22,354	3,10,612	4,72,238
Kistna	2,83,531	2,77,471	4,22,947
Nellore	1,37,312	1,35,947	1,69,235
Cuddapah...	1,54,488	1,45,465	1,81,625
Kurnool	85,143	77,544	73,424
Bellary	2,51,246	2,16,669	2,18,736
Presidency	2,85,991	3,10,918	4,25,512
Madras	3,23,490	3,30,737	4,88,050
North Arcot	1,74,132	1,76,792	2,62,052
South Arcot	1,75,993	1,75,814	2,77,140
Salem	1,08,167	1,02,997	1,42,375
Bangalore...	2,35,146	2,36,737	1,78,618
Tanjore	2,64,274	2,46,657	2,46,525
Trichinopoly	1,90,611	1,84,069	2,67,705
Coimbatore	6,18,903	5,74,409	3,90,736
Malabar	3,73,373	3,84,554	3,96,274
South Canara	72,240	76,019	1,08,487
Madura	1,27,071	1,19,431	1,14,899
Tinnevelly	1,43,128	1,30,358	1,66,132
Municipal Commissioners ...	35,897	35,897	35,897
Total...	46,37,424	45,06,216	53,65,941

B.

*Statement shewing the Expenditure on New Works in each District
from Imperial Funds under the Budget heads.*

DISTRICTS.	Military.	Civil Buildings.	Agricultural.	Communications.	Miscellaneous Public Improvement.	Total.
	RS.	RS.	RS.	RS.	RS.	RS.
Ganjam	3,516	21,003	8,383	53,075	...	85,977
Vizagapatam ...	499	25,723	1,502	25,561	...	53,285
Godavery ...	...	48,819	18,838	37,193	2,666	1,07,516
Kistna	...	9,177	98,500	16,499	19,773	1,43,949
Nellore	...	8,744	18,099	41,881	...	68,724
Cuddapah	...	6,713	2,553	28,125	...	37,391
Kurnool	8,367	2,818	2,734	7,578	...	21,497
Bellary	51,736	3,805	494	3,977	...	60,012
Presidency ...	60,927	1,46,472	441	170	56	2,08,066
Madras	38,292	27,104	19,603	21,033	326	1,06,358
North Arcot ...	...	6,740	34,373	4,613	...	45,726
South Arcot ...	...	18,889	13,628	11,025	...	43,542
Salem	3,566	9,212	1,087	15,335	...	29,200
Bangalore... ...	1,94,995	4,576	...	...	...	1,99,571
Tanjore	...	19,429	45,505	11,913	122	76,969
Trichinopoly ...	32,264	20,745	10,080	5,741	...	68,830
Coimbatore ...	1,27,724	2,17,577	15,846	97,266	4,688	4,63,101
Malabar	84,013	25,950	...	1,91,276	70	3,01,309
South Canara ...	1,906	12,803	...	28,191	...	42,900
Madura	...	3,095	2,417	26,619	1,746	33,877
Tinnevelly ...	731	2,578	3,623	6,570	57	13,259
Total...	6,08,486	6,41,972	2,97,706	6,33,341	29,504	22,11,009

B.—*(Concluded.)*

Statement shewing the Expenditure on Repairs in each District from Imperial Funds under the Budget heads.

DISTRICTS.	Military.	Civil Buildings.	Agricultural.	Communications.	Miscellaneous Public Improvement.	Total.
	RS.	RS.	RS.	RS.	RS.	RS.
Ganjam ...	247	4,824	12,683	44,298	...	62,052
Vizagapatam ...	3,452	7,741	5,643	37,727	1,292	55,855
Godavery ...	2,254	5,332	1,60,415	19,101	15,994	2,03,096
Kistna ...	415	7,028	1,10,568	15,326	185	1,33,522
Nellore	...	2,636	25,247	39,340	...	67,223
Cuddapah ...	351	797	28,876	78,050	...	1,08,074
Kurnool ...	359	1,020	14,933	39,735	...	56,047
Bellary	13,775	1,499	63,849	77,534	...	1,56,657
Presidency ...	35,152	21,926	2,667	42,803	304	1,02,852
Madras	17,564	8,024	77,079	1,21,712	...	2,24,379
North Arcot ...	3,075	2,301	68,736	56,954	...	1,31,066
South Arcot ...	...	2,390	62,042	67,652	188	1,32,272
Salem	81	1,270	19,862	52,584	...	73,797
Bangalore	36,411	755	...	...	...	37,166
Tanjore	...	8,181	99,954	60,505	1,048	1,69,688
Trichinopoly ...	4,722	779	54,674	55,064	...	1,15,239
Coimbatore ...	9,800	3,475	34,543	63,201	289	1,11,308
Malabar	13,495	6,473	861	62,373	43	83,245
South Canara ...	374	2,393	...	30,178	174	33,119
Madura	...	1,569	32,074	51,860	51	85,554
Tinnevelly... ...	1,913	2,901	47,757	63,178	1,350	1,17,099
Municipal Commissioners ...	...	...	...	35,897	...	35,897
Total...	1,43,440	93,314	9,22,463	11,15,072	20,918	22,95,207

C.

Statement shewing the Expenditure in each District from Local Funds.

DISTRICTS.	Income Tax Fund.	District Road, Port, and other Funds.	Educational Funds.	Total.
	RS.	RS.	RS.	RS.
Ganjam	...	2,321	2,815	5,136
Vizagapatam	42	576	3,715	4,333
Godavery	45	58,728	3,441	62,214
Kistna	4,597	14,193	...	18,790
Nellore	4,293	26,655	...	30,948
Cuddapah	3,385	4,545	1,355	9,285
Kurnool	594	12,879	3,560	17,033
Bellary	3,739	10,276	...	14,015
Presidency	864	...	32,922	33,786
Madras	6,026	4,404	...	10,430
North Arcot	2,781	17,772	...	20,553
South Arcot	...	59,876	...	59,876
Salem	8,523	3,317	...	11,840
Tanjore	...	12,469	...	12,469
Trichinopoly	36	16,292	...	16,328
Coimbatore	1,573	22,469	...	24,042
Malabar	9,927	1,06,166	813	1,16,906
South Canara	1,119	16,582	...	17,701
Madura	2,453	1,630	105	4,188
Tinnevelly	2,656	32,850	...	35,506
Total...	52,653	4,24,000	48,726	5,25,379

D.

Statement shewing the Estimate, and the Allotment and Expenditure in 1865-66 on Important Public Works in the Madras Presidency.

DISTRICTS.	WORKS.	Estimate.	Expenditure up to 30th April 1865.	Allotment for 1865-66.	Expenditure during 1865-66.
	Military.	R.	RS.	RS.	RS.
Bellary	School room for the Artillery...	3,700	2,640	1,060	1,721
Do.	Apothecary's Quarters	3,446	1,979	1,467	2,178
Do.	Married Men's Quarters... ...	26,024	12,642	13,392 reduced to 12,466	9,878
Do.	Non-Commissioned Officer's do.	22,149	11,795	10,354	11,180
Do.	Alterations to Non-Commissioned Officer's Quarters occupied by the Artillery.	7,240	...	7,240	6,646
Do.	Alterations and improvements to the buildings occupied by the Artillery.	21,980	...	1,800 reduced to 17,900	9,170
Do.	Channel from a ruined tank to the Native Infantry Lines.	15,806	13,291	2,515 reduced to 515	498
Do.	Branch Supply Channel to the Fort Ditch.	2,440	2,196	...	96
Do.	Raising the Bund for a Channel from a ruined tank to the Native Infantry Lines.	9,700	3,065	6,632 reduced to 3,594	2,550
Kurnool	Levelling the Ramparts of the Kurnool Fort.	8,840	528	8,317	7,796
Presidency. ...	Alterations to the Sea face Batteries.	13,180	9,753	3,377 reduced to 2,800	2,771
Do.	Family Quarters in Fort Saint George.	1,68,780	1,42,500	10,680 increased to 21,304	21,304
Do.	Soojee Mill and Bakery	30,400	...	3,000 increased to 15,000	15,000
Madras	Alterations to the Horse Artillery Lines at Saint Thomas' Mount.	85,100	72,023	12,000 reduced to 5,007	5,007
Do.	Reserve Powder Magazine at do.	37,300	...	30,000 reduced to 21,930	19,863
Do.	Soldiers' Rest-house at Avady.	2,810	...	1,807 increased to 2,810	2,845
Salem	Rest-house at Jollarpett. ...	3,410	...	3,100 increased to 3,410	3,049
Bangalore	Race Course Barracks... ...	5,92,250	5,23,903	1,00,000 increased to 1,00,876	92,558
Do.	Three additional blocks at the old Dragoon Barracks.	1,05,200	...	20,000 increased to 45,824	47,027
Do.	Bakery...	...	...	18,415	18,823
Do.	Ulsoor Water Project... ...	72,000	32,132	20,341	18,083
Trichinopoly ...	Racket and Fives Court for the Artillery at Trichinopoly.	10,580	5,525	4,420 reduced to 3,688	3,638
Do.	Twenty-six Family Quarters for do.	17,400	12,626	3,800 increased to 4,047	4,047
Do.	Additions to the Court yards and Out-offices for the Artillery Family Quarters at Trichinopoly.	8,500	...	8,500	8,232
Do.	Removal of Parcherry and purchase of ground.	25,811	23,002	6,011 reduced to 2,809	2,817
Coimbatore ...	Lawrence Asylum at Ootacamund.	9,61,067	1,23,388	1,48,543 reduced to 1,15,304	1,15,541

D. PUBLIC WORKS.	DISTRICTS.	WORKS.	Estimate.	Expenditure up to 30th April 1865.	Allotment for 1865-66.	Expenditure during 1865-66.
		Military.—(Continued.)	Rs.	Rs.	Rs.	Rs.
	Malabar	Married Quarters at Cannanore	1,27,723	59,127	26,140 increased to 49,831	49,065
		Civil Buildings.				
	Vizagapatam ..	Constructing Zillah Jail at Vizagapatam.	60,324	16,202	3,801 increased to 7,550	7,479
	Godavery	Constructing Central Jail at Rajahmundry.	2,08,080	1,24,102	50,249 increased to 38,194	36,441
	Salem	Upper Story to Salem Jail ...	40,500	42,783	418	418
	Coimbatore. ...	Central Jail at Coimbatore ...	1,80,800	1,06,583	1,00,000 increased to 1,43,978	1,46,888
	Nellore	Taluk Cutcherry at Ongole ...	11,334	8,610	5,534	4,884
	Madras	Madrantacum Taluk Cutcherry.	11,300	10,458	842	2,742
	Cuddapah. ...	Pullumpett Taluk Cutcherry ...	7,300	2,243	5,057 reduced to 4,346	2,549
	Do.	Post Office at Cuddapah ...	3,240	..	3,240	2,878
	Bellary	Head Assistant Collector's Cutcherry at Hospett.	2,745	2,673	72	116
	Do.	Re-roofing the Taluk Cutcherry at Hospett.	2,150	...	2,150	1,205
	Kurnool	Enlarging the Cutcherries at Nandikotkur and Ravalcotta.	2,670	...	2,670	2,546
	Trichinopoly ...	Additions to the Collector's Cutcherry to provide accommodation for the Paper Currency Department.	4,900	...	4,900 reduced to 4,748	4,748
	Do.	Alterations to the old abandoned Jail to adapt it for a Lunatic Asylum.	11,980	10,564	1,032	1,414
	Presidency. ...	Adding two wings to the Government Office, Fort Saint George.	12,070	...	12,070 reduced to 11,624	11,620
	Do.	Completing the General Hospital New Wing and Upper Story.	2,57,809	2,14,204	29,709 increased to 37,105	36,311
	Do.	Public Works Stores and Workshops.	80,360	55,023	27,160	28,680
	Do.	Foundry in connection with do.	28,530	...	4,000 increased to 6,000	6,000
	Do.	Upper Story to the East face of the Revenue Board Office.	10,460	...	3,000 increased to 9,000	8,734
	South Arcot. ...	Court House at Cuddalore ...	48,780	36,281	12,498	12,698
	Presidency ...	Additional Storage room at the Salt Cotars.	61,300	35,279	26,021 reduced to 21,047	7,492
	Madras	Salt platform, &c., at Home's Garden.	5,600	...	1,771	1,771
	Tanjore	New Salt platform at Tranquebar.	5,720	...	2,000 reduced to 1,500	1,926
	Do.	Salt platform with watch house, Superintendent's Cutcherry, &c., at Negapatam.	9,300	1,200	8,150	8,275
	Madras	Guindy Government House Water Supply Project.	17,986	5,058	8,923	10,151
		Agricultural.				
	Godavery	Raising Godavery Anicut ...	3,00,000	2,16,506	81,745 reduced to 11,436	11,517
	North Arcot ...	Step in rear of the body of the Palar Anicut.	12,700	2,000	10,700	10,596
	Do. ...	Raising the Cheyár Anicut, &c.	29,700	9,587	6,000	5,997
	South do. ...	Cheyar Anicut...	3,280	...	3,280	3,280

DISTRICTS.	WORKS.	Estimate.	Expenditure up to 30th April 1865.	Allotment for 1865-66.	Expenditure during 1865-66.
	Agricultural.—(Continued.)	RS.	RS.	RS.	RS.
Kistna.	Channel from Peddavadlapudy to Nizampett.	2,90,214	2,75,284	12,000 increased to 14,000	13,908
Do.	Channel from Valapapooram to Tidewater.	1,46,479	80,049	14,000	15,701
Do.	Enlarging the head of the Main Channel from Sitanagram to Dugarrella.	2,69,774	1,49,521	4,000	4,298
Do.	Widening the lower portion of the Pullara Channel.	1,04,050	71,852	11,500	11,182
Do.	Continuation of Commanur Channel and Subsidiary Works.	1,85,460	33,113	18,253	18,254
Do.	Channel from Akamarru lock to Sultanagram bridge.	14,000	8,442	4,227	4,227
Do.	Reconstructing a Tunnel under the Masulipatam canal.	15,200	5,275	9,699	9,997
Nellore	Idur and Labur branches of Jaffer Sahib's Channel.	{ 27,100 30,600	} 51,657	5,000	4,495
Tanjore	Improving the Vadavar head...	4,800	...	4,800 reduced to 2,300	1,900
Do.	Rebuilding the fallen portions of the Lower Coleroon Anicut, &c.	74,000	...	45,250	22,598
Do.	Constructing additional laterite and rough stone apron with retaining walls at the advanced portion of three sluices in the south branch of the Lower Coleroon Anicut.	16,000	...	...	5,932
Trichinopoly ...	Constructing six surplus sluices on the south bank of the Coleroon.	7,920	...	7,920 reduced to 5,920	4,675
Do.	Constructing 10 surplus sluices on the North do.	12,380	...		2,420
	Communications.				
Ganjam	Road from Aska to Russelconda Branch road from Bullipadra to Kurchuly.	{ 44,640 22,470	} 15,662	{ 10,000 increased to 11,354	13,552
Do.	Road from Majagedda to Sankerakole.	49,700	34,623	5,076 reduced to 2,222	2,222
Do.	Road from Aska to Ganjam Port and Salt Pans.	62,700	22,500	20,000 increased to 26,025	28,090
Vizagapatam ...	Constructing road from Vizagapatam to Cassipur.	1,15,000	36,982	25,000 reduced to 15,000	14,773
Do.	Road from Vizianagram to Bowdara.	53,080	38,657	14,418 reduced to 11,338	8,798
Godavery	Works for the Cross drainage of the Ellore High Level Canal.	1,04,000	18,561	12,000 increased to 16,917	16,123
Do.	Iron Girder bridge at Cocanada.	75,000	39,976	35,000 reduced to 15,000	15,000
Kistna	Reconstructing Sultanagram bridge.	14,100	9,056	5,044	5,044
Do.	Bridge across the Commanur Channel.	11,900	6,008	6,000 reduced to 4,292	3,818
Nellore	Embanked road and Masonry works across the Musanur Valley.	68,630	11,898	5,000 increased to 10,817	10,815
Do.	Masonry works on Trunk road No. VI.	1,02,350	71,171	Imperial 7,000 Income Tax 2,796	6,934 2,796
Do.	Ongole and Kottapatur road...	50,200	40,535	4,996	4,994

DISTRICTS.	WORKS.	Estimate.	Expenditure up to 30th April 1865.	Allotment for 1865-66.	Expenditure during 1865-66.
	Communications.—(Continued.)	Rs.	Rs.	Rs.	Rs.
Nellore	Nellore and Dorenal road ...	1,01,000	51,470	Imperial 1,541 Income Tax 1,500	} 1,497
Cuddapah... ...	Road from Rajampett to Rajampett Railway Station.	2,695	633	2,062	2,061
Do.	Road from Ontimitta to Ontimitta do.	570	...	570	570
Do.	Road from Nandalur to Nandalur do.	7,312	1,762	5,550 reduced to 5,193	3,320
Do.	Bridges and Tunnels on Trunk road No. XI.	86,748	71,815	8,591 increased to 9,141	8,427
Do.	Road from Cuddapah to Bellary frontier.	1,06,431	82,303	Imperial 5,000 Income Tax 3,500	5,000 3,385
Bellary	Road from Bellary to the Cuddapah frontier.	1,02,200	93,788	Imperial 4,000 Income Tax 3,731	3,977 3,739
Cuddapah... ...	Road from Cuddapah to Kurnool frontier.	62,000	52,771	8,747	8,747
Kurnool	Road from Nundial to Cuddapah frontier.	60,000	40,911	11,289 reduced to 7,289	7,247
Do.	Nundy Canama Ghaut... ...	54,540	54,384	154	154
Madras	Road from Satiaved to Cowrapet.	19,000	5,500	Income Tax 2,075	2,182
Do. ...	Road from Trivellur to Nagalapuram.	21,400	7,153	Income Tax 1,847	1,847
Do. ...	Road from Utacotta to Satiaved.	13,300	1,000	Income Tax 1,997	1,997
North Arcot ...	Road from Arcot to Arni ...	32,600	30,445	Income Tax 2,154	2,082
South Arcot ...	Gaddilam Bridge	12,000	8,240	3,760	3,756
Do. ...	Widening do.	3,150	...	3,150 increased to 3,300	3,300
Salem...	Ussur and Malar road... ...	8,320	...	7,200 reduced to 6,000	4,478
Do.	Taramangalam and Suramangalam road.	11,300	6,301	5,000 reduced to 4,400	4,341
Do.	Bridge across the Vellan at Talavassal.	14,300	7,288	Income Tax 5,731	5,352
Do.	Cart Track between Palakode and the Morapur Railway Station.	18,200	11,535	Income Tax 4,165	2,574
Tanjore	Road from Negapatam Railway Station to Nagore.	25,730	21,738	4,387 reduced to 3,003	1,562
Do.	Road from the Railway Station at Kivalur to the Town of Kivalur.	3,690	2,634	645 increased to 1,056	394
Do.	Canal from Negapatam to Tirupundy.	24,165	14,820	{ 8,306 increased to 9,345 }	5,924 3,797
Do.	Completing the Navigation between Negapatam and Vedarniem.	64,000	...		
Coimbatore ...	Coonor Ghaut New Trace ..	1,60,000	49,331	40,000 increased to 41,790	51,491
Do.	Bargur Ghaut do. ...	72,100	11,101	15,000 reduced to 10,010	10,015
Do.	Gudalur Ghaut do. ...	81,400	13,000	Imperial 5,760 Income Tax 795 }	5,759

DISTRICTS.	WORKS.	Estimate.	Expenditure up to 30th April 1865.	Allotment for 1865-66.	Expenditure during 1865-66.
	Communications.—(Continued.)	Rs.	Rs.	Rs.	Rs.
Malabar	Tambracherry Ghaut and Road.	1,46,413	50,184	60,000 reduced to 26,930	26,378
Do.	Peria Ghaut New Trace ...	...	4,999	7,000 increased to 13,339	13,451
Do.	Karkur Ghaut and Road above and below.	3,17,024	62,057	55,000 reduced to 51,170	52,824
Do.	Kalpatty Bridge near Palghat.	30,000	24,735	3,590 increased to 5,128	5,759
Do.	Completing the Terriot road...	58,500	13,920	14,000 increased to 24,408	27,243
Do.	Road between Vythery and the Kalpatty river.	30,886	1,944	Imperial 10,154 Income Tax 2,052	Imperial 10,154 Income Tax 1,778
Do.	Road from Kalpatty bridge to Sultan's Battery.	} 76,700	...	{ Imperial 430 Income Tax 7,748	Imperial 806 Income Tax 5,290
Do.	Road from Sultan's Battery to Mysore frontier.				
South Canara ...	Road to connect Mangalore and Cannanore by Vitla.	79,640	31,245	3,462	3,462
Madura	Road from Tirumangalam to the Coimbatore boundary.	1,65,000	11,065	Imperial 10,910 Income Tax 1,567	10,908 1,566
Do.	Bridge across the Shanmuganadi river.	36,450	16,945	11,545 reduced to 8,545	8,545
	Miscellaneous Public Improvements.				
Godavery	Cocanada Light house, Groynes, Flag Staff, &c.	71,435	70,345	1,128 increased to 2,666	2,666
Kistna...	Fresh water Channel from Sultanagram bridge to Robertson's Pettah	18,080	2,524	8,403	8,403
Do.	Reconstructing Sea Embankment from tidal Calingulah to Gilkaldandy.	9,000	1,663	7,338	7,144
Madura	Cutting the inner angle of the Paumben Reef Channel.	43,340	23,107	11,597 reduced to 2,930	1,746

E.
PUBLIC
WORKS.

E.

Statement shewing the principal works which were undertaken from the District Road, Educational, and Port Funds by Officers of the Public Works Department, during the year 1865-66.

Districts.	Works.	Expenditure in 1865-66.	Remarks.
Ganjam	Road from Jagganathapore to Poorooshottapur.	1,986	Earth-work nearly finished for the whole district, viz., 13¼ miles, and 28 ... works ...
Do.	Anglo-Vernacular School at Chicacole...	1,879	Foundations ..., doors and windows ready at site, and materials being collected.
Do.	Zillah School at Berhampore	936	Mals being collected.
Vizagapatam...	Taluk School at Casimcottah	838	Roofing in progress.
Do.	Normal School at Vizagapatam.	2,877	Completed, ... ¾th of the stone floor; the building will shortly be ready for use.
Godavery	Road from Pemiguduru to Jaggarnathgerry	1,762	All ..., ... 3 small bridges and culverts, ...
Do.	Do. from Samulcottah to Cocanada	12,550	Completed, with the ... tion of turfing.
Do.	Do. from Ambojreapettah to Amalapur	9,168	..., with the exception of a bridge of 60 feet span.
Do.	Extending Guntay and Kottapettah Road	2,527	Completed.
Do.	Road from Tanukú via Doova to Pratipaud	3,198	Road completed from Parravelly to Tanakú (3 miles), earth-work and tun als completed from Tanakú to Doova.
Do.	Do. from Palcole to Doddiputta	6,707	Earth- wk from Palcole to ..., ard 5 tunnels biilt. Graveling of road through Palcole ... finished.
Do.	Do. from Nursapur to Veeravassarum.	4,319	Earth-work for 2½ miles ...; 3 tunnels built, and 1 in progress.

E.
PUBLIC
WORKS.

District	Work	Amount	Remarks
Godavery	School at Ellore	2,519	Walls raised 5 feet.
Do.	Do. at Rajahmundry	922	Completed.
Kistna	Road from Jagerlamoody to Tenally	1,438	Gravel collected, 1 tunnel built, and 3 others in progress.
Do.	Do. from Poonoor to Intoor	1,520	Earth-work completed.
Do.	Coast road from Vellatoor to Sandole	1,444	Embankment between Vellatoor and Buttepole completed.
Nellore	Allúr and Iskapilly Road	9,811	Nineteen tunnels and 3¾ miles of road completed.
Do.	Kanagherri, Kundookoor, and Oollapallam road to the beach	11,370	Road from 1st to 21st mile, and masonry works from 1st to 16th mile, completed.
Cuddapah	School at Cuddapah	1,355	Completed.
Kurnool	Road from Gadidamadugu to Bairlooty	8,699	Road made from Gadidamadugu to Nandikotcoor.
Do.	Do. from Cumbum to Narkapur	2,880	1½ miles of road metalled and gravelled, and 3 road dams and 1 tunnel built.
Do.	School at Kurnool	3,560	Two additional rooms completed.
Bellary	Road from Hoovinhudgally to Hurpunhally	1,715	Two masonry bridges built.
Do.	Do. from Herihall to Raidroog	3,557	Nearly completed.
Presidency	Alterations and improvements to the Medical College.	29,368	The southern wing has been completed with the exception of the Laboratory, furnace, and fittings, and the northern wing has been roofed.
North Arcot	Improving the Synagontah Ghaut	2,000	First trace completed, and the second in progress.
Do.	Road from Kunnamungalum to Polur	2,898	In progress.
Do.	Do. from Vandivash to Polur	1,920	In progress.
South Arcot	Do. from Vellapuram to Gingee	1,830	Completed.
Do.	Do from Trinomalay to Ooloorpettah	6,400	91,891 cubic yards of earth-work, and 15 tunnels, completed.

E.—(*Continued.*)

Statement shewing the principal works which were undertaken from the District Road, Educational, and Port Funds by Officers of the Public Works Department, during the year 1865-66.

Districts.	Works.	Expenditure in 1865-66.	Remarks.
South Arcot ...	Road from Chellumbrum and Manargudi road to Naivassal Village.	1,723	Completed.
Salem ...	Road from Trichengode to Kolleeputtee ...	1,425	8½ miles of road completed, and the remaining 3½ miles in progress.
Tanjore ...	Constructing a Jetty at Nagore...	2,820	Completed.
Trichinopoly ...	Road from Leulgoody to Chenganoor	4,830	Masonry works nearly completed. Four out of the seven miles of earth-work finished.
Do. ...	Bridge over the Wyacondam	4,003	Two arches turned and the third in progress.
Coimbatore ...	Road from Coimbatore Railway Station to Ootacamund and thence to the Seegoor Ghauts.	7,517	Kept in thorough repair.
Malabar ...	Road from Tambracherry to Areacode trace ...	4,141	Trace completed to river at Alliol.
Do. ...	Do. from Edwarra to Munjerry	4,291	Completed.
Do. ...	Do. from Munjerry to Mangotte	5,399	Completed.
Do. ...	Re-constructing the Annacayan Bridge.. ...	2,170	Completed.
Do. ...	Constructing the Kakadoocadoo Bridge on the road from Ellatoor to Tambracherry.	103	Completed.
Do. ...	Re-building the Pyolly Lock	613	Completed.
Do. ...	Constructing a truss bridge across the Toota river.	6,471	The whole of the masonry, with the exception of the parapets, completed.
Do. ...	Do. Tiroovatty Bridge	1,229	Planking nearly completed.
Do. ...	Road from the Backwater to Tambracherry ...	9,315	Most of the tunnels, as well as the earth-work as far as Chellaye, completed.

E.
PUBLIC
WORKS.

Do.	Road from Parakoomoo to Wadakantarrah in Palghaut.	2,890	Completed.
Do.	Road from Palghaut to the Cullengode Section as far as Poodoonagaram.	7,937	Section as far as Poodoonagaram completed.
Do.	Deepening Canal from Tanoor to Cootai.	7,235	Completed.
Do.	Road from Tirtallah to Chowghaut	6,977	Repaired and improved.
Do.	Light-house at Cochin	6,942	Wells sunk, foundations laid, and two feet of pedestal built.
South Gn ra...	Road from Moodbiddy to Beltangodi	1,896	Three miles of ad opened to bridle path, 2¾ miles f bridle path opened to 4 yards width, ad ½ mile fo ad pened to 6 yards width.
Do.	Do. from Pootoor by Vitla and Munigeshwar.	2,131	4¾ miles of road op ad to bridle path, 2¼ miles of road opened to 4 yards width, and 340 ai yards of rough stone revetment built.
Do.	Timber Bridge across the Cupetta Nulla on the Beltangady and Pootoor road.	1,775	Co ple ed, with the ception of 53 running feet of planking.
Do.	Reclamation of the fore-shore at Mangalore	5,673	14,123 cubic yards filled with sand, &c, and 243 bic yards of rough e rev ment built.
Tinnevelly	Shady Khan's Choultry and Traveller's Bungalow.	2,975	Completed.
Do.	Portion of road from Tinnevelly to Streevellipoothoor.	13,965	Two large bridges, and a Chuttrum, as well as the road work, if in progress.
Do.	Road between Nangunery and Kalakad	4,861	Completed, with the exception of the turfing.

G.

Abstract Statement shewing the entire Expenditure of Cash and
Stores during and up to the end of official year 1865-66.

G.
IRRIGATION
AND CANAL
COMPANY.

	From 1st May 1865 to 30th April 1866.	Previous as per Form P., 30th April 1865.	Total.
GENERAL MANAGEMENT.	RS. A. P.	RS. A. P.	RS. A. P.
Agent's Office.			
Salaries	39,201 9 8	1,38,228 1 7	1,77,429 11 3
Contingent expenses	6,848 14 3	25,773 2 1	32,622 0 4
Stores	1,303 3 8	7,236 1 4	8,539 5 0
Chief Engineer's Department.			
Salaries	50,301 8 7	2,48,764 5 5	2,99,065 14 0
Contingent expenses	7,785 3 5	30,032 15 5	37,818 2 10
Stores	1,522 8 5	12,648 11 9	14,171 4 2
Inspecting Engineer.			
Salaries	4,015 14 7	7,623 14 4	11,639 12 11
Contingent expenses	114 1 2	234 4 3	348 5 5
Stores	... ...	... ...	... ...
CONSTRUCTION.			
Executive Establishment.			
Salaries ... ...' ...	2,16,712 8 9	8,55,209 2 0	10,71,921 10 9
Contingent expenses	16,246 1 1	64,956 0 10	81,202 1 11
Stores	4,519 12 0	20,895 14 9	25,415 10 9
WORK.			
Main Supply.			
Anicut and Head Works at Kurnool ...	}	60,236 5 1	60,236 5 1
Stores			
Anicut and Head Works at Soonkasala...	27,284 0 2	} 3,5³'053 5 8	3,82,282 4 9
Stores	1,944 14 11		
Anicut and Head Works at Somasi- warum	... ...	} 56,821 2	56,963 1 2
Stores	141 14 7		
Hindry Aqueduct	15,285 1 2	} 2,43,981 7	2,59,943 1 8
Stores	676 11 11		
Canal for 1 mile from the Head sluice of the Kurnool Anicut	... ...	49,210 13 7	49,210 13 7
South Main Canal.			
1st Section, from 1st to 17½ Miles ...	51,551 11 11	} 7,94,629 14 9	8,55,271 7 0
Stores	9,089 12 4		
2nd and 3rd Sections, from 18th to 43rd Mile	4,07,420 13 3	} 16,73,462 7 6	21,08,163 5 9
Stores	27,280 1 0		
4th and 5th Sections, from 44th to 72nd Mile ... ... '	2,11,159 1 0	} 9,49,198 15 6	11,80,187 4 10
Stores	19,829 4 4		
6th Section, from 73rd to 92nd Mile ...	36,518 13 3	} 2,70,212 12 11	3,11,842 12 6
Stores	5,111 2 4		
7th Section, from 93rd to 113th Mile ...	41,688 11 4	} 1,49,771 1 5	2,06,010 10 0
Stores	14,550 13 3		

G.—(*Continued.*)

Abstract Statement shewing the entire Expenditure of Cash and Stores during and up to the end of official year 1865-66.

	From 1st May 1865 to 30th April 1866.	Previous as per Form P., 30th April 1865.	Total.
	RS. A. P.	RS. A. P	RS. A. P.
8th Section, from 114th to 143½ Miles ...	85,432 6 8	} 1,66,212 2 9	2,52,501 3 8
Stores	856 10 3		
Distribution.			
Branch Channels and Sluices between 1st to 17½ Miles	782 11 9	} 4,432 8 1	5,240 2 1
Stores	24 14 3		
Channels and Sluices for irrigating 30,000 acres between Bowanassy and Kistna Rivers	587 15 2	} 1,376 7 1	1·966 0 2
Stores	1 9 11		
Distribution works at 6th Section in the Bowanassy Division	99 13 10	... ...	99 13 10
Branch Channels and Sluices at Soonka-sala	583 14 0	... ...	583 14 0
Building.			
Central Hospital with Out-houses and compound wall	174 9 1	} 4,188 5 4	4,387 10 1
Stores	24 11 8		
Office and Store Workshop at Soonkasala	317 9 9	5,628 13 4	5,946 7 1
Office and Store-room and Artificers' shed at Bowanassy	135 15 1	7,469 8 1	7,333 9 0
Powder Magazine, Store, and Station roads at Bowanassy	491 13 8	3,867 8 1	4,359 5 9
Gun Powder Manufactory into an Hospital at Bowanassy	7 2 2	12 0 0	19 2 2
Office and Store building at Valapenoor..	82 2 0	5,196 2 8	5,114 0 8
Iron and Brass Foundry and rooms for receiving and despatching Stores at Kurnool.	{ 28 15 2 {16,991 4 7	}	17,020 3 9
Workshop building at Bowanassy ...	6,224 9 0	... ...	6,224 9 0
Office and Temporary Store Shed at Ayaloor	... ...	67 6 0	67 6 0
Office and Store building at Jupaud ...	2,308 4 6	5,532 5 7	3,224 1 1
Office and Store building at Puggydial ...	626 12 2	3,206 5 9	3,833 1 11
Office and Store building at Chintagontla.	157 11 2	5,260 7 9	5,102 12 7
Quarters for Sub-Assistant Engineers and Assistant Surveyor's Bungalow ...	135 13 1	697 1 11	561 4 10
Hospital and Apothecary's residence at Somaiswaram	893 0 8	1,566 5 4	2,459 6 0
Office building at Apothecary's residence at Somaiswaram	... ...	1,470 0 0	1,470 0 0
Repairs to the anicut Office at Zorapoor..	... ...	307 12 0	307 12 0
Overseers' Quarters, Store Workshop, Clerk and Pay Office at Somaiswaram.	4,841 1 7	... ...	4,841 1 7
Office, Store, and Workshop at Kurnool...	1,653 8 3	... ...	1,653 8 3
Repairing Central Hospital and out-houses at Kurnool	60 0 0	... ...	60 0 0
Improvement of the road approaching to Bowanassy building	{ 266 10 9 { 6 1 5	} 24 14 10	297 11 9

G.—(*Concluded.*)

Abstract Statement shewing the entire Expenditure of Cash and Stores during and up to the end of official year 1865-66.

G.
IRRIGATION
AND CANAL
COMPANY.

	From 1st May 1865 to 30th April 1866.			Previous as per Form P., 30th April 1865.			Total.		
	RS.	A.	P.	RS.	A,	P.	RS.	A.	P.
Manufacture of Stores.									
Salaries									
Contingent expenses	*43,026	10	2	79,079	10	7	36,053	0	5
Stores									
Work done on private account	889	7	1	3,315	15	11	2,426	8	10
Store Charges.									
Salaries									
Contingent expenses	4,207	10	4	1,00,756	13	10	1,04,964	8	2
Stores									
General Plant on Works	36,519	12	6	3,75 865	6	3	4,12,385	2	9
Steamer " Thistle"	0	0	0	10,616	11	10	10,616	11	10
Stores sold and recoverable in cash ...	21	6	11	9.13		4	31	4	3
Stores lost or damaged	62	2	6	228	13	8	161	11	2
Profit and Loss	7,305	13	1	305	6	5	7,000	6	8
Revenue Account.									
Irrigation Establishment at Kurnool ...	1,379	12	2	2,644	11	6	4,024	7	8
Establishment for working Anicut Sluices at Soonkasala	938	0	0	1,819	0	9	2,757	0	9
Inefficient Balance.									
Amount disbursed under this head ...	54,503	12	3	1,62,425	9	7	2,16,929	5	10
	13,89,916	9	2						
	7,367	15	7						
Total	18,82,548	9	7	69,65,760	1	7	83,48,308	1	2
Add amount of Expenditure on Stores...		...			...		4,99,450	11	7
Grand Total...							†88,47,759	6	9

(Signed) F. H. HENSLOWE,

Agent and Manager.

* 48,361 11 5 Expended during the year.
91,418 13 4 Adjusted do. do.

43,02 6 10 2 Difference.

† The difference between this sum and that, Rupees 88,54,759-13-5, shewn in paragraph 205 of the Report, arises from the deduction in the former of a sum of Rupees 7,000-6-8, which stands in the account to the credit of the head Profit and Loss, and as this sum should stand as a set off against future debits to that head, it has not been thought proper to reduce the actual expenditure under other heads.

16 cxxi

H.

Estimates sanctioned during 1865-66.
MAIN SUPPLY.

	Amount sanctioned by Government.		
	RS.	A.	P.
Repairs to the Soonkasala anicut ...	37,180	0	0
Embankment at the north end north breach of the Soonkasala anicut ...	818	0	0
Cutting a supply channel to Rajoly on the north bank of the Toombuddra a little below the Soonkasala anicut ...	144	0	0
Construction of a wall to protect the unfinished at the breach in the Soonkasala anicut	3,200	0	0
Coping the crest of the Soonkasala anicut	59,300	0	0
Second supplemental sanction for the Hindry aqueduct	27,277	0	0
Supplemental estimate for 20th mile or second Section	43,938	0	0
Earthworks and revetment in the fourth Section	4,52,918	0	0
Revised estimate for earthwork and revetment, fifth Section	1,62,329	0	0
Revised estimate for the completion of earthworks of the eighth Section	1,78,220	0	0
	9,65,324	0	0

H.—*(Continued.)*

Estimates sanctioned during 1865-66.

MAIN SUPPLY.

	Amount sanctioned by Government.		
	RS.	A.	P.
DISTRIBUTION.			
Buildings.			
Supplemental sanction for the Hospital at Kurnool	1,648	5	4
Overseer's hut at Kurnool	1,244	13	3
Office, Workshop and Store buildings at Kurnool	30,612	0	0
Iron and Brass Foundry at Kurnool 9,127 5 1			
Room for receiving and despatching Stores at do. 1,759 3 3			
	10,886	8	4
Roads, Bridges, &c., at Bowanassy ...	4,359	5	9
Second supplemental sanction for Donapaud Office	1,731	0	0
Clerk and Pay Office at Somaiswaram...	575	0	0
Store and Workshop at do. ...	2,046	1	7
Overseer's quarters at do. ...	2,220	0	0
Office and Store at Jupad (supplemental sanction)	1,679	0	0
Do. do. at Puggydial (do.)	947	7	7
	57,949	9	10
Line of Telegraph from Soonkasala to Cuddapah	44,116	0	0
Total...	10,67,389	9	10

APPENDIX V.

A.

Particulars of the Trade of the Ports in the

Districts.	NAMES OF PORTS.	BRITISH				
		Vessels.	Tonnage.	Dues.		
				RS.	A.	P.
Ganjam.	Ganjam	3	1,550	96	14	0
	Munsoorcottah ...	46	34,705	1,604	4	0
	Sonnapore... ...	...	...	...	...	...
	Barwah	...	...	...	...	...
	Calingapatam ...	6	3,818	220	2	6
	Pudi	...	...	...	...	...
	Bapanapaudu ...	...	...	...	...	...
	Total...	55	40,073	1,921	4	6
Vizaga-patam.	Vizagapatam ...	87	56,962	1,874	8	6
	Bimlipatam ...	101	68,295	2,456	6	11
	Pudimadakah ...	1	685	...	...	...
	Pentacottah ...	1	407	...	...	...
	Total...	190	1,26,349	4,330	15	5
Godavery District	Coringa	...	...	...	...	...
	Cocanada	127	83,461	6,717	1	1
	Narasapore ...	...	...	...	...	...
	Total...	127	83,461	6,717	1	1
Kistna Distri dt.	Masulipatam ...	62	39,348	1,345	8	1
	Nizampatam ...	...	...	...	...	...
	Kottapollem ...	...	...	...	...	...
	Epurupollem ...	...	...	...	...	...
	Motupalli	...	...	...	...	...
	Total...	62	39,348	1,345	8	1

A.—(Continued.)

Madras Presidency, for the official year 1865-66.

FOREIGN					COUNTRY, OR NATIVE				
Vessels.	Tonnage.	Dues.			Vessels.	Tonnage.	Dues.		
		RS.	A.	P.			RS.	A.	P.
...	...	...	...	...	18	1,051	32	13	6
6	2,989	186	13	0	55	4,996	139	7	0
...	...	...	...	...	10	1,160	...	...	...
...	...	...	...	...	49	5,934	...	...	...
10	5,731	313	12	6	31	5,971	180	10	6
...	...	...	...	...	38	3,483	...	...	...
...	...	...	...	...	12	1,569¼	...	...	...
16	8,720	500	9	6	213	24,164¾	352	15	0
4	1,647	102	15	0	201	14,524	734	13	5
19	9,787	549	1	5	75	5,634	290	5	2
..	...	...	...	...	7	382	...	...	...
5	2,268	...	...	...	7	361	...	...	...
28	13,702	652	0	5	290	20,901	1025	2	7
...	...	...	...	...	227	33,426	3680	3	2
40	17,911	2212	12	1	92	8,511	888	9	3
...	...	...	...	...	106	5,406	...	...	...
40	17,911	2212	12	1	425	47,343	4568	12	5
3	976½	61	0	6	152	7,393	314	12	9
...	...	...	...	...	76	3,226	...	...	...
1	178	...	...	...	74	7,225	...	...	...
...	...	...	...	...	65	8,556	...	...	...
...	...	...	...	...	11	795	...	...	9
4	1,154½	61	0	6	378	27,195	314	12	

A.—(*Continued.*)

Particulars of the Trade of the Ports in the

Districts.	NAMES OF PORTS.	TOTAL				
		Vessels.	Tonnage.	Dues.		
				RS.	A.	P.
Ganjam.	Ganjam	21	2,601	129	11	6
	Munsoorcottah ...	107	42,690	1,930	8	0
	Sonnapore... ...	10	1,160	...	...	...
	Barwah	49	5,934	...	...	...
	Calingapatam ...	47	15,520	714	9	6
	Pudi	38	3,483	...	...	...
	Bapanapaudu ...	12	1,569¾	...	...	...
	Total...	284	72,957¾	2,774	13	0
Vizaga-patam.	Vizagapatam ...	292	73,133	2,712	4	11
	Bimlipatam ...	195	83,716	3,295	13	6
	Pudimadakah ...	8	1,067	...	...	...
	Pentacottah ...	13	3,036	...	...	...
	Total...	508	1,60,952	6,008	2	5
Godavery District.	Coringa	227	33,426	3,680	3	2
	Cocanada	259	1,09,883	9,818	6	5
	Narasapore ...	106	5,406	...	...	...
	Total -	592	1,48,715	13,498	9	7
Kistna District.	Masulipatam ...	217	47,717½	1,721	5	4
	Nizampatam ...	76	3,226	...	...	...
	Kottapollem ...	75	7,403	...	...	...
	Epurupollem ...	65	8,556	...	...	...
	Motupalli	11	795	...	...	...
	Total...	444	67,697½	1,721	5	4

A.—(*Continued.*)

Madras Presidency, for the official year 1865-66.

VALUE OF						DUTY ON						Sea Custom Revenue.		
Exports.			Imports.			Exports.			Imports.					
RS.	A.	P.	RS.	A.	P.	RS.	A.	P.	RS.	A.	P.	RS.	A.	P.
1,07,130	15	1	16,381	0	0	5,430	8	0	15	2	11	...	...	...
19,84,429	8	8	8,79,411	0	2	17,599	4	2	526	8	4	...	...	...
11,783	0	10	5,296	0	0	...	...	...	...	...	...	...	...	...
58,651	6	4	68,408	9	10	...	...	...	...	...	...	...	...	...
3,67,575	13	1	63,461	5	1	8,879	10	11	53	13	6	...	...	...
28,147	5	2	23,215	2	4	...	...	...	567	0	3	...	...	...
11,469	5	8	8,136	8	0	...	...	...	...	...	...	...	...	...
25,69,187	6	10	10,64,309	9	5	31,909	7	1	1,162	9	0	...	...	...
7,29,730	13	2	14,28,538	11	3	1,529	10	4	784	7	3	2,314	1	7
22,18,698	10	11	9,26,650	5	2	31,187	3	1	2,048	2	6	33,235	5	7
13,560	0	0	14,766	3	3	270	1	7	...	...	...	270	1	7
1,12,078	0	9	7,180	6	0	3,338	12	11	...	...	...	3,338	12	11
30,74,067	8	10	23,77,135	9	8	36,325	11	11	2,832	9	9	39,158	5	8
5,57,853	0	0	3,55,299	0	0	2,882	11	10	66	13	2	2,949	9	0
80,13,377	0	0	6,99,722	0	0	31,638	4	8	8,977	5	6	40,615	10	2
3,03,091	0	0	1,12,604	0	0	1	7	5	265	15	4	267	6	9
88,74,321	0	0	11,67,625	0	0	34,522	7	11	9,310	2	0	43,832	9	11
24,67,250	13	4	10,08,545	9	4	1,182	4	6	715	2	5	...	...	...
2,09,574	0	9	73,663	1	5	...	...	...	...	...	...	...	...	...
36,856	9	4	50,420	2	0	...	...	...	...	...	...	...	...	...
2,18,431	9	0	6,11,473	9	7	...	...	...	...	...	...	...	...	...
23,412	7	0	12,723	9	6	...	...	...	...	...	...	...	...	...
29,55,525	7	5	17,56,825	15	10	1,182	4	6	715	2	5	...	...	...

A.
MARINE.

A.—(*Continued.*)

Particulars of the Trade of the Ports in the

Districts	NAMES OF PORTS.	BRITISH				
		Vessels.	Tonnage.	Dues.		
				RS.	A.	P.
Nellore.	Kottapatnam... ...	...	...	...	...	...
	Itamukala	...	...	...	...	...
	Pakala...	...	...	...	...	...
	Ramayapatnam ...	29	3,778	...	...	...
	Chemayapalem ...	4	722	...	...	...
	Iskapalli ,.. ...	29	6,702	...	...	...
	Ponnapudi	34	5,286	...	...	...
	Joovaladinna ...	6	708	...	...	...
	Kristnapatnam ...	74	4,903	...	...	...
	Mypadu	20	1,492	...	...	...
	Dugarazapatam ...	6	542	...	...	...
	Tupili...	4	532	...	...	...
	Pamanji	4	626	...	...	...
	Pudi	6	654	...	...	...
	Total...	216	25,945	...	...	...
South Arcot.	Cuddalore	17	3,351¼	197	14	9
	Porto Novo	54	7,533¾	...	...	...
	Total...	71	10,885	197	14	9
Tanjore.	Negapatam	708	1,24,216	3,046	5	10
	Nagore	85	15,600	...	...	...
	Thoputoray	19	3,008	...	...	...
	Mutupetai	178	15,878	...	...	...
	Terumalavassal ...	104	11,131	...	...	...
	Tranquebar	155	18,925	299	11	6
	Total...	1,249	1,88,758	3,346	1	4
Madura	Keelakarry	...	...	...	...	...
	Davepatam	...	...	...	...	...
	Paumben	3	1,006	...	...	...
	Tondy \	...	...	...	...	...
	Total...	3	1,006	..	...	...

A.—(Continued.)

Madras Presidency, for the official year 1865-66.

Vessels	Tonnage	Dues RS.	A.	P.	Vessels	Tonnage	Dues RS.	A.	P.
2	118	41	0	8	188	16,470	...	...	...
...	...	...	...	...	70	10,201	...	...	...
...	...	...	...	...	25	4,013	...	...	...
...	...	...	...	...	...	...	...	...	...
...	...	...	...	...	...	...	...	...	...
...	...	...	...	...	...	...	...	...	...
...	...	...	...	...	...	...	...	...	...
...	...	...	...	...	...	...	...	...	...
...	...	...	...	...	34	933	...	...	...
...	...	...	...	...	3	108	...	...	...
...	...	...	...	...	...	...	...	...	...
...	...	...	...	...	...	...	...	...	...
...	...	...	...	...	3	292	...	...	...
...	...	...	...	...	...	...	...	...	...
2	118	41	0	8	323	32,017	...	...	...
2	63	1	15	6	157	8,886	234	5	1
8	1,533	...	...	...	424	17,750½	...	...	...
10	1,596	1	15	6	581	26,636½	234	5	1
4	1,714	53	9	0	339	15,846	482	1	0
6	732	...	...	...	32	1,000	...	...	...
...	...	...	...	...	717	15,008	...	...	...
2	79	...	...	...	544	18,238	...	...	...
...	...	...	...	...	45	2,031	...	...	...
29	10,897	311	11	6	26	1,094	65	14	8
41	13,422	365	4	6	1,703	53,217	547	15	8
...	...	...	...	...	841	36,183	...	...	...
...	...	...	...	...	1,679	72,189	...	...	...
...	...	...	...	...	3,244	2,69,993	...	...	...
...	...	...	...	...	690	24,224	...	...	...
...	...	...	...	...	6,454	4,02,589	...	...	...

A.
MARINE.

A.—(*Continued.*)

Particulars of the Trade of the Ports in the

Districts.	NAMES OF PORTS.	TOTAL				
		Vessels.	Tonnage.	Dues.		
				RS.	A.	P.
Nellore.	Kottapatnam ...	190	16,588	41	0	8
	Itamukala ...	70	10,201	...	...	...
	Pakala	25	4,013	...	...	...
	Ramayapatnam ...	29	3,778	...	...	...
	Chennayapalem ...	4	722	...	...	...
	Iskapalli	29	6,702	...	...	...
	Ponnapudi	34	5,286	...	...	...
	Joovaladinna ...	6	708	...	...	...
	Kristnapatnam ...	123	7,756	..	...	...
	Mypadu	23	1,600	...	...	...
	Dugarazapatam ...	6	542	...	...	...
	Tupili	4	532	...	..	...
	Pamanji	7	918	...	...	...
	Pudi	6	654	...	...	...
	Total...	556	60,000	41	0	8
South Arcot.	Cuddalore... ...	176	12,300¼	434	3	4
	Porto Novo... ...	486	26,817½	...	...	...
	Total...	662	39,117½	434	3	4
Tanjore.	Negapatam ...	1,051	1,41,776	3,581	15	10
	Nagore	123	17,332	...	...	...
	Thoputoray ...	736	18,016	...	...	...
	Mutupetai	724	34,195	...	...	...
	Terumalavassal ...	149	13,162	...	...	...
	Tranquebar ...	210	30,916	677	5	8
	Total...	2,993	2,55,397	4,259	5	6
Madura.	Keelakarry... ...	841	36,183	...	...	...
	Davepatam... ...	1,679	72,189	...	...	...
	Paumben	3,247	2,70,999	...	...	...
	Tondy	690	24,224	...	...	...
	Total...	6,457	4,03,595	...	...	...

A.—(*Continued.*)

Madras Presidency, for the official year 1865-66.

| Value of | | | | | | Duty on | | | | | | Sea Custom Revenue. | | |
| Exports. | | | Imports. | | | Exports. | | | Imports. | | | | | |
RS.	A.	P.	RS.	A.	P.	RS.	A.	P.	RS.	A.	P.	RS.	A.	P.
2,84,264	8	3	4,29,000	12	0	41	0	8	...	..	...	41	0	8
1,68,590	12	3	2,72,909	15	3	...	...	...	...	...	...	..	...	...
46,184	12	0	4,932	14	0	...	...	...	...	...	...	...		
6,907	13	0	4,373	8	0	...	...	...	...	...	...	...	...	...
...	...	...	...	...	...	...	...	...	...	...	...	...	...	...
43,520	11	7	6,560	12	0	...	...	...	...	...	...	...	...	...
69,263	0	2	1,440	3	11	...	...	...	...	...	...	...	...	...
2,952	3	3	...	...	...	...	...	...	...	...	...	...	...	...
7,842	5	10	11,887	8	0	...	...	...	...	...	...	...	...	...
29,242	10	11	...	...	...	...	...	...	...	...	...	...	...	...
125	0	0	34,520	8	0	...	...	...	...	...	...	...	...	...
2,150	11	0	1,000	0	0	...	..	...	...	...	...	...	...	...
5,915	8	0	2,000	0	0	...	...	...	...	...	...	...	...	...
702	10	11	...	...	...	...	...	...	...	...	...	...	...	...
6,67,662	11	2	7,68,626	1	2	41	0	8	...	...	...	41	0	8
3,46,707	0	0	14,807	0	0	13,245	12	6	1,099	5	1	14,345	1	7
1,48,012	8	5	77,465	15	1	20,860	12	2	5,794	6	10	26,655	3	0
4,94,719	8	5	92,272	15	1	34,106	8	8	6,893	11	11	41,000	4	7
23,83,793	0	0	30,42,437	0	0	75,741	4	8	1,11,237	7	11	1,90,560	12	5
5,53,621	0	0	74,503	0	0	30,224	3	5	1,439	3	3	31,663	6	8
6,745	0	0	1,54,816	0	0	504	11	3	7,529	1	1	8,033	12	4
47,847	0	0	12,26,957	0	0	3,294	11	0	44,117	12	6	47,412	7	6
30,715	0	0	6,09,410	0	0	896	4	1	27,778	17	11	28,674	15	0
9,500	0	0	6,82,221	0	0	863	2	2	27,165	0	3	28,705	15	1
30,32,221	0	0	57,90,344	0	0	1,11,524	4	7	2,19,267	10	11	3,35,051	5	0
3,79,835	7	6	5,27,500	9	11	8,990	7	10	13,103	14	10	...	...	...
53,402	0	0	3,04,082	7	5	684	5	4	825	6	0	...	...	...
2,73,527	4	8	2,91,521	14	2	385	6	11	1,419	8	6	...	...	...
49,398	0	0	1,36,850	1	0	856	4	2	2,652	2	11	...	...	...
7,56,162	12	2	12,59,955	0	6	10,916	8	3	18,001	0	3	...	...	...

A.—(*Continued.*)

Particulars of the Trade of the Ports in the

Districts.	NAMES OF PORTS.	BRITISH				
		Vessels.	Tonnage.	Dues.		
				RS.	A.	P.
Tinne-velly.	Tuticorin	79	48,755	7,050	10	6
Malabar.	Cannanore... ...	144	64,387	2,210	12	0
	Tellicherry ...	103	38,745	1,285	4	9
	Kalay	...	...	...	...	...
	Baragaree	12	5,839	...	...	...
	Quilandy	11	4,205	...	...	...
	Calicut	148	62,046	1,911	7	0
	Beypore	32	15,664	...	...	...
	Tanore	...	...	...	...	...
	Ponany	...	...	...	...	...
	Chowghat	...	...	...	...	...
	Cochin	241	81,308	6,778	4	0
	Total...	691	2,72,194	12,185	11	9
South Canara.	Mangalore... ...	233	1,02,153	1,431	12	6
	Mulki	...	...	...	...	...
	Munjeshwar ...	...	...	...	...	...
	Cumbla	...	...	...	...	...
	Cassergode ...	...	...	...	...	...
	Udipi	...	...	...	...	...
	Barkur	...	...	...	...	...
	Kundapur... ...	...	...	...	...	...
	Baidur	...	...	...	...	...
	Naikenkotta ...	...	...	...	...	...
	Total...	233	1,02,153	1,431	12	6
	Madras	378	2,92,337	40,458	0	0

A.—(*Continued.*)

Madras Presidency, for the official year 1865-66.

FOREIGN					COUNTRY, OR NATIVE				
Vessels.	Tonnage.	Dues.			Vessels.	Tonnage.	Dues.		
		RS.	A.	P.			RS.	A.	P.
3	1,740	326	4	0	647	34,773½	1,699	10	1
3	1,571	98	3	0	1,353	27,228	495	9	0
14	5,826	256	11	0	1,247	17,855	217	3	4
...	...	...	...	...	415	6,085	...	...	...
1	998	..	...	...	646	15,891	...	...	...
3	2,124	...	...	...	276	5,249	...	...	...
5	2,495	155	15	0	2,044	74,465	1,843	1	4
...	...	...	...	...	735	25,054	...	...	...
...	...	...	...	...	222	6,177	...	...	...
...	...	...	...	...	584	21,521	...	...	...
...	...	...	...	...	63	4,890	...	...	...
9	3,527	418	4	6	1,182	36,888	1,601	12	9
35	16,541	929	1	6	8,767	2,41,303	4,157	10	5
514	42,365	821	11	9	2,957	60,332	574	14	4
2	76	...	...	...	486	7,891	...	...	...
2	62	...	...	...	201	6,414	...	...	...
3	57	...	...	...	361	7,323	...	...	...
1	16	...	...	...	505	7,081	...	...	...
22	501	...	...	...	739	9,720	...	...	...
359	6,444	...	...	...	1,162	17,844	...	...	...
196	11,260	...	...	...	1,268	24,734	...	...	...
28	248	...	...	...	444	4,430	...	...	...
...	...	...	...	...	106	1,116	...	...	...
1,127	61,029	821	11	9	8,229	1,46,885	574	14	4
64	42,335	4,273	0	0	674	76,174	6,265	0	0

A.—(*Continued.*)

Particulars of the Trade of the Ports in the

Districts.	NAMES OF PORTS.	TOTAL				
		Vessels.	Tonnage.	Dues.		
				RS.	A.	P.
Tinne-velly. {	Tuticorin	729	85,268¼	9,076	8	7
Malabar. {	Cannanore ...	1,500	93,186	2,804	8	0
	Tellicherry ...	1,364	62,426	1,759	3	1
	Kalay	415	6,085	...	...	...
	Baragaree	659	22,728	...	...	...
	Quilandy	290	11,578	...	...	...
	Calicut	2,197	1,39,006	3,910	7	4
	Beypore	767	40,718	...	...	...
	Tanore	222	6,177	...	...	...
	Ponany	584	21,521	...	...	...
	Chowghat... ...	63	4,890	...	...	...
	Cochin	1,432	1,21,723	8,798	5	3
	Total...	9,493	5,30,038	17,272	7	8
South Canara. {	Mangalore	3,704	2,04,850	2,828	6	7
	Mulki	488	7,967	...	...	...
	Munjeshwar ...	203	6,476	...	...	...
	Cumbla	364	7,380	...	...	...
	Cassergode ...	506	7,097	...	...	...
	Udipi	761	10,221	...	...	...
	Barkur	1,521	24,288	...	...	...
	Kundapur... ...	1,464	35,994	...	...	...
	Baidar	472	4,678	...	...	...
	Naikenkotta ...	106	1,116	...	...	...
	Total...	9,589	3,10,067	2,828	6	7
	Madras	1,116	4,10,846	50,996	0	0

A.—(*Concluded.*)

...dras *Presidency, for the official year* 1865-66.

Value of						Duty on						Sea Custom Revenue.		
Exports.			Imports.			Exports.			Imports.					
RS.	A.	P.	RS.	A.	P.	RS.	A.	P.	RS.	A.	P.	RS.	A.	P.
5,08,239	0	0	22,42,066	0	0	14,557	15	0	32,322	5	2	...	...	...
1,09,204	0	0	24,77,994	0	0	2,642	14	10	1,844	1	9	4,487	0	7
3,69,440	0	0	23,10,596	0	0	13,581	5	1	617	13	10	14,199	2	11
73,495	0	0	3,38,881	0	0	441	10	9	4	9	11	446	4	8
5,14,312	0	0	7,31,290	0	0	1,148	2	1	152	2	11	1,300	5	0
2,02,308	0	0	2,02,814	0	0	1,169	3	6	97	0	7	1,266	4	1
8,76,491	0	0	50,99,862	0	0	22,211	12	5	8,476	0	11	30,687	13	4
9,10,155	0	0	10,14,462	0	0	3,871	7	0	1,687	13	0	5,559	4	0
2,02,656	0	0	41,674	0	0	526	5	9	...	...	...	526	5	9
7,95,979	0	0	1,32,154	0	0	510	12	9	...	...	...	510	12	9
85,011	0	0	17,141	0	0	...	...	...	...	...	...	...	...	...
8,70,549	0	0	54,83,373	0	0	42,615	14	5	15,417	1	9	58,033	0	2
0,09,600	0	0	178,50,241	0	0	88,719	8	7	28,296	12	8	1,17,016	5	3
1,40,877	0	0	19,10,055	0	0	12,898	10	11	9,757	11	11	25,484	13	5
3,02,393	0	0	44,230	0	0	721	2	0	...	...	...	721	2	0
36,702	0	0	17,122	0	0	298	0	7	...	...	...	298	0	7
1,20,774	0	0	9,137	0	0	527	3	1	...	...	...	527	3	1
75,899	0	0	64,606	0	0	236	4	0	...	...	...	236	4	0
3,03,910	0	0	2,17,844	0	0	709	11	1	561	5	1	1,271	0	2
3,09,037	0	0	1,44,769	0	0	21,632	10	11	127	15	10	21,760	10	9
3,85,746	0	0	1,38,866	0	0	8,770	2	0	149	11	9	8,919	13	9
1,19,573	0	0	21,084	0	0	143	14	2	...	...	...	143	14	2
38,398	0	0	3,419	0	0	...	...	...	...	...	...	...	...	...
3,33,309	0	0	25,71,132	0	0	45,937	10	9	10,596	12	7	59,362	13	11
3,26,707	0	0	311,27,785	0	0	1,79,128	0	0	9,95,954	0	0	11,75,082	0	0

B.
MARINE.

B.

Statement shewing the receipts and disbursements of Coals at Madras and the Out-ports, during the official year 1865-66.

	Tons.	Cwt.	lbs.	Qrs.
Madras.				
Balance on hand on the 30th April 1865 ...	2,011	...	3	6
Receipts...	3,168	6	3	5
	5,179	7	2	11
Tons. Cwt. lbs. Qrs.				
Expenditure including coals sold 3,392 13 0 1				
Dryage and wastage during a long series of years as per report to Government of 29th November 1865, No.4069 516 4 ... 5				
	3,908	17	...	6
Balance on hand on the 30th April 1866 ...	1,270	10	2	5
Cocanada.				
Balance on hand on the 30th April 1865 ...	301	...	2	22
No Receipts	...	...	...	...
Disbursements	30	...	...	...
Balance on hand on the 30th April 1866 ...	271	...	2	22
Bimlipatam.				
Balance on hand on the 30th April 1865 ...	9	19	...	...
No Receipts	...	...	...	...
Tons. Cwt. lbs. Qrs.				
Dryage and wastage as per report to Government of 7th August 1865, No. 2845 7 19				
Quantity of coal sold ... 2				
	9	19	...	...
Balance on hand on the 30th April 1866 ...	...	...	...	...
Munsoorcottah.				
Balance on hand on the 30th April 1865 ...	126	...	...	...
No Receipts and Disbursements	...	...	...	...
Balance on hand on the 30th April 1866 unserviceable and unsalable	126	...	...	...
Cochin.				
Balance on hand on the 30th April 1865 ...	154	9	3	17
Add surplus quantity of coal	115	10	...	11
	270	...	...	...
Quantity of coal sold	270	...	...	...
Balance on hand on the 30th April 1866 ...	...	...	...	...

C.

Table shewing the number of Boats and Rafts using the Pier each month, from May 1865 to April 1866.

Months.	No. of Boats.		Total.	No. of Rafts.
	Export.	Import.		
1865.				
May	2,174	1,698	3,882	22
June	2,497	2,085	4,572	60
July	3,027	1,289	4,316	8
August	4,338	1,461	5,799	17
September	3,331	2,295	5,626	4
October	3,972	881	4,853	20
November	3,230	741	3,971	5
December	2,338	1,137	3,475	4
1866.				
January	3,722	1,440	5,162	26
February	2,180	1,593	3,773	...
March	1,245	860	2,105	27
April	1,148	521	1,669	19
Total. ...	33,202	16,001	49,203	- 212

D.

Statement of Tolls levied on the Madras Pier, from 1st May 1865 to 30th April 1866.

Months.	On Passengers.			On Goods.			Tarpaulin hire.			Total.		
	RS.	A.	P.	RS.	A.	P.	RS.	A.	P.	RS.	A.	P.
1865.												
May	1,055	13	6	445	6	0	...	...	...	1,501	3	0
June	1,157	7	0	572	14	0	...	...	...	1,730	5	0
July	1,158	2	0	567	6	0	...	..	..	1,725	8	0
August	1,092	2	0	824	14	0	...	...	..	1,917	0	0
September ...	874	10	0	664	8	0	67	5	0	1,606	7	0
October ...	693	1	0	687	8	0	68	9	0	1,449	2	0
November ...	442	10	0	501	2	6	59	1	0	1,002	13	6
December ...	472	4	6	444	0	0	...	...	...	916	4	6
1866.												
January ...	844	5	0	769	15	6	15	1	0	1,629	5	6
February ...	711	10	0	711	15	1	9	11	0	1,433	4	1
March ...	570	5	0	467	14	10	10	12	0	1,048	15	10
April	547	3	1	367	15	10	2	11	0	917	13	10
Total. ...	9,619	8	6	7,025	7	9	233	2	0	16,878	2	3

18

E.
MARINE.

E.

Statement shewing the Receipts, Disbursements, and Balances connected with Port charges and Dues in the various Ports of the Presidency of Fort Saint George under the operations of Act XXII of 1855, from 1st May 1865 to 30th April 1866.

Names of the Ports.	Receipts.			Disbursements.			Excess for this year.			Deficit for this year.			Total balance to credit of the Port.			Total deficit against the Port.		
	RS.	A.	P.	RS.	A.	P.	RS.	A.	P.	RS.	A.	P.	RS.	A.	P.	RS.	A.	P.
Ganjam	129	11	6	576	9	3	...			446	13	9	...			97	6	7
Monsoorcottah	1,930	8	0	591	12	9	1,338	12	0	...			3,376	0	1	...		
Calingapatam	714	9	6	626	11	9	87	13	9	...			2,123	6	11	...		
Bimlipatam	3,334	13	6	1,736	3	6	1,598	10	0	...			6,822	0	8	...		
Vizagapatam	2,724	12	11	2,094	9	4	630	3	7	...			...			629	13	5
...la	14,179	15	11	8,102	6	6	6,077	9	5	...			20,081	12	4	...		
...m	1,720	7	2	429	8	3	1,290	14	11	...			5,608	0	9	...		
Madras	74,938	8	4	69,534	3	11	5,404	4	5	...			1,20,362	0	0	...		
...re	434	3	4	421	14	0	12	5	4	...			1,486	8	1	...		
Tranquebar	677	5	8	711	12	0	...			34	7	4	3,528	4	3	...		
N...gm	3,586	6	10	5,094	8	10	...			1,508	2	0	4,258	3	0	...		
Tuticorin	9,092	7	11	3,222	8	8	5,869	15	3	...			17,034	15	0	...		
...dn	10,754	14	0	13,961	9	8	...			3,206	11	8	16,473	2	9	...		
Calicut	3,977	6	6	5,062	0	4	...			1,084	10	4	5,787	2	8	...		
...ry	1,785	3	1	1,151	11	9	633	7	4	...			3,005	6	4	...		
...e	2,830	3	0	905	4	8	1,924	14	4	...			13,535	11	0	...		
Mangalore	8,542	3	11	5,885	9	6	2,656	10	5	...			11,574	15	8	...		
Total...	1,41,353	12	7	1,20,109	0	11	27,525	8	9	6,280	13	1	2,35,057	15	3	727	4	0

F.

Statement shewing the Wrecks which have occurred at various Ports under this Presidency during the year 1865-66.

Date of Wreck.	Name of Vessel.	Tons.	REMARKS.
1865. 12th May	Brig "Vencataswerloo" ...	101	Left Moulmein with a cargo of timber for Vizagapatam, and having experienced bad weather during the voyage she anchored near the village of Opada, in a leaky state, where she soon after foundered from being water-logged. The crew landed safely, and the cargo was washed ashore.
13th do.	Ship "Fatel Rozack"	485	Foundered off Alleppy while on her voyage from Jeddah to Calcutta. She grounded and filled immediately, thus rendering it impossible to save her cargo, but all hands were rescued.
14th do.	French Ship "Tanrean" ...	228	This vessel sailed from Madras on the 12th May for Cocanada and Bimlipatam, and missing her reckoning she ran ashore near Narsapore, becoming a total wreck. Part of her cargo was saved. No lives were lost.
— November...	French Ship " Rawmur" ..	..	This vessel put to sea from Pondicherry in the Cyclone of 25th and 26th November last, and was wrecked off the Coleroon river.

G.
MARINE.

G.

Statement of Vessels passing through the Paumben Channel from 1849 to 1865 inclusive.

Calendar year.	Square-rigged vessels.	Tonnage.	Dhonies.	Tonnage.	Total Vessels.	Total Tonnage.	Average size. Vessels.	Average size. Dhonies.
							Tons.	Tons.
1849	1,003	79,234	1,114	58,700	2,117	1,37,934	79	53
1850	1,142	90,656	1,004	60,807	2,146	1,51,457	79½	60½
1851	1,092	82,697	939	57,084	2,031	1,39,781	75¾	60¾
1852	1,178	94,109	924	59,565	2,112	1,53,674	80	64½
1853	1,192	98,189	920	54,264	2,122	1,52,453	82½	59
1854	1,035	78,746	879	59,140	1,914	1,39,886	76	67½
1855	1,220	1,09,326	947	60,771	2,169	1,70,097	89½	64⅛
1856	1,353	1,21,810	990	54,867	2,343	1,76,677	90	55½
1857	1,506	1,38,090	1,025	57,214	2,531	1,95,304	91¾	55¾
1858	1,108	1,13,814	803	43,720	1,911	1,57,534	102¾	54½
1859	974	88,574	742	38,414	1,716	1,26,988	91	51¾
1860	1,366	1,43,082	950	48,763	2,316	1,91,845	104¾	51⅓
1861	1,335	1,33,897	905	45,916	2,240	1,79,813	100¼	50⅔
1862	1,050	1,00,907	894	38,994	1,944	1,39,901	96	43⅔
1863	1,226	1,18,816	789	38,960	2,015	1,57,776	96¾	54½
1864	1,265	1,26,471	672	34,313	1,937	1,60,784	100	51
1865	1,359	1,31,165	774	42,298	2,133	1,73,463	96½	49⅓

Statement shewing the numbers carried on each trip by the Vessels employed in the movement of Troops, and the dates of their arrivals and departures.

Arrived	Sailed	From and to what Ports	Vessels' Names	Corps	Officers	Men	Women	Children	Convicts	Horses	Bullocks
1865.	**1865.**										
24th November	...	From Rangoon and Port Blair to Madras	Ship "Devonport"	H. M.'s 50th Rifles	8	407	24	40	...	1	...
30th do.	...	From Rangoon to Madras	Ship "Star of India"	Do	11	321	25	38	...	...	...
	1866.										
	6th January	From Madras to Penang via Vizagapatam and Port Blair	Steamer "Busheer"	No. 5 Battery 23rd Brigade Royal Artillery	3	107	16	19	45	...	...
23rd January	...	From Penang to Madras	Do.	Different Corps and Depts, No. 2 B. 17th Brig. R. A. Rifle Department	3	61	1	9	...	...	...
					4	96	19	17	...	...	...
						1	1	3	...	...	...
29th do.	...	From Port Blair to Madras	Transport "Tubal Cain"	21st Regiment Bengal N.I.	17	94					
	31st January	From Madras to Calcutta	Steamer "Hydaspes"	H. M.'s 8th Regiment Head Quarters, and 6 with volunteers		625	103	146			
...	2nd February	From Madras to Rangoon	Steamer "Arracan" and Transport "Tubal Cain"	16th Regiment N.I. Different Depts & Departments	7	718	4	7	...	2	...
					3	40	4	4	...		
...	12th do.	From Negapatam to Calcutta	Str. "Governor Higginson"	Remaining Company of the 104th Regiment	3	87	13	23	...	6	...
22nd February	27th February	From Rangoon to Madras / From Madras to Singapore	Transport "Tubal Cain" / Steamer "Arabia"	Different Corps / 8th Regiment N.I.	8	19	1	8	...	5	...
					8	499	6	9	...	4	...
	27th do.	From Madras to Rangoon	Steamer "Arracan" and Transport "Tubal Cain"	30th Regt N.I. / Different Depts	1	337	11	7	...		
						31	2				
18th March	...	From Singapore to Madras	Steamer "Arabia"	34th Regiment N.I. Shni Corps	33	351	6		...		
						4	1				
...	23rd March	From Madras to Singapore	Do.	8th Regiment N.I. Defnt Corps	3	388	8	8	...		
						23					
1st April	...	From Rangoon to Madras	Steamer "Arracan" and Transport "Tubal Cain"	6th Regiment N.I.	7	689			...	18	...
...	7th April	From Madras to Port Blair and Rangoon	Do.	C. Co. Sappers and Miners / Different Corps & Departments	1	135			213		
						71	7	13			
13th April	...	From Singapore to Madras	Steamer "Arabia"	Left Wing 34th N.I. Different Corps & Departments	3	353			...	5	...
						46					
23rd do.	...	From Rangoon to Madras	Steamer "Arracan" and Transport "Tubal Cain"	3rd Regiment L.I. / Different Corps & Departments	9	762	1	21	...	6	...
					9	19	1	7			
	5th May	From Madras to Negapatam and Moulmein	Transport "Tubal Cain"	25th Regiment N.I. Camp Equipage	1	778	7	7	...		
						4					
6th & 11th June	...	From Moulmein to Negapatam	Do.	9th Regiment N.I.	18	796	19	16	...	3	...
				Total.	159	8,217	278	399	258	62	...

I.

Statement of Troops, &c., arrived from England during the year 1865-66.

Name of Vessels.	Date of arrival.	Rate.			Number of				Remarks.
		£	s.	d.	Officers.	Men.	Women.	Children.	
Steamer "Golden Fleece"	1865. September 9th	9	17	6	23	503	68	94	16th Lancers.
Ship "Middlesex"	Do. 29th	9	19	3	10	340	9	6	Details.
	Total...			......	33	843	71	99	

I.—(*Continued.*)

Statement of Troops, Invalids, &c., embarked for England and the Cape during the year 1865-66.

Names of Vessels.	Date of Departure.	Rate for Invalids.	Rate for Effectives.	Off. cers.	Men.	Women.	Children.	Insanes Number.	Insanes Rate.	Convicts Num-ber.	Convicts Rate.	Remarks.
		Rs.	Rs.						Rs.		Rs.	
Ship..... "Mary Shepherd"	1865. June 3rd	300	300	2	84	8	17	2 / *1	450 / 1,400	5	450	* Mr. G. Smith, M.C.S.
Do. ... "Theron" Invalids and Effectives / Invalids and Time-expired men	September 1st	...	294½ / †400 / 240	1	67 / 1 / 1	3	2 / 2			3	400	† Warrant Officer of H. M.'s Naval Service.
Do. ... "Barham" Time-expired men and Invalids	Do. 9th	363	...	...	1	1	1	...	...	...	...	
Do. ... "Blenheim" Invalids	December 23rd	294½	...	...	1	1	...	...	...	...	...	
Do. ... "Nile" Effectives	Do. 8th	294½	215 / 235	...	1	1	...	...	...	...	...	
Do. ... "Cornwallis" Invalids and Effectives	1866. January 13th	275	235	3	†108	15	33	...	...	9	950	‡ Nine Naval Invalids included.
Steamer... "Golden Fleece" Invalids and Effectives	February 1st	294½ / 300	300	...	1 / 3	1 / 2 / 2	3	...	...	...	...	
Ship. ... The "Lord Warden" 2 Batteries 17th Brigade R.A.	Do. 13th	294½	260	**7	151	25	70	...	...	...	...	
Do. ... "Star of India" Invalids	Do. 18th	300	280	3	156	14	28	4	340	...	...	
Do. ... "Lady Melville" 1st King's Dragoon Guards	March 8th	...	252½ / 272½ / 500	10	236 / 8 / 1	24	40	...	...	...	...	§ Staff Serjeants. ‖ School Master.
Do. ... "Ivanhoe" Left Wing King's Dragoon Guards and other details	Do. 20th	310	268 / ¶300	7	148 / 1	15	30	...	...	...	...	¶ A Midshipman of the York.
Steamer... "Hydaspes" Effectives and Invalids	April 11th	294½ / 319½ / 294½	200 / 250	3	**2 / 108	1 / 12 / 1	32	...	...	...	...	** To Cape.
Ship ... "Dare" Effectives and Invalids	Do. 17th	320	250	3	95	13	21	4	500	...	...	
	Total...			39	1,173	141	279	11		10		

J.

Statement of Pilotage levied at Paumben, from
1849 to 1865 inclusive.

CALENDAR YEARS.	Pilotage levied.			Pilot's share.			Credited to Government.		
	RS.	A.	P.	RS.	A.	P.	RS.	A.	P.
1849	7,247	2	0	1,811	12	6	5,435	5	6
1850	4,684	8	0	1,171	2	0	3,513	6	0
1851	10,525	5	0	2,628	8	.6	7,896	12	6
1852	11,456	12	3	2,861	14	9	8,594	13	6
1853	11,569	5	9	2,890	1	0	8,679	4	9
1854	11,153	1	9	2,786	7	5	8,366	10	4
1855	12,486	8	3	3,120	9	8	9,365	14	7
1856	13,168	5	0	3,292	1	3	9,876	3	9
1857	15,575	5	6	3,891	13	9	11,683	7	9
1858	12,820	8	0	3,203	2	0	9,617	6	0
1859	10,647	1	0	2,661	0	3	7,986	0	9
1860	17,144	5	0	4,286	1	3	12,858	3	9
1861	16,193	9	0	4,048	6	3	12,145	2	9
1862	14,598	4	0	3,177	0	7	11,421	3	5
1863	17,312	10	0	3,461	8	9	13,851	1	3
1864	17,055	6	0	3,410	2	8	13,045	3	4
1865	19,419	2	0	3,883	13	1	15,535	4	11

K.

Statement of the Pilotage levied between Paumben and Keelacarry, for the year 1865.

Months and Year.	From Paumben to Keelacarry.									From Keelacarry to Paumben.									Total.								
	Pilotage levied.			Pilot's share.			Credited to Government.			Pilotage levied.			Pilot's share.			Credited to Government.			Pilotage levied.			Pilot's share.			Credited to Government.		
	RS.	A.	P.	RS.	A.	P.	RS.	A.	P.	RS.	A.	P.	RS.	A.	P.	RS.	A.	P.	RS.	A.	P.	RS.	A.	P.	RS.	A.	P.
1865.																											
January	89	8	6	71	10	0	17	14	6	52	10	6	42	2	0	10	8	6	142	3	0	113	12	0	28	7	0
February	46	6	6	37	0	2	9	6	4	121	6	6	97	2	0	24	4	6	167	13	0	134	2	2	33	10	10
March	47	8	0	38	0	0	9	8	0	109	6	0	87	8	0	21	14	0	156	14	0	125	8	0	31	6	0
April	191	9	0	153	4	0	38	5	0	228	9	6	183	6	0	45	3	6	420	2	6	336	10	0	83	8	6
May	111	9	0	89	4	0	22	5	0	181	1	0	145	4	0	35	13	0	292	10	0	234	8	0	58	2	6
June	400	5	0	320	4	0	80	1	0	70	7	6	56	6	0	14	1	6	470	12	6	376	10	0	94	2	6
July	438	9	6	350	14	0	87	11	6	50	10	0	40	8	0	10	2	0	489	3	6	391	6	0	97	13	6
August	472	13	0	378	4	0	94	9	0	70	5	0	56	2	0	14	3	0	543	2	0	434	6	0	108	10	0
September	438	14	6	351	2	0	87	12	6	98	14	6	79	12	0	19	2	6	537	13	0	430	14	0	107	0	10
October	372	0	6	297	10	0	74	6	6	35	15	0	28	4	0	7	11	0	407	15	6	325	14	0	81	9	6
November	81	14	0	65	8	0	16	6	0	30	5	0	24	4	0	6	1	0	112	3	0	89	12	0	22	0	0
December	62	8	0	50	0	0	12	8	0	40	5	0	32	4	0	8	1	0	102	13	0	82	4	0	20	9	0
Total...	2,753	9	6	2,202	12	2	550	13	4	1,089	15	6	872	14	0	217	1	6	3,843	9	0	3,075	10	2	767	14	10

L.
MARINE.

Statement of Vessels built at Cochin, with their estimated value, from 1st May 1865 to 30th April 1866.

Year.	Names of Vessels.	Tonnage of square rigged vessels.	Rate of building.	Estimated value.	Tonnage of Fatimars and other Coasting crafts.	Rate of building.	Estimated value.	Wood.	Remarks.
				Rs. A. P.			Rs. A. P.		
1865-66.	Schooner "Mira Mather"	28	At 125 Rs. ⅌ ton	3,500 0 0	...	...	...	Anjelly and Benteak	Measured under Act No. X of 1841.
	Brig "Ammanthoola"	155	" 90 "	13,950 0 0	...	...	...	Do. Teak, and Benteak	Merchant Shipping Act, 1854.
	Schooner "Hiral"	55	" 150 "	8,250 0 0	...	...	...	Do. do. do.	Do.
	Pattimar "Slamathy"	...	...	...	99	At 66 Rs. ⅌ ton	2,494 0	Benteak	Act No. X of 1841.
	Do. "Shaool Ahmid"	...	...	...	38	" 66 "	2,608 0	Do.	Do.
	Do. "Moydin"	57	At 106 Rs. ⅌ ton	6,042 0 0	76	" 40 "	3,040 0	Anjelly, Benteak, and Teak	Do.
	Gral Brig "Canderbaut"	...	...	...	125	At 83 Rs. ⅌ ton	4,125 0	Benteak and White Cedar.	Do.
	Bugalow "Jebrab Kahilake"	...	...	...	53	" 66 "	3,498 0	Do. and Teak	Do.
	Pattimar "Mooydin Cap"	...	...	...	47	" 43 "	2,021 0	Benteak	Do. Arab Colors.
	"Munjee Miskin"	...	...	...	214	" 47 "	10,068 0	Do. and White Cedar...	Do.
	Bugalow "Falel Mahin"	...	...	...	...	...	...	Teak and Benteak	Do. Arab Colors.
	Total...	295		31,742 0 0	582		27,744 0		

Statement exhibiting the difference between the official year 1864-65 and 1865-66.

Years.	Total new tonnage of square rigged vessels.	Difference in decrease.	Value of the new tonnage.	Difference in decrease.	Total new tonnage of coasting crafts.	Difference in increase.	Value of the new tonnage.	Difference in increase.	Remarks.
			Rs. A. P.	Rs. A. P.			Rs. A. P.	Rs. A. P.	
1864-65.	1,292		2,06,998 0 0		250		17,641 0 0		
1865-66.	295	997	31,742 0 0	1,74,256 0 0	582	332	27,744 0 0	10,103 0 0	

M.

Statement of Vessels built in Malabar, Travancore, &c., but registered at Cochin, from 1st May 1865 to 30th April 1866.

Year.	Name of Vessel.	Tonnage of square-rigged vessels.	Rate of building.	Estimated value.			Tonnage of Pattimars & other coasting crafts.	Rate of building.	Estimated value.			Wood.	Remarks.
				RS.	A.	P.			RS.	A.	P.		
1865-66.	Padows "Slamathy"	...	...	...	...	...	24	At 34Rs. ℔ ton	816	0	0	Anjelly, Benteak, and white Cedar.	Measured under Act No. X of 1841. Built at Quilon.
	Total...		...	...	...	...	24		816	0	0		

Statement exhibiting the difference between the official years 1864-65 and 1865-66.

Years.	Total new tonnage of square rigged vessels.	Difference in increase.	Value of the new tonnage.			Difference in increase.			Total new tonnage of coasting crafts.	Difference in decrease.	Value of the new tonnage.			Difference in decrease.		
			RS.	A.	P.	RS.	A.	P.			RS.	A.	P.	RS.	A.	P.
1864-65.	......	...	...	...	...	...	...	...	310		17,984	0	0			
1865-66.	......	...	...	...	...	...	...	...	24		816	0	0			
										286				17,168	0	0

N.

Statement shewing the Pilotage, Tonnage and Fees levied at Cochin during the year 1865-66.

Month and Year.	Inward tonnage and fees.			Outward tonnage and fees.			Total monthly tonnage and fees.			⅗ths Pilot's share.	⅖ths Govt. share.
	No. of vessels.	Tons.	Rs.	No. of vessels.	Tons.	Rs.	No. of vessels.	Tons.	Rs.	Rs.	Rs.
1865.											
May	8	2,162	245	8	2,163	225	16	4,325	470	282	188
June... ...	2	415	60	1	120	25	3	535	85	51	34
July	1	487	40	3	1,020	110	4	1,507	150	90	60
August ...	...	...	...	3	1,08 6	100	3	1,086	100	60	40
September ...	8	2,478	260	6	1,505	185	14	3,983	445	267	178
October ...	5	1,350	150	7	2,144	220	12	3,494	370	222	148
November ...	10	3,226	305	6	1,733	175	16	4,959	480	288	192
December ...	7	2,469	220	8	2,666	250	15	5,135	470	282	188
1866.											
January ...	8	2,536	245	6	2,221	190	14	4,757	435	261	174
February ...	10	3,205	320	11	3,144	335	21	6,349	655	393	262
March ...	9	2,590	270	12	3,721	380	21	6,311	650	390	260
April ...	4	919	120	8	2,475	250	12	3,394	370	222	148
Total...	72	21,837	2,235	79	23,998	2,445	151	45,835	4,680	2,808	1,872

APPENDIX VI.

A.

Statement shewing the Receipts and Disbursements at the Bank of Madras on account of Government, during the official year 1865-66.

RECEIPTS.

	RS.	A.	P.
Land Revenue...	1,10,795	2	9
Abkaree	8,666	10	8
Income Tax	52,608	2	9
Stamps...	1,26,329	10	10
Law and Justice...	1,76,377	13	2
Police...	71,316	8	4
Marine	2,164	5	5
Education...	13,344	10.	11
Interest...	80,059	11	7
Local Loans	4,60,000	0	0
Service Funds	11,70,793	9	11
Local Funds	67,994	6	3
Deposits...	51,07,361	13	5
Revenue Cash Remittances	234,84,837	3	6
Public Works Department	62,407	2	7
Bills drawn	140,91,069	1	3
Military Department, Madras...	4,88,268	4	7
Bills drawn on the Secretary of State for India in Council... ...	24,408	10	9
Madras Railway Company...	47,66,062	11	0
Madras Irrigation and Canal Company	38,185	0	0
Remittances from other Governments...	8,49,692	12	2
Postal Department...	17,281	7	7
Electric Telegraph Department	1,26,874	4	10
Miscellaneous...	1,62,758	7	3
	515,54,657	11	6

DISBURSEMENTS.

	RS.	A.	P.
Interest on Service Funds and other Accounts	2,51,095	12	9
Allowances, Refunds, and Drawbacks...	9,247	13	4
Land Revenue...	2,00,431	14	1
Forest...	29,069	13	2
Income Tax...	4,683	12	0
Customs...	43,985	4	4
Salt...	2,903	3	8
Stamps...	30,241	1	0
Mint...	1,70,640	5	9
Administration and Public Departments	11,85,994	10	10
Law and Justice...	7,81,123	9	10
Police...	6,53,058	15	9

cxlix

A.
FINANCIAL.

DISBURSEMENTS.

	RS.	A.	P.
Marine...	1,73,007	14	0
Education, Science, and Art...	4,15,668	5	4
Ecclesiastical...	1,84,436	1	6
Medical Services	2,44,251	15	0
Stationery and Printing...	2,73,898	13	1
Political Agencies and other Foreign Services...	16,426	12	6
Allowances and Assignments under Treaties and Engagements ...	8,51,416	7	5
Superannuation, Retired, and Compassionate Allowances...	1,24,826	10	9
Service Funds ..	10,49,223	4	4
Local Funds...	1,04,765	6	6
Deposits...	51,24,944	2	0
Revenue Cash Remittances...	23,21,913	12	1
Public Works Department...	7,93,445	15	6
Bills discharged...	28,72,307	10	11
Bullion certificates...	52,41,785	9	5
Military Department, Madras...	73,91,688	0	11
Do. Bengal..	41,095	12	6
Do. Bombay..	1,332	7	1
Bills drawn by the Secretary of State for India in Council ...	42,72,832	12	3
Madras Railway Company...	44,39,340	8	5
Madras Irrigation and Canal Company...	11,44,548	6	7
Great Southern of India Railway	1,31,597	2	5
Interest on Imperial Loans...	34,31,838	11	10
Remittances to other Governments...	67,04,780	9	5
Postal Department...	1,63,657	13	9
Electric Telegraph Department ..	75,945	10	10
Miscellaneous...	4,10,783	5	7
	513,64,236	6	5
Balance on the 30th April 1865...	31,31,609	0	10
Receipts during the official year 1865-66 ...	515,54,657	11	6
	546,86,266	12	4
Disbursements during do. do.	513,64,236	6	5
Balance on the 30th April 1866...	33,22,030	5	11

16th June 1866.

B.

B.

Abstract of Receipts and Disbursements from
1st May 1863 *to* 30th *April* 1866.

	Receipts.			Disbursements.		
	Amount.			Amount.		
	RS.	A.	P.	RS.	A.	P.
Official year 1863-64	623,37,566	7	8	625,43,319	9	2
„ 1864-65............................... ...	598,70,336	7	5	559,36,022	3	2
„ 1865-66..............................	515,54,657	11	6	513,64,236	6	5

F. LUSHINGTON, *Accountant General.*

cl

C.

Statement shewing the Estimated and the Actual Income for 1865-66.

	Heads of Receipt.	Estimated Income.	Actual Income.	Increase.	Decrease.	Per Centage.
I	Land Revenue... ...	4,26,00,000	4,30,69,000	4,69,000	......	62·6
II	Tributes & Contributions from Native States.........	34,46,400	34,46,400	... ...	......	5·
III	Forest...	4,00,000	3,12,000	......	88,000	·5
IV	Abkaree...	41,00,000	41,47,000	47,000	......	6·
V	Income Tax...	* 7,51,600	6,11,000	......	1,40,600	·9
VI	Customs...	26,18,000	20,85,000	......,	5,33,000	3·
VII	Salt......	106,00,000	101,29,000	......	4,71,000	14·7
IX	Stamps...	28,00,000	30,65,000	2,65,000	......	4·5
X	Mint............	11,00,000	6,84,000	......	4,16,000	·9
XIII	Law and Justice. ...	7,42,000	6,01,000	......	1,41,000	·9
XIV	Police.........	33,000	74,000	41,000	......	·1
XV	Marine.........	26,900	31,200	4,300	....	·1
XVI	Education............	37,800	40,500	2,700	... ...,	.1
XVII	Interest......... .·...	1,15,100	1,08,000	... ...	7,100	·2
XVIII	Miscellaneous........	5,79,200	4,06,900	......,	1,72,300	·6
	Total, Cl. Dept. Rs.	699,50,000	688,10,000	......	11,40,000	100
	Military Department	15,60,000	† 11,50,000	......	4,10,000	...
	Public Works do...,	5,00,000	5,54,000	54,000	......	...
	Postal do....	5,44,000	5,45,000	1,000	....	...
	Telegraph do....	2,05,000	2,86,000	81,000	......	...
	Total Rupees ..	727,59,000	713,45,000	......	14,14,000	...

* This is exclusive of Rs. 98,400, realizable in the Military Department.
† This is exclusive of money paid into the Treasuries of other Presidencies on account of Madras Stores, but inclusive of the same, it amounts to Rs, 13,82,000, as ascertained from the Controller of Military Accounts,

C.
FINANCIAL.

C.—*(Concluded.)*

Statement shewing the Estimated and the Actual Expenditure for 1865-66.

	Heads of charge.	Budget Grant.	Actual Expenditure.	Increase.	Decrease.	Per-centage.
2	Interest on Service Funds, &c.	8,41,200	9,04,800	63,600	......	3·5
3	Allowances, Refunds, and Drawbacks....	1,61,000	3,01,300	1,40,300	......	1·2
4	Land Revenue... ...	39,82,700	39,34,700	......	48,000	15·5
5	Forest......	3.00,000	2,56,500	......	43,500	1·
6	Abkaree......	2,70,000	2,70,400	400	... ...	1·
7	Income Tax..........	19,500	17,400	... ...	2,100	·0
8	Customs.............	1,69,500	1,65,700	......	3,800	·6
9	Salt	14,47,000	14,98,800	51,800	....	6·
11	Stamps...............	1,13,980	1,24,100	10,120	......	·4
12	Mint	2,28,300	2,14,800	......	13,500	·8
15	Allowances to District and Village Officers........ ..	3,67,610	3,58,900	·	8,710	1·4
16	Administration and Public Depts ...	13,20,010	12,78.700	......	41,310	5·0
17	Law and Justice.....	40,11,090	38,80,000	....	1,31,090	15·2
18	Police...............	38,91,000	38,41,400	... ...	49,600	15·1
19	Marine..........	1,70,000	2,30,000	60,000	... ...	·9
20	Education, Science, and Art............	9,12,190	7,86,000	......	1,26,190	3·2
21	Ecclesiastical......,....	3,70,000	3,97,100	27,100	......	1·6
22	Medical Services.	5,93,360	4,93,700	......	99,660	2·
23	Stationery and Printing........	3,24,970	3,50,000	25,030	......	1·4
24	Political Agencies, &c.................	1,01,700	98,800	......	2,900	·4
25	Allowances and Assignments..	30,96,000	29,71,900	... ..	1,24,100	11·7
26	Miscellaneous.... ...	7,14,760	6,76,100	......	38,660	2·7
27	Superannuations, &c	24,22,130	23,80,900	......	41,230	9·4
	Total, Cl. Dept. Rs.	258,28,000	254,32,000	......	3,96,000	100
	Military Dept*...	227,72,500	215,46,200	......	12,26,300	...
	Public Works do....	79,23,000	74,73,800	...∧..	4,49,200	...
	Postal do....	6,19,800	5,93,800	......	26,000	...
	Telegraph do....	3,04,600	2,91,900	......	12,700	...
	Total Rupees	574,47,900	553,37,700	˙:.....	21,10,200	...

* The amounts entered under this head are exclusive of payments made at other Presidencies on account of Madras Troops serving there, but the amounts inclusive of them are Rs. 338,68,000 and 310,53,000, respectively, as ascertained from the Controller of Military Accounts.

APPENDIX VII.

A.

OPERATIONS OF COURTS.

Statement shewing number of Original Suits instituted, disposed of, and pending during the year 1039, as compared with the year 1040.

Courts.	1039.			1040.		
	Previous Balance and those filed.	Disposed of.	Remaining on the 1st Avani, 1040.	Previous balance and those filed.	Disposed of.	Remaining on the 1st Avani, 1041.
Zillah Civil Courts........	1,435	946	489	1,601	831	773
Do. Small Cause Courts.	637	542	95	781	523	258
Moonsiffs' Courts.........	10,184	9,169	1,015	11,214	9,943	1,271
Total...	12,256	10,657	1,599	13,599	11,297	2,302

A.
TRAVAN-
CORE.

Statement shewing the number of Criminal Cases pending, filed, and disposed of in the four Criminal Courts of Travancore during the year 1040.

A.—(*Concluded.*)

COURTS.	Pending on the 31st Carcadagam 1039.		Filed during the year 1040.		Total.		Disposed of.		Decrees received from the Sudr Court after confirmation.		Total.		No. of prisoners flogged.	The Decision of the Criminal Court.							Do. flogged.	The Decision of the Sudr Court.											Released.	Average delay from filing until the disposal of the cases.			Balance.						
	No. of cases.	No. of prisoners.	No. of cases.	No. of prisoners.	No. of cases.	No. of prisoners.	No. of cases.	No. of prisoners.	No. of cases.	No. of prisoners.	No. of cases.	No. of prisoners.		No. sentenced to rigorous or simple imprisonment not exceeding one year.	No. sentenced above one and within two years.	Do. above two and within three years.	Do. sentenced to pay a fine.	Do. sentenced to furnish security.	Do. acquitted.			Do. sentenced to rigorous or simple imprisonment not exceeding one year.	Do. above one year and within three years.	Do. above three years and within seven years.	Do. above seven and within ten years.	Do. above ten and within fourteen years.	Do. for life.	Do. to capital punishment.	Do. sentenced to pay a fine.	Do. sentenced to furnish security.		Years.	Months.	Days.	No. of Decrees referred to the Sudr Court under Section 11 of 1038.	Remaining on the file of the Criminal Court.	Total.	Under one month.	Above one month and under three months.	Above three months.	Total.
Palpanapoorum Criminal Court	...	...	80	202	80	202	77	186	3	16	80	202	2	37	10	1	32	18	91		...	...	...	4	...	...	...	...	...	...	18	...	...	5	...	...	...	...	...	...	...
Trevandrum ..... do.	2	3	106	238	108	241	95	209	12	30	107	239	3	40	21	7	8	7	128	1	...	4	9	...	...	8	2	...	2	2,11	...	...	11	...	1	1	...	...	1	1
Quilon ..... do.	...	...	181	410	81	410	174	385	6	23	180	408	4	81	19	5	91	95	230	...	...	2	1	9	...	1	1	...	...	9	...	...	15	...	1	1	...	...	1	1
Alleppy ..... do.	...	...	209	529	209	599	192	475	17	41	209	516	1	128	19	6	100	56	185	...	...	5	4	1	...	4	2	1	1	23	...	...	19	...	4	4	6	...	4	4
Total	2	3	576	1,379	58	1,889	538	1,255	38	110	576	1,365	10	286	69	19	161	81	629	1	...	13	18	10	...	4	2	...	2	9,55	...	...	...	...	6	6	6	...	6	6

B.

THE following is a brief explanation of the tenure called Circar Pauttum.

The Circar or Government was considered the sole Jenmie, Merassi-holder, or landlord of these lands. The Ryots in possession of these lands held them of the Circar, just as the tenants of an ordinary Jenmie or Merassidar hold lands of him.

Many serious disadvantages attached to this tenure in consequence of its character. The Circar was supposed to have the absolute domi-nion of a landlord over these lands, limited only by its own considera-tions of self interest. It seems that the Circar was not bound to respect possession. It was thought that the lands could, in some cases, be resumed at the Circar's pleasure, though this was not often done in practice. Circar Pauttum lands could not be legally sold by one Ryot to another, for the reason that he was a simple tenant, and could not act as a proprietor. If a sale were nevertheless effected, it was deemed invalid, and the Circar had the right to ignore the transaction altogether. When a sale was executed, it was done clandestinely, and in a most circuitous manner, involving an infraction of the truth at almost every step. As Circar Pauttum land could not be legally sold, such land was no security for the tax payable on it. When the tax on such land had to be levied by coercive process, the land could not of course be brought to sale, but the Circar had to seek out other pro-perty of the defaulter, and on failure, the demand had to be remitted. As sales were illegal, mortgages were also equally so, and thus the tenant was unable to borrow capital on the security of his Pauttum land, though such capital were required for the improvement of those very lands. The pernicious principle involved was carried out by refusal to accept Pauttum lands as security for public servants, for public contracts, &c. Nor could Pauttum lands be sold by the Civil Courts of the country in execution of decrees. The judgment creditor was not, there-fore, at liberty to regard the Pauttum lands in the possession of his debtor, as assets available for the satisfaction of just debts. The Circar steadily refused to assent to any action on the part of the tenant, such as was calculated to give him any pecuniary interest in the Pauttum lands forming his holding. This was carried so far, that if a ryot asked to be permitted to spend capital in improving his lands, the Circar told him that he might do so if he liked, but that the Cir-car would not recognize the improvement, or respect any claim to consequent pecuniary interest in the property. Following out the system, no price, or a mere nominal price, was paid by the Circar for Pauttum lands resumed for public purposes, such as for roads, canals, and public buildings.

It is easy to see how adverse such a state of things must have been to the permanent improvement of this important class of lands.

C.

C.

Notification issued by His Highness the Maha Rajah, relative to interportal arrangements :—

" Whereas it has been found expedient to revise, in communication with the British Indian Government, and the Cochin Circar, the system of duties hitherto levied on the trade of Travancore, it is notified that from and after the 20th Vycausy 1040,(1st of June 1865,) no customs duties on account of this Circar will be levied on goods imported by land, sea, or backwater into Travancore, and being the produce and manufacture of British India or of the territories of the Cochin State, excepting on

Tobacco raw and manufactured,

Salt,

Opium,

Spirits,

which will be treated as heretofore.

" The British Indian and Cochin Governments will also give up their customs duties on all goods imported by land, sea, or backwater into Travancore from their territories. The British Indian Government will permit Bombay salt to be exported to Travancore on the same terms as to the British Provinces, such as Malabar and Canara.

" On imported goods other than those which are the produce or manufacture of British India, or the territories of the Cochin State, the Travancore Government will levy the British Indian rates of duty, except when they shall have already paid duty to British India or the Cochin State, in which case they will be exempted from duty.

" The duty that this Government will levy on goods exported from Travancore will be ten per cent. on timber ; fifteen Rupees per candy of 500 English lbs. on pepper and betel-nut ; and five per cent. on all other goods. But Tinnevelly cloths exported from Travancore to British India or to Circar Cochin will be free. And also only a limited number of commodities will be liable to export duty at the Chowkies of Ramaswarem Cotah, Bagavathy Cotah, and Eddapully ; the said commodities being notified from time to time.

" Neither the British Indian Government, nor the Cochin State will levy any duty on goods imported into their territories from Travancore, whether by land, sea, or backwater, and whether the produce and manufacture of Travancore or foreign goods, which have already paid import duty to this State, excepting

Salt,
Opium,
Spirits.

This Circar will not tax Coimbatore or other British Indian produce passing through the Travancore backwater to British Cochin or to the Cochin State, nor tax the produce of the territories of the Cochin Circar directly proceeding through Travancore to British Cochin, or to some other part of the territories of the Cochin State itself.

" The British Indian Tariff of valuations will supersede the Tariffs hitherto in force in the Chowkies of this Circar."

———

D.

D.

THE ceremony of laying the first stone for the foundation of the new Government Offices took place last evening, at half past 5 o'clock.

At 5 o'clock precisely, His Highness the Maha Rajah arrived, followed by His Highness the First Prince and the two junior Princes. His Highness the Maha Rajah was received by the British Resident, and His Highness the First Prince by the Assistant Resident, the troops paying due honors, and the Band playing "God save the King."

Every thing being announced ready, His Highness rose and proceeded to the spot where the stone was to be laid, accompanied by the Resident and others.

At His Highness' desire, the Dewan then read the following address in His Highness' name :—

" The occasion which has drawn us together here is one of great importance. For a long time the want of suitable public offices has been felt in regard to almost all departments of the Government, and happily the finances of the State are in a condition to enable it to supply this long standing want.

D.
TRAVAN-
CORE.

"It is proposed to erect one large edifice, so as to have under one roof all the principal departments of the Government at the capital.

"The position for these offices has been selected with great care. It is centrical, airy, and adjoins a main thoroughfare.

"We have had before us the plan of the proposed buildings. The skill and good taste of the Engineer, Mr. Barton, are conspicuous in the general design, and also in the details to suit the requirements of the several departments; and I have every confidence that his practical energy will bring this important undertaking to a successful conclusion at as early a period as possible.

"The offices will be commodious, substantial, and handsome, without extravagant ornament. While they are calculated to answer highly useful purposes in facilitating the administration, by promoting punctuality, order, and despatch of business, they will largely contribute to raise the character of the capital of the Travancore State in its architectural aspect.

"For so large an undertaking it is intended to procure from Europe a steam engine, and several important mechanical appliances; and these aids to manual labor, while greatly contributing to facilitate the work, will have the beneficial effect of demonstrating the advancement made in mechanical ingenuity in the western world, and of encouraging progress in this direction, which is much needed in. Travancore.

"It is gratifying to me to be enabled to press forward improvements in various directions. It is true that no limits can be assigned to our progress, and it can never be given to any ruler, however powerful or favored, to say that he has done every thing for his subjects. On the contrary, what a single ruler can possibly do in a life of incessant activity, must form but a small fraction of what may be due to the country. The lifetime of an individual is but as a day in the lifetime of a nation. Yet, it is no less our duty to exert our utmost energies to prove useful in our generation.

"Secure under the ægis of the British Queen from external violence, it is our pleasant, and, if rightly understood, by no means difficult task, to develope prosperity and to multiply the triumphs of peace in our territories.

"Nor are the Native States left to pursue this task in the dark, alone, and unaided. It is not necessary for them to try system after system, principle after principle, to undergo long and anxious trials, to pass through the pains and penalties of a succession of failures, with

a view to the determination of the best conditions of progressive happiness. The Native Princes have but to cast their eyes abroad, and the
results of the long and checkered experience of nations, as well as of
the speculations of the profoundest thinkers, are ready to hand.

" More immediately they have the advantage of the enlightened
guidance of the British Government itself. Looking at that Government as a reflex of the British nation, it is undoubtedly true that it is
actuated by the noblest philanthrophy, that it sincerely wishes for the
greatest happiness of the greatest portion of the globe. Of course
small States, like the Native States of India, come under the beneficial
influence of that comprehensive feeling as much as great countries,
and hence we may rest assured that we cannot establish a stronger
claim to the sympathy and support of that great Government, than
by a full conception, and a steady performance of the duty of securing
the greatest happiness of those whose welfare is in our hands.

" It would no longer do for Native Princes to remain in profound
ignorance of what passes around, to care little about their subjects,
and to concentrate their attention upon selfish enjoyments. The
notion that the State is made but for the personal happiness of the
sovereign is quite obsolete in this age.

" These are mere commonplaces in the view of the European
part of the community I have the pleasure of addressing; but they
require to be expressed, repeated, and enforced, till they come to be
regarded as commonplaces by all Native States.

" Such being my views, I am prepared to do all that lies in my
power towards making Travancore an honorable example of Native
good Government, and in this endeavour I trust to have the hearty
co-operation of all parties.

" I must take this opportunity to impress one important truth
on my native subjects, and this is that the realization of our hopes
depends, not in a great measure, but *entirely*, upon their advancement in moral and intellectual culture. If knowledge is power in
individuals, it is equally a source of power to communities. It is
knowledge that now chiefly constitutes the difference between one
nation and another. The supremacy of violence and fraud has
almost wholly passed away ; it has at least passed away so far as the
ordinary affairs of civilized communities are concerned. Reason and
justice have succeeded. An enlightened public law, generally recognized and respected, ensures security and consideration to communities irrespective of their extent, wealth, or power. Hence, there

is nothing upon which the position and happiness of a community so much depend as upon its ówn knowledge, as manifested in knowing and maintaining its own rights, in respecting those of others, and, generally, in making itself as happy as possible, consistently with the happiness of other communities.

" What is required then, is that education should permeate all the parts of this community. The higher classes, who have the necessary means and leisure, should study generally what it is that constitutes the happiness of a community, and what the means are by which that happiness is best secured. They should learn, in particular, what the true sources of national wealth are, and the way to improve those sources. In the pursuit of such enquiries, they must cast off all prejudices, and follow reason to those great practical principles, which are the boast of the more advanced of the European nations. The science of legislation is also full of practical interest, and deserving of study, inasmuch as it shows what the foundation of laws should be, what institutions should be discouraged, and what fostered and improved.

" Minds thus fortified are alone capable in these days, of claiming a share in the management of public affairs of the highest order. It is only such minds that are at all capable of sustaining the respecta- bility of a State in the view of the enlightened public. And I must add, that the vigor, if not the vitality of Native States, largely depends upon the number of such minds that are brought to bear upon the administration.

" The bulk of the people, too, should advance in knowledge suited to their position. They must know every thing about their own country, and something about other countries. Unless communities are able to compare themselves with others better advanced, there will be little improvement. It is such comparison that creates a wholesome discontent with a state of stagnation, and inspires a desire for pro- gress. It is that which enables a community to form for itself, by degrees, an ideal of perfection, to be kept constantly before it, reced- ing as it is approached, and ensuring incessant progress, which is the law of all healthy communities.

" The facilities for such comparison on the spot will not be wanting. Travancore is no longer a secluded corner of India. The broad ocean on the one side, and the alpine forests on the other, which used to complete its isolation, are now operating just in the opposite direction ; they are only inviting foreign capital and foreign enterprise. The natives of the country in general should learn to profi by these great and irresistible phenomena. The preliminary step for this is to cast off those erroneous notions, which have indeed been generated and fostered by long insulation, but which are incompatible with the association of races. Let each by all means enjoy to the fullest extent possible the freedom of thought and action, let each have his own views on all subjects, but let none interfere with another's liberty of the same nature.

"Turning now to the immediate object of our meeting, I proceed to lay the first foundation stone of the public offices. In doing so, I fervently implore the blessing of Almighty God. May He ever guide, with His boundless wisdom, those who are to administer the affairs of the country in these buildings."

E.
TRAVAN-
CORE.

E.

Comparative Statement of the Revenue, Collections, and Disbursements of the Travancore Circar, during the years 1039 and 1040.

Revenue and Collections

		1039. RS.	1040. RS.
1	Land Revenue	16,51,208	16,45,470
2	Miscellaneous do.	4,94,796	4,92,412
3	Customs	4,57,907	3,78,213
4	Arrack and Opium	81,789	80,451
5	Tobacco	7,88,901	7,85,709
6	Pepper	76,172	43,426
7	Salt	5,15,748	5,48,724
8	Cardamoms and other goods	95,321	1,41,998
9	Timber	89,309	40,029
10	Arrears of Revenue collected in the year	59,576	54,708
		43,10,727	42,11,140

Disbursements

		1039. RS.	1040. RS.
1	The Davasom or Religious Institution	5,70,843	5,47,689
2	The Ootaperrah or Charitable do	2,95,192	3,06,869
3	The Palace	4,57,460	4,65,585
4	Huzzoor Cutcherry and the Civil Establishments.	...	...
5	Judicial Establishment	4,90,696	4,14,126
6	Police do.	85,984	97,669
7	Nair Troops	74,375	1,07,382
8	Elephant and Horse Establishments	1,25,969	1,26,119
9	Ed... , Science, and Art	30,107	29,705
10	Pensions	...	57,039
11	Public Works...	1,06,498	1,16,113
12	Gift and charges of goods sold and advances made for purchase of goods	2,60,169	4,76,305
13	Contingent	3,05,263	3,30,746
14	Subsidy to the British Indian Government	2,21,044	1,60,919
15	Amount for Pooliooody ceremony of Her Highness the Junior Ranee	8,10,127	8,11,475
	Do. for Moorajeppum do.	2,659	
		1,63,611	
		39,99,997	40,47,784

A.

The following Statement exhibits the Receipts and Disbursements of the Cochin Circar for the year 1040.

RECEIPTS.	RS.	A.	P.	DISBURSEMENTS.	RS.	A.	P.
Amount of Land Revenue...	5,83,154	0	1	Expenses of the Palace ...	1,61,760	0	0
„ of Customs' Collections	92,246	15	1	„ of Religious Institutions	51,176	18	9
„ Abkarry Rs. 17,377-5-9				„ of Charitable do.	48,111	4	11
and Opium „ 2,600-0-0	19,977	5	9	Administrative Establishment.	1,05,643	5	7
„ of sale of Salt	1,70,470	8	1	Judicial do.	37,950	0	0
„ of Teak Timber ...	55,668	4	0	Police do.	13,352	10	18
„ of Miscellaneous Reve-				Military do.	20,058	3	10
nue	1,53,713	9	4	Pensions	10,208	14	3
				Public Works	1,75,795	7	7
				Miscellaneous expenses ...	2,50,830	5	0
				Subsidy to British Government	2,00,000	0	0
Total...	10,75,230	10	4	Total...	10,74,881	1	7
Amount Balance of 1039 ...	4,50,225	15	9	Balance to be carried to the account of the year 1041.	4,50,575	8	6
Grand Total...	15,25,456	10	1	Grand Total...	15,25,456	10	1

A.
EDUCA-
TIONAL.

APPENDIX VIII.
A.

Distribution of Schools connected with the Department of Public Instruction in the Madras Presidency, classified with reference to the Agency by which they are managed.

Name of District	Government Colleges and Schools	Number of Pupils	Schools supported by a rate	Number of Pupils	Private Colleges and Schools which either now receive or have received grants-in-aid			Private Schools under inspection which have not received grants-in-aid	Number of Pupils	Total Colleges and Schools	Total number of Pupils	Divisions	Total number of Pupils according to Divisions	Total number of Pupils in Government Schools according to Divisions	Remarks
					Established by Missionary Societies	Established by other than Missionary Societies	Number of Pupils								
Ganjam	24	822	…	…			149	…	…	27	963	First	5,303	1,488	
Vizagapatam	7	339	72	1,241			857	…	…	21	1,196				
Godavery	4	299	…	…			777	…	…	91	2,317				
Kistna	1	28	…	…			800	…	…	12	828				
Bellary	4	425	…	…			479	…	…	18	904	Second	3,893	714	
Kurnool	1	116	…	…			81	1	44	5	241				
Cuddapah	1	173	…	…			211	17	209	24	593				
Nellore	…	…	…	…			2,155	…	…	117	2,155				
Madras	*16	1,893	1	202			6,263	9	535	85	8,893	Third	10,042	2,546	
South Arcot	10	653	…	…			399	3	97	19	1,149				
North Arcot	7	1,069	…	…			753	14	289	55	2,111	Fourth	7,337	2,921	
Salem	6	650	…	…			…	…	…	6	650				
Tanjore	7	923	…	…			1,968	5	513	55	3,404				
Trichinopoly	2	279	…	…			753	20	140	20	1,172				
Coimbatore	6	382	…	…			2,132	18	3,397	328	5,921	Fifth	16,385	846	
Madura	3	454	…	…			1,118	38	449	44	2,021				
Tinnevelly	…	…	…	…			7,863	2	578	314	8,441				
South Canara	4	176	1	135			108	…	…	9	501	Mal. & Canara	2,098	919	
Malabar	6	743	5	373			439	…	42	16	1,597				
Total	109	9,434	79	1,951	519	347	27,351	377	6,320	1,261	45,056		45,056	9,434	

Remarks: * In last year's Table the Taluk School of Tripaty was erroneously included in the District of Madras; a correction has been made in the present Table.

The Presidency, Medical, and Civil Engineering Colleges, which are included here, are reckoned as single institutions, although they consist each of a College Proper and a Collegiate School.

N. B.—The Trichinopoly and Vellore Normal Schools are under the Inspector of the 3rd Division, though they are here included among the Schools of the 4th Division : the number of Pupils in them is 179 and 221, respectively.

The Calicut Provincial School is included among the Schools in the Sub-Division of Malabar and South Canara, but it is actually supervised by the Inspector of the 5th Division; the number of Pupils in it is 345.

B.

Distribution of Schools connected with the Department of Public Instruction in the Madras Presidency, classified with reference to the Standard of Instruction imparted in them.

Name of District.	Number of Schools of the Higher Class.	Number of Pupils.	Number of Schools of the Middle Class.	Number of Pupils.	Number of Schools of the Lower Class.	Number of Pupils.	Number of Female Schools.	Number of Pupils.	Number of Normal Schools.	Number of Pupils.	Number of Schools for special Education.	Number of Pupils.	Total Number of Schools.	Total Number of Pupils.	Remarks.
Ganjam ...	1	111	9	356	16	487	...	...	1	8	...	...	27	962	
Vizagapatam	1	258	8	472	11	497	...	...	1	39	...	...	21	1,196	The Nursapur Central School, the Church Mission School at Elur, and the Vizianagram Samusthanum School are reckoned as belonging to the 2nd Class.
Godavery ...	1	181	17	980	72	1,139	1	30	1	137	...	...	91	2,317	
Kistna ...	2	384	5	222	5	232	...	...	...	...	...	...	12	828	
Bellary ...	1	246	10	586	1	42	...	...	...	...	...	...	13	904	
Kurnool ...	1	116	4	125	...	...	...	...	...	...	...	...	5	241	
Cuddapah ...	1	173	6	211	17	209	...	...	...	...	...	...	24	693	
Nellore ...	...	...	4	270	111	1,802	1	83	1	320	...	...	117	2,155	
Madras ...	10	2,561	44	704	1	40	25	1,489	1	...	4	431	85	8,893	
South Arcot	1	218	12	533	4	174	2	53	...	221	...	...	19	1,149	
North Arcot	1	332	6	376	45	933	2	92	...	...	...	...	55	2,111	
Salem ...	1	274	5	890	...	...	5	193	1	24	...	...	6	650	
Tanjore ...	3	850	22	1,890	24	448	2	48	1	179	...	...	55	3,404	
Madura ...	...	143	4	454	12	348	1	49	...	...	...	...	20	1,172	
...	...	...	13	573	314	4,999	2	76	...	77	...	...	328	5,921	
Tinnevelly	1	262	16	854	24	752	94	1,635	2	316	...	...	44	2,021	
South ...	1	197	33	1,508	184	4,785	2	27	...	...	...	...	314	8,441	
Malabar...	...	...	6	372	1	102	1	49	...	...	...	...	9	501	
	1	345	13	983	...	...	...	...	1	227	...	...	16	1,597	
Total ...	28	6,651	237	5,821	842	16,909	189	3,816	11	1,428	4	431	1,261	45,056	

N. B.—The figures in Column 11 include the Pupils in the Practising Schools attached to Normal Schools. The number of Normal Students proper is 205 for Government Schools, and 207 for Private Schools.

www.ingramcontent.com/pod-product-compliance
Lightning Source LLC
Chambersburg PA
CBHW060328100426
42812CB00003B/909